Language
Network

Grammar • Writing • Communication

McDougal Littell
A HOUGHTON MIFFLIN COMPANY

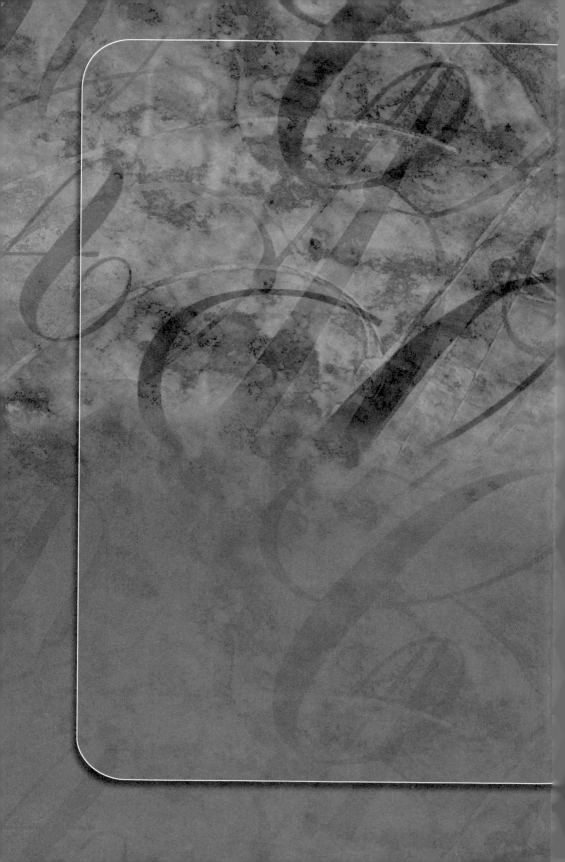

Language
Network

- **Grammar, Usage, and Mechanics**
- **Essential Writing Skills**
- **Writing Workshops**
- **Communicating in the Information Age**

McDougal Littell

A HOUGHTON MIFFLIN COMPANY

2006 Impression.
ISBN-13: 978-0-395-96738-6   ISBN-10: 0-395-96738-4

Acknowledgments begin on page 701.

40049692

17 18 19 – DCI– 09   08 07

Teacher Panels

The teacher panels helped guide the conceptual development of *Language Network*. They participated actively in shaping and reviewing prototype materials for the pupil edition, determining ancillary and technology components, and guiding the development of the scope and sequence for the program.

Gloria Anderson, Campbell Junior High School, Houston, Tex.
Luke Atwood, Park Junior High School, LaGrange, Ill.
Donna Blackall, Thomas Middle School, Arlington Heights, Ill.
Karen Bostwick, McLean Middle School, Fort Worth, Tex.
Rebecca Hadavi, Parkland Middle School, El Paso, Tex.
Sandi Heffelfinger, Parkland Junior High School, McHenry, Ill.
Diane Hinojosa, Alamo Middle School, Pharr, Tex.
Patricia Jackson, Pearce Middle School, Austin, Tex.
Sue Kazlusky, Lundahl Middle School, Crystal Lake, Ill.
Tom Kiefer, Cary Junior High School, Cary, Ill.
Keith Lustig, Hill Middle School, Naperville, Ill.
Joanna Martin, Haines Middle School, St. Charles, Ill.
Sandy Mattox, Coppell Middle School, Lewisville, Tex.
Susan Mortensen, Deer Path Junior High School, Lake Forest, Ill.
Adrienne Myers, Foster Middle School, Longview, Tex.
Kathy Powers, Welch Middle School, Houston, Tex.
Patricia Smith, Tefft Middle School, Streamwood, Ill.
Frank Westerman, Jackson Middle School, San Antonio, Tex.
Bessie Wilson, Greiner Middle School, Dallas, Tex.
Kimberly Zeman, Hauser Junior High School, Riverside, Ill.

Content Specialists

Dr. Mary Newton Bruder, Former Professor of Linguistics, University of Pittsburgh, Pittsburgh, Pa. (creator of the Grammar Hotline Web site)
Rebekah Caplan, High School and Middle Grades English/Language Arts Specialist for the New Standards Project, National Center on Education and the Economy, Washington, D.C.
Dr. Sharon Sicinski Skeans, Assistant Professor, University of Houston-Clear Lake, Houston, Tex.
Richard Vinson, Retired Teacher, Provine High School, Jackson, Miss.

Technology Consultants

Dr. David Considine, Media Studies Coordinator, Appalachian State University, Boone, NC (author of *Visual Messages: Integrating Imagery into Instruction*)
Heidi Whitus, Teacher, Communication Arts High School, San Antonio, Tex.
Anne Clark, Riverside-Brookfield High School, Riverside, Ill.
Pat Jurgens, Riverside-Brookfield High School, Riverside, Ill.
Ralph Amelio, Former teacher, Willowbrook High School, Villa Park, Ill.
Cindy Lucia, Horace Greeley High School, New York, N.Y.
Aaron Barnhart, Television writer for the *Kansas City Star* and columnist for *Electronic Media,* Kansas City, Mo.

ESL Consultants

Dr. Andrea B. Bermúdez, Professor of Studies in Language and Culture; Director, Research Center for Language and Culture; Chair, Foundations and Professional Studies, University of Houston-Clear Lake, Clear Lake, Tex.
Inara Bundza, ESL Director, Kelvyn Park High School, Chicago, Ill.
Danette Erickson Meyer, Consultant, Illinois Resource Center, Des Plaines, Ill.
John Hilliard, Consultant, Illinois Resource Center, Des Plaines, Ill.
John Kibler, Consultant, Illinois Resource Center, Des Plaines, Ill.
Barbara Kuhns, Camino Real Middle School, Las Cruces, N.M.

Teacher Reviewers

Gloria Anderson, Campbell Junior High School, Houston, TX
Patricia Jackson, Pearce Middle School, Austin, TX
Sandy Mattox, Coppell Middle School, Lewisville, TX
Adrienne Myers, Foster Middle School, Longview, TX
Frank Westerman, Jackson Middle School, San Antonio, TX
Bessie Wilson, Greiner Middle School, Dallas, TX

Student Reviewers

Saba Abraham, Chelsea High School
Julie Allred, Southwest High School
Nabiha Azam, East Kentwood High School
Dana Baccino, Downington High School
Christianne Balsamo, Nottingham High School
Luke Bohline, Lakeville High School
Nathan Buechel, Providence Senior High School
Melissa Cummings, Highline High School
Megan Dawson, Southview Senior High School
Michelle DeBruce, Jurupa High School
Brian Deeds, Arvada West High School
Ranika Fizer, Jones High School
Ashleigh Goldberg, Parkdale High School
Jacqueline Grullon, Christopher Columbus High School
Dimmy Herard, Hialeah High School
Sean Horan, Round Rock High School
Bob Howard, Jr., Robert E. Lee High School

Rebecca Iden, Willowbrook High School
Agha's Igbinovia, Florin High School
Megan Jones, Dobson High School
Ed Kampelman, Parkway West High School
David Knapp, Delmar High School
Eva Lima, Westmoor High School
Ashley Miers, Ouachita High School
Raul Morffi, Shawnee Mission West High School
Sakenia Mosley, Sandalwood High School
Sergio Perez, Sunset High School
Jackie Peters, Westerville South High School
Kevin Robischaud, Waltham High School
Orlando Sanchez, West Mesa High School
Selene Sanchez, San Diego High School
Sharon Schaefer, East Aurora High School
Mica Semrick, Hoover High School
Julio Sequeira, Belmont High School
Camille Singleton, Cerritos High School
Solomon Stevenson, Ozen High School
Tim Villegas, Dos Pueblos High School
Shane Wagner, Waukesha West High School
Swenikqua Walker, San Bornardino High School
Douglas Weakly, Ray High School
Lauren Zoric, Norwin High School

Student Writers

Echo Bergquist, Oak Hill Middle School
Aleah Dillard, Foster Middle School
Jessica Dussling, Thomas Middle School
Caitlyn Fox, Lake Forest Country Day School
Ann Marie Gasparro, Coppell Middle School
Danny Krantz, Charlo School
Katelyn Peters, Target Range High School
Julia Risk, Wood Oaks Junior High School
Carlos Thoma, Highland Middle School
Angela Tressler, Jane Addams Middle School

Contents Overview

Grammar, Usage, and Mechanics

Essential Writing Skills

Writing Workshops: Writing for Different Purposes

Communicating in the Information Age

Student Resources

Grammar, Usage, and Mechanics

6 Prepositions, Conjunctions, Interjections 150

7 Verbals and Verbal Phrases 168

8 Sentence Structure

11 Punctuation 248

Quick-Fix Editing Machine

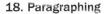

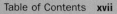

Essential Writing Skills

Student Help Desk   340

Crafting Sentences at a Glance
   Combining Sentences *Weld Those Words*
   Expanding Sentences *Fine-Tune with Precision*
   Conjunctions
   The Bottom Line *Checklist for Crafting Sentences*

14 Building Paragraphs

Student Help Desk   352

Building Paragraphs at a Glance
   Types of Paragraphs *Paragraph Profiles*
   Test for Paragraph Unity *Does It Make the Grade?*
   Transition Words *Bridge the Gap*
   The Bottom Line *Checklist for Building Paragraphs*

Writing Workshops

xxix

Communicating in the Information Age

Critical Thinking

Special Features

Grammar Across the Curriculum

Grammar in Literature

Power Words: Vocabulary for Precise Writing

Quick-Fix Editing Machine

Student Resources

Grammar, Usage, and Mechanics

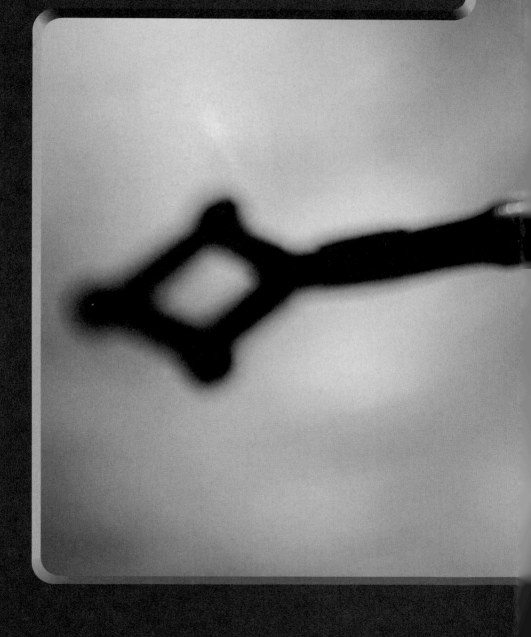

The Key to Good Writing

If you don't have the key to a house, you can't get in it. Grammar is the key to the house of language. By learning proper grammar and usage, you'll have the keys to unlock your imagination in words.

The Sentence and Its Parts

Theme: Cities and Towns

Parts of a Whole

This postcard shows photographs of several parts of San Francisco. How are the neighborhoods different from each other? How are they parts of a whole? Just as cities are made up of neighborhoods, sentences are composed of subjects and predicates. These basic parts can appear in different kinds of sentences that add variety to writing.

Write Away: Picture This

If you were asked to create a postcard showing different parts of your city or town, what pictures would you include in it? Write a paragraph explaining your choices. Save your paragraph in your 🗀 **Working Portfolio.**

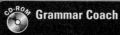 **Grammar Coach**

Choose the letter of the term that correctly identifies each underlined item in the paragraph below.

Most <u>Americans</u> live in urban areas. Cities offer <u>people</u> a wide
(1)   (2)
variety of activities. They also <u>provide</u> many job opportunities.
                                      (3)
<u>Offices and factories</u> are often located in cities. Yet rural life has
         (4)
<u>advantages</u>. Small towns <u>can seem</u> friendlier. <u>People</u> usually know
    (5)   (6)   (7)
their neighbors. <u>There is more open space, the pace is slower</u>. <u>What</u>
                                          (8)
<u>kind of place should you live in?</u> <u>Let your heart be your guide</u>.
         (9)   (10)

---

1. A. simple subject
   B. simple predicate
   C. complete subject
   D. complete predicate

2. A. predicate noun
   B. predicate adjective
   C. direct object
   D. indirect object

3. A. simple subject
   B. simple predicate
   C. complete subject
   D. complete predicate

4. A. direct object
   B. simple predicate
   C. compound subject
   D. compound verb

5. A. predicate noun
   B. predicate adjective
   C. direct object
   D. indirect object

6. A. verb phrase
   B. helping verb
   C. main verb
   D. compound subject

7. A. simple subject
   B. simple predicate
   C. compound subject
   D. compound verb

8. A. fragment
   B. run-on sentence
   C. exclamatory sentence
   D. interrogative sentence

9. A. fragment
   B. run-on sentence
   C. exclamatory sentence
   D. interrogative sentence

10. A. imperative sentence
    B. exclamatory sentence
    C. fragment
    D. declarative sentence

Complete Subjects and Predicates

❶ Here's the Idea

In order to share ideas and information successfully, you need to use complete sentences.

▶ **A sentence is a group of words that expresses a complete thought.**

Here is a group of words.

cities   central
suburbs   around
develop

The words cannot get a message across unless they have a structure. Here is a sentence built from the same words. Notice that the sentence communicates a complete idea.

Suburbs develop around central cities.

▶ **Every complete sentence has two basic parts: a subject and a predicate.**

1. The **complete subject** includes all the words that tell whom or what the sentence is about.

COMPLETE SUBJECT

Metropolitan areas include suburbs.

2. The **complete predicate** includes the verb and all the words that complete the verb's meaning.

COMPLETE PREDICATE

Metropolitan areas **include suburbs.**

Here's How **Finding Complete Subjects and Predicates**

Metropolitan areas include suburbs.

1. **To find the complete subject, ask who or what does something (or is something).**

What includes suburbs? **Metropolitan areas**

2. **To find the complete predicate, ask what the subject does (or is).**

What do metropolitan areas do? include suburbs

---

❷ Why It Matters in Writing

Writers often use isolated words and phrases when jotting down ideas and information. For example, when writing about Tokyo, you might jot down "metropolitan population more than 27 million" and "highways, public transportation strained." To turn these notes into thoughts that you can share with others, you must use complete sentences.

STUDENT MODEL

> Tokyo is a very crowded city. More than 27 million people live in the metropolitan area. Commuters often jam the highways. The public transportation system is also strained.

❸ Practice and Apply

CONCEPT CHECK: Complete Subjects and Predicates

In separate columns on a sheet of paper, write the complete subject and complete predicate of these sentences.

Urban Sprawl
1. Species of plants and animals are disappearing near cities.
2. Urban sprawl harms their habitats.
3. Growing families want bigger houses and yards.
4. Many of them move from dense central cities into suburbs.
5. Real-estate developers need land for new housing.
6. Some projects take over forests and woodlands.
7. New policies limit growth in some areas.
8. State and local governments buy undeveloped land.
9. Some cities encourage development on old industrial sites.
10. Every reclaimed acre saves about seven acres of unspoiled land.

➡ **For a SELF-CHECK and more practice, see the EXERCISE BANK, p. 602.**

Simple Subjects

❶ Here's the Idea

You have learned that one basic part of a sentence is the complete subject. Now you will learn about the key part of the complete subject.

▶ **The simple subject is the main word or words in the complete subject.** Descriptive words are not part of the simple subject.

COMPLETE SUBJECT

> **Some small towns** hold town meetings.
>
> SIMPLE SUBJECT

> **Adult residents** vote directly on community issues.
> SIMPLE SUBJECT

When a proper name is used as a subject, all parts of the name make up the simple subject.

> **New England** is the birthplace of town meetings.
> SIMPLE SUBJECT

❷ Why It Matters in Writing

The simple subject is one of the key words in a sentence. Make sure that you have chosen a precise one so that readers will know whom or what the sentence is about.

STUDENT MODEL

DRAFT

Democracy is simple in some parts of New England. **People** make decisions at town meetings instead of electing officials to make them. **This** helps ordinary people feel in charge.

REVISION

Democracy is simple in some parts of New England. **Voters** make decisions at town meetings instead of electing officials to make them. This **system** helps ordinary people feel in charge.

❸ Practice and Apply

A. CONCEPT CHECK: Simple Subject

On a separate sheet of paper, write the simple subject of each sentence. Remember, descriptive words are not part of the simple subject.

Example: Many large universities have urban planning programs.
Simple subject: universities

City Planning
1. The Industrial Revolution transformed old cities.
2. Healthy new industries attracted people from the countryside.
3. Most workers had to live in overcrowded, filthy slums.
4. Some leaders recognized the need for improvements.
5. Early planners focused on preventing disease.
6. City officials passed laws to improve sanitary conditions.
7. Urban reformers also tackled problems in housing and education.
8. These groundbreaking efforts led to the urban planning movement.
9. Any modern city can experience rapid change.
10. A good plan allows a city to meet this challenge.

➜ For a SELF-CHECK and more practice, see the EXERCISE BANK, p. 602.

B. REVISING: Using Specific Subjects

Read the following passage. Then replace the underlined words with more specific subjects.

Bettles Field is a small town in Alaska. The <u>number of people</u> is only 51. <u>Those who come from other places</u> usually must take a plane to get there. The <u>degree of coldness</u> can plunge to 70 degrees below zero in winter. Some <u>24-hour periods</u> have only three hours of sunlight. The <u>ones who live there</u> often schedule town dinners to keep their spirits up.

Simple Predicates, or Verbs

❶ Here's the Idea

You have learned about the simple subject of a sentence. You also need to know about the simple predicate.

▶ **The simple predicate, or verb, is the main word or words in the complete predicate.**

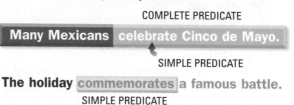

COMPLETE PREDICATE

Many Mexicans celebrate Cinco de Mayo.

SIMPLE PREDICATE

The holiday commemorates **a famous battle.**

SIMPLE PREDICATE

Verb

▶ **A verb is a word used to express an action, a condition, or a state of being.** A **linking verb** tells what the subject *is.* An **action verb** tells what the subject *does,* even when the action cannot be seen.

The Mexicans fought **a French army.** (action you can see)

They wanted **independence.** (action you cannot see)

Cinco de Mayo is **very popular in Mexico City.** (linking)

❷ Why It Matters in Writing

People sometimes drop verbs from sentences when they write quickly. Watch out for missing verbs when you revise.

STUDENT MODEL

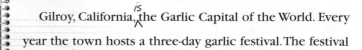

Gilroy, California, *is* the Garlic Capital of the World. Every

year the town hosts a three-day garlic festival. The festival

organizers *build* a huge flaming model of a garlic bulb.

❸ Practice and Apply

A. CONCEPT CHECK: Simple Predicates, or Verbs

On a separate sheet of paper, write the simple predicate, or verb, of each sentence.

A Small-Town Festival
1. Stahlstown, Pennsylvania, is the home of an old-time ritual.
2. Residents hold a flax-scutching festival every year.
3. This festival preserves the skills of their ancestors.
4. Pioneer settlers created fabric from flax plants.
5. First they dried the plants.
6. Then they separated the plant fibers.
7. Scutching is the name for the separation process.
8. The settlers spun the scutched flax into thread.
9. They wove the thread into linen fabric.
10. The resourceful pioneers made clothing from this fabric.

➡ **For a SELF-CHECK and more practice, see the EXERCISE BANK, p. 603.**

B. WRITING: Communicating Information

Use the following information to write a five-sentence paragraph about Atlanta. Underline the verb in each sentence. Include at least three different verbs in your paragraph.

Example: the Jimmy Carter Library
Atlanta <u>contains</u> the Jimmy Carter Library.

Facts About Atlanta
- the capital of Georgia
- in the foothills of the Blue Ridge Mountains
- about 3 million people in the metropolitan area
- the birthplace of Martin Luther King, Jr.
- host of the 1996 Summer Olympic Games

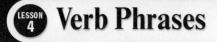

Verb Phrases

LESSON 4

❶ Here's the Idea

The simple predicate, or verb, may consist of two or more words. These words are called a verb phrase.

▶ **A verb phrase is made up of a main verb and one or more helping verbs.**

VERB PHRASE

We **can imagine** the city of the future.

HELPING VERB ↗   ↖ MAIN VERB

Main Verbs and Helping Verbs

A **main verb** can stand by itself as the simple predicate of a sentence.

Technology **changes** cities. (action)
MAIN VERB

The changes **are** rapid. (linking)
MAIN VERB

Helping verbs help main verbs express action or show time.

VERB PHRASE

Technology **will change** cities.
HELPING VERB ↗   ↖ MAIN VERB

The changes **will be occurring** rapidly.

City dwellers **should have been preparing** for change.

Notice that sometimes the main verb changes form when it is used with helping verbs. For more on these changes, see pages 100–104.

Common Helping Verbs	
Forms of *be*	is, am, are, was, were, be, been
Forms of *do*	do, does, did
Forms of *have*	has, have, had
Others	may, might, can, should, could, would, shall, will

❷ Why It Matters in Writing

Writers often use verb phrases to show time. Notice how the verb phrases convey past, present, and future time in the following paragraph.

PROFESSIONAL MODEL

This year, a team of students from New Morning School in Plymouth, Michigan, designed a city of the future. Residents of Terrania will travel on computer-guided hover shuttles. This system can reduce traffic and pollution.

                                          —Randy Vickers

PAST

PRESENT

FUTURE

❸ Practice and Apply

CONCEPT CHECK: Verb Phrases

Write the verb phrase in each sentence below.

Pollution Problems
1. Modern industries have allowed cities and towns to flourish.
2. However, they can cause serious problems as well.
3. Chemical wastes from factories can poison our environment.
4. Pollution is endangering animals and plants.
5. Automobiles have been polluting the air for decades.
6. Industries and individuals can prevent pollution.
7. The Environmental Protection Agency was created in 1970.
8. It has been overseeing federal action against pollution since then.
9. Laws have tightened standards for pollutants like carbon monoxide.
10. Such laws should have a substantial effect in the future.

➡ **For a SELF-CHECK and more practice, see the EXERCISE BANK, p. 603.**

Compound Sentence Parts

❶ Here's the Idea

Sentences can have **compound subjects** and **compound verbs**.

▶ **A compound subject is made up of two or more subjects that share the same verb.** The subjects are joined by a conjunction, or connecting word, such as *and, or,* or *but.*

COMPOUND SUBJECT

Tornadoes and hurricanes are dangerous.
SUBJECT   SUBJECT

   A flood or an earthquake can devastate a city.

▶ **A compound verb is made up of two or more verbs that have the same subject.** The verbs are joined by a conjunction such as *and, or,* or *but.*

COMPOUND VERB

The swollen river rose and crested.
         VERB   VERB

   Rescue workers located and evacuated residents.

❷ Why It Matters in Writing

Sometimes two sentences contain similar information. You can use compound subjects and verbs to combine such sentences and avoid repetition in your writing.

STUDENT MODEL

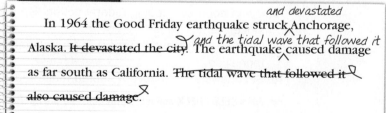

                    and devastated

In 1964 the Good Friday earthquake struck Anchorage,

Alalaska. ~~It devastated the city~~. *and the tidal wave that followed it* The earthquake caused damage

as far south as California. ~~The tidal wave that followed it~~

~~also caused damage~~.

CHAPTER 1

❸ Practice and Apply

A. CONCEPT CHECK: Compound Sentence Parts

On a separate sheet of paper, write the compound subject or the compound verb for each sentence.

The Alaska Gold Rush

1. Juneau and other Alaskan cities owe their existence to the gold rush.
2. Joseph Juneau and Richard Harris discovered gold in southeastern Alaska in 1880.
3. This area and the nearby Yukon region proved rich in gold deposits.
4. Professional prospectors and amateurs soon flooded into Alaska.
5. Some of these adventurers survived and profited.
6. Others froze or starved in the harsh environment.
7. Jack London and Robert Service wrote about the prospectors' hardships.
8. Their writings preserve and glorify this exciting period.
9. Tourism and government are the big industries in Juneau today.
10. However, stories of the gold rush still excite and captivate residents.

➡ **For a SELF-CHECK and more practice, see the EXERCISE BANK, p. 603.**

B. REVISING: Combining Sentences

Luisa tried to write this note on a postcard, but she ran out of space. Make it more compact by using compound subjects and verbs to combine sentences.

Dear Ahmed,

Jeff is having a great time in Seattle. So am I. The parks are great. The restaurants are great, too. Yesterday we swam at a beach along Puget Sound. We also sunbathed. The water surrounding the city makes it beautiful. So do the mountains.

Love,

Luisa

Kinds of Sentences

❶ Here's the Idea

▶ **A sentence can be used to make a statement, to ask a question, to make a request or give a command, or to show strong feelings.**

Four Kinds of Sentences

	What It Does	Examples
Declarative .	Makes a statement; always ends with a period	I went to Honolulu last week. My hotel was on Waikiki Beach.
Interrogative ?	Asks a question; always ends with a question mark	What did you do there? Did you surf?
Imperative . or !	Tells or asks someone to do something; usually ends with a period but may end with an exclamation point	Show me your photographs. Take me with you next time!
Exclamatory !	Shows strong feeling; always ends with an exclamation point	What a lucky person you are! That beach looks gorgeous!

❷ Why It Matters in Writing

Writers use the different kinds of sentences in dialogue to imitate how people speak. Notice which sentences in this dialogue express Henry's anxiety during his stay in London.

LITERARY MODEL

Henry. When will they be back? — INTERROGATIVE
Servant. In a month, they said. — EXCLAMATORY
Henry. A month! This is awful! Tell me how — IMPERATIVE
to get word to them. It's of great importance. — DECLARATIVE

—from Mark Twain, *The Million-Pound Bank Note*, dramatized by Walter Hackett

❸ Practice and Apply

A. CONCEPT CHECK: Kinds of Sentences

Identify each of the following sentences as declarative (D), interrogative (INT), exclamatory (E), or imperative (IMP).

Cherry Blossom Time

1. Do you know whose idea it was to plant cherry trees in Washington, D.C.?
2. Writer and photographer Eliza Scidmore came up with the idea.
3. Scidmore admired the flowering cherry trees she saw in Japan.
4. The city government had recently dredged the Potomac River and piled the dirt along the river.
5. Wouldn't blooming trees hide that sight nicely?
6. The city of Tokyo gave Washington 3,020 cherry trees in 1912.
7. Come to the Cherry Blossom Festival next spring and see them for yourself.
8. You would love Washington in the spring!
9. Look at the trees' reflections in the Tidal Basin.
10. The delicate pink blossoms look beautiful!

➡ **For a SELF-CHECK and more practice, see the EXERCISE BANK, p. 604.**

B. WRITING: Describing a Photograph

The famous gateway arches in Mombasa, Kenya, are shaped like giant elephant tusks. Write a declarative, interrogative, imperative, and exclamatory sentence about what you see in this photograph.

Subjects in Unusual Order

❶ Here's the Idea

In most declarative sentences, subjects come before verbs. In some kinds of sentences, however, subjects can come between verb parts, follow verbs, or not appear at all.

Questions

▶ **In a question, the subject usually comes after the verb or between parts of the verb phrase.**

⌐ VERB PHRASE ⌐
Are **you** walking to the Brooklyn Bridge?
⤴ SUBJECT

Is **it far away?** When will **you** arrive there?

To find the subject, turn the question into a statement. Then ask who or what is or does something.

Can **I** go with you?

I can go with you. (Who can go? *I*)

Commands

▶ **The subject of a command, or an imperative sentence, is usually *you*.** Often, *you* doesn't appear in the sentence because it is implied.

(You) Put on your comfortable shoes.
⤴ IMPLIED SUBJECT

(You) Meet me in the lobby.

Inverted Sentences

In an inverted sentence, the subject comes after the verb. Writers use inverted sentences to emphasize particular words or ideas.

Inverted Subject and Verb	
Normal	The **bridge** extends across the East River.
Inverted	Across the East River extends the **bridge**.
Normal	Its **towers** are reflected in the water.
Inverted	Reflected in the water are its **towers**.

Sentences Beginning with *Here* or *There*

▶ **In some sentences beginning with *here* or *there*, subjects follow verbs.** To find the subject in such a sentence, look for the verb and ask the question *who* or *what*.

WHAT IS?

There is the world-famous bridge.
    VERB   SUBJECT

WHAT COMES?

Here comes the bus to Brooklyn.
    VERB   SUBJECT

❷ Why It Matters in Writing

Inverting the word order enables you to add variety to your sentences. Notice how the changes in the revision below make it more interesting to read.

STUDENT MODEL

DRAFT

We have walked all the way to the tip of Manhattan. The Brooklyn Bridge stands before us. Brooklyn lies beyond the river.

REVISION

We have walked all the way to the tip of Manhattan. **Before us stands the Brooklyn Bridge. Beyond the river lies Brooklyn.**

❸ Practice and Apply

A. CONCEPT CHECK: Subjects in Unusual Order

In separate columns on a sheet of paper, write the simple subject and the verb (or verb phrase) of each sentence below.

Coney Island: King of Amusement Parks

1. Have you heard of Coney Island?
2. On the edge of Brooklyn lies this famous amusement park.
3. Among its attractions are many rides.
4. Test your courage on the old-fashioned wooden roller coaster.
5. There is a ride worth taking.
6. Do you like games of skill?
7. Then walk down the midway at Coney Island.
8. On both sides are games like the ring toss.
9. There are not too many winners in those games.
10. Here is a map of the amusement park.

➔ For a SELF-CHECK and more practice, see the EXERCISE BANK, p. 604.

B. REVISING: Adding Variety

Rewrite the following sentences according to the instructions given in parentheses.

1. You would like to learn more about Brooklyn. (Change the sentence to a question.)
2. Your chance has arrived. (Rewrite the sentence to begin with *Here is*)
3. You come on a walking tour of the borough. (Change the sentence to a command.)
4. Many fascinating neighborhoods are scattered throughout Brooklyn. (Begin the sentence with *Scattered throughout* and place the subject after the helping verb.)
5. You meet your guide on the Brooklyn side of the bridge. (Change the sentence to a command.)

In your 🗀 **Working Portfolio,** find the paragraph that you wrote for the **Write Away** on page 4. Add variety to the sentences by changing the positions of some of their subjects.

Complements: Subject Complements

❶ Here's the Idea

A complement is a word or a group of words that completes the meaning of a verb. Two kinds of complements are **subject complements** and **objects of verbs**.

▶ **A subject complement is a word or group of words that follows a linking verb and renames or describes the subject.** A linking verb links the subject with a noun or an adjective that tells more about the subject.

LINKING VERB
Pennsylvania is the Keystone State.
SUBJECT   COMPLEMENT

Common Linking Verbs	
Forms of *be*	am, is, are, was, were, being, been
Other linking verbs	appear, feel, look, sound, seem, smell, taste, grow, become

Predicate Nouns and Predicate Adjectives

Both nouns and adjectives can serve as subject complements.

▶ **A predicate noun follows a linking verb and defines or renames the subject.**

DEFINES
Philadelphia is the largest city in Pennsylvania.
SUBJECT   PREDICATE NOUN
RENAMES

The capital of Pennsylvania is Harrisburg.

▶ **A predicate adjective follows a linking verb and describes a quality of the subject.**

DESCRIBES
Philadelphia cheesesteaks taste great.
SUBJECT   PREDICATE ADJECTIVE
DESCRIBES

The Liberty Bell is historic.

❷ Why It Matters in Writing

Subject complements can provide important information and vivid details about your subjects.

PROFESSIONAL MODEL

The town of Hershey smells delicious. A huge candy factory is the source of this pleasurable sensation. Tourists seem happy just to breathe in the air.

PREDICATE NOUN

PREDICATE ADJECTIVES

—Rachel Robinson

❸ Practice and Apply

A. CONCEPT CHECK: Subject Complements

Find the subject complement in each sentence and identify it as a predicate noun (PN) or a predicate adjective (PA).

By Any Other Name

1. Chicago is the Windy City.
2. This nickname is a reference to loud and windy promoters.
3. Denver is the Mile-High City.
4. It is high above sea level.
5. Paris became the City of Light long ago.
6. It looks so beautiful at night.
7. Molde, Norway, is the Town of Roses.
8. Its rose gardens smell fragrant.
9. Tin Can Island is the nickname for Niuafo'ou, Tonga.
10. Tin cans are the containers that islanders used for exchanging letters with passing ships.

➜ For a SELF-CHECK and more practice, see the EXERCISE BANK, p. 605.

B. REVISING: Replacing Subject Complements

Find each subject complement below and replace it with a synonym. Identify your replacement as a predicate noun or predicate adjective.

Los Angeles seems glamorous. It has become the heart of the entertainment industry. The presence of movie stars is a delight for tourists.

Complements: Objects of Verbs

❶ Here's the Idea

In addition to subject complements, there are objects of verbs. Action verbs often need complements called direct objects and indirect objects to complete their meaning.

Direct Objects

▶ **A direct object is a word or group of words that names the receiver of the action.** A direct object answers the questions *what* or *whom.*

RIDE WHAT?

Many Beijing residents ride bicycles.
DIRECT OBJECT ↗

New Yorkers take the subway. (take what? *subway*)

Indirect Objects

▶ **An indirect object is a word or group of words that tells to whom or what (or for whom or what) an action is performed.** An indirect object usually comes between a verb and a direct object.

TO WHOM?

Mass transit offers people easy commutes.
INDIRECT OBJECT ↗   ↖ DIRECT OBJECT

Gondolas give Venetians romantic rides.

Verbs that are often followed by indirect objects include *bring, give, hand, lend, make, offer, send, show, teach, tell, write,* and *ask.*

> **Here's How** Finding Direct and Indirect Objects
>
> **The conductor hands us our change.**
>
> 1. Find the action verb in the sentence. *hands*
> 2. To find the **direct object**, ask, Hands what? *change*
> 3. To find the **indirect object**, ask, Hands to or for whom? *us*

❷ Why It Matters in Writing

Direct objects and indirect objects are important when you are describing the effects of actions.

LITERARY MODEL

Grady Bishop had just been hired as a driver for Metro Bus Service. When he put on the gray uniform and boarded his bus, nothing mattered, not his obesity, not his poor education, not growing up the eleventh child of the town drunk. Driving gave him power. And power mattered.

— "The Woman in the Snow," retold by Patricia C. McKissack

DIRECT OBJECTS

INDIRECT OBJECT

❸ Practice and Apply

CONCEPT CHECK: Objects of Verbs

For each sentence below, write each object and identify it as either a direct object (DO) or an indirect object (IO).

Easy Riding
1. The interstate highway system offers American cities a connection with each other.
2. State governments began building the system in the 1950s.
3. The federal government gave the states funds for their portions of the interstate highway system.
4. Builders poured concrete by the ton during the project.
5. They moved enough soil to cover Connecticut.
6. The project gave many towns an economic boost.
7. The system now reaches all areas of the country.
8. Astronauts can even see it from space.
9. It brought Americans increased mobility.
10. Drivers can cross the country without stopping for a traffic light.

➡ For a SELF-CHECK and more practice, see the EXERCISE BANK, p. 605.

Fragments and Run-Ons

❶ Here's the Idea

Sentence fragments and run-on sentences are writing errors that can make your writing difficult to understand.

Sentence Fragments

▶ **A sentence fragment is a part of a sentence that is written as if it were a complete sentence.** A sentence fragment is missing a subject, a predicate, or both.

FRAGMENTS

Ghost towns usually around deserted mines and oil fields. (missing a predicate)

Abandoned them after the mines or fields were exhausted. (missing a subject)

Numerous in the western states. (missing both)

To make a complete sentence, add a subject, a predicate, or both.

REVISION

Ghost towns usually can be found around deserted mines and oil fields. Residents abandoned them after the mines or fields were exhausted. Such towns are numerous in the western states.

For more help, see the **Quick-Fix Editing Machine, p. 290.**

The Sentence and Its Parts

Run-On Sentences

▶ **A run-on sentence consists of two or more sentences written as though they were a single sentence.**

RUN-ON

Most ghost towns are **in ruins, some** have been restored **to their original condition.**

REVISION

Most ghost towns are **in ruins. Some** have been restored **to their original condition.**

REVISION

Most ghost towns are **in ruins, but some** have been restored **to their original condition.**

For more help, see the Quick-Fix Editing Machine, p. 291.

When combining two sentences with a conjunction, insert a comma before the conjunction.

❷ Why It Matters in Writing

Fragments and run-on sentences can confuse and frustrate readers. Fixing these problems will make your writing clearer.

STUDENT MODEL

DRAFT

The town of Garnet flourished for a while. During the second half of the 19th century. One thousand people lived there in 1898, seven years later the population was only 200. Now a ghost town.

REVISION

The town of Garnet flourished **during the second half of the 19th century.** One thousand people lived there in 1898, **but** seven years later the population was only 200. **Garnet is** now a ghost town.

❸ Practice and Apply

A. CONCEPT CHECK: Sentence Fragments and Run-Ons

On a separate sheet of paper, identify each of the following sentences as a fragment (F), a run-on (RO), or a complete sentence (CS).

Ink, Arkansas

1. A tiny village in Arkansas had no name, residents walked to the next town for their mail.
2. Tired of walking such a distance.
3. They wanted their own post office.
4. The U.S. Postal Service replied to the residents, it sent them questionnaires.
5. Asked what name the village wanted.
6. Every family in town received a questionnaire, the instructions said, "Please write in ink."
7. The residents did just that.
8. Wrote in the word "Ink" for the name of their town.
9. Now Ink, Arkansas, has a name and a post office.
10. Just 12 miles from Pencil Bluff, Arkansas.

➜ For a SELF-CHECK and more practice, see the EXERCISE BANK, p. 606.

B. REVISING: Frustrating Fragments and Ridiculous Run-Ons

A friend of yours is going to Montana. You have dashed off a note with suggestions on visiting ghost towns. Complaining that it is confusing, she hands back the note. Correct the fragments and run-on sentences so that your note is easier to understand.

Suggestions for Visiting Ghost Towns

You will need comfortable shoes. Be careful as you. Many of the buildings are badly deteriorated, there may be old mine shafts you can fall into. Rattlesnakes another danger. Never remove any items from a ghost town, leave them for other visitors to enjoy.

Grammar in Literature

Using Different Types of Sentences

When you write for school or for fun, you can use different types of sentences to create dialogue. Using different types of sentences makes dialogue more interesting and realistic. Notice the types of sentences author Amy Tan uses in the dialogue from "Rules of the Game."

from

RULES of the GAME

BY AMY TAN

"Let me! Let me!" I begged between games ...
Vincent explained the rules, pointing to each piece.
"You have sixteen pieces and so do I. One king and queen, two bishops, two knights, two castles, and eight pawns. The pawns can only move forward one step,

IMPERATIVE SENTENCES

DECLARATIVE SENTENCE

except on the first move. Then they can move two. But they can only take men by moving crossways like this, except in the beginning, when you can move ahead and take another pawn."

"Why?" I asked as I moved my pawn. "Why can't they move more steps?"

INTERROGATIVE SENTENCES

Chinese Girl, Emil Orlik. Oil on canvas. Christie's Images/SuperStock.

Practice and Apply

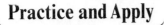

WRITING: Using Different Types of Sentences

Some of the rules for the board game checkers are listed below. Create a dialogue between two people about the game. You might have a sister explain the rules to her sister, a friend explain the rules to another friend, or one stranger explain the rules to another stranger. Be sure to use different types of sentences. Save your dialogue in your 📁 **Working Portfolio.**

Rules for Checkers

The object of the game is to capture all of your opponent's pieces.

1. The first player moves a black piece diagonally toward the red pieces.
2. The second player moves a red piece diagonally toward the black pieces.
3. The pieces can only be moved diagonally on the black squares.
4. Players can only move the pieces forward, toward the opponent's starting place.
5. To capture a piece, a player must "jump" diagonally, from one square, over the opponent's piece, landing on the closest empty square.
6. When a player captures a piece, that piece is removed from the board.

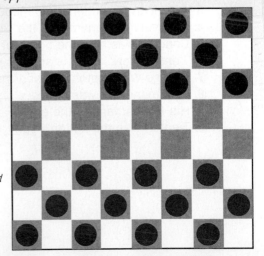

SENTENCE PARTS

Mixed Review

A. Subjects, Predicates, and Compound Sentence Parts Read the passage, and then write the answers to the questions below it.

Riding Underground

(1) A subway is an underground railway. **(2)** Electricity powers the trains. **(3)** Subways are very convenient in crowded urban areas. **(4)** Some large cities have built extensive subway systems. **(5)** They must plan and construct those systems carefully. **(6)** Cost and efficiency are the main concerns. **(7)** There are several different methods for building subway tunnels. **(8)** Construction crews often tear apart and rebuild streets over subway lines. **(9)** Can you imagine the traffic problems such construction would create? **(10)** However, the benefits will outweigh any inconvenience.

1. What is the simple subject of sentence 1?
2. What kind of sentence is sentence 2?
3. What is the simple predicate of sentence 3?
4. What is the main verb in sentence 4?
5. What is the compound part of sentence 5?
6. What is the compound part of sentence 6?
7. What is the simple subject of sentence 7?
8. What is the complete subject of sentence 8?
9. What kind of sentence is sentence 9?
10. What is the complete predicate in sentence 10?

B. Complements Identify each underlined word as a predicate adjective (PA), a predicate noun (PN), a direct object (DO), or an indirect object (IO).

1. Concord is a <u>town</u> in Massachusetts.
2. The town is <u>famous</u>.
3. American revolutionaries encountered British <u>soldiers</u> there.
4. The revolutionaries gave the <u>British</u> a good fight.
5. Concord was also the <u>home</u> of several important writers.
6. Trenton, New Jersey, is another <u>site</u> of a Revolutionary War battle.
7. George Washington crossed the <u>Delaware River</u> near the city.
8. This maneuver was <u>daring</u>.
9. His troops handed the <u>enemy</u> a major defeat.
10. Trenton was the nation's <u>capital</u> for a brief period.

Choose the letter of the term that correctly identifies each underlined part of this passage.

Cities <u>are home to a variety of wildlife</u>. Pigeons <u>have thrived</u> in
                        (1)   (2)
cities. They build <u>nests</u> on ledges. Squirrels are hardy <u>acrobats</u>.
                    (3)   (4)
<u>Many people appreciate their playful behavior, others consider</u>
                                  (5)
<u>them pests</u>. <u>More exotic forms of wildlife</u> are appearing in cities.
                        (6)
<u>Los Angeles, New York, and other cities</u> attract coyotes. These
                   (7)
creatures <u>hunt and scavenge</u> for food. <u>One coyote in New York</u>
                   (8)   (9)
enjoyed shrimp lo mein and spaghetti! <u>What would you do if you</u>
                                                              (10)
<u>saw a coyote in your neighborhood</u>?

1. A. simple subject
   B. complete subject
   C. simple predicate
   D. complete predicate

2. A. main verb
   B. helping verb
   C. verb phrase
   D. compound verb

3. A. simple predicate
   B. complete predicate
   C. direct object
   D. indirect object

4. A. predicate adjective
   B. predicate noun
   C. direct object
   D. indirect object

5. A. compound subject
   B. compound verb
   C. fragment
   D. run-on sentence

6. A. complete subject
   B. simple subject
   C. complete predicate
   D. compound subject

7. A. compound subject
   B. compound verb
   C. complement
   D. predicate noun

8. A. compound subject
   B. compound verb
   C. complement
   D. predicate noun

9. A. declarative sentence
   B. interrogative sentence
   C. exclamatory sentence
   D. imperative sentence

10. A. declarative sentence
    B. interrogative sentence
    C. exclamatory sentence
    D. imperative sentence

SENTENCE PARTS

Student Help Desk

The Sentence at a Glance

A sentence has two parts: a complete subject and a complete predicate.

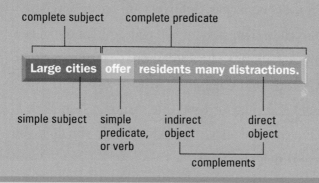

complete subject   complete predicate

Large cities **offer** **residents many distractions.**

simple subject   simple predicate, or verb   indirect object   direct object

complements

Subjects and Predicates   Central City

Term or Concept	Example	How to Find It
Complete subject	**Most cities** have a downtown area.	Ask who or what is or does something.
Simple subject	**cities**	Find the key word(s) in the complete subject.
Complete predicate	Skyscrapers tower over pedestrians.	Ask what the subject is or does.
Simple predicate	tower	Find the verb(s) or verb phrase(s).

Complements Outer Neighborhoods

	Term or Concept	Example	What It Does
Linking verbs	Predicate noun	This is my **neighborhood.**	Renames or defines the subject
	Predicate adjective	It is **peaceful.**	Describes the subject
Action verbs	Direct object	I ride my **bike** downtown.	Completes the verb's action
	Indirect object	A map shows **me** the route.	Tells to whom/what or for whom/what the action is done

Kinds of Sentences Seeking Variety

Declarative sentence	I'm going to the museum.
Interrogative sentence	Will it be interesting**?**
Imperative sentence	**(You)** Come with me.
Exclamatory sentence	The show is fascinating**!**

The Bottom Line

Checklist for Editing Sentences

Have I . . .

____ made sure that each sentence has a subject and a predicate?

____ corrected any fragments or run-on sentences?

____ combined any sentences with similar ideas by using compound subjects or verbs?

____ used different kinds of sentences and different orders of sentence parts for variety?

____ used complements to make the meanings of sentences clear?

Nouns

The Big Dipper

Theme: Stars and Planets

Naming It

For thousands of years, astronomers have been giving names to stars, planets, constellations, and other objects in the sky. How many different ones can you list? All of these names are nouns. Nouns allow us to communicate our ideas about places that are far away from our planet. Without nouns, you might say that we would be lost in space—unable to talk or write about the world around us.

Write Away: Travel Plans
Write about a planet you would like to visit. Why does it interest you? What would you like to learn about it? Save your work in your 📁 **Working Portfolio.**

CD-ROM Grammar Coach

For each underlined item, choose the letter of the term that correctly identifies it.

The first <u>telescopes</u> were built about 1608 by lens makers in the
(1)
<u>Netherlands</u>. An Italian scientist, <u>Galileo Galilei</u>, used this new
(2)   (3)
<u>invention</u> to observe heavenly <u>bodies</u>. Galileo's telescope had little
(4)   (5)
power by today's standards. However, this remarkable <u>instrument</u>
(6)
allowed Galileo to make important discoveries about the <u>solar</u>
(7)
<u>system</u>. Over the <u>centuries</u>, our knowledge of the universe has
(8)
been greatly expanded by <u>astronomers'</u> observations through
(9)
telescopes. We now know that the stars, planets, and galaxies we

see as <u>pinpoints</u> of light may be many light-years away.
(10)

1. A. proper noun
   B. common noun
   C. collective noun
   D. compound noun

2. A. predicate noun
   B. proper noun
   C. collective noun
   D. possessive noun

3. A. noun as direct object
   B. noun as indirect object
   C. noun as appositive
   D. noun as object of
      preposition

4. A. noun as subject
   B. noun as direct object
   C. noun as indirect object
   D. noun as object of
      preposition

5. A. concrete noun
   B. abstract noun
   C. proper noun
   D. compound noun

6. A. noun as object of
      preposition
   B. noun as subject
   C. noun as direct object
   D. noun as indirect object

7. A. proper noun
   B. collective noun
   C. compound noun
   D. abstract noun

8. A. noun as indirect object
   B. noun as direct object
   C. noun as subject
   D. noun as object of
      preposition

9. A. collective noun
   B. singular noun
   C. compound noun
   D. possessive noun

10. A. possessive noun
    B. collective noun
    C. singular noun
    D. compound noun

Kinds of Nouns

❶ Here's the Idea

▶ **A noun is a word that names a person, place, thing, or idea.** There are several ways to classify nouns.

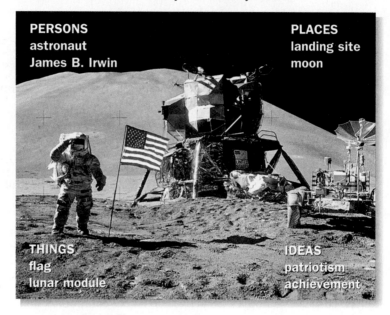

PERSONS
astronaut
James B. Irwin

PLACES
landing site
moon

THINGS
flag
lunar module

IDEAS
patriotism
achievement

Common and Proper Nouns

A **common noun** is a general name for a person, place, thing, or idea. Common nouns are usually not capitalized.

A **proper noun** is the name of a particular person, place, thing, or idea. Proper nouns are always capitalized.

Common	astronaut	planet	mission
Proper	Sally Ride	Jupiter	*Apollo 11*

Concrete and Abstract Nouns

A **concrete noun** names a thing that can be seen, heard, smelled, touched, or tasted. Examples include *sunlight, explosion, fuel, rocks, moon,* and *ice.*

The astronauts collected rocks from the moon.

An **abstract noun** names an idea, feeling, quality, or characteristic. Examples include *exploration, excitement, lightness,* and *courage.*

They felt great excitement as they explored.

Every noun is either common or proper and also concrete or abstract. For example, *planet* is common and concrete. *Mars* is proper and concrete.

Collective Nouns

A **collective noun** is a word that names a group of people or things. Examples include *community, audience, panel, crowd, class, government,* and *staff.*

A panel of scientists presented their findings.

Some collective nouns name specific groups of animals or sometimes people. Examples include *pack, herd,* and *colony.*

They hope to establish a colony on the moon.

➋ Why It Matters in Writing

Without concrete common and proper nouns, writing is often too vague. Notice how the highlighted concrete nouns in the following description help make it specific.

PROFESSIONAL MODEL

Early on the morning of July 20, 1969, I was circling the moon with Neil Armstrong and Buzz Aldrin in our spacecraft *Columbia.* We had just awakened from a short sleep and were sucking lukewarm coffee out of plastic tubes and munching on bacon which had been squeezed into little cubes, like lumps of sugar.

PROPER NOUNS

COMMON NOUNS

—Michael Collins, *Flying to the Moon: An Astronaut's Story*

❸ Practice and Apply

A. CONCEPT CHECK: Kinds of Nouns

Write the nouns in these sentences, identifying each as common or proper. Then identify three collective nouns.

Dining in Orbit

1. The first astronauts squeezed food from tubes.

2. Astronauts in the Space Shuttle Program eat from a tray with forks and spoons.

3. They use straws to drink beverages from sealed pouches.

4. NASA employs a team of dietitians to make sure the astronauts eat properly.

5. Before the flight, each astronaut chooses food from a large group of items.

6. There is a supply of snacks available to the crew.

7. Yet most astronauts crave certain favorite foods.

8. Shannon Lucid missed her favorite candy during her six-month mission.

9. Astronauts cannot gain weight in space.

10. The extra fat will show up on their return to Earth.

➡ For a SELF-CHECK and more practice, see the EXERCISE BANK, p. 606.

B. WRITING: Using Nouns

Read the following biographical facts about Mae Jemison. Then write a paragraph about her, using common and proper nouns.

Mae Jemison

Born: October 17, 1956

Birthplace: Decatur, Alabama

Family: one of three children of Charlie and Dorothy Jemison; father, a maintenance worker; mother, a teacher

Education:

- Stanford University, Palo Alto, California, 1977
  Bachelor of Science in Chemical Engineering
- Cornell University, Ithaca, New York, 1981
  Doctor of Medicine

Achievement: first African-American female astronaut

Advice to Students: encourages students to pursue careers in science and engineering

Singular and Plural Nouns

❶ Here's the Idea

▶ **A singular noun names one person, place, thing, or idea. A plural noun names more than one person, place, thing, or idea.**

One astronomer saw a star. (singular nouns)

The astronomers saw many stars. (plural nouns)

One of the hardest things about plural nouns is spelling them correctly. Use these rules in the Quick-Fix Spelling Machine.

QUICK-FIX SPELLING MACHINE: PLURALS OF NOUNS

SINGULAR	RULE	PLURAL
① star planet	Add -s to most nouns.	stars planets
② gas dish	Add -es to a noun that ends in s, sh, ch, x, or z.	gases dishes
③ radio	Add -s to most nouns that end in o.	radios
	hero	Add -es to a few nouns that end in o.	heroes
④ galaxy	For most nouns ending in y, change the y to an i and add -es.	galaxies
	ray	When a vowel comes before the y, just add -s.	rays
⑤ half life	For most nouns ending in f or fe, change the f to v and add -es or -s.	halves lives
	belief	Just add -s to a few nouns that end in f or fe.	beliefs
⑥ sheep species	For some nouns, keep the same spelling.	sheep species

▶ **The plurals of some nouns are formed in irregular ways.**

Singular	man	child	foot	mouse
Plural	men	children	feet	mice

❷ Why It Matters in Writing

Writing plural nouns can be tricky. Note the various ways plural nouns are spelled in the model.

PROFESSIONAL MODEL

When you look up at the night sky, the **stars** seem like tiny **points** of light. Yet many of them are much larger than the sun. All **varieties** of life on Earth depend on the heat and light of a star that is no different from **billions** of other stars in the billions of **galaxies** in the universe.

—Gerald Ng

❸ Practice and Apply

A. CONCEPT CHECK: Singular and Plural Nouns

Rewrite the nouns in parentheses in their plural forms.

The Exciting Lives of Stars
 1. Stars are made of hydrogen, helium, and small (quantity) of other elements.
 2. They create enormous (amount) of energy when their hydrogen atoms join together and change into helium.
 3. Like human (being), stars go through a life cycle.
 4. Stars fall into (category), mainly based on their size.
 5. Many stars shrink as they age into smaller (body) known as white dwarfs.
 6. Other stars, called supergiants, may end their (life) in explosions called supernovas.
 7. (Astronomer) believe our sun is a middle-aged star.
 8. Most of the sun's surface consists of (wave) of energy.
 9. There are also dark (patch) on its surface, called sunspots.

10. The sun's powerful (ray) can damage your eyes.

➡ **For a SELF-CHECK and more practice, see the EXERCISE BANK, p. 607.**

B. PROOFREADING: Spelling Plural Nouns

Ten plural nouns in the following passage are misspelled. Find them, and write the correct spellings.

Twinkle, Twinkle

Ancient observers thought stars were the flickering torchs of the gods. These old beliefs are poetic. However, the real reason stars twinkle is that their light must pass through Earth's atmosphere. Moving air currentes and dust cause starlight to bend. Our ancestorcs may not have understood why stars twinkle. However, they could enjoy seeing thousands of them while watching their flocks of sheeps. During our lifes artificial lighting has brightened the night sky over citys. Rayes from streetllghts and neon signs of factorys obscure our view. Today pollution interferes with our searchs of the night skys.

C. WRITING: Comparing Photographs

One of Many

Astronomers estimate that there are 100 billion galaxies in the universe. Look at the pictures of two galaxies below. Write a paragraph comparing their shapes. Underline the plural nouns in your comparison. Be sure you spell plural nouns correctly.

Possessive Nouns

① Here's the Idea

▶ **The possessive form of a noun shows ownership or relationship.**

Rudy's teacher discussed the Martian atmosphere.
RELATIONSHIP

Inez could see Mars through her father's telescope.
OWNERSHIP

You may use possessive nouns in place of longer phrases.

Mars's

We saw photos of ~~the~~ moons ~~of Mars.~~

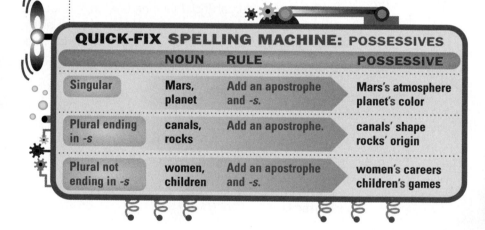

QUICK-FIX SPELLING MACHINE: POSSESSIVES

	NOUN	RULE	POSSESSIVE
Singular	Mars, planet	Add an apostrophe and *-s*.	Mars's atmosphere planet's color
Plural ending in *-s*	canals, rocks	Add an apostrophe.	canals' shape rocks' origin
Plural not ending in *-s*	women, children	Add an apostrophe and *-s*.	women's careers children's games

② Why It Matters in Writing

Possessive nouns can make your writing less wordy and easier to understand. Be sure not to make spelling errors by putting apostrophes in the wrong places.

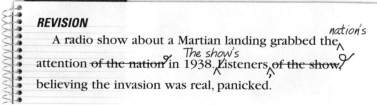

STUDENT MODEL

REVISION

nation's

A radio show about a Martian landing grabbed the∧

The show's

attention ~~of the nation~~ in 1938. ~~Listeners of the show,~~

believing the invasion was real, panicked.

❸ Practice and Apply

A. CONCEPT CHECK: Possessive Nouns

Write the possessive form of each noun in parentheses. Then label each possessive noun singular or plural.

Astronomy: The Early Years

1. (Astronomy) history dates back 5,000 years to Babylon.
2. The (Babylonians) calendar was based on their observations of the stars and planets.
3. (Men) and (women) lives were governed by the stars.
4. Ancient (Egypt) builders may have used the stars to guide their placement of the pyramids.
5. The Greek philosopher Aristotle claimed that Earth was the (solar system) center.
6. He used the (sun) movement across the sky as proof.
7. His theory was accepted for more than a thousand (years) time.
8. The Polish astronomer Copernicus pointed out (Aristotle) errors in the 1500s.
9. He showed that (Earth) rotation makes it seem as if the sun revolves around it.
10. All of the (planets) orbits are actually centered around the sun.

➡ For a SELF-CHECK and more practice, see the EXERCISE BANK, p. 607.

B. REVISING: Labeling a Science Display

Use possessive nouns to make these phrases short enough to fit as photo captions.

Example: The Moons of Jupiter

Answer: Jupiter's Moons

1. Soil Samples from the Mission
2. The Rings of Saturn
3. The Cabin in the Spacecraft
4. The Atmosphere of Venus
5. The Fuel Tanks of the Rocket Boosters

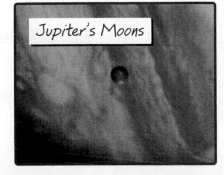

Jupiter's Moons

NOUNS

LESSON 4 · Compound Nouns

① Here's the Idea

▶ **A compound noun is made of two or more words used together as a single noun.** The parts of a compound noun may be written as

- a single word: **liftoff, spacecraft**
- two or more separate words: **rocket engine, peanut butter**
- a hyphenated word: **light-year**

Plural Compound Nouns

QUICK-FIX SPELLING MACHINE: COMPOUND NOUNS			
	SINGULAR	**RULE**	**PLURAL**
One word	liftoff	Add -*s* to most words.	liftoffs
	wristwatch	Add -*es* to words that end in *ch, sh, s, x,* or *z*.	wristwatches
Two or more words or hyphenated words	rocket engine mother-in-law	Make the main noun plural. The main noun is the noun that is modified.	rocket engines mothers-in-law

② Why It Matters in Writing

Many spelling errors in writing involve compound nouns. Note how these are spelled correctly in the following model.

> **LITERARY MODEL**
>
> My father ... was not impressed by the growing enthusiasm for parachute-jumping as a sport. Young **daredevils** like my brother could call it "**sky-diving**" if they wanted to, but the aviation pioneers referred to it disgustedly as "jumping out of a perfectly good **airplane**."
>
> —Reeve Lindbergh, "Flying"

❸ Practice and Apply

Write each compound noun in the sentences, and label it singular or plural.

Telescopes

1. The world's most powerful optical telescope is located on the volcanic mountaintop of Mauna Kea in Hawaii.
2. Mauna Kea's remote location can cause headaches and forgetfulness for workers not used to the lack of oxygen at more than 13,000 feet above sea level.
3. Gary Puniwai, who is very much the commander in chief at the Keck I telescope site, keeps a notebook as a memory backup.
4. Melted snow can also freeze on a telescope dome and cause a shutdown.
5. Astronomers do not have to work at this rugged outpost.
6. They can radio their instructions to workers from a communication hookup in a warm village 50 miles away.
7. Radio telescopes were another breakthrough for astronomers.
8. These telescopes collect radio waves from objects light-years away and turn them into computer images.
9. Astronomers can sit in a comfortable workplace as they analyze the images with sophisticated software.
10. Astronomers hope spacecraft will provide even better telescopes to help solve the mysteries of the universe.

➡ For a SELF-CHECK and more practice, see the EXERCISE BANK, p. 608.

B. REVISING: Plural Compound Nouns

Write the plural for each singular compound noun in parentheses.

On dark nights in the countryside, you can usually see the stars. Sirius is the brightest. It is 8.6 (light-year) away. You and your friends can set your (wristwatch) for midnight. Wear your (sweatsuit) and (windbreaker). Bring your (flashlight), your (notebook), and maybe some (leftover) from dinner, and see if you can find it.

LESSON 5 — Nouns as Subjects and Complements

❶ Here's the Idea

▶ **A noun can be the subject of a sentence or it can work as a complement.**

Nouns as Subjects

A **subject** tells whom or what a sentence is about. Nouns are often subjects, as this description shows.

PROFESSIONAL MODEL

Comets are made of ice, dust, and gas.
Astronomers often describe them as dirty snowballs.
The **tails** only appear when comets come near the sun.

—Helen Witowski

Nouns as Complements

A **complement** is a word that completes the meaning of the verb. Three kinds of complements are *predicate nouns, direct objects,* and *indirect objects.*

Nouns as Complements		
Predicate noun	Renames or defines the subject after a linking verb	Carolyn Shoemaker is an **astronomer.**
Direct object	Names the receiver of the action of the verb	She has discovered many **comets.**
Indirect object	Tells *to whom or what* or *for whom or what* an action is done	One of her discoveries gave **astronomers** a thrill.

❷ Why It Matters in Writing

Specific complements are needed in your writing, particularly in informative writing. Notice how the nouns acting as complements complete the meaning and add information.

STUDENT MODEL

Jupiter is the **king** of planets, bigger than all the others put together. In 1994 a comet named Shoemaker-Levy 9 hit the **planet** with enormous force. The Hubble Space Telescope sent **astronomers** spectacular photographs of the collision.

> **PREDICATE NOUN**

> **DIRECT OBJECTS**

> **INDIRECT OBJECT**

❸ Practice and Apply

CONCEPT CHECK: Nouns as Subjects and Complements

Identify each underlined noun as a subject or a complement.

Target Earth
1. <u>Comets</u> orbit the <u>sun</u> just as planets do.
2. However, their <u>orbits</u> are not very predictable.
3. A small <u>comet</u> gave <u>human beings</u> a <u>scare</u> in 1908.
4. The <u>comet</u> destroyed a <u>forest</u> when it crashed into Siberia.
5. <u>People</u> felt its <u>impact</u> hundreds of miles away.
6. <u>Asteroids</u> are another potential <u>danger</u> to us.
7. These rocky <u>objects</u> can be as wide as 600 miles.
8. Sometimes their <u>orbits</u> bring them very close to Earth.
9. An <u>asteroid</u> could destroy all <u>life</u> on our planet if it crashed here.
10. Such a <u>collision</u> may have killed off the <u>dinosaurs</u> about 65 million years ago.

➜ **For a SELF-CHECK and more practice, see the EXERCISE BANK, p. 608.**

Further label each complement as *predicate noun, direct object,* or *indirect object.*

LESSON 6 — Nouns in Phrases

① Here's the Idea

Nouns often appear in prepositional phrases and appositive phrases. Such phrases add information to a sentence.

Nouns as Objects of Prepositions

An **object of a preposition** is the noun or pronoun that follows the preposition. Nouns often appear in sentences as objects of prepositions.

Mount Wilson is an observatory in California.

PREPOSITION ↗   ↖ OBJECT OF PREPOSITION

Edwin Hubble made many discoveries at the famous observatory.

Nouns as Appositives

An **appositive** is a noun or pronoun that identifies or renames another noun or pronoun. An **appositive phrase** is made up of an appositive and its modifiers.

APPOSITIVE PHRASE

The Milky Way, our galaxy, is one of many.

↖ APPOSITIVE

Edwin Hubble, the famous astronomer, proved this.

Hubble showed that the Milky Way, a galaxy with billions of stars, is only one of many galaxies in the universe.

Note that you should use commas before and after the appositive phrase if the information isn't essential to understanding the preceding noun or pronoun.

Cosmology, the study of the universe, owes a great debt to Hubble.

② Why It Matters in Writing

The use of nouns in prepositional phrases and appositives can provide the specific details you need to support the statements you make in explanatory writing.

STUDENT MODEL

Henrietta Leavitt, an astronomer, discovered the way to measure how far away stars are from our planet. Her observations provided Edwin Hubble with a method for finding other galaxies.

APPOSITIVE

OBJECT OF PREPOSITION

③ Practice and Apply

CONCEPT CHECK: Nouns in Phrases

Identify each underlined noun as an object of a preposition or an appositive.

Working Overtime in Space
1. Shannon Lucid, an experienced <u>astronaut</u>, was chosen for a joint American-Russian space mission in 1996.
2. She spent a year in Russia preparing for her duties on *Mir*, a Russian <u>space station</u>.
3. She flew to *Mir* on a <u>space shuttle</u>.
4. Two Russians aboard *Mir* showered her with <u>greetings</u>.
5. Lucid grew used to eating Russian foods such as borscht, a beet <u>soup</u>.
6. She did experiments to see how plants grow in <u>space</u>.
7. Her mission was supposed to last for four <u>months</u>.
8. Her return was delayed by seven <u>weeks</u>.
9. Lucid's 188 days in space set a record for <u>Americans</u>.
10. She was delighted to return to Houston, her home <u>city</u>.

➡ **For a SELF-CHECK and more practice, see the EXERCISE BANK, p. 609.**

For each sentence, write the phrase in which the object of a preposition or the appositive is found.

Nouns **49**

Grammar in Physical Education

Using Specific Nouns

For a physical education class, some students have gathered information about physical requirements for astronauts. They plan to use this information to create a brochure encouraging all students to become competent swimmers. Notice the specific nouns the students have used in their notes.

All **candidates** for the astronaut **corps** must pass a swimming **test** before they receive physical **training** at the **Johnson Space Center** near **Houston, Texas.**

Candidates must swim a total of 75 **meters**, or about 225 **feet.** During the **test** they must wear **tennis shoes** and a flight **suit,** a one-piece **garment** that combines **pants** with a long-sleeved **shirt.**

Swimmers may swim the **sidestroke, breaststroke,** or **freestyle.** For the final **requirement** of the **test,** they must tread **water** for 10 **minutes.**

Only when astronaut **candidates** have successfully passed this swimming **test** can they go on to learn more advanced **skills.** The next **steps** in their physical **training** are to become scuba-qualified and to complete military water-survival **training.**

As part of her training, astronaut Eileen M. Collins attended water-survival training school. Here she is shown in a parachute dropping into water.

National Aeronautics and Space Administration

Practice and Apply

A. DRAFTING: Plan a Brochure

Create a brochure encouraging students to learn to swim. The following steps will help you plan your brochure.

1. Make a list of reasons for learning to swim. Use specific nouns to name the reasons. (Exercise and enjoyment are two possible reasons.)
2. Use specific nouns to name careers that require swimming.
3. Provide information about the swimming test that astronaut candidates must pass.
4. Provide information about where in your town or school students can learn to swim. Use specific nouns to name people or places students should contact.
5. Write a slogan for the cover of your brochure. Use a very specific noun in your slogan. (Swim for Success is a possible slogan.)

B. WRITING: Create a Brochure

1. Turn an $8\frac{1}{2}$ by 11 inch sheet of paper horizontally. Fold it into thirds.
2. On your first panel, place your slogan (and an illustration if you wish).
3. Provide reasons for being a competent swimmer on another panel. You might want to list all the occupations that require swimming along with the reasons, or you may choose to devote one panel to this information.
4. Describe the swimming test given to astronaut candidates. Use the information to convince students of the importance of swimming. (You may decide to use two panels for the text about astronauts.)
5. Provide information about where students can learn to swim.

Be sure to use specific nouns on your brochure. Save your brochure in your 📁 **Writing Portfolio.**

NOUNS

A. Plurals, Possessives, and Compounds Read the following help-wanted ad and correct ten errors in spelling. Remember an error in placing an apostrophe is a spelling error.

Section

Astronauts' Wanted

Must be strong enough to lift rocksamples. Should have knowledge of nine planet's orbites and nearby galaxys. Preference will be given to applicants' who can pilot a space craft. People of all age's and ethnic backgrounds welcome. Send application to NASAs department of human resourcies.

B. Nouns and Their Jobs In each group of sentences, the same underlined noun is used in different ways. Label each noun as subject, direct object, indirect object, predicate noun, object of a preposition, or appositive.

Group 1
1. <u>Saturn</u> is the second largest planet in the solar system.
2. At least eighteen moons orbit <u>Saturn</u>.
3. The sun's rays give <u>Saturn</u> its bright appearance.
4. The planet <u>Saturn</u> is encircled by thousands of rings.
5. The rings around <u>Saturn</u> are made of water, ice, and rock.

Group 2
6. The seventh planet from the sun is <u>Uranus</u>.
7. The atmosphere of <u>Uranus</u> is so thick that we cannot see the planet's surface.
8. The astronomer William Herschel discovered <u>Uranus</u> in 1781.
9. Another astronomer gave <u>Uranus</u> its name.
10. <u>Uranus</u> has rings that are less noticeable than Saturn's rings.

For each underlined item, choose the letter of the term that correctly identifies it.

> Lunar eclipses occur when <u>Earth's</u> shadow falls on the moon.
> (1)
> They give the <u>moon</u> a beautiful reddish <u>glow</u>. Solar <u>eclipses</u> occur
> (2) (3) (4)
> when the moon comes between the sun and Earth. The moon
> blocks out the sun, and <u>daylight</u> fades dramatically. Many ancient
> (5)
> peoples believed eclipses were signs of evil. The ancient <u>Chinese</u>
> (6)
> feared a dragon was devouring the sun during solar eclipses. They
> would make <u>noise</u> to scare away the dragon. Emperors hired
> (7)
> astronomers to predict <u>eclipses'</u> arrivals. Two Chinese <u>astronomers</u>
> (8) (9)
> failed to predict an eclipse in 2136 B.C. The emperor, <u>Chung K'ang</u>,
> (10)
> had them executed.

1. A. common noun
   B. possessive noun
   C. compound noun
   D. plural noun

2. A. noun as subject
   B. noun as direct object
   C. noun as indirect object
   D. noun as predicate noun

3. A. compound noun
   B. possessive noun
   C. common noun
   D. collective noun

4. A. possessive noun
   B. compound noun
   C. plural noun
   D. proper noun

5. A. proper noun
   B. plural noun
   C. possessive noun
   D. compound noun

6. A. noun as direct object
   B. noun as indirect object
   C. noun as predicate noun
   D. noun as subject

7. A. noun as predicate noun
   B. noun as direct object
   C. noun as indirect object
   D. noun as object of preposition

8. A. singular noun
   B. possessive noun
   C. predicate noun
   D. compound noun

9. A. noun as subject
   B. noun as predicate noun
   C. noun as object of preposition
   D. noun as direct object

10. A. noun as object of preposition
    B. noun as appositive
    C. noun as predicate noun
    D. noun as indirect object

NOUNS

Student Help Desk

Nouns at a Glance

A noun names a person, place, thing, or idea. There are several ways to classify nouns.

Benjamin Banneker studied stars through a skylight near his parents' farm.

| proper noun | common noun | compound noun | possessive noun |

QUICK-FIX SPELLING MACHINE: PLURALS OF NOUNS

	SINGULAR	RULE	PLURAL
1	comet	Add -s to most nouns.	comets
2	crash	Add -es to a noun that ends in s, sh, ch, x, or z.	crashes
3	photo	Add -s to most nouns that end in o.	photos
	echo	Add -es to a few nouns that end in o.	echoes
4	discovery	For most nouns ending in y, change the y to an i and add -es.	discoveries
	way	When a vowel comes before the y, just add -s.	ways
5	wharf	For most nouns ending in f or fe, change the f to v and add -es or -s.	wharves
	reef	Just add -s to a few nouns that end in f or fe.	reefs
6	salmon	For some nouns, keep the same spelling.	salmon

Classifying Nouns Classifying Your Collection

Possessives of Nouns

Relationship	Ownership
Linus's brother	Tim's automobile

Collective Nouns

Collective Noun	Group
colony	colony of ants or badgers
flock	flock of birds or sheep
herd	herd of cattle or elephants

More Noun Types

Concrete	Abstract
rock	love

NOUNS

Nouns and Their Jobs

Nouns as . . .	Example
Subject	**Saturn** was spectacular.
Predicate noun	The student astronomer was our **guide.**
Direct object	We studied the **planet** with a powerful telescope.
Indirect object	The scientists gave **Saturn** a long look.
Object of preposition	The rings of **Saturn** are colorful.
Appositive	The planet **Saturn** is the sixth from the sun.

The Bottom Line

Checklist for Nouns

Have I . . .

____ chosen precise nouns?

____ spelled plural nouns correctly?

____ spelled possessive nouns correctly?

____ used nouns to provide specific details in explanatory writing?

____ used possessive nouns to show ownership or relationship?

____ spelled compound nouns correctly?

Pronouns

You folks listen to me! Who has survived on this planet for millions of years?

We have!

We have!

We have!

And which is the toughest species around?

We are!

We are!

Theme: Survival

Hanging On

Imagine this conversation without the words *you, me, who, we,* and *which.* These words are called **pronouns**. They take the place of other nouns or pronouns. Be careful, though. If you don't use pronouns correctly, your meaning may not survive.

Write Away: Survival Instincts

Humans, like all living species, have a strong survival instinct. Every day, people survive injury, illness, natural disaster, and plain old tough times. Write a paragraph describing the survival of someone you know. Place the paragraph in your 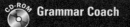 **Working Portfolio**.

CD-ROM **Grammar Coach**

Choose the letter of the best revision for each underlined word or group of words.

At age eighteen, Daniel Huffman was a football star planning to play football in college. But <u>they</u> had a problem. <u>His</u> grandmother,
(1)   (2)
Shirlee Allison, was dying. She needed a kidney transplant. <u>Would someone donate his</u> kidney? <u>Whom would help?</u> <u>His grandmother</u>
     (3)   (4)   (5)
<u>and him</u> discussed it. Huffman decided that he <u>himself</u> would give
                                      (6)
her a kidney, even though that meant he would never play college ball. Right after the transplant, Allison began to regain her health. Daniel <u>had made herself</u> a very lucky person. "That was happiness
       (7)
for <u>me</u>," said Daniel. <u>It was him</u> who then received a full
  (8)   (9)
scholarship to Florida State and an appointment as athletic trainer for <u>it's football team</u>.
         (10)

1. A. he
   B. she
   C. someone
   D. Correct as is

2. A. Their
   B. Her
   C. They're
   D. Correct as is

3. A. Would someone donate their
   B. Would someone donate his or her
   C. Would someone donate her
   D. Correct as is

4. A. Who would help?
   B. Whose would help?
   C. Who would help who?
   D. Correct as is

5. A. Him and his grandmother
   B. Him and her
   C. His grandmother and he
   D. Correct as is

6. A. hisself
   B. himselves
   C. themselves
   D. Correct as is

7. A. Daniel had made her
   B. Daniel had made him
   C. Daniel had made she
   D. Correct as is

8. A. I
   B. us
   C. myself
   D. Correct as is

9. A. It was his
   B. It was he
   C. It was himself
   D. Correct as is

10. A. their football team
    B. his football team
    C. its football team
    D. Correct as is

What Is a Pronoun?

❶ Here's the Idea

▶ **A pronoun is a word that is used in place of a noun or another pronoun.** Like a noun, a pronoun can refer to a person, place, thing, or idea. The word that a pronoun refers to is called its **antecedent.**

REFERS TO

Maria was lost. She didn't panic.

REFERS TO

She checked the flashlight. It still worked.

Personal Pronouns

▶ **Pronouns such as *we, I, she, them*, and *it* are called personal pronouns.** Personal pronouns have a variety of forms to indicate different **persons, numbers,** and **cases.**

Person and Number There are first-person, second-person, and third-person personal pronouns, each having both singular and plural forms.

Singular	Plural
I shivered.	**We lit a fire.**
You slept.	**You all fell asleep.**
She saw a light.	**They ran toward it.**

Case Each personal pronoun forms has three cases: subject, object, and possessive. Which form to use depends on the pronoun's function in a sentence.

Subject: **She took a deep breath.**

Object: **Jerry told her about the problem.**

Possessive: **I like your story better than mine.**

The chart on the next page shows all the forms of the personal pronouns.

Personal Pronouns			
	Subject	**Object**	**Possessive**
Singular			
First person	I	me	my, mine
Second person	you	you	your, yours
Third person	he, she, it	him, her, it	his, her, hers, its
Plural			
First person	we	us	our, ours
Second person	you	you	your, yours
Third person	they	them	their, theirs

❷ Why It Matters in Writing

Pronouns often are used to make writing flow smoothly from sentence to sentence. Notice how some of the pronouns in this paragraph connect one sentence to the sentence before it.

STUDENT MODEL

My friend Jan and I barely survived last summer. **We** were sailing with **her** family off the coast of Florida when a storm came up. **It** capsized our boat. Fortunately, we had life jackets, which saved our lives.

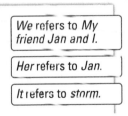

We refers to *My friend Jan and I.*

Her refers to *Jan.*

It refers to *storm.*

❸ Practice and Apply

A. CONCEPT CHECK: What Is a Pronoun?

List the personal pronoun(s) in each sentence.

Wilderness Survival

1. Hannah Nyala is known for her tracking expertise.
2. She has found many lost hikers before they got into real trouble.
3. She wrote a book called *Point Last Seen*.
4. She learned some of her skills in the Mojave and Kalahari deserts.

5. Other experts remind us to plan ahead for danger.
6. To them, a first-aid kit is a necessity.
7. They advise us to find out before we go whether the water is safe to drink.
8. We are also advised to conserve our energy.
9. We are told to find shelter and avoid becoming too hot or too cold.
10. They say that all hikers should carry plenty of water with them.

➜ For a SELF-CHECK and more practice, see the EXERCISE BANK, p. 609.

Name the antecedents for the personal pronouns in sentences 1–4 and 6.

B. REVISING: Substituting Pronouns for Nouns

Rewrite this student's draft of a science report. Change the underlined nouns to pronouns to connect the sentences smoothly.

Experts say we will run out of natural resources some day. **(1)** <u>Experts</u> point out that Americans use nearly 25 percent of the world's resources, but **(2)** <u>Americans</u> make up only four percent of the world's population. This overuse is not fair, environmentalists say. **(3)** <u>Environmentalists</u> say that **(4)** <u>this overuse</u> is leading to a shortage of resources and too much pollution.

C. WRITING: Dialogue

Based on the photograph below, write a short dialogue between two people who are hiking. Use pronouns to make the dialogue sound natural.

Example:
Speaker 1: Do **you** see that moose?
Speaker 2: Yes, **I** do. In fact, **I** see a mother moose and **her** calf.
Speaker 1: **I** can't see the calf. Shall **we** get closer to **them?**

Subject Pronouns

❶ Here's the Idea

▶ **A subject pronoun is used as the subject of a sentence or as a predicate pronoun after a linking verb.**

Subject Pronouns	
Singular	**Plural**
I	we
you	you
he, she, it	they

Pronouns as Subjects

Use a subject pronoun when the pronoun is a subject or part of a compound subject.

The Apollo program was a great success.

It got us to the moon. (*It,* referring to *The Apollo program,* is the subject of the sentence.)

A pronoun can be part of a compound subject.

You and I both think we should go on to Mars.

Predicate Pronouns

A predicate pronoun follows a linking verb and identifies the subject. Use the subject case for predicate pronouns.

IDENTIFIES

The greatest astronauts were they.
↑ SUBJECT   ↑ PREDICATE PRONOUN

IDENTIFIES

The biggest supporters were she and I.

IDENTIFIES

The first astronaut on Mars will be I.

Remember, the most common linking verbs are forms of the verb *be,* including *is, am, are, was, were, has been, have been, can be, will be, could be,* and *should be.*

PRONOUNS

❷ Why It Matters in Writing

It's sometimes difficult to know which pronoun forms to use in writing because many people use them incorrectly in speech. Always double-check the pronouns in your writing, and make sure you've used the correct forms.

STUDENT MODEL

Neil Armstrong commanded Apollo 11, the first mission to reach the moon. Buzz Aldrin and ~~him~~ *he* spent hours on the moon. They were trailblazers.

❸ Practice and Apply

CONCEPT CHECK: Subject Pronouns

Write the correct form of the pronoun(s) to complete each sentence.

Apollo 13: A Close Call
1. Some big fans of space exploration are Sam and (I, me).
2. (We, Us) learned that in April 1970, the Apollo 13 astronauts almost didn't make it back to Earth.
3. (They, Them) never did land on the moon.
4. Two hundred thousand miles from home, (they, them) heard an explosion.
5. Jim Lovell was the mission commander; it was (he, him) who radioed the message "Houston, we've had a problem."
6. Then (he, him), Jack Swigert, and Fred Haise were forced to abandon the main ship for the lunar module.
7. The tiny module was designed to keep two people alive for just two days, but (they, them) were four days from Earth.
8. (They, Them) finally splashed down in the Pacific Ocean four days later, having overcome crisis after crisis.
9. (We, Us) watched the movie about their dangerous journey.
10. It was (they, them) who won our respect and admiration.

➡ **For a SELF-CHECK and more practice, see the EXERCISE BANK, p. 610.**

Object Pronouns

❶ Here's the Idea

▶ **An object pronoun is used as a direct object, an indirect object, or an object of a preposition.**

Object Pronouns	
Singular	**Plural**
me	us
you	you
him, her, it	them

Direct Object The pronoun receives the action of a verb and answers the question *whom or what*.

SCARE WHOM?

Bad storms scare me.
⬆ DIRECT OBJECT

Do you like them? (like what? *them*)

Indirect Object The pronoun tells to whom or what or for whom or what an action is performed.

TO WHOM? ◀ DIRECT OBJECT

Give me an explanation of how hurricanes form.
⬆ INDIRECT OBJECT

I told him the story of Hurricane Floyd.

Object of a Preposition The pronoun follows a preposition (such as *to, from, for, against, by,* or *about*).

When he sees big storms, he runs from them.
PREPOSITION ⬆ ⬆ OBJECT

The storm is coming straight at us.

HOT TIP

Always use object pronouns after the preposition *between*.

It's a contest between him and me. (NOT between he and I.)

❷ Why It Matters in Writing

People commonly misuse subject and object pronouns in conversation, especially *I* and *me*. Pay attention to your use of these words when they are part of compound subjects or objects.

My mother and ~~me~~ listened to a radio program about Hurricane Floyd.

❸ Practice and Apply

MIXED REVIEW: Subject and Object Pronouns

Write the correct pronoun(s) for each sentence. Label each pronoun *subject* or *object*.

Hurricane Floyd
1. Hurricane Floyd ravaged the East Coast in 1999; the extent of the damage horrified my friends and (I, me).
2. My brother and (I, me) read that Floyd was 600 miles across and had winds of 155 miles an hour.
3. Gerald Keeth is a U.S. sailor; the hurricane gave (he, him) the scare of his life.
4. "The bad weather started pounding (we, us) Tuesday night," he wrote.
5. "(We, Us) launched our life raft in . . . 55-foot seas with 60-knot winds."
6. The raft accidentally left (he, him) and two others behind.
7. (They, Them) had only life jackets and an emergency locator beacon.
8. "I could hear each wave from behind (I, me) like a freight train coming."
9. Then a helicopter rescued (they, them).
10. "Rescue swimmer Shad Hernandez put a harness on each of (we, us), and (we, us) were hauled into the helicopter."

➡ **For a SELF-CHECK and more practice, see the EXERCISE BANK, p. 611.**

Tell how each pronoun functions in the sentence.

Possessive Pronouns

❶ Here's the Idea

▶ **A possessive pronoun is a personal pronoun used to show ownership or relationship.**

Possessive Pronouns	
Singular	**Plural**
my, mine	our, ours
your, yours	your, yours
her, hers, his, its	their, theirs

The possessive pronouns *my, your, her, his, its, our,* and *their* come before nouns.

OWNERSHIP

The dog pricked up its little ears.

RELATIONSHIP

It saw the boy and heard his loud cry for help.

RELATIONSHIP

The owner and his best friend came to the rescue.

The possessive pronouns *mine, ours, yours, his, hers, its,* and *theirs* can stand alone in a sentence.

This cat is mine. That cat is his.

Is the striped cat yours? No, mine is all black.

What color is his? Hers hasn't come home yet.

Possessive Pronouns and Contractions

Some possessive pronouns sound like contractions (*its/it's, your/you're, their/they're*). Because these pairs sound alike, writers often confuse possessive pronouns and contractions.

Remember, a possessive pronoun *never* has an apostrophe. A contraction, however, *always* has an apostrophe. The apostrophe shows where a letter or letters have been left out in a combination of two words. Look on the next page to see how this works.

QUICK-FIX SPELLING MACHINE

POSSESSIVE PRONOUNS		CONTRACTIONS	
its	Its paws are muddy.	it's	It's been a long day.
your	Your dog is nice.	you're	You're all right.
their	Their dog is smart.	they're	They're proud of her.

❷ Why It Matters in Writing

Proofread your work carefully to see that you haven't confused contractions and possessive pronouns. Remember that the spell-checker on a computer won't catch these mistakes.

STUDENT MODEL

Many Alpine travelers owe ~~they're~~ *their* survival to the trusty St. Bernard dog. This dog was first used in the 1600s by a group of monks at the St. Bernard monastery in the Swiss Alps. The dog's intelligence and ~~it's~~ *its* keen sense of smell enable it to find lost travelers or warn them of dangerous footing.

Even today, the monks of St. Bernard and ~~they're~~ *their* dogs rescue many travelers every winter.

❸ Practice and Apply

A. CONCEPT CHECK: Possessive Pronouns

Write the correct pronoun or contraction for each sentence.

Bustopher, the Rescue Cat
1. Has (your, you're) pet ever saved a life?
2. David and Marjorie Giles can say yes; a woman survived an accident because of (their, they're) cat.
3. One morning in Dobbins, California, Bustopher was in (its, it's) yard.
4. Birds were calling, but amidst (their, they're) songs David Giles heard a peculiar noise.
5. Then he noticed Bustopher; (its, it's) front paw was pointing.
6. There is a steep drop-off to a canyon beyond the Gileses' lawn; (its, it's) not far away.
7. When Giles walked over to the drop-off, he heard the noise again; (its, it's) source was in the canyon.
8. He looked and saw (they're, their) neighbor, an 84-year-old woman who had fallen and broken her hip.
9. "(Your, You're) going to be all right," Giles assured her.
10. (Its, It's) amazing how animals can help people to survive.

➡ **For a SELF-CHECK and more exercises, see the EXERCISE BANK, p. 611.**

B. PROOFREADING: Using Possessive Pronouns

Correct the possessive pronoun errors in the paragraph below. If a sentence contains no error, write *Correct*.

Marie Murphy was paralyzed, and she used an iron lung to help her breathe. **(1)** It's mechanism breathed for her at night, while she and her family slept. **(2)** One night she awoke and realized that they're electricity had gone out— she could no longer hear the machine's electrical hum. **(3)** You're probably wondering what someone who couldn't move or breathe would do. **(4)** Its remarkable, but she had just enough breath to whisper to her dog, Rosie, whose barking woke Murphy's family. **(5)** Their quick response, putting the iron lung on batteries, saved her life.

Reflexive and Intensive Pronouns

LESSON 5

❶ Here's the Idea

A pronoun that ends in *self* or *selves* is either a **reflexive** or an **intensive** pronoun.

Reflexive and Intensive Pronouns		
myself	yourself	herself, himself, itself
ourselves	yourselves	themselves

Reflexive Pronouns

▶ **A reflexive pronoun refers to the subject and directs the action of the verb back to the subject.** Reflexive pronouns are necessary to the meaning of a sentence.

REFLECTS

The Carson family tried to lift themselves out of poverty.

REFLECTS

Ben Carson dedicated himself to becoming a doctor.

Notice that if you drop the reflexive pronoun, the sentence no longer makes sense. (*Ben Carson dedicated to becoming a doctor.*)

Intensive Pronouns

▶ **An intensive pronoun emphasizes a noun or another pronoun within the same sentence.** Intensive pronouns are not necessary to the meaning of the sentence.

You yourself have overcome many hardships.

Dr. Carson himself has survived great poverty.

Notice that when you drop the intensive pronoun, the sentence still makes sense. (*Dr. Carson has survived great poverty.*)

Avoid the use of *hisself* and *theirselves,* which are grammatically incorrect. Use *himself* and *themselves* instead.

❷ Why It Matters in Writing

You can use an intensive pronoun to stress a point. In the following model, the writer used the pronoun *himself* to emphasize that Ben Carson knew something just as well as the other students knew it.

> **PROFESSIONAL MODEL**
>
> When Ben Carson was in fifth grade, his classmates considered him the dumbest kid in the class. They teased him, but he didn't seem to mind. He **himself** knew that he couldn't read very well.

❸ Practice and Apply

CONCEPT CHECK: Intensive and Reflexive Pronouns

Write the reflexive or intensive pronoun in each sentence. Then identify it as reflexive (R) or intensive (I).

Beyond Survival to Success
1. By fifth grade, Ben Carson considered himself the dumbest kid in his class.
2. His mother was raising Ben and his brother herself.
3. When she saw his report card, she decided that she herself would give him extra homework assignments: two book reports every week.
4. She also told her sons to limit themselves to only two TV shows each week.
5. Ben outdid himself.
6. He learned to love reading and then to love learning itself.
7. He promised himself he would rise to the top of his class.
8. Carson went on to become a first-rate doctor, surprising even himself with some of his successful cases.
9. He has performed many operations that other doctors feared to try themselves.
10. He himself likes the challenge of difficult surgery.

➡ **For a SELF-CHECK and more practice, see the EXERCISE BANK, p. 612.**

LESSON 6 | Interrogatives and Demonstratives

❶ Here's the Idea

Interrogative Pronouns

▶ **An interrogative pronoun is used to introduce a question.** The interrogative pronouns are *who, whom, what, which,* and *whose.*

Who used up all the water?

Whose cup is this?

Using *Who* and *Whom*

▶ ***Who* is always used as a subject or a predicate pronoun.**

Subject: **Who called the power company?**

Predicate pronoun: **The electrician is who?**

▶ ***Whom* is always used as an object.**

Direct object: **Whom did you call?**

Indirect object: **You gave whom my number?**

Object of preposition: **To whom did you speak?**

Here's How Choosing *Who* or *Whom* in a Question

(Who, Whom) will you see?

1. Rewrite the question as a statement.
   You will see (who, whom).
2. Decide if the pronoun is used as a subject or an object. Choose the correct form. The pronoun in the sentence above is an object.
   You will see whom.
3. Use the correct form in the question.
   Whom will you see?

 Don't confuse *whose* with *who's. Who's* is a contraction that means *who is.* ("Who's missing?") *Whose* is an interrogative pronoun. ("Whose book is gone?")

CHAPTER 3

Demonstrative Pronouns

▶ **A demonstrative pronoun points out a person, place, thing, or idea.**

The demonstrative pronouns—*this, that, these,* and *those*—are used alone in sentences as shown below.

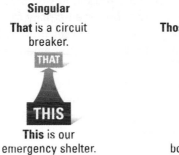

Singular	**Plural**
That is a circuit breaker.	**Those** are electrical appliances.
This is our emergency shelter.	**These** are bottles of water.

Never use *here* or *there* with a demonstrative pronoun. The pronoun already tells which one or ones. *This* and *those* point out people or things that are near, or *here*. *That* and *those* point out people or things that are far away, or *there*.

This ~~here~~ is a dead refrigerator.

That ~~there~~ is five pounds of rotting food.

❷ Why It Matters in Writing

In dialogue, questions can show a character's mood, such as curiosity, shock, or anger. The author in this model uses interrogative pronouns in questions to show Sammy's confusion.

PROFESSIONAL MODEL

"**What** just happened?" Sammy cried.

"The lights went out. We must have lost power," said Gilberto. There was a knock at the door.

"**Who**'s there?" Sammy called out.

"It's your neighbor." Sammy's heart began to beat fast.

"**Which** neighbor? I don't have any neighbors!" he said.

❸ Practice and Apply

A. CONCEPT CHECK: Interrogatives and Demonstratives

Choose the correct word in parentheses.

Urban Emergency

1. (What, Whose) would you do if a natural disaster like an earthquake or blizzard struck close to home?
2. (That, Those) is a good question.
3. (These, That) is a situation in which you might not have access to water, food, or electricity for days.
4. To (who, whom) should you turn for advice?
5. The Federal Emergency Management Agency (FEMA) has a plan. (This, That) is its most important advice: store lots of clean water ahead of time.
6. (What, Who) do you need to purify your water?
7. (What, Whom) does FEMA recommend? They advise a two-week supply of water for each person.
8. For food, you'll need a manual can opener and a camp stove or grill. Make sure you have (these, this).
9. (Who, Whom) will be responsible for your family's emergency plan?
10. (Whose, Who's) most organized and knowledgeable? You should choose that person.

➡ For a SELF-CHECK and more practice, see the EXERCISE BANK, p. 612.

B. WRITING: Using Demonstrative Pronouns

You are a TV reporter showing your audience some things they should have on hand for emergencies. Write a one-paragraph script naming the necessary items and explaining why they are necessary. Use four demonstrative pronouns in your paragraph and underline them.

Pronoun-Antecedent Agreement

❶ Here's the Idea

▶ **The antecedent is the noun or pronoun that a pronoun replaces or refers to.** The antecedent and the pronoun can be in the same sentence or in different sentences.

REFERS TO

The Hopi people made their homes in the desert.
　　　　　　▲ ANTECEDENT　▲ PRONOUN

REFERS TO

The Hopi settled what is now Arizona. They have been here for more than ten centuries.

Pronouns must agree with their antecedents in number, person, and gender.

Agreement in Number

▶ **Use a singular pronoun to refer to a singular antecedent.**

REFERS TO

Hopi culture, in all its forms, is alive and well.

▶ **Use a plural pronoun to refer to a plural antecedent.**

REFERS TO

Traditional members keep cattle on their farms.

Agreement in Person

▶ **The pronoun must agree in person with the antecedent.**

3RD PERSON

Tribal elders tell the myths of their people.

1ST PERSON

We like to listen to our grandparents' stories.

Avoid switching from one person to another in the same sentence or paragraph.

Incorrect

Visitors realize you can learn from other cultures.

(*Visitors* is third person; *you* is second person.)

Correct

Visitors realize they can learn from other cultures.

(*Visitors* and *they* are both third person.)

Agreement in Gender

▶ **The gender of a pronoun must be the same as the gender of its antecedent.**

Personal pronouns have three gender forms: masculine (*he, his, him*), feminine (*she, her, hers*), and neuter (*it, its*).

Derrick Davis performs his hoop dances.

Laurel Mansfield teaches her students at Hopi High.

Don't use only masculine or only feminine pronouns when you mean to refer to both genders.

DRAFT:

Each dancer has his favorite moves.

(The dancer could be male or female.)

There are two ways to make this sentence more accurate.

1. Use the phrase *his or her*.

Each dancer has his or her favorite moves.

2. Rewrite the sentence using a plural antecedent and a plural pronoun. Be careful! Other words in the sentence, especially verbs, may also need to be made plural.

The dancers have their favorite moves.

❷ Why It Matters in Writing

For many years, people used the pronoun *he* to refer to nouns or pronouns of unclear gender. This custom is changing. Often, the problem can be fixed by changing the subject to the plural form.

~~The~~ Native American artist̲ ̲i̲s̲ becoming better known.
(s) (are)

They are
~~He is~~ working with traditional ideas in new materials.

❸ Practice and Apply

Write the pronouns in these sentences, along with their antecedents.

Old Cultures Survive in a New World
1. Native cultures have faced great threats to their survival.
2. For years, Native Americans were pushed to adopt a white, industrial way of life. They have had to fight to hold on to their own cultural and spiritual traditions.
3. Rose Robinson was a member of the Hopi tribe. She founded the Native American Journalists' Association.
4. Robinson monitored and resisted nuclear-waste dumping in her tribal lands.
5. Raymond Cross is a lawyer for the Mandan, Arikara, and Hidatsa nations. He sued the government for flooding tribal land with a dam. He won $150 million for the tribes.
6. Other tribes have gone to court to get back the rights to their land, minerals, and other valuable resources.
7. Native languages are another important issue; speaking them helps people keep their heritages alive.
8. Each person follows his or her own spiritual path based on respect for nature.
9. Native arts and crafts continue to celebrate both function and beauty; they also earn income.
10. Self-determination is the right of a group to make decisions about its future. It is becoming a reality for Native American nations.

➡ For a SELF-CHECK and more practice, see the EXERCISE BANK, p. 613.

Write the number, person, and gender of each pronoun.

B. REVISING: Correcting Errors in Agreement

The paragraph below contains four errors in pronoun-antecedent agreement. Rewrite the paragraph, correcting the errors.

> Lance Polingyouma works at a Native American learning center, where he teaches tourists about the customs of his or her people, the Hopi. The tourists hope to expand her knowledge of the Hopi culture. Lance often asks his elders for his advice about how to explain the Hopi ways. If a tourist asks a question, Lance wants to give him a thorough answer.

Indefinite-Pronoun Agreement

❶ Here's the Idea

▶ **An indefinite pronoun does not refer to a specific person, place, thing, or idea.**

Indefinite pronouns often do not have antecedents.

Nothing lasts forever.

Anyone can make a time capsule.

▶ **Some indefinite pronouns are always singular, some are always plural, and some can be either singular or plural.**

Indefinite Pronouns		Plural	Singular or Plural
Singular		**Plural**	**Singular or Plural**
another	much	both	all
anybody	neither	few	any
anyone	nobody	many	most
anything	no one	several	none
each	nothing		some
either	one		
everybody	somebody		
everyone	someone		
everything	something		

Pronouns containing *one, thing,* or *body* are always singular.

Singular Indefinite Pronouns

▶ **Use a singular personal pronoun to refer to a singular indefinite pronoun.**

REFERS TO

Everyone added his or her favorite item to the capsule.
(*Everyone* could be male or female.)

REFERS TO

One of the girls put her soccer ball in the box.

Plural Indefinite Pronouns

▶ **Use a plural personal pronoun to refer to a plural indefinite pronoun.**

REFERS TO

Many contributed their favorite CDs or video games.

REFERS TO

Few realized that their electronics may become completely outdated.

Singular or Plural Indefinite Pronouns

▶ **Some indefinite pronouns can be singular or plural.** The phrase that follows the indefinite pronoun will often tell you whether it is singular or plural.

Some of the time capsule looks like it is very old.

♠ SINGULAR   ♠ SINGULAR NOUN   ♠ SINGULAR
INDEFINITE PRONOUN   PERSONAL PRONOUN

Some of the time capsules list their contents outside.

♠ PLURAL   ♠ PLURAL NOUN   ♠ PLURAL PERSONAL PRONOUN
INDEFINITE PRONOUN

❷ Why It Matters in Writing

You can use indefinite pronouns in your writing when you want to show how a whole group of people is acting or feeling.

LITERARY MODEL

She heard the irritability in their voices, knew that soon **someone** would refuse to go on. . . . **No one** commented. **No one** asked any questions.

—Ann Petry, *Harriet Tubman: Conductor on the Underground Railroad*

❸ Practice and Apply

A. CONCEPT CHECK: Indefinite-Pronoun Agreement

Choose the pronoun that agrees with the indefinite-pronoun antecedent.

A Message to the Future

1. Everyone likes to think that (he or she, they) will leave a mark on the world.

2. We all want to create something, and we hope (it, they) will outlive us.

3. Some take an unusual approach; for (him or her, them), a time capsule is the answer.

4. Anyone who assembles a time capsule hopes that (he or she, they) can send a message to the future.

5. Each of the people who planned the time capsule at the New York World's Fair in 1939 had (his or her, their) opinion about what should go into it.

6. What did all of those experts finally agree on? (He or she, They) put nineteen items in the capsule.

7. Most of the items would be familiar to us today. (They, It) included an alarm clock, a safety pin, and a dollar bill.

8. However, none of the people knew at the time that (his or her, their) slide rules would become outdated in just a few decades.

9. One of California's tar pits acts as a time capsule because (it, they) contains people's throwaways.

10. Although time capsules often remain sealed for decades, few are meant to keep (their, its) treasures hidden for as long as the Crypt of Civilization. Completed in 1940, it is meant to last until the year 8113!

➡ **For a SELF-CHECK and more practice, see the EXERCISE BANK, p. 614.**

B. WRITING: Using Correct Indefinite-Pronoun Agreement

Write a paragraph describing what you would choose to put in a time capsule and why. Use at least one singular indefinite pronoun, one plural indefinite pronoun, and one indefinite pronoun that could be singular or plural. Underline all of the indefinite pronouns.

Pronoun Problems

❶ Here's the Idea

We and *Us* with Nouns

The pronoun *we* or *us* is sometimes followed by a noun that identifies the pronoun (*we students*, *us students*).

▶ **Use *we* when the pronoun is a subject or a predicate pronoun. Use *us* when the pronoun is an object.**

We humans don't always appreciate trees.
↑SUBJECT

Trees can feed and shelter us humans.
↑ OBJECT OF VERB

> **Here's How** **Choosing *We* or *Us***
>
> Some trees depend on (us, we) humans for survival.
>
> 1. Drop the identifying noun from the sentence.
>
>   Some trees depend on (us, we) for survival.
>
> 2. Decide whether the pronoun is used as a subject or an object. In this sentence, the pronoun is the object of the preposition *on*.
>
>   Some trees depend on us for survival.
>
> 3. Use the correct pronoun with the noun.
>
>   Some trees depend on us humans for survival.

Unclear Reference

▶ **Be sure that each personal pronoun refers clearly to only one person, place, or thing.** If there is any chance your reader will be confused about whom or what you are talking about, use a noun instead of a pronoun.

Confusing
   Sara and Anne want to become tree farmers. She works after school at an orchard. (Who works? Sara or Anne?)

Clear
   Sara and Anne want to become tree farmers. Anne works after school at an orchard.

PRONOUNS

❷ Why It Matters in Writing

Readers get frustrated and may give up if your writing is too confusing. To get your ideas across, you must be clear about who is doing what. This is especially important when there is more than one noun that a pronoun could be replacing.

STUDENT MODEL

Until a century ago, humans competed with animals in the eastern United States. ~~They~~ *Animals* needed the nuts to get through hard winters. Farmers saw them as a cash crop.

❸ Practice and Apply

A. CONCEPT CHECK: Pronoun Problems

Choose the correct noun or pronoun from the words in parentheses.

The Majestic Chestnut Tree
1. For decades, (we, us) carpenters used the wood from chestnut trees to build houses and furniture.
2. Chestnuts were a nutritious food for both (we, us) country dwellers and wildlife. The trees provided bushels of them.
3. Then in 1904, a fungus began killing (them, the trees).
4. Now scientists are crossbreeding American chestnut trees with Chinese chestnut trees. (They, Chinese chestnut trees) resist the blight.
5. (They, Scientists) hope the new hybrid trees will survive for centuries.

➜ For a SELF-CHECK and more practice, see the EXERCISE BANK, p. 614.

B. REVISING: Correcting Pronoun Errors

Correct the five pronoun errors in the following paragraph.

If Trees Could Talk . . .
Us chestnut trees are very generous. We give you boards for building and nuts for eating and even flowers in the spring. They make fine furniture. They taste sweet and crunchy. However, a fungus is killing us. What do we ask you to do for we trees in return? Just help us fight it.

More Pronoun Problems

1 Here's the Idea

Using Pronouns in Compound

Pronouns sometimes cause difficulty when they are parts of compound subjects and compound objects.

▶ **Use the subject pronoun *I*, *she*, *he*, *we*, or *they* in a compound subject or with a predicate noun or pronoun.**

Greg and she decided to learn more about Sacajawea.

The researchers are Polly and I.

▶ **Use the object pronoun *me*, *her*, *him*, *us*, or *them* in a compound object.**

Her story has always fascinated Polly and me.

The research was divided between Greg and her.

To choose the correct case of a pronoun in a compound part, read the sentence with only the pronoun in the compound part. Mentally screen out the other pronoun or other noun. Then choose the correct case.

My grandmother told the story to ~~Ron and~~ me.

Phrases That Interfere

Sometimes a group of words comes between a noun and a pronoun that refers to it. Don't be confused by the words in between.

REFERS TO

Sacajawea, ~~who guided Lewis and Clark,~~ never lost her way. (*Her* agrees with *Sacajawea* and not with *Lewis* and *Clark*.)

REFERS TO

About 40 men started ~~up the Missouri River~~ on their voyage. (*Their* agrees with *men* and not with *Missouri River*.)

② Why It Matters in Writing

Many people think it sounds better to use *I* rather than *me* in a compound object. This isn't true—use *me* as part of a compound object.

STUDENT MODEL

> When our friends go camping, they always like to take
> along my sister and ~~I~~ *me.* She and I have a lot of experience.

③ Practice and Apply

A. CONCEPT CHECK: More Pronoun Problems

Write the correct word to complete each sentence. Choose from those given in parentheses.

Sacajawea, Young Explorer

1. Meriwether Lewis is a favorite topic for Polly and (I, me).
2. In 1803, President Jefferson sent (he, him) and William Clark to explore thousands of miles of wilderness.
3. Lewis and Clark met Sacajawea, a young Shoshone woman, in 1804; (they, she) hired her as a guide.
4. They had first hired her husband, Toussaint Charbonneau, as an interpreter. Both Sacajawea and (he, him) translated their conversations with Native Americans.
5. Lewis, Clark, a band of soldiers, and (she, her) headed west when she was around 17.
6. She survived near starvation and illness as (she, they) accompanied the explorers.
7. Greg, Polly, and (I, me) learned that she was very important to the expedition.
8. The baby on Sacajawea's back made (her, it) much less threatening to Native Americans than the white soldiers alone would have been.
9. At one point, she, Lewis, and Clark visited (her, their) people's summer home.
10. The expedition, short on food and medicines, was able to restock (its, their) supplies from her tribe's stores.

➜ For a SELF-CHECK and more practice, see the EXERCISE BANK, p. 615.

B. PROOFREADING: Correct Use of Pronouns

Rewrite the passage below, correcting the pronoun errors.

Sacajawea: Explorer and Survivor

Polly and me read Lewis and Clark's journals. Sacajawea and them met at Fort Mandan, near present-day Bismarck, North Dakota. Several months later, Lewis described how their supplies were washed overboard as he traveled by boat. Sacajawea's quick thinking saved journals, instruments, and medicines.

Sacajawea introduced Lewis and Clark to their tribe, the Shoshone, in the summer of 1805. Lewis had left she, Clark, and most of the other men behind while he scouted ahead, looking for the Shoshone villages. Finally, he met a Shoshone leader named Cameahwait. When Clark and Sacajawea rejoined Lewis, she recognized Cameahwait; he was her brother! Now Lewis and him could be friends.

C. WRITING: Using Pronouns Correctly

The map shows milestones in Sacajawea's journey. Working with a partner, use it and the information in exercises A and B to write a paragraph, explaining in your own words what she survived and accomplished.

Underline the pronouns you use. Proofread your work to be sure you have used the pronouns correctly.

Example: No one could have guessed how hard the journey would be.

Sacajawea's Journey West with Lewis and Clark, 1805
Shown on a current map of the western United States

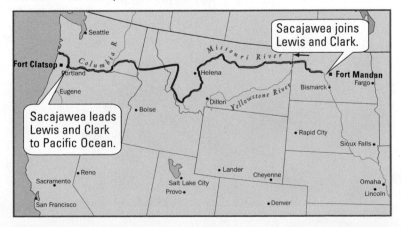

Grammar in Literature

Using Personal Pronouns Effectively

When you write, you have a choice about pronouns. You might choose to use first-person pronouns—like *I, me, we* and *us*—or you might find it better to use third-person pronouns—including *he, she, him, her, they, them.* First-person pronouns show a close relationship between writer and reader. In the passage below, actor Christopher Reeve uses first-person pronouns to reveal his reactions to a horse-riding accident that left him paralyzed.

from

Still Me
by Christopher Reeve

[T]he chief radiologist . . . showed me that the damage to my spinal cord was only one centimeter wide, and said that if I had landed with my head twisted only a fraction further to the left, I would have been killed instantly. If I had landed with my head slightly more to the right, I probably would have sustained a bruise and been up on my feet within a few weeks. I just happened to hit the rail at an angle that turned me into a C2 vent-dependent quadriplegic. The irony of it hit me very hard, although I kept my emotions to myself. I knew there was no point dwelling on it. But now I knew on a visceral level how fragile our existence is.

> **FIRST PERSON**
> pronouns create a sense of closeness. You are there with Reeve, reading his innermost thoughts.

> What effect does Reeve produce by using the pronoun *our?* How would the last sentence change if the pronoun were omitted?

Christopher Reeve with his wife after his injury left him paralyzed.

Practice and Apply

WRITING: Using Pronouns

The following passage is from a news story about Reeve's accident. Read the passage; then follow the directions below.

Section

"He was in the middle of the pack . . . , and he was pretty excited about it," says Lisa Reid, [who] witnessed his May 27 ride. "The horse was coming into the fence beautifully. The rhythm was fine and Chris was fine, and they were going at a good pace." But then, Reid says, . . . "The horse put his front feet over the fence, but his hind feet never left the ground." . . . "Chris is such a big man. He was going forward, his head over the top of the horse's head. He had committed his upper body to the jump. But the horse . . . backed off the jump. . . . Reeve kept moving, pitching forward over the horse's neck." To Reid it appeared that Reeve first hit his head on the rail fence, then landed on the turf on his forehead.

—"Fallen Rider," *People Weekly*, June 12, 1995

1. The passage is written from an observer's point of view. What pronouns does the observer use?
2. Imagine that Reeve himself wrote the report, and revise the passage, using first-person pronouns like *I* and *me*.
3. Compare your revision with the original. Which version is more personal and immediate? Why?

Save your revision in your 📁 **Working Portfolio.**

PRONOUNS

A. Pronouns Write the pronoun that correctly completes the sentence. Choose the correct pronoun from those in parentheses.

1. E. L. Konigsburg tells an unusual survival story in (her, its) book *From the Mixed-Up Files of Mrs. Basil E. Frankweiler.*
2. It's the story of Claudia Kincaid; (she, herself) ran away to live in the Metropolitan Museum of Art.
3. (She, Her) and her brother Jamie lived there for a week.
4. They slept in an antique bed and took (their, they're) baths in a fountain.
5. The fountain had coins all over (it's, its) base.
6. (These, This) is where both of the children collected (their, his or her) lunch money.
7. There was a new statue; (its, it's) origin was a mystery to everyone.
8. Claudia and Jamie decided to solve the mystery (theirselves, themselves).
9. They contacted Mrs. Basil E. Frankweiler. That statue had come from (her, his) private collection.
10. (Who, Whom) made the statue? You'll have to read the book (yourself, itself)!

B. Pronoun Use This student report about the novel *Island of the Blue Dolphins* contains nine errors in pronoun usage. Rewrite the passage to correct the errors.

> **STUDENT MODEL**
>
> What if my brother and me were abandoned by my entire community on our island home? How would us castoffs survive? What would we do with ourself?
>
> In *Island of the Blue Dolphins,* by Scott O'Dell, the heroine was left behind with her brother, who was soon killed by wild dogs. It was her who remained on the island for eighteen years. She tamed one of the island dogs herself and named it Rontu; it's friendship was invaluable to her.
>
> Few of the people I know would take such good care of himself or herself if left alone on an island. Even these who know the wilderness might not have the mental strength to last alone for such a long time. O'Dell's heroine showed great skill, courage, and patience. Whom else would be so strong?

Choose the correct replacement for each underlined word in the passage, or indicate if it is correct as is.

> Who is Thomas Eisner? Him and his wife Maria are
> (1)   (2)
> entomologists, or insect experts. Their concerned about the survival
> (3)
> of endangered insects. Himself and writer Diane Ackerman explored
> (4)
> insect life in Florida. Ackerman describes what she learned in her
> (5)
> book *The Rarest of the Rare: Vanishing Animals, Timeless Worlds*. It
> was him who proved that some insects contain medicines that can
> (6)
> cure human diseases. That has encouraged drug companies to help
> (7)
> protect the rain forests for insect research. Eisner has also testified
> before members of the U.S. Senate, asking them to reauthorize the
> (8)
> Endangered Species Act. Eisner reminded the Senate that us
> (9)
> humans share the planet with many other species. In helping them
> survive, we may ultimately help themselves.
> (10)

1. A. Whom
   B. Which
   C. Whose
   D. Correct as is

2. A. Himself
   B. He
   C. His
   D. Correct as is

3. A. There
   B. They're
   C. Them are
   D. Correct as is

4. A. Him
   B. Them
   C. He
   D. Correct as is

5. A. his
   B. their
   C. hers
   D. Correct as is

6. A. he
   B. himself
   C. his
   D. Correct as is

7. A. These
   B. His discovery
   C. This
   D. Correct as is

8. A. it
   B. those
   C. they
   D. Correct as is

9. A. our
   B. my
   C. we
   D. Correct as is

10. A. ourselves
    B. we
    C. humans
    D. Correct as is

Student Help Desk

Pronouns at a Glance

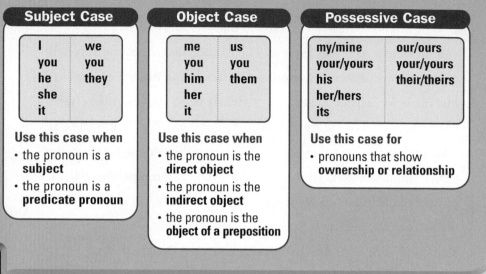

Subject Case

I	we
you	you
he	they
she	
it	

Use this case when
- the pronoun is a **subject**
- the pronoun is a **predicate pronoun**

Object Case

me	us
you	you
him	them
her	
it	

Use this case when
- the pronoun is the **direct object**
- the pronoun is the **indirect object**
- the pronoun is the **object of a preposition**

Possessive Case

my/mine	our/ours
your/yours	your/yours
his	their/theirs
her/hers	
its	

Use this case for
- pronouns that show **ownership or relationship**

Pronoun-Antecedent Agreement

We'll Do Our Best

A pronoun should agree with its antecedent in number, person, and gender.

A singular antecedent takes a singular pronoun.

Marisella is saving **her** candles for a power outage. (singular)

A plural antecedent takes a plural pronoun.

The **Garcias** have boarded up **their** house against the hurricane. (plural)

Avoid incorrect gender reference.

Everyone has **his or her** favorite precautions.

We all have **our** favorite precautions.

Types of Pronouns
Everything in Its Place

Intensive & Reflexive	Interrogative	Demonstrative	Indefinite
myself	who	this	someone
yourself	whom	that	anyone
herself	what	these	each
himself	which	those	several
itself	whose		many
ourselves			all
yourselves			most
themselves			none

For a full list of indefinite pronouns, see page 76.

Pronoun Problems   A Clear-cut Case

We: Subject/Predicate Pronoun

We Californians have survived many natural disasters.

Us: Object

So many natural disasters have struck **us** Californians.

Who: Subject/Predicate Pronoun

Who has ever survived a tornado?

Whom: Object of verb or preposition

To **whom** will we turn for advice?

The Bottom Line

Checklist for Pronouns

Have I . . .

____ used the subject case for pronouns that are subjects and predicate pronouns?

____ used the object case for pronouns that are objects of verbs or prepositions?

____ used the possessive case to show ownership or relationship?

____ used *who* and *whom* correctly?

____ made sure that pronouns agree with their antecedents in number, person, and gender?

____ used the correct cases in compound subjects and objects?

Verbs

Hold on!

Theme: Great Rides
Three Thrilling Minutes

How does it feel to speed through the air on a roller coaster?
Does your skin tingle? Does your stomach churn? Do your ears
pop? Verbs help you recreate how real-life experiences feel,
look, sound, smell, and taste. What verbs do you think the
passenger in this picture would use to recreate his real-life
experience on a roller coaster?

Write Away: Want a Ride?
Write a paragraph describing the most thrilling ride you can
imagine. It could be a roller coaster ride, a train trip through a
wild animal preserve, or a drive along a twisting mountain
road. Put the paragraph in your 🗁 **Working Portfolio.**

CD-ROM **Grammar Coach**

Choose the best way to rewrite each underlined word or group of words.

> Amazing things <u>happen</u> on roller coasters. In 1949, a West
> (1)
> Virginian coal miner <u>ride</u> the Cyclone at Coney Island. For six
> (2)
> years before, the miner <u>will be</u> mute. After the ride, he <u>speaks</u>
> (3) (4)
> again. He <u>said</u>, "I feel sick." While this man found his voice on a
> (5)
> roller coaster, other people <u>are losing</u> things. In 1994, workers at
> (6)
> an amusement park in England <u>have drained</u> a pool beneath two
> (7)
> roller coasters. Twenty-five sets of false teeth <u>lay</u> at the bottom of
> (8)
> the pool. Amusement park workers also <u>has found</u> glass eyes,
> (9)
> hearing aids, and toupees beneath coaster tracks. Who knows what
> workers <u>discovered</u> under future rides.
> (10)

1. A. will have happened
   B. were happening
   C. had happened
   D. Correct as is

2. A. will ride
   B. rode
   C. is riding
   D. Correct as is

3. A. had been
   B. will have been
   C. was being
   D. Correct as is

4. A. will be speaking
   B. has spoken
   C. spoke
   D. Correct as is

5. A. says
   B. will say
   C. had said
   D. Correct as is

6. A. lose
   B. have lost
   C. will be losing
   D. Correct as is

7. A. will drain
   B. drained
   C. drains
   D. Correct as is

8. A. laid
   B. has laid
   C. are laying
   D. Correct as is

9. A. have found
   B. will be finding
   C. must find
   D. Correct as is

10. A. are discovering
    B. were discovering
    C. will discover
    D. Correct as is

VERBS

What Is a Verb?

LESSON 1

❶ Here's the Idea

▶ **A verb is a word used to express an action, a condition, or a state of being.** The two main types of verbs are **action verbs** and **linking verbs.** Both kinds can be accompanied by helping verbs.

Action Verbs

An **action verb** tells what its subject does. The action it expresses may be either **physical** or **mental.**

The roller coaster climbs up a hill. (physical action)

Then the coaster plunges straight down. (physical action)

Some people hate amusement parks. (mental action)

Others enjoy them. (mental action)

Linking Verbs

A **linking verb** links its subject to a word in the predicate. The most common linking verbs are forms of the verb *be.*

Linking Verbs	
Forms of *be*	be, is, am, are, was, were, been, being
Verbs that express condition	appear, become, feel, grow, look, remain, smell, sound, taste

LINKS

The Cyclone is a roller coaster.

LINKING VERB

Its name sounds dangerous.

Some verbs can serve as either action or linking verbs.

LINKS

A passenger looks at the roller coaster. She looks eager.
ACTION VERB   LINKING VERB

She feels ready. She feels the steel bar across her lap.
LINKING VERB   ACTION VERB

Helping Verbs and Verb Phrases

Helping verbs help main verbs express precise shades of meaning. The combination of one or more helping verbs with a main verb is called a **verb phrase.**

VERB PHRASE

Many people will ride the Cyclone this weekend.
HELPING   MAIN

They must want some thrills in their lives.

Some verbs can serve both as main verbs and as helping verbs. For example, *has* stands alone in the first sentence below but is a helping verb in the second sentence.

Rich Rodriguez has no fear of roller coasters.
MAIN VERB

He has set a world roller coaster record.
HELPING VERB

Common Helping Verbs	
Forms of *be*	be, am, is, are, was, were, been, being
Forms of *do*	do, does, did
Forms of *have*	have, has, had
Others	could, should, would may, might, must can, shall, will

② Why It Matters in Writing

You often can express strong feelings by using action verbs instead of linking verbs. Notice the difference that the change to an action verb makes in the sentence below.

The Cyclone ~~is scary to~~ *petrifies* me.

③ Practice and Apply

A. CONCEPT CHECK: What Is a Verb?

Write the verb or verb phrase in each of the following sentences.

The King of Coaster Jockeys

1. Rich Rodriguez has ridden a roller coaster longer than anyone else in the world.
2. He set the record on the Big Dipper in Blackpool, England.
3. His record is 1,013.5 hours over 47 days.
4. Guidelines allow a rider two hours a day off a coaster.
5. Rodriguez slept on the roller coaster.
6. By the end, Rodriguez had traveled 11,362 miles.
7. The wind rubbed his face raw.
8. The Big Dipper is a complete-circuit roller coaster.
9. It travels about 65 miles per hour.
10. But Rodriguez calls the Cyclone his favorite.

➡ **For a SELF-CHECK and more practice, see the EXERCISE BANK, p. 616.**

Label each verb above as *Action* or *Linking*.

B. WRITING: Using Action Verbs

Write an action verb for each numeral in the paragraph below.

The Chiller

Imagine a trip on the Chiller, a roller coaster in New Jersey. The coaster **(1)** from 0 to 70 miles per hour in four seconds. Its launch **(2)** you. Ahead **(3)** a tunnel and then a sharp rise. Halfway through the ride, the train **(4)** and hurtles you backwards. The ride **(5)** only 45 seconds.

Action Verbs and Objects

❶ Here's the Idea

Action verbs are often accompanied by words that complete their meaning. These complements are **direct objects** and **indirect objects**.

Direct Objects

▶ **A direct object is a noun or pronoun that names the receiver of a verb's action.** The **direct object** answers the question *what* or *whom.*

GAINED WHAT?

Evel Knievel gained much fame.
ACTION VERB   DIRECT OBJECT

He performed **dangerous stunts on a motorcycle.**

Indirect Objects

▶ **An indirect object tells *to what* or *whom* or *for what* or *whom* an action is done.** Verbs that often take indirect objects include *bring, give, hand, lend, make, send, show, teach, tell,* and *write.*

Knievel gave a thrill. (Gave a thrill to whom?)

TO WHOM?

Knievel gave **his fans a thrill.**
INDIRECT OBJECT   DIRECT OBJECT

Knievel taught **his son some stunts.**

If the word *to* or *for* appears in the sentence, the word that follows is **not** an indirect object. It is the object of a preposition.

Show the stunt to us.
                OBJECT OF PREPOSITION

Show us the stunt.
     INDIRECT OBJECT

Transitive and Intransitive Verbs

An action verb that has a direct object is called a **transitive verb**. An action verb that does not have a direct object is called an **intransitive verb**.

Knievel cleared nineteen cars in one stunt.

TRANSITIVE VERB 🠝   🠝 DIRECT OBJECT

His motorcycle sailed through the air.

🠝 INTRANSITIVE VERB (NO OBJECT)

Sometimes an intransitive verb is followed by a word that looks like a direct object but is really an adverb. An adverb tells where, when, how, or to what extent, but a direct object answers the question *what* or *whom*.

CRASHED WHAT?

Knievel crashed his motorcycle.

TRANSITIVE VERB 🠝   🠝 DIRECT OBJECT

CRASHED WHEN?

He crashed frequently.

INTRANSITIVE 🠝   🠝 ADVERB
VERB

❷ Why It Matters in Writing

Use direct objects that are specific nouns to make your writing clearer and more interesting to readers. Notice how the model below uses specific nouns as direct objects.

PROFESSIONAL MODEL

Knievel became as tough as Butte [Montana]. He held **school records** for push-ups and sit-ups. He played **pro hockey**.... He raced **stock cars, sprint cars,** and **motorcycles.** ...

—Jerry Garrett, "Midnight in the Garden of Good and Evel"

❸ Practice and Apply

A. CONCEPT CHECK: Action Verbs and Objects

Write the 15 complements in these sentences, identifying each as a direct object or an indirect object.

Jumping a Canyon

1. In 1974, Evel Knievel staged the most famous feat of his career.
2. He chose the Snake River Canyon in Idaho.
3. He bought himself a steam-powered vehicle.
4. Knievel's promoter publicized the danger of the jump.
5. Fans wished Knievel good luck.
6. TV cameras showed viewers the quarter-mile-wide chasm.
7. The launch gave spectators a fright.
8. A parachute opened its canopy early.
9. The vehicle hit the floor of the canyon.
10. The failure gave the famous daredevil no desire for another try at the canyon.

➜ For a SELF-CHECK and more practice, see the EXERCISE BANK, p. 616.

B. WRITING. Using Specific Nouns

The photograph below shows Evel Knievel's son Robbie jumping his motorcycle over the Grand Canyon. Write a short description of him in action based on what you see in the photo. Use some of the nouns in this list as direct objects.

air, Grand Canyon, ground, helmet, motorcycle, record, reputation, rocks, scaffold, stunt

Linking Verbs and Predicate Words

① Here's the Idea

The word that a linking verb connects its subject to is called a **subject complement.** The subject complement identifies or describes the subject. Some common linking verbs are *is, feel, seem,* and *look.*

IDENTIFIES

Paul Revere's mount was **a** saddle horse.
SUBJECT   VERB   SUBJECT COMPLEMENT

DESCRIBES

The mare seemed **very** fast.
SUBJECT   VERB   SUBJECT COMPLEMENT

Predicate Nouns and Predicate Adjectives

A subject complement can be a **predicate noun** or a **predicate adjective.**

▶ **A predicate noun is a noun that follows a linking verb and identifies, renames, or defines the subject.**

IDENTIFIES

Brown Beauty was **the mare's name.**
SUBJECT   VERB   PREDICATE NOUN

Mr. Larkin was **the horse's owner.**

▶ **A predicate adjective is an adjective that follows a linking verb and modifies the subject.**

MODIFIES

Saddle horses are powerful.
SUBJECT   VERB   PREDICATE ADJECTIVE

They look **distinctive.**

❷ Why It Matters in Writing

You can use predicate adjectives to evaluate a subject or show judgment. Notice author William Saroyan's use of a predicate adjective to evaluate a horse.

"I do not know what to think," he said. "The horse is **stronger** than ever. Better-tempered, too. I thank God."

—William Saroyan, "The Summer of the Beautiful White Horse"

❸ Practice and Apply

CONCEPT CHECK: Linking Verbs and Predicate Words

Identify each linking verb, predicate noun, and predicate adjective in the sentences below.

A Narrow Escape
1. On the night of Paul Revere's ride, the weather was mild.
2. His mount's canter was graceful.
3. Revere himself felt calm.
4. Suddenly, Revere's horse became nervous.
5. The two horsemen on the road ahead were enemy soldiers.
6. The result was a brief chase off the original route.
7. A clay pit became a trap for one soldier's horse.
8. Brown Beauty was faster than the other soldier's horse.
9. Revere's detour seemed a nuisance.
10. But his new route was safer.

➡ **For a SELF-CHECK and more practice, see the EXERCISE BANK, p. 617.**

Principal Parts of Verbs

❶ Here's the Idea

▶ **Every verb has four basic forms called its principal parts: the present, the present participle, the past, and the past participle.** These principal parts are used to make all of the forms and tenses of the verb. Here are some examples.

PRESENT
Balloonists sail **on wind currents.**

PRESENT PARTICIPLE
They often are riding **jet streams.**

PAST
Bertrand Piccard and Brian Jones circled **the earth in a balloon in 1999.**

PAST PARTICIPLE
Many balloonists have tried **the feat.**

The Four Principal Parts of a Verb			
Present	**Present Participle**	**Past**	**Past Participle**
sail	(is) sail**ing**	sail**ed**	(has) sail**ed**
lift	(is) lift**ing**	lift**ed**	(has) lift**ed**

Notice that helping verbs are used with the present participle and the past participle.

Regular Verbs

There are two kinds of verbs: regular and irregular.

▶ **A regular verb is a verb whose past and past participle are formed by adding -ed or -d to the present.** It forms the present participle by adding -ing to the present.

Present	**Present Participle**	**Past**	**Past Participle**
succeed	(is) succeed + **ing**	succeed + **ed**	(has) succeed + **ed**

You will learn about irregular verbs in the next lesson.

② Why It Matters in Writing

The principal parts of verbs help you show changes in time in your writing. In the model below, notice how the writer uses the past and the present to show two different times.

PROFESSIONAL MODEL

Piccard and Jones finished their around-the-world trip in 20 days. Their feat stands as a world record.

PAST

PRESENT

—Martha Schmitt

VERBS

③ Practice and Apply

CONCEPT CHECK: Principal Parts of Verbs

Identify each underlined principal part as the present, the present participle, the past, or the past participle.

An Around-the-World Balloon Flight

Piccard and Jones **(1)** traveled in a combination hot-air and helium balloon called *Breitling Orbiter 3*. In terms of comfort, the balloon greatly **(2)** outclasses earlier aircraft. Inside a pressurized, heated cabin, engineers have **(3)** equipped the balloon with a bunk bed, toilet, and kitchen. When one pilot is **(4)** sleeping, the other **(5)** sits at the control panel. Then the pilots **(6)** switch places. Other equipment on the flight **(7)** included a fax machine and satellite telephones. Solar-charged batteries **(8)** provided power for the onboard equipment. Other pilots have **(9)** used similar balloons in around-the-world attempts. Engineers are continually **(10)** improving the design of high-altitude balloons.

➡ For a SELF-CHECK and more practice, see the EXERCISE BANK, p. 617.

Irregular Verbs

❶ Here's the Idea

▶ **Irregular verbs are verbs whose past and past participle forms are not made by adding *-ed* or *-d* to the present.**

The following chart shows you how to form the past and past participle forms of many irregular verbs.

Common Irregular Verbs			
	Present	**Past**	**Past Participle**
Group 1 The forms of the present, the past, and the past participle are all the same.	**burst** cost cut hurt let put set shut	**burst** cost cut hurt let put set shut	(has) **burst** (has) cost (has) cut (has) hurt (has) let (has) put (has) set (has) shut
Group 2 The forms of the past and the past participle are the same.	**bring** build catch feel keep lay leave lend make pay say sell shine sit sting swing teach think win wind	**brought** built caught felt kept laid left lent made paid said sold shone sat stung swung taught thought won wound	(has) **brought** (has) built (has) caught (has) felt (has) kept (has) laid (has) left (has) lent (has) made (has) paid (has) said (has) sold (has) shone (has) sat (has) stung (has) swung (has) taught (has) thought (has) won (has) wound

Common Irregular Verbs *(continued)*

	Present	Past	Past Participle
Group 3 The past participle is formed by adding *-n* or *-en* to the past.	**bite** break choose freeze lie speak steal tear wear	**bit** broke chose froze lay spoke stole tore wore	(has) **bitten** (has) broken (has) chosen (has) frozen (has) lain (has) spoken (has) stolen (has) torn (has) worn
Group 4 The past participle is formed from the present, often by adding *-n* or *-en*.	**blow** do draw drive eat fall give go grow know rise run see shake take throw write	**blew** did drew drove ate fell gave went grew knew rose ran saw shook took threw wrote	(has) **blown** (has) done (has) drawn (has) driven (has) eaten (has) fallen (has) given (has) gone (has) grown (has) known (has) risen (has) run (has) seen (has) shaken (has) taken (has) thrown (has) written
Group 5 The last vowel changes from *i* in the present to *a* in the past, to *u* in the past participle.	**begin** drink ring shrink sing sink spring swim	**began** drank rang shrank sang sank sprang swam	(has) **begun** (has) drunk (has) rung (has) shrunk (has) sung (has) sunk (has) sprung (has) swum

The Irregular Verb *Be*

	Present	Past	Past Participle
The past and past participle do not follow any pattern.	**am, are, is**	**was, were**	(has) **been**

VERBS

❷ Why It Matters in Writing

Skilled writers use irregular verb forms correctly. You probably already know the principal parts of many irregular verbs. To avoid mistakes, memorize any that you do not know. Notice the student writer's correct use of irregular verbs in the model below.

> **STUDENT MODEL**
>
> My brother Mike **took** part in "Ride the Rockies," Colorado's famous bike ride through the Rocky Mountain range. In one day he **rode** 67 miles. "Half of that **was** uphill!" **said** my brother when I congratulated him after the event.

❸ Practice and Apply

CONCEPT CHECK: Irregular Verbs

In the sentences below, choose the correct forms of the verbs in parentheses.

On the Rebound

1. American bicyclist Lance Armstrong (win, won) the 2,287-mile Tour de France in 1999.
2. Several years earlier, doctors (give, gave) him less than a 40 percent chance of surviving cancer.
3. Armstrong (chose, chosen) an aggressive treatment plan.
4. Now Armstrong has (beat, beaten) the disease.
5. After the cancer, he (began, begun) his career all over.
6. The experience has (gave, given) him a different outlook.
7. It also has (leave, left) him with a leaner body.
8. Armstrong's lighter weight (pay, paid) off when he had to cycle through the mountains.
9. So (did, done) his training, in which he cycled the toughest portions of the course.
10. Armstrong's amazing victory has (teach, taught) other cancer patients to maintain hope.

➡ **For a SELF-CHECK and more practice, see the EXERCISE BANK, p. 618.**

Simple Tenses

❶ Here's the Idea

> **A tense is a verb form that shows the time of an action or condition.** Verbs have three **simple tenses:** the present, the past, and the future.

Understanding Simple Tenses

Simple Tenses

The hatch of the lunar module opens.	The **present tense** shows that an action or condition occurs now.
The module reached Tranquillity Base 30 minutes ago.	The **past tense** shows that an action or condition was completed in the past.
Soon the occupants will walk on the moon.	The **future tense** shows that an action or condition will occur in the future.

A **progressive form** of a verb expresses an action or condition in progress. The progressive forms of the three simple tenses are used to show that actions or conditions were, are, or will be in progress.

Progressive Forms

You are operating a virtual-reality model of the Apollo 11 mission.	Present Progressive
You were blasting off before.	Past Progressive
You will be sharing the game with a friend.	Future Progressive

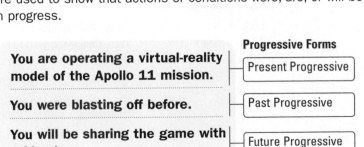

VERBS

Forming Simple Tenses

The **present tense** of a verb is the present principal part. The **past tense** is the past principal part. To form the **future tense,** add *will* to the present principal part.

Forming Simple Tenses		
	Singular	**Plural**
Present (present principal part)	I moonwalk you moonwalk he, she, it moonwalks	we moonwalk you moonwalk they moonwalk
Past (past principal part)	I moonwalked you moonwalked he, she, it moonwalked	we moonwalked you moonwalked they moonwalked
Future (*will* + present part)	I will moonwalk you will moonwalk he, she, it will moonwalk	we will moonwalk you will moonwalk they will moonwalk

To make the progressive form of one of these tenses, add the present, past, or future form of *be* to the present participle.

Present Progressive: **I am moonwalking.**

Past Progressive: **I was moonwalking.**

Future Progressive: **I will be moonwalking.**

❷ Why It Matters in Writing

The simple tenses help you express basic time frames. Notice how the model uses the past and present tenses to shift between the writer's childhood and her adulthood.

> **LITERARY MODEL**
>
> I held on to the knowledge tightly afterward, and I still hold it to this day. I learned what flying was for my father and for the other early aviators....
>
> —Reeve Lindbergh, "Flying"
>
> PAST
> PRESENT

❸ Practice and Apply

A. CONCEPT CHECK: Simple Tenses

Identify each underlined verb as present, past, future, present progressive, past progressive, or future progressive.

The *Eagle* Has Landed
1. What <u>was</u> the first moon landing like?
2. A virtual-reality game <u>recreates</u> the experience.
3. Inside the lunar module *Eagle,* you <u>head</u> for a plain called the Sea of Tranquillity.
4. A computer <u>sounds</u> several alarms.
5. Mission Control <u>will override</u> the alarms.
6. You <u>are running</u> out of fuel in the search for a good landing spot.
7. You <u>will have</u> only thirty seconds left.
8. But you <u>will land</u> without a bump.
9. Before the real take-off, Neil Armstrong <u>doubted</u> the mission's likelihood of success.
10. He <u>set</u> the odds at 50-50.

Rewrite sentences 2, 3, 4, 5, and 8, changing the verbs to progressive forms.

➜ For a SELF-CHECK and more practice, see the EXERCISE BANK, p. 618.

B. WRITING: Using Simple Tenses

Use time frame clues to write each verb in parentheses in the correct simple tense: present, past, or future.

Shuttle Commander Collins
NASA (select) Eileen Collins as the first female space-shuttle pilot in 1990. She (pilot) her first mission in February 1995. In 1997, she (return) to space, piloting *Atlantis* to the *Mir* space station. Today, Collins's husband, Pat Youngs, (take) care of their daughter during her space missions. He (handle) that job during Collins's future flights for NASA.

Perfect Tenses

❶ Here's the Idea

Understanding Perfect Tenses

The **present perfect tense** places an action or condition in a stretch of time leading up to the present.

Many people have rafted through the Grand Canyon.	People rafted through the canyon at unspecified times before the present.

The **past perfect tense** places a past action or condition before another past action or condition.

After the guide had straightened the raft, we entered the rapids.	The straightening occurred before the entering.

The **future perfect tense** places a future action or condition before another future action or condition.

We will have cleared many rapids before the trip ends.	The clearing will occur before the ending.

Rafters will have passed this point soon.

Forming Perfect Tenses

To form the present perfect, past perfect, or future perfect tense, add the present, past, or future form of *have* to the past participle.

Forming Perfect Tenses		
	Singular	**Plural**
Present Perfect (*has* or *have* + past participle)	I have rafted you have rafted he, she, it has rafted	we have rafted you have rafted they have rafted
Past Perfect (*had* + past participle)	I had rafted you had rafted he, she, it had rafted	we had rafted you had rafted they had rafted
Future Perfect (*will* + *have* + past participle)	I will have rafted you will have rafted he, she, it will have rafted	we will have rafted you will have rafted they will have rafted

In a perfect form, the tense of the helping verb *have* shows the verb's tense.

❷ Why It Matters in Writing

When writing a narrative, you can use the perfect tenses to make the timing of events clear. Notice how the use of the past perfect tense and the future perfect tense makes the time relationships clear in the model.

STUDENT MODEL

Just before the trip began, our guide had warned us about Lava Falls, the largest rapid in the Grand Canyon. He now says that by the time the trip ends, at least one raft will have flipped in its churning currents.

PAST PERFECT

FUTURE PERFECT

VERBS

❸ Practice and Apply

A. CONCEPT CHECK: Perfect Tenses

Identify the verb in each sentence, and indicate whether its tense is present perfect, past perfect, or future perfect.

A Grand Ride

1. The guide had compared a trip through the Grand Canyon to a roller coaster.
2. Soon I will have experienced the journey myself.
3. Within eight days, we will have ridden more than 70 rapids.
4. I have taken other rafting trips.
5. But the Grand Canyon trip will have been the longest and wildest.
6. At Hermit Rapid, huge waves had swept over our boat.
7. The roar of the waves had muffled our voices.
8. Someone has called Lava Falls the world's fastest navigable white-water rapid.
9. I never have rafted through anything like it.
10. By the end of Lava Falls, the river had dropped 37 feet.

➡ **For a SELF-CHECK and more practice, see the EXERCISE BANK, p. 619.**

B. WRITING: Using Perfect Tenses

Add verbs to this narrative in the tense indicated in parentheses. Choose verbs from this list:

climb, travel, see, return, take

The Best Trip

The ride through the Grand Canyon was the best trip I ever (present perfect). Before it was over, we (past perfect) nearly 280 miles in just eight days. We (past perfect) up the rocks along waterfalls and jumped into the pools below. We (past perfect) mule deer and bighorn sheep as well as fossils of sea creatures millions of years old. I hope that by the time I graduate from college I (future perfect) to the Grand Canyon.

Using Verb Tenses

1 Here's the Idea

A good writer uses different verb tenses to indicate that events occur at different times. If you do not need to indicate a change of time, do not switch from one tense to another.

Writing About the Present

▶ **The present tenses convey actions and conditions that occur in the present.** When you write about the present, you can use the present tense, the present perfect tense, and the present progressive form.

People ride many animals besides horses. **Tourists in India sightsee on the backs of elephants.**	The **present tense** places the actions in the present.
Indians have trained elephants for thousands of years. **They have used elephants for transportation and work.**	The **present perfect tense** places the actions in a period of time leading up to the present.
Elephant handlers are continuing an old tradition. **They are passing the tradition on to their children.**	The **present progressive form** shows the actions in progress now.

Writing About the Past

▶ **The past tenses convey actions and conditions that came to an end in the past.** When you write about the past, you can use past verb forms to indicate the order in which events occurred. Using these forms correctly will make it easier for readers to follow the events.

In 218 B.C., Hannibal's army crossed the Alps with elephants.

His army included thirty-eight elephants.

> The **past tense** shows actions that began and were completed in the past.

Other generals had used elephants in war before Hannibal did.

Almost a century after Persians had ridden elephants in battle, Hannibal led elephants against Rome.

> The **past perfect tense** places the actions before other past actions.

Hannibal's elephants were scaring the Roman army's horses, as well as its soldiers.

Hannibal was winning battle after battle.

> The **past progressive forms** show that the actions were in progress in the past.

Elephants were frightening Hannibal's opponents.

Writing About the Future

▶ **The future tenses convey actions and conditions that are yet to come.** By using the different future verb forms, you can show how future events are related in time.

Maybe you will ride an elephant one day.

You will mount the largest land animal on earth.

> The **future tense** shows that the actions have not yet occurred.

By the time you are an adult, perhaps elephants will have survived threats to their existence.

With luck, people will have protected enough elephants to keep the species from becoming extinct.

> The **future perfect tense** places the actions before other future actions.

Elephant herds will be prospering with protection.

Their numbers will be growing.

> The **future progressive forms** show that the actions will be continuing in the future.

❷ Why It Matters in Writing

The present tense is useful when you are describing or explaining something. Notice how the writer consistently uses the present tense in the model below.

PROFESSIONAL MODEL

A mahout . . . is one who **trains** and **drives** an elephant. The mahout **sits** on the elephant's neck, just behind the head, and **guides** the animal through a series of spoken and physical commands.

—Malcolm C. Jensen, "Elephants of War"

❸ Practice and Apply

A. CONCEPT CHECK: Using Verb Tenses

In the sentences below, choose the correct tense or form for each verb in parentheses.

Park Rangers on Elephants

1. In the Kanha National Park in India, mahouts (patrol, will patrol) the park every day.
2. In India, mahouts (have ridden, had ridden) elephants for centuries.
3. On their daily patrols, the mahouts at Kanha (protect, will protect) the park's Bengal tigers from poachers.
4. Bengal tigers (are becoming, became) increasingly rare.
5. A mahout and his elephant (remained, will remain) together for life.
6. Yesterday, a mahout (takes, took) several tourists into the jungle.
7. They (were hoping, will be hoping) for a glimpse of the tigers.
8. During the ride, the mahout (was pointing, have pointed) out tigers in the bamboo and elephant grass.
9. By the end of the ride, the tourists (had learned, were learning) a great deal about tigers.
10. Every day for the next month, the mahout (will have taken, will be taking) tourists on elephant rides.

➡ For a SELF-CHECK and more practice, see the EXERCISE BANK, p. 620.

B. EDITING: Correcting Verb Tenses

Rewrite this paragraph, correcting inconsistencies in the use of verb tenses. There are five errors.

The Elephants at Kanha

At Kanha, each elephant has a caretaker. What do the caretakers do? In the late afternoon, the caretakers have given the elephants their baths and fed them. Then they set the elephants free in the jungle. In the middle of the night, the caretakers woke up and will round up the elephants. They dust off the animals and will be saddling them for the mahouts.

📂 **Working Portfolio:** Find your **Write Away** from page 90 or a sample of your most recent work. Identify any errors in the use of verb tenses and correct them.

Troublesome Verb Pairs

LESSON 9

❶ Here's the Idea

Some verbs seem similar but are actually different words with different meanings. Troublesome verb pairs include *lie* and *lay, sit* and *set, rise* and *raise,* and *let* and *leave.*

Lie and *Lay*

Lie means "to rest in a flat position." It does not take an object. *Lay* means "to put or place." It does take an object.

The worker lies near the tree.

He lays a bucket near the tree.

Lie and *Lay*		
Present	**Past**	**Past Participle**
lie Al **lies** down.	lay Al **lay** down.	lain Al has **lain** down.
lay Al **lays** the sponge down.	laid Al **laid** the sponge down.	laid Al has **laid** the sponge down.

 WATCH OUT

Lie and *lay* are confusing because the present principal part of *lay* has the same spelling as the past principal part of *lie.*

Sit and *Set*

Sit means "to be seated." It does not take an object.

Set means "to put or place." It does take an object.

The worker sits by the window.

He sets the squeegee near the sill.

Sit and *Set*		
Present	**Past**	**Past Participle**
sit He **sits** on the ledge.	sat He **sat** on the ledge.	sat He has **sat** here often.
set Amy **sets** down the screen.	set Amy **set** down the screen.	set Amy has **set** down the screen.

VERBS

Rise and Raise

Rise means "to move upward" or "to get out of bed." It does not take an object. *Raise* means "to lift" or "to care for or bring up." It does take an object.

Lee rises before dawn every morning.

Lee raises the window.

Rise and Raise		
Present	**Past**	**Past Participle**
rise The hot air **rises.**	rose The hot air **rose.**	risen The hot air has **risen.**
raise Irene **raises** the screen.	raised Irene **raised** the screen.	raised Irene has **raised** the screen.

Let and Leave

Let means "to allow" or "to permit." *Leave* means "to depart" or "to allow something to remain where it is." Both *let* and *leave* may take an object.

Frank let his son operate the rig.

Marta leaves the windows closed.

Let and Leave		
Present	**Past**	**Past Participle**
let Anna **lets** me help.	let Anna **let** me help.	let Anna has **let** me help.
leave Tom **leaves** for work at noon.	left Tom **left** for work at noon yesterday.	left Tom has **left** for work.

❷ Practice and Apply

A. CONCEPT CHECK: Troublesome Verb Pairs

Choose the correct verb in parentheses for each of the following sentences.

Riding to the Top

1. (Let, Leave) me tell you about the job of washing the windows of a skyscraper.
2. On some buildings, the window washer (sits, sets) in a chair attached by ropes to the top of the building.
3. To move the chair up and down the building, a worker (rises, raises) and lowers the ropes.
4. From this high perch, a window washer can watch the sun (rise, raise).
5. On some skyscrapers, sliding scaffolds (rise, raise) the workers up and down.
6. One window washer began work at 5:00 A.M. and (let, left) work before the afternoon sun got too hot.
7. Another (lay, laid) asleep during the day and worked at night.
8. Would you like to (lie, lay) on a scaffold along the Sears Tower and watch the stars?
9. Window washers have to watch where they (sit, set) their tools.
10. They cannot just (lie, lay) them anywhere.

➜ For a SELF-CHECK and more practice, see the EXERCISE BANK, p. 620.

B. PROOFREADING: Correcting Errors in Verb Usage

List the five verbs that are used incorrectly in the following paragraph. Then change them to the correct verb forms.

At the Top

Imagine what it's like to set in a window-washing rig 70 stories up in the air. The cement sidewalk lays far below. As you look down, goose bumps raise on your skin. Don't sit your squeegee on that bird's nest on the window ledge! Let the nest alone, or you may be attacked by an angry bird.

Grammar in Social Studies

Using Verbs Effectively

In social studies you study major events in history. You use verbs—especially action verbs—to relate what happened. Creating an annotated map is a good way to describe a series of unfolding events. The map itself shows important locations. The annotations allow you to describe important events that took place at those locations. Below is an annotated map of part of the Oregon Trail, a pathway that settlers followed to get to the West in the mid-1800s.

Moving West Along the Oregon Trail

5 **Three Island Crossing.** Here settlers **can risk** a direct river crossing, or they **can travel** the long route around the river bend.

4 **South Pass.** South Pass **marks** the halfway point.

2 **Ash Hollow.** Most travelers **rest** here. They **taste** fresh water and **gaze** at the first trees in 100 miles.

n
w ← → *e*
s

3 **Ft. Laramie.** This fort **is** the gateway to the Rocky Mountains. Some people **decide** to go back.

1 **Shawnee Mission.** Oxen or mules **pull** wagons along the overland trail. Many settlers **walk** alongside them, barefoot. They **begin** a 2,000-mile journey.

Practice and Apply

A. USING VERBS TO RELATE EVENTS

Use your own ideas and the information on the map to write an imaginary journal entry by a settler on the Oregon Trail. Choose one of the landmarks on the map. Write what the settler might do, think, feel, or say upon arriving at that location. Your journal entry may answer questions like these:

• What might the settler do when he or she first arrives?

• What might the settler see?

• What might the settler wish?

B. WRITING: Making A Map

Draw a map of the route you follow to go to school or to go to another local spot. Label at least three landmarks along the route, and write a one-sentence annotation to indicate what you do at each one. You might include landmarks such as these:

• buildings

• natural features, such as rivers, hills, and lakes

• constructed features, such as bridges, overpasses, and railroad tracks

VERBS

home

I **meet** a friend at 7:35.

I **start** my trip at 7:30.

We always **check** the clock on the bank.

Mixed Review

A. Correcting Errors in Verb Usage Find and correct the 15 incorrect verbs in the following sentences. Watch out for irregular verbs and members of troublesome verb pairs.

An Unusual Soap-Box Derby

1. Each year, the Sand Hill Challenge, a soap-box derby race in California, promoted driver safety among teenagers.
2. For several years, business firms sponsor the race teams, and technology companies build the race cars.
3. In the past, some cars will be having high-tech designs.
4. For a race in 1997, designers build a three-wheeled car.
5. Driver Amy Han laid down in the car and will steer it.
6. In the Whimsy Division, car designers typically will be worrying more about style than speed.
7. One year, a group will have made a car from bread.
8. In the past, both adult and high school teams participate in the races, but they will be having separate divisions.
9. Besides the driver, a typical team will be including two people who have pushed the car for the first 40 yards down a hill.
10. A "catcher" at the bottom of the hill slowed down and stopped the car.

B. Using Verb Tenses Imagine yourself in a soap-box derby race in a car of your own design. Write five sentences answering the following questions about the race. Be sure to use verb tenses correctly.

1. What thoughts or feelings did you have before the race?
2. What is your prediction about the outcome of the race?
3. How does the race start?
4. How does your car perform during the race?
5. What is the outcome of the race?

Choose the best way to rewrite each underlined word or group of words.

Nannette Baker admits to a fear of heights. Nevertheless, she takes up the sport of parachuting a number of years ago. When she (1) skydives, Baker lets her fears behind. In a typical dive, she free-falls (2) (3) for about 60 seconds and then opens her parachute. As she free-falls, she sometimes will be attaining a speed of 200 miles per hour. (4) In 1995, while she was skydiving with 102 other women, Baker (5) helped set a record for most women in a free-fall formation. But she will have jumped in even larger formations. For Baker, this sport (6) was the greatest thrill of all. According to Baker, it feels like she (7) floated, not falls, through the air. Although Baker is one of the few (8) African-American women in this sport, she gains company. In the (9) future, others probably will be drawn to the thrill of this sport. (10)

1. A. is taking
   B. took
   C. will take
   D. Correct as is

2. A. leaves
   B. has left
   C. had let
   D. Correct as is

3. A. has free-fallen
   B. had free-fallen
   C. was free-falling
   D. Correct as is

4. A. is attaining
   B. was attaining
   C. attains
   D. Correct as is

5. A. skydives
   B. will skydive
   C. is skydiving
   D. Correct as is

6. A. has jumped
   B. was jumping
   C. is jumping
   D. Correct as is

7. A. is
   B. will be
   C. had been
   D. Correct as is

8. A. will float
   B. had floated
   C. floats
   D. Correct as is

9. A. may gain
   B. was gaining
   C. gained
   D. Correct as is

10. A. were drawn
    B. are drawn
    C. had drawn
    D. Correct as is

VERBS

Student Help Desk

Verbs at a Glance

A verb expresses action, condition, or state of being.
The two main kinds of verbs are **action verbs** and **linking verbs**.

People **ride** many kinds of vehicles.   A glider **is** a quiet craft.
    ↑ ACTION VERB   LINKING VERB ↗

Principal Parts of Regular Verbs

Present	Present Participle	Past	Past Participle
present	present + *-ing*	present + -*ed* or -*d*	present + -*ed* or -*d*
coast	**(is) coasting**	**coasted**	**(has) coasted**
bicycle	(is) bicycling	bicycled	(has) bicycled
gallop	(is) galloping	galloped	(has) galloped
land	(is) landing	landed	(has) landed
race	(is) racing	raced	(has) raced
raft	(is) rafting	rafted	(has) rafted
roll	(is) rolling	rolled	(has) rolled
steer	(is) steering	steered	(has) steered
trot	(is) trotting	trotted	(has) trotted
walk	(is) walking	walked	(has) walked
cry	(is) crying	cried	(has) cried

Time to Sail

Keeping Tenses Straight

Tense	What It Conveys	Example
Present	Action or condition occurring in the present	I **sail** the boat.
Past	Action or condition occurring in the past	I **sailed** the boat.
Future	Action or condition occurring in the future	I **will sail** the boat.
Present perfect	Action or condition occurring in the period leading up to the present	I **have sailed** the boat.
Past perfect	Past action or condition preceding another past action or condition	I **had sailed** the boat before my sister did.
Future perfect	Action or condition preceding another future action or condition	I **will have sailed** the boat nine times by the weekend.

The Bottom Line

Checklist for Verb Usage

Have I . . .

____ used action verbs to express actions?

____ used linking verbs with predicate nouns and predicate adjectives?

____ used direct objects and indirect objects to answer the questions *whom, what,* and *to whom* or *to what*?

____ used the correct principal parts of irregular verbs?

____ used tenses correctly to express the times of actions and conditions?

____ used *sit* and *set, lie* and *lay, rise* and *raise,* and *let* and *leave* correctly?

Chapter 5

Adjectives and Adverbs

goblet — ceremonial
golden
ornate
concave
bejeweled

Theme: One of a Kind

Following the Clues

Can you find the particular goblet that this treasure hunter has been seeking? Use the words listed on the treasure map to learn what makes this goblet different from the others.

What makes something one of a kind? To explain why something is unique, you would need to describe it by answering questions like *what kind, which one,* and *to what extent.* Words that do this are called **adjectives** and **adverbs.**

Write Away: One of a Kind
Pick another object in the treasure box. Write a description of the object without naming it. Be sure your description is so complete that someone could find the object you have in mind. Save the paragraph in your 🗀 **Working Portfolio.**

CD-ROM Grammar Coach

For each numbered item, choose the letter of the term that identifies it.

In 1926 Benny Benson was in <u>seventh</u> grade. Benny's ethnic
(1)
background was a combination of <u>Aleutian, Russian</u>, and Swedish
(2)
ancestry. The teenager decided to enter a contest to create a design
for the territory of Alaska. The contest asked people to make a
design that would fit <u>artistically</u> on a flag. Benny Benson was <u>shy</u>.
(3)   (4)
He loved nature and looking at the stars. All these things came
<u>together</u>, and he began <u>very</u> quickly to sketch his design. He wrote,
(5)   (6)
"The blue field is for the Alaska sky and the forget-me-not, an
Alaska flower." Benny <u>also</u> explained that the big star showed
(7)
Alaska's future as the <u>most northern</u> state. Both houses of the
(8)
Alaska legislature voted <u>unanimously</u> to accept this design for the
(9)
flag. No one stood <u>more proudly</u> than Benny Benson the day his
(10)
flag was first raised outside his school.

ADJ. & ADV.

1. A. adjective
   B. predicate adjective
   C. adverb
   D. intensifier

2. A. proper adjectives
   B. demonstrative pronouns
   C. predicate adjectives
   D. comparative adjectives

3. A. adverb telling when
   B. adverb telling where
   C. adverb telling how
   D. adverb telling to what extent

4. A. demonstrative pronoun
   B. comparative adjective
   C. predicate adjective
   D. proper adjective

5. A. adverb modifying *things*
   B. adverb modifying *All*
   C. adjective modifying *things*
   D. adverb modifying *came*

6. A. adverb modifying adjective
   B. adverb modifying adverb
   C. adverb modifying verb
   D. adjective modifying pronoun

7. A. adverb modifying verb
   B. adverb modifying adverb
   C. adverb modifying adjective
   D. adjective modifying noun

8. A. superlative adjective
   B. superlative adverb
   C. comparative adjective
   D. comparative adverb

9. A. adjective
   B. adverb modifying verb
   C. adverb modifying adjective
   D. adverb modifying adverb

10. A. comparative adjective
    B. comparative adverb
    C. superlative adjective
    D. superlative adverb

LESSON 1 · What Is an Adjective?

❶ Here's the Idea

▶ **An adjective is a word that modifies, or describes, a noun or a pronoun.**

MODIFIES   MODIFIES

Extraordinary weather can cause strange events.
ADJECTIVE   NOUN   ADJECTIVE   NOUN

Adjectives help you see, feel, taste, hear, and smell all the experiences you read about. Notice how adjectives make the second sentence in this pair more descriptive.

> **During a storm, a boat capsized in the waves.**

> **During a violent storm, a large boat capsized in the enormous waves.**

Adjectives answer the questions *what kind, which one, how many,* and *how much.*

Adjectives			
What kind?	a **sudden** blizzard	a **brisk** wind	a **destructive** flood
Which one or ones?	the **first** warning	the **Mexican** earthquake	the **last** weather report
How many or how much?	**several** tornadoes	a **few** drifts	**more** ice

What kind? a **deadly** storm

Which one? the **worst** storm of the decade

How many? **three** men

Articles

The most commonly used adjectives are the **articles** *a, an,* and *the. A* and *an* are forms of the **indefinite article.** The indefinite article is used before a noun that names an unspecified person, place, thing, or idea.

A weather radar can predict an unusual storm.
⬆INDEFINITE ARTICLE　　　　　　　⬆INDEFINITE ARTICLE

Use *a* before a word beginning with a consonant sound ("a ball"); use *an* before a word beginning with a vowel sound ("an egg").

The is the **definite article.** It points to a particular person, place, thing, or idea.

The six-o'clock news predicted the tornado.
⬆DEFINITE ARTICLE　　　　　　　⬆DEFINITE ARTICLE

Proper Adjectives

Many adjectives are formed from common nouns.

Nouns and Adjectives

Common Noun	Common Adjective
cloud	cloudy
nation	national
statue	statuesque
friend	friendly

A **proper adjective** is formed from a proper noun. Proper adjectives are always capitalized.

Proper Nouns and Proper Adjectives

Proper Noun	Proper Adjective
Honduras	Honduran
Olympus	Olympian
North America	North American
(Queen) Elizabeth	Elizabethan

❷ Why It Matters in Writing

Fiction writers use adjectives to supply important details that help set a scene and provide background for a story.

> **LITERARY MODEL**
>
> It was a **dark autumn** night. The **old** banker was pacing from corner to corner of his study, recalling to his mind the party he gave in the autumn **fifteen** years ago. There were many **clever** people at the party and much **interesting** conversation. They talked among **other** things of **capital** punishment.
>
> —Anton Chekhov, "The Bet"

❸ Practice and Apply

CONCEPT CHECK: What Is an Adjective?

Write each adjective in these sentences, along with the noun or pronoun it modifies. Do not include articles.

How Strong Was It?

1. Scientists are amazed by the terrific power of a tornado.
2. The circular winds in strong tornadoes cause more damage than winds in other storms of a similar size.
3. Large hailstones often accompany a typical tornado.
4. One hailstone weighed two pounds, or about one kilogram.
5. It fell in the small Kansan town of Coffeyville.
6. A Chinese newspaper reported a rain of monstrous hailstones that killed a hundred people.
7. Tornadoes can drive large pieces of timber into thick walls.
8. A tornado hit the Midwestern town of Coralville.
9. The winds carried a heavy mechanical part a long way through the air.
10. Another tornado in 1875 carried a metal coop four miles.

➡ **For a SELF-CHECK and more practice, see the EXERCISE BANK, p. 621.**

Write and label the proper adjectives in your answers above. For each proper adjective, write the proper noun from which it is formed.

Predicate Adjectives

❶ Here's the Idea

▶ **A predicate adjective is an adjective that follows a linking verb and describes the verb's subject.** The linking verb connects the predicate adjective with the subject.

DESCRIBES

Some people are extraordinary.
SUBJECT　　　LINKING VERB

DESCRIBE

They are very energetic or calm.

Predicate adjectives can follow linking verbs other than forms of *be*. Forms of *taste, smell, feel, look, become,* and *seem* are often used as linking verbs.

DESCRIBES

You usually feel lucky to know such a person.
LINKING VERB　　　PREDICATE ADJECTIVE

❷ Why It Matters in Writing

Writers often use predicate adjectives to supply key details about characters. Notice how predicate adjectives capture in just a few words the personality and appearance of this writer's teacher.

PROFESSIONAL MODEL

Miss Bindle . . . was **tiny, scrawny,** and **fierce,** with an eighty-year-old face and twenty-year-old red hair. . . .

Miss Bindle was extremely **short,** only about half the size of some of the larger boys. When Miss Bindle grabbed them by the hair and took off for the office, they had to trail along behind her in a bent-over posture. . . .

—Patrick F. McManus, "The Clown"

❸ Practice and Apply

A. CONCEPT CHECK: Predicate Adjectives

Write each predicate adjective in these sentences, along with the noun or pronoun it modifies. There may be more than one predicate adjective in a sentence.

Barreling Along!

1. Anna Edson Taylor was brave.
2. She grew certain that she could achieve fame by trying a dangerous feat.
3. Taylor had been a teacher, but she was now financially independent.
4. She felt eager to go over Niagara Falls in a barrel.
5. Her barrel was wooden and contained a rubber hose so that she could breathe.
6. According to the press, Taylor was "intelligent and venturesome."
7. When the barrel reached the edge of the falls, it appeared motionless for a moment.
8. After the plunge, the wait for the appearance of the barrel seemed endless.
9. Meanwhile, the daredevil herself was unconscious.
10. As the only woman survivor of a plunge over Niagara Falls, Anna Taylor remains unique.

→ For a SELF-CHECK and more practice, see the EXERCISE BANK, p. 621.

CHALLENGE

Rewrite five of the sentences above by substituting a new predicate adjective.

B. WRITING: Creating a Character Description

Describe a person who you think is one of a kind. Use predicate adjectives and linking verbs in your description.

Other Words Used as Adjectives

❶ Here's the Idea

In addition to their usual uses, many pronouns and nouns can be used as adjectives. They can modify nouns to make their meanings more specific.

Pronouns as Adjectives

Demonstrative Pronouns *This, that, these,* and *those* are demonstrative pronouns that can be used as adjectives.

LOOP

MODIFIES

This fingerprint is a loop.

MODIFIES

That fingerprint is a whorl.

PLAIN WHORL

Possessive Pronouns *My, our, your, her, his, its,* and *their* are possessive pronouns that are used as adjectives.

MODIFIES   *MODIFIES*

My thumbprint is a double loop, but your thumbprint is a tented arch.

DOUBLE LOOP

Indefinite Pronouns Indefinite pronouns such as *all, each, both, few, most,* and *some* can be used as adjectives.

MODIFIES

All fingerprints fit one of seven patterns.

MODIFIES

But each fingerprint is unique.

TENTED ARCH

ACCIDENTAL

PLAIN ARCH

CENTRAL POCKET LOOP

ADJ. & ADV.

Nouns as Adjectives

Like pronouns, nouns can be used as adjectives. In the expression "crime story," for example, the word *crime* (normally a noun) is used to modify *story*. Notice the examples of nouns used as adjectives in the sentences below.

MODIFIES

The fingerprint evidence convicted the murderer.

MODIFIES

She was convicted on murder charges.

❷ Why It Matters in Writing

By using nouns as adjectives, writers can convey a lot of descriptive information in a single word. Notice how much information is contained in the nouns used as adjectives in the passage below.

LITERARY MODEL

The country is India. A large **dinner** party is being given in an **up-country** station by a colonial official and his wife. The guests are **army** officers and **government** attachés and their wives, and an American naturalist.

—Mona Gardner, "The Dinner Party"

Detail of Dinner at Haddo House (1884), Alfred Edward Emslie. National Portrait Gallery, London

➌ Practice and Apply

A. CONCEPT CHECK: Other Words Used as Adjectives

Write each noun or pronoun that is used as an adjective in these sentences, along with the word it modifies.

Don't Touch!
1. Why do your fingerprints leave their marks on objects?
2. The fingers have skin ridges on their surface.
3. These ridges are coated with both sweat and body oil.
4. When a criminal touches a surface with his fingers, these ridges leave an impression.
5. These impressions are often not visible to the human eye.
6. But detectives in a crime investigation use special chemicals to reveal those fingerprints.
7. Police can also reveal these clues by using laser light.
8. The first criminal convicted on fingerprint evidence was Alfred Stratton.
9. He left his fingerprint on a cash box at the crime scene.
10. Many criminals do not make this mistake anymore, because they wear latex gloves.

➡ For a SELF-CHECK and more practice, see the EXERCISE BANK, p. 622.

Write five sentences using nouns as adjectives and five sentences using pronouns as adjectives.

B. REVISING: Using Nouns as Adjectives

Make this e-mail message more detailed by adding a noun from the list below to modify each of the nouns in boldface type.

city   super-sleuth   ridge   foot-sole   leather   body

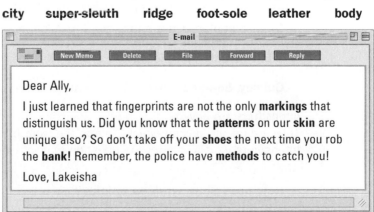

Dear Ally,

I just learned that fingerprints are not the only **markings** that distinguish us. Did you know that the **patterns** on our **skin** are unique also? So don't take off your **shoes** the next time you rob the **bank**! Remember, the police have **methods** to catch you!

Love, Lakeisha

Adjectives and Adverbs   **133**

What Is an Adverb?

❶ Here's the Idea

▶ **An adverb is a word that modifies a verb, an adjective, or another adverb.**

MODIFIES

Teenagers often make a unique impression.
ADVERB ⬆   ⬆ VERB

MODIFIES

They wear very creative clothing.
ADVERB ⬆   ⬆ ADJECTIVE

MODIFIES

They nearly always have their own way of talking.
⬆ ADVERBS ⬆

Adverbs answer the questions *how, when, where,* or *to what extent*.

Adverbs			
How?	successfully	quietly	terribly
When?	soon	later	now
Where?	inside	close	together
To what extent?	nearly	completely	quite

Adverbs can appear in several different positions.

Shari completed the exam quickly. (after verb)

Shari quickly completed the exam. (before verb)

Quickly, Shari completed the exam. (beginning of sentence)

Intensifiers are adverbs that modify adjectives or other adverbs. They are usually placed directly before the word they modify. Intensifiers usually answer the question *to what extent*.

MODIFIES

How does Shari work so quickly?

Intensifiers				
almost	extremely	quite	so	usually
especially	nearly	really	too	very

Forming Adverbs

Many adverbs are formed by adding the suffix -ly to adjectives. Sometimes a base word's spelling changes when -ly is added.

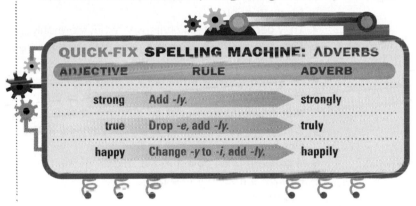

QUICK-FIX SPELLING MACHINE: ADVERBS

ADJECTIVE	RULE	ADVERB
strong	Add -ly.	strongly
true	Drop -e, add -ly.	truly
happy	Change -y to -i, add -ly.	happily

ADJ. & ADV.

❷ Why It Matters in Writing

Adverbs can add information that makes verbs clearer and more specific. What would be lost if the adverbs in the model below were removed?

PROFESSIONAL MODEL

Yehudi Menuhin played the violin spectacularly. He began to study quite early, at the age of four. When he performed onstage, he always received thunderous applause. He first appeared in *Who's Who* at the age of 15 and was written about frequently in the world's press throughout his long career.

—C. Podojil

ANSWERS HOW

ANSWERS WHEN

ANSWERS WHERE

ANSWERS TO WHAT EXTENT

❸ Practice and Apply

A. CONCEPT CHECK: What Is an Adverb?

Write each adverb and the word it modifies. Identify the modified word as a verb, an adjective, or an adverb. There may be more than one adverb in a sentence.

The Green Scene

1. Alison and James Henry climb trees professionally.
2. To some people, this seems quite extraordinary.
3. This is because Alison and James are unusually young for such a job.
4. They became professionals when they were only 17 and 16.
5. They are certified arborists, and they care for trees expertly.
6. They may ascend trees daily if their services are needed.
7. The two teenagers climb high in order to cut branches that might suddenly fall on a house or wire.
8. They work very carefully when they are up in the tops of trees.
9. They were once called in the middle of the night to remove a tree that had fallen dangerously close to a house.
10. So far, Alison and James are the only teenagers to have this particularly impressive professional title.

➜ **For a SELF-CHECK and more practice, see the EXERCISE BANK, p. 623.**

B. WRITING: Adding Adverbs

Add adverbs to modify the numbered words in the paragraph below. Choose adverbs that will make the words clear and specific.

Julie **(1)** walked to the library. She had **(2)** thought she would **(3)** win the math contest. She was **(4)** good at math. But the new student from across town also **(5)** completed her math assignments. She would be a **(6)** tough competitor for Julie. I'll just have to **(7)** work, Julie thought as she **(8)** entered the library.

In your 🗐 **Working Portfolio,** find the description you wrote for the **Write Away** on page 124. Use verbs and adverbs to expand your description.

Making Comparisons

① Here's the Idea

Special forms of modifiers are used to make comparisons.

▶ **Use the comparative form of an adjective or adverb when you compare a person or thing with one other person or thing.**

> **Earth is larger than Venus.**
>
> **Earth orbits the sun more slowly than Venus.**

▶ **Use the superlative form of an adjective or adverb when you compare someone or something with more than one other person or thing.**

> **Which of the four inner planets is the hottest?**
>
> **Which of the five outer planets rotates most quickly?**

Regular Forms of Comparisons

For most one-syllable modifiers, add -er to form the comparative and -est to form the superlative.

One-Syllable Modifiers	Base Form	Comparative	Superlative
Adjective	light	lighter	lightest
	slow	slower	slowest
Adverb	close	closer	closest
	soon	sooner	soonest

You can also add -er and -est to some two-syllable adjectives. With other two-syllable adjectives, and with all two-syllable adverbs, use the words *more* and *most*.

Two-Syllable Modifiers	Base Form	Comparative	Superlative
Adjectives	windy	windier	windiest
	massive	more massive	most massive
Adverbs	brightly	more brightly	most brightly
	quickly	more quickly	most quickly

With adjectives and adverbs having three or more syllables, use *more* and *most*.

Modifiers with More than Two Syllables			
	Base Form	**Comparative**	**Superlative**
Adjectives	successful	**more** successful	**most** successful
	mysterious	**more** mysterious	**most** mysterious
Adverbs	awkwardly	**more** awkwardly	**most** awkwardly
	eloquently	**more** eloquently	**most** eloquently

Use only one sign of comparison at a time. Don't use *more* and *-er* together or *most* and *-est* together.

INCORRECT: **Earth is the most greenest planet.**

CORRECT: **Earth is the greenest planet.**

Irregular Forms of Comparisons

The comparatives and superlatives of some adjectives and adverbs are formed in irregular ways.

Irregular Modifiers			
	Base Form	**Comparative**	**Superlative**
Adjectives	good	better	best
	bad	worse	worst
Adverbs	much	more	most
	little	less	least
	well	better	best

❷ Why It Matters in Writing

When you write about science or technology, you can often explain your subject more clearly by comparing it to another.

PROFESSIONAL MODEL

Venus is **hotter** than Earth—about 800 degrees **hotter.** The atmosphere on Venus is **more unfriendly** too. It rains sulfuric acid, and the pressure is 90 times **greater** than that on Earth. —T. Bagwell

❸ Practice and Apply

A. CONCEPT CHECK: Making Comparisons

Choose the correct comparative or superlative form to complete each sentence.

Nine of a Kind

1. Which do you think is the (fascinatingest/ most fascinating) planet in the solar system?
2. Earth is (wettest/wetter) than Mars.
3. Venus orbits the sun (quicker/more quickly) than it rotates on its axis.
4. This means that a day on Venus is (longer/longest) than its year.
5. Mars has a volcano that is (taller/more taller) than any one on Earth.
6. It also has a canyon that is (longer/longest) than the Grand Canyon.
7. Jupiter is the (most massive/more massive) planet in the system.
8. If Jupiter were many times (larger/more large) than it is, it might have ignited to become a star.
9. Neptune is the planet on which winds blow the (most rapidly/more rapidly).
10. If Neptune had a solid surface, you'd never be able to stand upright on this (windiest/windier) of planets.

➡ **For a SELF-CHECK and more practice, see the EXERCISE BANK, p. 623.**

B. WRITING: Creating Comparisons

Write five sentences in which you compare and contrast the planets shown, using comparative and superlative forms. Use the information given.

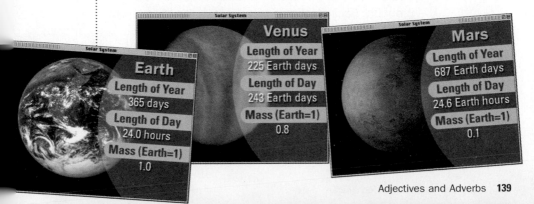

Solar System

Earth
Length of Year
365 days
Length of Day
24.0 hours
Mass (Earth=1)
1.0

Solar System

Venus
Length of Year
225 Earth days
Length of Day
243 Earth days
Mass (Earth=1)
0.8

Solar System

Mars
Length of Year
687 Earth days
Length of Day
24.6 Earth hours
Mass (Earth=1)
0.1

ADJ. & ADV.

Adjective or Adverb?

LESSON 6

① Here's the Idea

Some pairs of adjectives and adverbs are often a source of confusion and mistakes in speaking and writing.

Good or Well *Good* is always an adjective; it modifies a noun or pronoun. *Well* is usually an adverb, modifying a verb, an adverb, or an adjective. *Well* is an adjective when it refers to health.

MODIFIES
Poetry is a good way to express your individuality.
ADJECTIVE ↗ ↖ NOUN

MODIFIES
Good poems can communicate ideas well.
VERB ↗ ADVERB ↗

MODIFIES
You can write poems even when you don't feel well.
PRONOUN ↗ ADJECTIVE ↗

Real or Really *Real* is always an adjective; it modifies a noun or pronoun. *Really* is always an adverb; it modifies a verb, an adverb, or an adjective.

MODIFIES
Reciting poetry is a real talent.
ADJECTIVE ↗ ↖ NOUN

MODIFIES
If you really work at it, you can become good at it.
ADVERB ↗ ↖ VERB

Bad or Badly *Bad* is always an adjective; it modifies a noun or pronoun. *Badly* is always an adverb; it modifies a verb, an adverb, or an adjective.

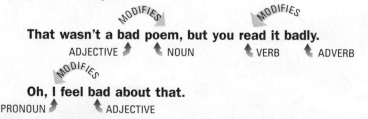

MODIFIES   MODIFIES
That wasn't a bad poem, but you read it badly.
ADJECTIVE ↗ ↖ NOUN   ↖ VERB ↖ ADVERB

MODIFIES
Oh, I feel bad about that.
PRONOUN ↗ ↖ ADJECTIVE

❷ Why It Matters in Writing

The pairs of words you have just studied are often misused in everyday speech. When you find yourself using one of these words in writing, stop and make sure you have the correct one.

STUDENT MODEL

My sister wants to be in the *Guinness Book of Records.*
really badly   *well*
She wants this ~~real bad~~. She swims ~~good~~, so she thinks she

will try to tread water longer than anyone else. I will feel
bad   *good*
~~badly~~ for her if she fails but ~~well~~ if she succeeds.

ADJ. & ADV.

❸ Practice and Apply

CONCEPT CHECK: Adjective or Adverb?

For each sentence, choose the correct modifier from those given in parentheses. Identify each word you choose as an adjective or an adverb.

Setting Real Records
1. If you are (good/well) at something, you can try to get into the *Guinness Book of Records.*
2. You may climb (bad/badly) or be a (real/really) poor runner.
3. But maybe you grow vegetables or flowers that are large and make a (real/really) statement.
4. Or maybe you blow big bubble-gum bubbles (good/well).
5. It helps if you attempt a (real/really) feat in public.
6. At least you must have (good/well) documentation by a person with (real/really) excellent community standing.
7. If it's just you and the huge bubble, that's (bad/badly).
8. The Guinness people will react (bad/badly) to your claim.
9. Those same folks also suggest that you take (good/well) safety precautions when you try to set a record.
10. After all, you don't want to get your award while lying in a hospital bed, feeling (bad/badly).

➡ **For a SELF-CHECK and more practice, see the EXERCISE BANK, p. 624.**

Avoiding Double Negatives

❶ Here's the Idea

A **negative word** is a word that implies that something does not exist or happen. Some common negative words are listed below.

Common Negative Words				
barely	never	none	nothing	can't
hardly	no	no one	nowhere	don't
neither	nobody	not	scarcely	hasn't

If two negative words are used where only one is needed, the result is a **double negative.** Avoid double negatives in your speaking and writing.

NONSTANDARD:
You don't have no business climbing Mt. Rushmore.

STANDARD:
You don't have any business climbing Mt. Rushmore.

You have no business climbing Mt. Rushmore.

❷ Why It Matters in Writing

Many of the situations where success counts most—school, work, and interviews—require language that is free of double negatives. The following model is an example of what NOT to say in an interview.

PROFESSIONAL MODEL

For example, suppose you are being interviewed for a job as an airline pilot, and your prospective employer asks you if you have any experience, and you answer: "Well, I ain't never actually flied no actual airplanes or nothing, but I got several pilot-style hats and several friends who I like to talk about airplanes with."

—Dave Barry, "What Is and Ain't Grammatical"

A. CONCEPT CHECK: Avoiding Double Negatives

Write the word in parentheses that correctly completes each sentence.

Big Foot or Big Fake?

1. You (can/can't) scarcely imagine how many people believe in one-of-a-kind monsters.
2. You (can't/can) barely read a newspaper or a magazine without seeing a reference to one.
3. The "abominable snowman" (is/isn't) nothing like the kind you build.
4. No one has (never/ever) been able to prove it exists.
5. Researchers investigating the Loch Ness Monster (haven't/have) had nothing to show for their efforts.
6. People trying to prove the existence of Bigfoot haven't come up with (nothing/anything) either.
7. Evidence of such creatures (is/isn't) nowhere to be found.
8. Nobody has ever taken a photograph of one (either/neither).
9. No one (has/hasn't) ever gotten one on videotape.
10. Some people believe in such creatures, but I don't think there are (none/any).

→ For a SELF-CHECK and more practice, see the EXERCISE BANK, p. 624.

B. PROOFREADING: Eliminating Double Negatives

In the draft below, find and correct five double negatives. There is more than one way to correct each double negative.

STUDENT MODEL

You won't find no animal more unusual than the duck-billed platypus. Since it lays eggs, you wouldn't hardly guess that it's a mammal. It has a bill like a duck, but it can't fly neither. You shouldn't never judge things by appearances. Duck-billed platypuses are odd looking, but there isn't an animal better designed for its environment nowhere.

ADJ. & ADV.

143

Grammar in Literature

Using Adjectives and Adverbs to Describe

When you write a character description, using adjectives and adverbs allows you to make a person come alive. Adjectives and adverbs help writers clearly express what they see, think, and feel. As you read the following passage from a science-fiction story, notice how writer Daniel Keyes uses adjectives and adverbs to describe an adult student's impressions of his special-education teacher. The student, Charlie, has had brain surgery that has made him more intelligent, and he feels as if he is seeing his teacher clearly for the first time.

Flowers for Algernon
by Daniel Keyes

April 28 I don't understand why I never noticed how beautiful Miss Kinnian really is. She has brown eyes and feathery brown hair that comes to the top of her neck. She's only thirty-four! I think from the beginning I had the feeling that she was an unreachable genius—and very, very old. Now, every time I see her she grows younger and more lovely.

We had dinner and a long talk. When she said that I was coming along so fast that soon I'd be leaving her behind, I laughed.

"It's true, Charlie. You're already a better reader than I am. You can read a whole page at a glance while I can take in only a few lines at a time. And you remember every single thing you read. I'm lucky if I can recall the main thoughts and the general meaning."

"I don't feel intelligent. There are so many things I don't understand."

Max Seabaugh/MAX

ADJECTIVES
describe Miss Kinnian's appearance.

ADVERBS
add to the description of changes in Charlie by telling how and when actions occur.

ADJECTIVES
compare the skills of Miss Kinnian and Charlie.

CHAPTER 5

Practice and Apply

A. USING ADJECTIVES AND ADVERBS

The following passage is a possible journal entry describing the dinner from Miss Kinnian's point of view. Follow the directions below to make the entry clearer. Add adjectives and adverbs to the numbered sentences.

April 28 Today, Charlie was not in class. **(1)** His absence worried me, so I decided to call him. I asked him to meet me at City Restaurant. **(2)** We had a dinner and a talk. **(3)** The surgery has changed him. **(4)** Just weeks ago, he could not carry on a conversation. **(5)** Now, he expresses himself. He can read a book in just minutes. I believe that he will be smarter than his doctors.

1. Add an adverb that emphasizes that Miss Kinnian was worried.
2. Add adjectives to describe what kind of dinner and what kind of talk you think they had.
3. Add an adverb to emphasize that Charlie has changed.
4. Use your imagination and add adjectives to describe how many weeks ago and what kind of conversation he used to make.
5. Add an adverb to describe how Charlie expresses his ideas now, and when he may become smarter than his doctors.

B. WRITING: Description

Charlie uses a variety of adjectives and adverbs to describe his favorite teacher. Write a paragraph in which you use adjectives and adverbs to describe someone whom you admire. Save your paragraph in your
📁 **Working Portfolio.**

ADJ. & ADV.

A. Using Adjectives Write each adjective in the sentences below and give the word it modifies. Do not include articles. Then add as many of the following descriptions as apply (may be none).

predicate adjective   noun used as adjective
proper adjective   comparative form of adjective
demonstrative pronoun   superlative form of adjective
indefinite pronoun   possessive pronoun

1. The animal world is full of unique characteristics.
2. Most insects are small, and many mammals are large.
3. But a kind of mammal is actually a smaller creature than a bumblebee.
4. This creature—the Kitti's hog-nosed bat—is the tiniest mammal.
5. Actually, the honeybee makes the food with the most impressive additive.
6. That's right, honey tastes fresher after time on the shelf than some foods because of its natural preservatives.
7. Despite the purple dinosaur you see on television, the African blesbok is unique.
8. His coat is purple, and he is the only land animal to have that color.
9. When you think of sharks, you probably see them in their wide oceans and their salty seas.
10. But the bull shark also likes fresh water, such as Mississippi River water.

B. Using Adverbs Write each adverb in the paragraph below, tell what word it modifies, and tell whether the word it modifies is a verb, an adverb, or an adjective.

LITERARY MODEL

    When I had waited a long time, very patiently, without hearing him lie down, I resolved to open a little—a very, very little crevice in the lantern. So I opened it—you cannot imagine how stealthily, stealthily—until, at length, a single dim ray, like the thread of the spider, shot from out the crevice and fell full upon the vulture eye.

        —Edgar Allan Poe, "The Tell-Tale Heart"

For each numbered item, choose the letter of the term that identifies it.

Satchel Paige, who played in both the Negro Leagues and the major leagues, was one of the greatest players in <u>American</u> baseball.
(1)
He is the only person who played <u>professionally</u> into his sixties.
(2)
He is also the <u>oldest</u> player ever to play in the All-Star Game. As if
(3)
that were not enough, Paige pitched <u>more</u> games than anyone in the
(4)
history of baseball—about 2,500!

Satchel Paige pitched <u>more distinctively</u> than other pitchers.
(5)
Batters gritted <u>their</u> teeth when they were up against "Satch." His
(6)
"bee ball" was <u>extremely</u> fast, and batters swore they could hear it
(7)
buzz. His "pea ball" appeared <u>small</u> as it zipped over the plate. Some
(8)
people remember Paige <u>best</u> for his words of wisdom. He said, "If your
(9)
stomach disputes you, lie <u>down</u> and pacify it with cool thoughts."
(10)

1. A. pronoun used as adjective
   B. comparative adjective
   C. proper adjective
   D. predicate adjective

2. A. adverb modifying *person*
   B. adverb modifying *is*
   C. adverb modifying *played*
   D. intensifier

3. A. comparative adjective
   B. superlative adjective
   C. comparative adverb
   D. superlative adverb

4. A. adjective modifying *pitched*
   B. adjective modifying *games*
   C. adjective modifying *anyone*
   D. adjective modifying *Paige*

5. A. superlative adjective
   B. comparative adverb
   C. comparative adjective
   D. superlative adverb

6. A. demonstrative pronoun
   B. noun used as adjective
   C. possessive pronoun
   D. proper adjective

7. A. adverb telling to what extent
   B. adverb telling how
   C. adverb telling where
   D. adverb telling when

8. A. predicate adjective
   B. comparative adjective
   C. superlative adjective
   D. pronoun used as adjective

9. A. comparative adverb
   B. superlative adjective
   C. superlative adverb
   D. comparative adjective

10. A. adverb telling when
    B. adverb telling where
    C. adverb telling how
    D. adverb telling to what extent

Student Help Desk

Adjectives and Adverbs at a Glance

Adjectives modify nouns and pronouns.

> The Jamaican runner finished first. She was fast!

Adverbs modify verbs, adverbs, and adjectives.

> The usually quiet student spoke very emphatically.

Modifiers in Comparisons

Bigger and Better

	Comparative	Superlative
fast	faster	fastest
speedy	speedier	speediest
unusual	more unusual	most unusual
original	more original	most original
quickly	more quickly	most quickly
good	better	best
bad	worse	worst

Avoiding Double Forms

Double Trouble

Double Negative	Fix
we can't never	we can never we can't
we don't hardly	we hardly we don't

Double Comparison	Fix
more better	better
most luckiest	luckiest

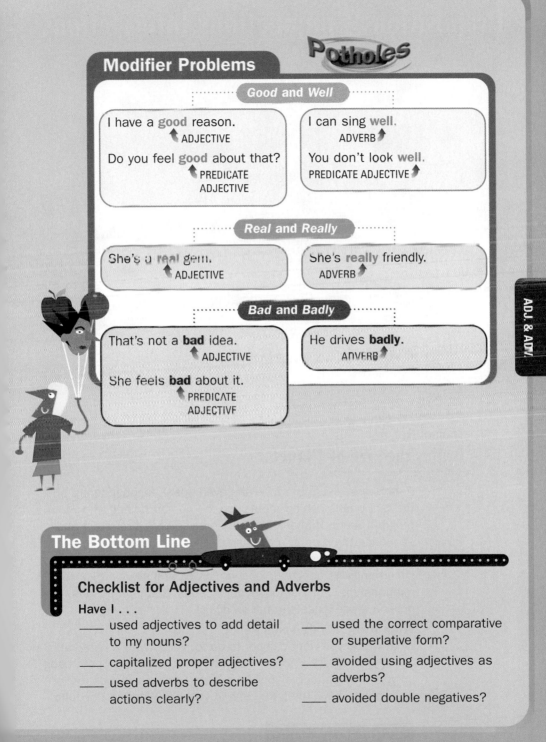

Modifier Problems

Potholes

Good and Well

I have a **good** reason.
↑ ADJECTIVE

Do you feel **good** about that?
↑ PREDICATE
ADJECTIVE

I can sing **well**.
ADVERB ↗

You don't look **well**.
PREDICATE ADJECTIVE ↗

Real and Really

She's a **real** gem.
↑ ADJECTIVE

She's **really** friendly.
ADVERB ↗

Bad and Badly

That's not a **bad** idea.
↑ ADJECTIVE

She feels **bad** about it.
↑ PREDICATE
ADJECTIVE

He drives **badly**.
ADVERB ↗

ADJ. & ADV.

The Bottom Line

Checklist for Adjectives and Adverbs

Have I . . .

____ used adjectives to add detail to my nouns?

____ capitalized proper adjectives?

____ used adverbs to describe actions clearly?

____ used the correct comparative or superlative form?

____ avoided using adjectives as adverbs?

____ avoided double negatives?

Prepositions, Conjunctions, Interjections

Theme: Robots

Brains the Size of Planets

Robots may seem to move and even speak independently, but the real brains behind robots are the human beings who program them. Humans use very precise codes to direct and sequence the robots' movements. Like computer codes, our language includes small but critical signals that communicate such things as direction, location, order, and even relationships. Prepositions, conjunctions, and interjections provide those signals in our language.

Write Away: My Personal Robot
What would you want a robot to do for you? Write a paragraph about your personal robot. Describe what it does. Does it hang up your clothes, serve your food, entertain your friends, or pitch balls? Save the paragraph in your 🗁 **Working Portfolio.**

CD-ROM Grammar Coach

Choose the letter of the term that correctly identifies each underlined item.

How great would it be if you had a robot? It isn't such a wild idea. People <u>around the world</u> have robots. One teenager designed
(1)
a robot that responded to musical <u>tones</u>. There were different
(2)
tones <u>for different commands</u>. It had claws that opened and closed.
(3)
The robot <u>not only</u> picked up objects <u>but also</u> moved them from
(4)   (4)
place to place. Another teenager designed a robot with sonar. This robot bumped <u>into</u> objects <u>and</u> learned where the objects were
(5)   (6)
located. <u>Wow!</u> Unfortunately, sometimes the bumper switches
(7)
would stick. The robot dashed <u>across the room</u> wildly. It looked
(8)
frantically for a way <u>out</u>. These robots may seem primitive, <u>but</u>
(9)   (10)
they are really complex systems that operate independently.

1. A. coordinating conjunction
   B. correlative conjunction
   C. prepositional phrase
   D. preposition

2. A. coordinating conjunction
   B. correlative conjunction
   C. object of a preposition
   D. preposition

3. A. correlative conjunction
   B. coordinating conjunction
   C. adjective phrase
   D. adverb phrase

4. A. coordinating conjunction
   B. correlative conjunction
   C. prepositional phrase
   D. interjection

5. A. coordinating conjunction
   B. preposition
   C. interjection
   D. adverb

6. A. coordinating conjunction
   B. correlative conjunction
   C. preposition
   D. adjective

7. A. correlative conjunction
   B. preposition
   C. subordinating conjunction
   D. interjection

8. A. coordinating conjunction
   B. correlative conjunction
   C. adverb phrase
   D. adjective phrase

9. A. correlative conjunction
   B. preposition
   C. adverb
   D. adjective

10. A. coordinating conjunction
    B. correlative conjunction
    C. preposition
    D. adjective

PREPOSITIONS

What Is a Preposition?

❶ Here's the Idea

▶ **A preposition is a word that shows a relationship between a noun or pronoun and some other word in the sentence.**

Robots in outer space perform useful functions.

⬆ PREPOSITION

Here, the preposition *in* shows the relationship between *robots* and *space*. In the sentences below, notice how each preposition expresses a different relationship between the robot and the spacecraft.

The robot is above the spacecraft.

The robot is below the spacecraft.

The robot is beside the spacecraft.

The robot is inside the spacecraft.

Common Prepositions				
about	at	despite	like	to
above	before	down	near	toward
across	behind	during	of	under
after	below	except	off	until
against	beneath	for	on	up
along	beside	from	out	with
among	between	in	over	within
around	beyond	inside	past	without
as	by	into	through	

Some prepositions, called **compound prepositions,** are made up of more than one word. These include *according to, instead of,* and *apart from.*

Prepositional Phrases

▶ **A prepositional phrase consists of a preposition, its object, and any modifiers of the object.** The object of the preposition is the noun or pronoun following the preposition.

PREPOSITIONAL PHRASE

Robots conduct missions for the space program.
PREPOSITION   OBJECT

Among their many tasks is photographing the planets.
PREPOSITION   MODIFIER   OBJECT

Compound Objects in Prepositional Phrases

A preposition may have a compound object made up of two or more nouns or pronouns joined by *and* or *or,* as shown below.

PREPOSITIONAL PHRASE

Robots conduct a series of tests and experiments.
PREPOSITION   COMPOUND OBJECT

Experiments can be performed by robots or people.
COMPOUND OBJECT

Preposition or Adverb?

Sometimes the same word can be used as a preposition or as an adverb. If the word has no object, then it is an adverb.

PREPOSITIONAL PHRASE

The spacecraft has no gravity within its walls.
PREPOSITION   OBJECT

The spacecraft has no gravity within.
ADVERB

For more on adverbs, see pp. 134–135.

PREPOSITIONS

❷ Why It Matters in Writing

When writing for science, you can use prepositions to describe where objects are located in relation to other objects. Notice how the prepositions in the model show the robot's location in relation to Mars.

PROFESSIONAL MODEL

The *Sojourner* microrover rolled **onto** the planet Mars. Controllers guided it **over** the rough terrain.

—R. Golub

❸ Practice and Apply

CONCEPT CHECK: What Is a Preposition?

Write the preposition in each sentence, along with its object or objects.

A Viking in Space

1. The *Viking 1* lander used a robot arm in outer space.
2. Scientists encoded computer programs with instructions and rules.
3. The instructions inside the computer's memory directed the robot.
4. They designed the lander according to the functions it would perform.
5. It communicated data between Mars and Earth.
6. The lander's mechanical arm reached beyond the spacecraft.
7. The lander photographed the surface of Mars.
8. The robot arm reached below the surface.
9. For later tests and analysis, the robot arm collected soil and rocks.
10. Unfortunately, a faulty command from Earth caused the lander to malfunction.

➜ For a SELF-CHECK and more practice, see the EXERCISE BANK, p. 625.

🗐 **Working Portfolio:** Find your **Write Away** from page 150 or a sample of your most recent work. Add at least one prepositional phrase that helps explain the location of your robot or other topic.

Using Prepositional Phrases

❶ Here's the Idea

A prepositional phrase is always related to another word in a sentence. It modifies the word in the same way an adjective or adverb would.

Adjective Phrases

▶ **An adjective prepositional phrase modifies a noun or a pronoun.** Like an adjective, a prepositional phrase can tell which one, how many, or what kind.

WHAT KIND?

Robots perform several jobs **in the automobile industry.**
NOUN   ADJECTIVE PHRASE

WHICH ONE?

The sprayer **on an assembly line** is an industrial robot.

Adverb Phrases

▶ **An adverb prepositional phrase modifies a verb, an adjective, or an adverb.** An adverb prepositional phrase can tell where, when, how, why, or to what extent.

WHERE?

Industrial robots operate **from fixed positions.**
VERB   ADVERB PHRASE

HOW?

These robots are reprogrammable **for various tasks.**
ADJECTIVE

Several prepositional phrases can work together. Often, each phrase after the first modifies the object in the phrase before it.

Some industrial robots load frozen slabs **of meat** **in meat lockers** **with subzero temperatures.**

PREPOSITIONS

Placement of Prepositional Phrases

When you write, try to place each prepositional phrase as close as possible to the word it modifies. Otherwise, you may confuse—or unintentionally amuse—your readers.

Unclear

In a chorus line, we watched 15 robots.

(Who or what was in a chorus line?)

Clear

We watched 15 robots in a chorus line.

(Now the readers know who or what was in a chorus line.)

② Why It Matters in Writing

When you write technical information that shows how to do something or how something works, prepositional phrases can help make your explanations clear. Use them to tell *where, how, which one,* and *what kind.* Notice that the prepositional phrases in the model tell *where, how,* and *which one.*

PROFESSIONAL MODEL

The wheels, located on the bottom of the robot's body, are set in a triangular pattern. The two back wheels are the "drive" wheels, and they propel the robot either forward, backward, or sideways. Each drive wheel can be driven independently of the other, allowing the robot to turn right or left.

—Margaret Baldwin and Gary Pack, *Robots and Robotics*

TELLS WHERE

TELLS WHICH ONE

TELLS HOW

---

❸ Practice and Apply

A. CONCEPT CHECK: Using Prepositional Phrases

Write the prepositional phrase in each sentence, along with the word it modifies. Then write whether the phrase is an adjective phrase or an adverb phrase.

On the Job

1. Automobile manufacturers around the world have installed robots.
2. In factories, robots work quickly and efficiently.
3. Many factory robots are arms on moving rails.
4. Mechanical arms move systematically down an assembly line.
5. Robots work chiefly under hazardous conditions.
6. With great precision, robots spray-paint cars.
7. They are immune to dangerous paint fumes.
8. Mold-maker robots inject red-hot metal into molds.
9. Robots handle materials that would cause damage to human flesh.
10. Arc welding is another job among the many risky jobs that robots perform.

➜ For a SELF-CHECK and more practice, see the EXERCISE BANK, p. 625.

B. WRITING: Explaining with Prepositional Phrases

Write the prepositional phrase that best completes each sentence in the paragraph.

a. below the surface
b. on shore
c. between the coral reef and some large rocks
d. of the sea exploration team
e. with cameras

As a member ___(1)___ , the robot plunged into the deep icy water. It sank quickly ___(2)___ . Equipped ___(3)___ , it scanned the ocean floor. The broken oil pipeline ___(4)___ was identified. Scientists ___(5)___ received the data.

A diving robot works under the water.

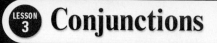

LESSON 3   Conjunctions

❶ Here's the Idea

▶ **A conjunction is a word used to join words or groups of words.** Different kinds of conjunctions are used in different ways.

Coordinating Conjunctions

▶ **A coordinating conjunction connects words used in the same way.** The words joined by a conjunction can be subjects, objects, predicates, or any other kind of sentence parts.

◀ SUBJECTS ▶
Motors and software control a robot named Cog.
▲ COORDINATING CONJUNCTION

Common Coordinating Conjunctions						
and	but	for	or	nor	so	yet

Use *and* to connect similar ideas. Use *but* or *yet* to contrast ideas.

Cog can make eye contact and track motion.
(*And* connects two of Cog's abilities.)

Cog is a computer-driven machine, but it acts like a human being.
(*But* contrasts what Cog is with how it acts.)

Use *or* or *nor* to introduce a choice.

Kismet, another robot, can smile or look sad.
(*Or* introduces another choice for a facial expression.)

Correlative Conjunctions

▶ **Correlative conjunctions are pairs of words that connect words used in the same way.** Like coordinating conjunctions, correlative conjunctions can join subjects, objects, predicates, and other sentence parts.

OBJECTS
Cog moves not only its head but also its arms.
CORRELATIVE CONJUNCTION

SUBJECTS
Both Cog and Kismet are robots with intelligence.
CORRELATIVE
CONJUNCTION

Common Correlative Conjunctions		
both . . . and	either . . . or	not only . . . but also
neither . . . nor	whether . . . or	

You will learn about conjunctions of another type—subordinating conjunctions—in Chapter 8.

❷ Why It Matters in Writing

When writing descriptions, you can use conjunctions to help the reader know how details relate to each other. Notice how the conjunctions in the model help you picture the arrangement of features on the monster.

LITERARY MODEL

It had a flat head **and** the overhanging brows of a Neanderthal man. Its face was crisscrossed with crude stitching, **and** two electrodes stuck out of its neck.

—Daniel Cohen, "Man-Made Monsters," from *A Natural History of Unnatural Things*

❸ Practice and Apply

A. CONCEPT CHECK: Conjunctions

Write the conjunction in each sentence, along with the words or groups of words that it joins.

Cog and Kismet

1. Cog and Kismet are two robots developed at MIT, the Massachusetts Institute of Technology.

2. The robot Cog has an upper body, but it doesn't have any legs.

3. Cog's achievements are few, yet they are impressive.

4. Cog not only stares at strangers but also follows them with its gaze as they cross a room.

5. Cog can play drums and even played them in a rock video.

6. It can move a toy or pick up a stuffed animal.

7. Kismet needs constant stimulation, yet it is easily amused.

8. Its features are cartoon-like, and its big blue eyes open wide.

9. Kismet can respond to its handlers' actions with a smile or a look of interest.

10. Neither Cog nor Kismet is programmed with emotions.

➜ For a SELF-CHECK and more practice, see the EXERCISE BANK, p. 626.

Identify each conjunction in items 1–10 above as a coordinating conjunction or a correlative conjunction.

B. REVISING: Changing Conjunctions

Using the right conjunctions helps you say what you mean. Rewrite the conjunctions so that the following paragraph makes sense.

Robot Danger?

(1) We may have a basic fear of robots, **nor** we depend on them. **(2)** Robots can work faster **but** are stronger than people. **(3)** They never grow tired **for** get bored. **(4)** All robots are cold **but** unfeeling. **(5)** They can injure a human being **nor** just keep working. Is our fear justified?

LESSON 4 Interjections

❶ Here's the Idea

▶ **An interjection is a word or phrase used to express emotion.**

Hey, how do you like my automatic scanner?

It's fast! Wow!

> An interjection can stand alone or be set off by a comma.

❷ Why It Matters in Writing

The 5th Wave by Rich Tennant

"Shoot, that's nothing! Watch me spin him!"

Writers often use interjections to express strong emotions, such as anger, joy, concern, surprise, terror, and disgust. What emotion is the crew member on the left in the cartoon expressing?

> *Shoot* is an interjection.

❸ Practice and Apply

📁 **Working Portfolio:** Find your **Write Away** from page 150 or a sample of your most recent work. Add to your writing three interjections that express emotions. Use the interjections in the Student Help Desk on page 167 for ideas.

Grammar in Science

Using Prepositions to Write About Science

When you take notes on a science book or a documentary film, the proper use of prepositions can help you keep things straight in your mind. Prepositions are especially important when you are describing how a machine works. In the notebook below, a student has used notes and a diagram to describe the movement of *Dante II*, a robot used to explore the inside of volcanoes.

Dante II

The frames are connected **by a track** Each frame can slide **along the track, toward the ends of the other frame.** Most of the time, **at least** one frame has all four **of its legs on the ground.**

Dante consists **of two frames;** there are four legs attached **to each frame.**

How Dante Walks
It begins **with all eight legs on the ground.** Then one frame lifts its four legs **from the ground** and slides forward **on the track** When it can slide no further, it stops, planting its legs **on the ground** again. **At that point,** the second frame lifts its legs and repeats the process.

Practice and Apply

WRITING: Using Prepositions

For a project on robots, your class has designed robots for a variety of tasks. Your robot, shown below, is meant to answer the door. Using the information provided in the labels, write a short description of how the robot functions. Use prepositional phrases to describe the relationship between moving parts as well as the movements themselves. Useful prepositions might include the words *on, into, toward, from,* or *at.* Underline the prepositional phrases in your summary. Save your work in your 🗁 **Working Portfolio.**

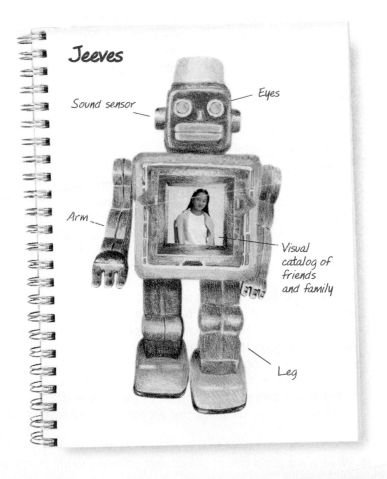

Jeeves

Sound sensor

Eyes

Arm

Visual catalog of friends and family

Leg

PREP. CONJ. INTER.

Mixed Review

A. **Prepositions, Conjunctions, Interjections** Choose the correct word in parentheses to complete each sentence. Then identify the word as a preposition, a conjunction, or an interjection.

The Future Is Now!
1. Someday scientists will develop robots that think. (Wow!, After!)
2. Many theorists believe that machine intelligence is possible, (yet, or) scientists are far from copying the human brain.
3. (Whether, Both) robots help their operators (or, to) perform new jobs, they hold the future.
4. The invention of (both, neither) smarter tools (and, nor) more exotic devices will happen.
5. (With, Between) advanced robot technology, labor-saving devices will be even more common.
6. We barely notice, (and, but) robots have already taken over many tedious tasks.
7. Factories hum (to, after) a steady robot rhythm.
8. Mine shafts are dug (by, from) tireless automated moles.
9. Our banking is done (below, at) automated terminals.
10. (During, Among) surgery, robots drill bones and assist doctors.

B. **Prepositional Phrases** Read the passage and answer the questions below it.

Can You Give Me a Hand?
(1) A jointed-arm robot can perform a number of complex actions. (2) The arm's various sections move the same way as a human arm. (3) With seven joints, the arm can change positions. (4) Its attached hand can grasp anything within reach. (5) The robot-arm can be trained by a human. (6) A person can stand beside the robot-arm, hold the arm, and repeat a motion. (7) After a few repetitions, the robot performs the job independently.

1. What is the prepositional phrase in sentence 1?
2. What is the prepositional phrase in sentence 2?
3. What word does the prepositional phrase modify in sentence 2?
4. What word does the prepositional phrase modify in sentence 3?
5. What is the preposition in sentence 4?
6. What is the object of the preposition in sentence 5?
7. What is the prepositional phrase in sentence 6?
8. What word or words does the prepositional phrase modify in sentence 6?
9. What is the prepositional phrase in sentence 7?
10. What word does the prepositional phrase modify in sentence 7?

Choose the letter of the term that correctly identifies each underlined item.

Have you heard the story <u>about ancient Egyptian robots</u>? Some
(1)
ancient Egyptians believed that statues could speak <u>and</u> that the
(2)
statues could also answer their questions. <u>According to early</u>
(3)
<u>accounts</u>, Egyptian statues <u>both</u> spoke <u>and</u> even moved their
(4)   (4)
arms. Archaeologists have discovered some of these <u>statues</u>, which
(5)
are hollow. A man would put his head <u>into the statue's head</u> and
(6)
talk <u>through</u> the mouth. <u>Alas!</u> What a ruse! Some people believed
(7)   (8)
that the statue spoke, but it was really a man <u>inside</u>. The man
(9)
made the arms move up and down <u>with strings</u> attached to the
(10)
statue's arms.

1. A. adverb phrase
   B. adjective phrase
   C. conjunction
   D. object of a preposition

2. A. conjunction
   B. interjection
   C. preposition
   D. adverb phrase

3. A. prepositional phrase
   B. preposition
   C. conjunction
   D. adverb

4. A. coordinating conjunction
   B. correlative conjunction
   C. compound preposition
   D. interjection

5. A. coordinating conjunction
   B. correlative conjunction
   C. object of a preposition
   D. adverb

6. A. coordinating conjunction
   B. correlative conjunction
   C. adverb phrase
   D. adjective phrase

7. A. object of a preposition
   B. preposition
   C. coordinating conjunction
   D. correlative conjunction

8. A. correlative conjunction
   B. coordinating conjunction
   C. adverb phrase
   D. interjection

9. A. correlative conjunction
   B. preposition
   C. adverb
   D. interjection

10. A. coordinating conjunction
    B. correlative conjunction
    C. adverb phrase
    D. adjective phrase

Student Help Desk

Prepositions, Conjunctions, Interjections at a Glance

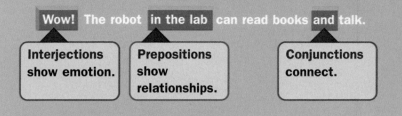

Wow! The robot in the lab can read books and talk.

Interjections show emotion.

Prepositions show relationships.

Conjunctions connect.

Prepositions, Conjunctions, Interjections Summary

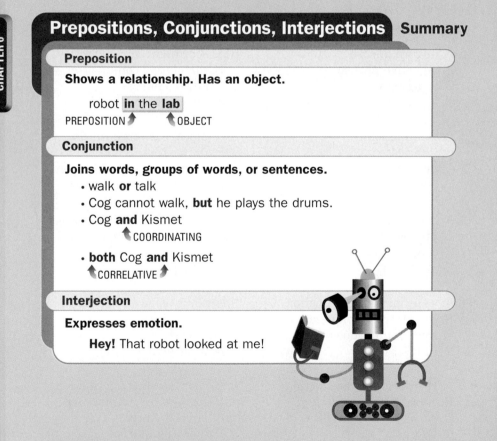

Preposition

Shows a relationship. Has an object.

robot **in** the **lab**
PREPOSITION   OBJECT

Conjunction

Joins words, groups of words, or sentences.
- walk **or** talk
- Cog cannot walk, **but** he plays the drums.
- Cog **and** Kismet
       COORDINATING
- **both** Cog **and** Kismet
       CORRELATIVE

Interjection

Expresses emotion.

Hey! That robot looked at me!

Prepositional Phrases

Adjective Phrases

Modify a noun or a pronoun.

Tell *which one*	The robot known **as ROBODOC**
Tell *what kind*	is a type **of industrial robot.**

Adverb Phrases

Modify a verb, an adjective, or another adverb.

Tell *when*	Surgeons use it **during surgery**
Tell *where*	**at the hospital**
Tell *why*	**for precise work**
Tell *how* or *to what extent*	**with a drill.**

Interjections! Just a Few Ideas . . .

To express concern	oh-oh, oh no, oops
To express terror	eek, help, yipes
To express disgust	yuck, ick, gross
To express joy	awesome, hooray, yea
To express surprise	wow, what, whoops
To draw attention to	hey

The Bottom Line

Checklist for Prepositions and Conjunctions

Have I . . .

____ used prepositions to show relationships between things?

____ placed prepositional phrases close to the words they modify?

____ used coordinating conjunctions to connect words and groups of words?

____ used both parts of correlative conjunctions?

____ used interjections to express strong emotions?

Chapter 7

Verbals and Verbal Phrases

> Hurrying down the dark street, Jeff knew that someone—or something—was right behind him. To turn and look seemed like a bad idea. He kept walking, but suddenly . . .

Theme: Scary Stories

It Was a Dark and Stormy Night . . .

What happens next? Chances are, your favorite character will be running headlong into . . . verbals! A verbal is a verb form that acts as another part of speech. Can you spot two verbals in the passage above? You already know that strong verbs can make your writing livelier. Verbals, too, can add further interest and excitement to anything you write.

Write Away: A Tale of Terror
Copy the story starter above and write a paragraph that describes what happens next. Or, if you prefer, freewrite a paragraph about a scary event of your own choosing, either real or imagined. Save your thriller in your
📁 **Working Portfolio**.

💿 CD-ROM **Grammar Coach**

For each numbered item, choose the letter of the answer that correctly identifies it.

<u>Driving</u> home late one night, a man was startled to see a girl
(1)
<u>dressed in white</u> appear in front of his car. The driver stopped;
(2)
<u>screeching</u> echoed in the night air. He stopped just in front of the
(3)
girl, whose <u>torn</u> coat hung from her shoulder. The man got out
(4)
<u>to offer help</u>. The girl said that she had been in an accident and
(5)
asked the man <u>to drive her</u> home. Her only wish was <u>to get home</u>.
(6)   (7)
After <u>giving directions to her house</u>, the girl did no further talking.
(8)
When they arrived, the man turned—and saw that the girl had
vanished! The girl's mother told him that her daughter had been
killed in a car accident two months earlier!

---

1. A. gerund
   B. present participle
   C. past participle
   D. infinitive

2. A. past participial phrase
   B. gerund phrase
   C. infinitive phrase
   D. present participle

3. A. infinitive
   B. past participle
   C. gerund
   D. present participle

4. A. past participle
   B. present participle
   C. gerund
   D. infinitive

5. A. gerund phrase
   B. gerund
   C. infinitive phrase
   D. participial phrase

6. A. infinitive phrase used as subject
   B. infinitive phrase used as adjective
   C. infinitive phrase used as direct object
   D. infinitive phrase used as adverb

7. A. gerund used as subject
   B. infinitive phrase used as subject
   C. gerund used as direct object
   D. infinitive phrase used as predicate noun

8. A. gerund phrase used as object of a preposition
   B. gerund phrase used as direct object
   C. gerund phrase used as subject
   D. gerund phrase used as predicate noun

LESSON 1 — Gerunds and Gerund Phrases

❶ Here's the Idea

A **verbal** is a word that is formed from a verb and that acts as a noun, an adjective, or an adverb. There are three kinds of verbals: gerunds, infinitives, and participles.

▶ **A gerund is a verbal that ends in *ing* and acts as a noun.** Like nouns, gerunds may be subjects, predicate nouns, direct objects, indirect objects, and objects of prepositions.

Inventing can be dangerous.

▶ **A gerund phrase consists of a gerund plus its modifiers and complements.** Like a gerund, a gerund phrase functions as a noun.

GERUND PHRASE

Writing *Frankenstein* must have given Mary Shelley goose bumps!

Using Gerund Phrases	
Subject	**Calling the monster Frankenstein** is a mistake.
Predicate noun	Frankenstein's error was **creating the monster.**
Direct object	I like **watching horror movies.**
Object of a preposition	The monster was responsible for **killing three people.**

❷ Why It Matters in Writing

A gerund can create a "special effect" in a sentence by adding a sense of motion or action. Notice how the gerund in the model communicates what the speaker is hearing.

> **LITERARY MODEL**
>
> My head ached, and I fancied a **ringing** in my ears: but still they sat and still chatted. The **ringing** became more distinct. . . .
>
> —Edgar Allan Poe, "The Tell-Tale Heart"

❸ Practice and Apply

A. CONCEPT CHECK: Gerunds and Gerund Phrases

Write the gerund or gerund phrase for each sentence.

Dream Story

1. Mary Shelley is famous for creating the Gothic novel *Frankenstein.*
2. Completing *Frankenstein* at 19 was an incredible accomplishment.
3. One night, after listening to ghost stories, Mary and three others agreed to write their own horror stories.
4. Mary Shelley heard her husband and a friend discuss the possibility of reviving a corpse.
5. Another idea was assembling a human being from various body parts.
6. Falling asleep was difficult for Mary that night.
7. She dreamed of a man who was responsible for creating a ghastly creature.
8. After seeing this mental image, Mary was terrified.
9. Opening her eyes reminded her that the vision was not real.
10. Imagining this ghastly creature inspired *Frankenstein.*

➡ **For a SELF-CHECK and more practice, see the EXERCISE BANK, p. 626.**

Tell how each gerund or gerund phrase functions in the sentences above.

B. REVISING: Using Gerunds for Concise Writing

In the following paragraph, replace the words in parentheses with gerunds or gerund phrases. You may need to add, change, or remove words.

Dr. Jekyll, the main character in *Dr. Jekyll and Mr. Hyde,* tries to transfer all of his own evil to another character. The young scientist concocts a potion to isolate his wicked impulses. However, after (he drinks) the liquid, he becomes a man controlled by those impulses. His dream (to improve) himself has failed. He has become Mr. Hyde, a villainous version of himself. (To break) all rules of society seems to be Hyde's goal. Jekyll's mistake is (that he fails) to foresee that his bad side might be stronger than his good side.

Verbals and Verbal Phrases **171**

Participles and Participial Phrases

① Here's the Idea

▶ **A participle is a verb form that acts as an adjective.** It modifies a noun or a pronoun.

MODIFIES   *MODIFIES*

The exhausted campers found a crumbling schoolhouse.

Present and Past Participles

There are two kinds of participles: present participles and past participles. The **present participle** always ends in *ing*.

MODIFIES

Creaking eerily, the door swung open.

The **past participle** of a regular verb ends in *ed*. Past participles of irregular verbs, such as *fall*, are formed in a variety of ways.

MODIFIES

The deserted building was old and decrepit. (regular verb)

MODIFIES

Fallen bricks blocked the entry. (irregular verb)

Gerunds, present participles, and main verbs in progressive forms all end in *ing*. Here's how you can tell them apart.

Using Words That End in *ing*		
	Example	**Clue**
Participle	What's that **scampering** sound?	Could be replaced by an adjective
Gerund	It's the **scampering** of rodents.	Could be replaced by a noun
Verb	Mice are **scampering** beneath the floorboards.	Always preceded by a helping verb

Need help in remembering past participles of irregular verbs? See page 102.

Participial Phrases

▶ **A participial phrase consists of a participle plus its modifiers and complements.** The entire phrase modifies a noun or pronoun.

MODIFIES

They spied a shape lurking in the dark shadows.

MODIFIES

Frightened by the sight, they stopped cold.

❷ Why It Matters in Writing

If your descriptive writing seems dull, you can use participial phrases to enliven it. Notice how the participial phrases in the model present strong visual images.

LITERARY MODEL

He was thin, nondescript, with a cap **pulled down over his eyes**. . . , I was just slowing down for one of the tunnels—when I saw him— **standing under an arc light by the side of the road.** I could see him quite distinctly. The bag, the cap, even the spots of fresh rain **spattered over his shoulders.**

—Lucille Fletcher, *The Hitchhiker*

❸ Practice and Apply

A. CONCEPT CHECK: Participles and Participial Phrases

Write the participles and participial phrases in these sentences, along with the words they modify.

"The Legend of Sleepy Hollow"

1. Washington Irving's "The Legend of Sleepy Hollow" is still a frightening story.
2. A schoolmaster named Ichabod Crane falls in love with the bewitching Katrina Van Tassel.
3. Handsome Brom Bones, annoyed by Ichabod's flirtations, turns against him.
4. Knowing of the schoolmaster's superstitious nature, Brom tells Ichabod of his encounter with the Headless Horseman of Sleepy Hollow.
5. The horseman is the ghost of a beheaded soldier who appears at night.
6. After that chilling story, Ichabod sets out for home through the woods.
7. Suddenly, he is confronted by a hideous figure riding on a horse!
8. The horseman hurtles something resembling a head at Ichabod!
9. Scared out of his wits, Ichabod Crane flees from Sleepy Hollow forever.
10. Did Brom, disguised as the ghost, scare Ichabod away?

➡ **For a SELF-CHECK and more practice, see the EXERCISE BANK, p. 627.**

B. REVISING: Using Participial Phrases

For each blank, choose the correct participial phrase.

a. learning about the house's history
b. known for sentencing many people to death
c. neglected for many years
d. staring at him

"An Account of Some Strange Disturbances in Aungier Street" is a ghost story by Sheridan Le Fanu. A house **(1)** _____ suddenly has new occupants. One night, one of them sees a huge, dark monster **(2)** _____, and he tries to learn the cause of the appearance. **(3)** _____, he finally begins to understand the odd events. Many years earlier, the house had belonged to an old judge **(4)** _____. Now the judge's ghost haunts the house.

Infinitives and Infinitive Phrases

❶ Here's the Idea

▶ **An infinitive is a verb form that usually begins with the word *to* and acts as a noun, an adjective, or an adverb.**

INFINITIVE
Mars is a place some people want to visit.

▶ **An infinitive phrase is an infinitive plus its modifiers and complements.** The entire phrase functions as a noun, an adjective, or an adverb.

INFINITIVE PHRASE
To believe in life on Mars was common in the 1930s.
(ACTS AS NOUN)

INFINITIVE PHRASE
Martians might use flying saucers to invade Earth.
(ACTS AS ADVERB)

INFINITIVE PHRASE
I took time to read an old science fiction book.
(ACTS AS ADJECTIVE)

Using Infinitive Phrases	
Noun	To colonize Mars is a real possibility. (SUBJECT)
	My dream is to live on Mars. (PREDICATE NOUN)
	Would you like to go there? (DIRECT OBJECT)
Adverb	Science fiction writers wrote about little green Martians to scare readers.
Adjective	Even some scientists believed Mars to be inhabited.

On some evenings, the planet Mars seems to be red.

VERBALS

Is the phrase an infinitive phrase or a prepositional phrase? If a verb follows *to,* the phrase is an infinitive phrase. If a noun or pronoun follows *to,* the phrase is a prepositional phrase.

PREPOSITIONAL PHRASE

Of all the planets, Mars is most similar to Earth.

NOUN

INFINITIVE PHRASE

It was easy to imagine creatures on Mars.

VERB

Would you like to travel to Mars?

VERB　　　　　NOUN

I prefer to go to libraries for information.

❷ Why It Matters in Writing

Infinitive phrases are useful for communicating goals, wishes, and plans. Notice how the infinitive phrases in the model let readers know what the old man wishes.

LITERARY MODEL

"I'd like **to go to India myself,**" said the old man, "just **to look round a bit,** you know."

"Better where you are," said the sergeant-major, shaking his head. . . .

"I should like **to see those old temples and fakirs and jugglers,**" said the old man.

—W. W. Jacobs, "The Monkey's Paw"

❸ Practice and Apply

A. CONCEPT CHECK: Infinitives and Infinitive Phrases

Identify the infinitives and infinitive phrases in the following sentences.

> **The War of the Worlds**
> 1. It's possible to scare an entire nation with an imaginary story.
> 2. One day in 1938, Orson Welles began to broadcast a radio play about a Martian invasion.
> 3. It was not Welles's intention to cause a nationwide panic, but that's what he did.
> 4. Welles had designed the play to sound like an actual broadcast with flash news bulletins.
> 5. People tuning in were shocked to hear that giants from Mars had landed in New Jersey!
> 6. A later bulletin reported that the invaders had started to destroy entire cities!
> 7. Ready to wade across the Hudson River, the Martians were headed to New York!
> 8. Many hysterical listeners tried to escape their homes.
> 9. Some rushed outside with wet handkerchiefs over their faces to protect them from the Martians' lethal gas.
> 10. The media's ability to influence the public is astonishing.

➡ For a SELF-CHECK and more exercises, see the EXERCISE BANK, p. 627.

B. WRITING: Using Infinitives and Infinitive Phrases

Use each of these infinitive phrases in a sentence of your own. Tell whether the infinitive phrase is used as a noun, an adjective, or an adverb.

1. to read mysteries
2. to be choosy
3. to surprise my friends
4. to entertain myself on the weekend
5. to find out the ending

C. REVISING: Using Verbal Phrases

🗂 Return to your **Write Away** assignment. Add three verbal phrases—gerund, participial, or infinitive—to make your writing more interesting and fluent. Then underline each verbal phrase you used.

Grammar in Literature

Using Verbals in Descriptive Writing

When you describe an eerie scene, you can use verbals to create energetic images. Because they are formed from verbs, verbals often lend a feeling of action to descriptions. Notice how Aiken's use of gerunds and participles shows the vivid actions of the struggling swan, as well as the quiet energy of Mr. Peters and the woods themselves.

from

The Third Wish

by JOAN AIKEN

As Mr. Peters entered a straight, empty stretch of road he seemed to hear a faint crying, and a struggling and thrashing, as if somebody was in trouble far away in the trees. He left his car and climbed the mossy bank beside the road. Beyond the bank was an open slope of beech trees leading down to thorn bushes through which he saw the gleam of water. He stood a moment waiting to try and discover where the noise was coming from, and presently heard a rustling and some strange cries in a voice which was almost human—and yet there was something too hoarse about it at one time and too clear and sweet at another. Mr. Peters ran down the hill and as he neared the bushes he saw something white among them which was trying to extricate itself; coming closer he found that it was a swan that had become entangled in the thorns growing on the bank of the canal.

> **GERUNDS**
>
> as direct objects of *hear* and *heard,* lend energy and vividness to the images.

> **PARTICIPIAL PHRASES**
>
> The first phrase modifies *trees;* although the trees are standing still, the phrase shows them in the act of leading.
>
> The second phrase modifies *He;* it shows that Mr. Peters waits and listens while he stands.

Practice and Apply

WRITING: Using Verbals

Follow the directions to write your own description of a person secretly watching or hearing a struggle. You can suggest what happens next to Mr. Peters, or you can create a passage about another character.

1. List four gerunds naming activities that are a part of the struggle being observed. You can describe a struggle that is bold and noisy, or one that is quiet and tense.
2. List four participles you might use as adjectives to describe both the character and his or her surroundings.
3. Use your responses to 1 and 2 to write a short scene about someone seeing or hearing a struggle. (You may decide not to use all of your participles or gerunds.)
4. Evaluate your work. How would your writing be different if you hadn't used participles or gerunds? Put your writing and your evaluation in your ▭ **Working Portfolio.**

VERBALS

1. Gerunds
   1. weeping
   2. whispering
   3.
   4.

2. Participles
   1. trapped
   2. darkening
   3.
   4.

Wallpaper design for *Swan, Rush and Iris,* Walter Crane (1845–1915). Victoria & Albert Museum, London, UK/Bridgeman Art Library, London/New York.

Mixed Review

A. Gerunds, Participles, and Infinitives In each of the following sentences, identify the word or words in italics as a gerund, a participle, or an infinitive.

1. *Writing* bestsellers has been Stephen King's specialty for a long time.
2. He seems to be able *to write* at least one book every year.
3. The *amazing* fact is that more than a hundred million copies of his books are in print.
4. King's popularity shows that people enjoy *scaring* themselves.
5. Every new King book results in a huge rush by customers *to buy* every copy.
6. Several successful movies are *adapted* versions of his books and stories.
7. King has played small parts in many of those films, because he enjoys *acting*.
8. His books are constructed to keep suspense *building* from beginning to end.
9. It is safe *to predict* that King's work will be popular for a long time.
10. By *achieving* such remarkable success, King has shown that he would deserve a place in the Scary Writers' Hall of Fame if one existed.

B. Writing with Verbal Phrases Write five sentences using the phrases below. Follow the directions in parentheses. You may choose to add more details to the phrases.

Example: to write five fresh sentences (Use as an infinitive phrase that acts as a direct object.)

Answer: I will soon begin to write five fresh sentences.

1. to walk home late one night (Use as an infinitive phrase that is the direct object in the sentence.)
2. shocked (Use as a participle.)
3. running away (Use as a gerund phrase that is the subject.)
4. speaking loudly (Use as a participial phrase.)
5. to advise you (Use as an infinitive phrase that acts as a noun.)

For each numbered item, choose the letter of the answer that correctly identifies it.

Not believing in ghosts, a reporter agreed to stay overnight in a
(1)   (2)
"haunted" house where events considered weird had occurred.
(3)
Finding natural causes of the events was her goal. The reporter
(4)
decided to take her niece along on the adventure. That night,
(5)
sitting in the front hall of the dark house, the woman and girl
(6)
heard an upstairs door open and close. Then, echoing footsteps
(7)
came down the stairs. After opening the lid of the piano in the
(8)
next room, *something* began to play music! When the music

stopped, the footsteps seemed to go back upstairs.

---

1. A. gerund phrase
   B. infinitive phrase
   C. present participial phrase
   D. past participial phrase

2. A. gerund
   B. past participle
   C. present participle
   D. infinitive

3. A. gerund
   B. present participle
   C. infinitive
   D. past participle

4. A. gerund phrase used as
      direct object
   B. gerund phrase used as
      object of a preposition
   C. gerund phrase used as
      predicate noun
   D. gerund phrase used as
      subject

5. A. infinitive phrase used as
      subject
   B. infinitive phrase used as
      direct object
   C. infinitive phrase used as
      adverb
   D. infinitive phrase used as
      adjective

6. A. past participial phrase
   B. past participle
   C. present participial phrase
   D. present participle

7. A. past participial phrase
   B. past participle
   C. present participial phrase
   D. present participle

8. A. gerund phrase used as
      direct object
   B. gerund phrase used as
      object of a preposition
   C. gerund phrase used as
      predicate noun
   D. gerund phrase used as
      subject

Student Help Desk

Verbals and Verbal Phrases at a Glance

Verbal	Job	Example
Gerund	Noun	**Seeing** a horror show can jangle your nerves.
Participle	Adjective	The **terrifying** plot will make you gasp.
Infinitive	Noun	**To scare** you out of your wits is the director's aim.
	Adjective	The dark and lonely scenes are the ones **to watch.**
	Adverb	When a door slams shut, you're sure **to jump.**

Gerund, Participle, or Verb? Rolling, Rolling, Rolling

	Example	Clue
Gerund	**Running** was Jason's best sport.	Could be replaced by a noun
Participle	His daily **running** schedule was rigorous.	Could be replaced by an adjective
Verb	Friday night, Jason was **running** out of the horror movie!	Always preceded by a helping verb

Infinitives vs. Prepositional Phrases

To Cut to the Chase

	Example	Clue
Infinitive	He started **to run home.** VERB	A verb follows *to*.
Prepositional phrase	Instead, he returned **to work.** NOUN	A noun or pronoun follows *to*.

Understanding Infinitives   To Weave a Plot

Noun

SUBJECT
To save the victims required a genius.

DIRECT OBJECT
An eccentric scientist tried **to find** a solution.

PREDICATE NOUN
His brilliant idea was **to catch** the spiders in their own webs.

Adjective

Victims' struggles in the mammoth sticky webs were a horrible sight **to see.**

Adverb

In the horror show, giant spiders were able **to trap** people in their webs.

The Bottom Line

Checklist for Verbals and Verbal Phrases

Have I . . .

____ used gerunds and gerund phrases to name actions and activities?

____ used participles and participial phrases to modify nouns and pronouns?

____ understood the different jobs of words that end in *ing*?

____ understood the difference between infinitives and prepositional phrases beginning with *to*?

____ used infinitives and infinitive phrases as nouns, adjectives, and adverbs?

____ used verbals and verbal phrases to add fluency and excitement to my writing?

Sentence Structure

Dark and slippery
Formed a chain to bring in gear
Started mapping from entrance
Sketched view of passage
Need to wear helmets with lights
Found stalagmites and stalactites
If lost

CHAPTER 8

Theme: A Day in the Life . . .

One Step at a Time

How exactly will Brandon and Taylor describe their experience as underground cave explorers? The notes they made while helping their team map the cave are sketchy and brief. How could they turn these notes into sentences that give a better description of their experience? You, too, often have to translate sketchy thoughts into complete ideas. Knowing how sentences are structured can help you explore the best possible way to say what you want.

Write Away: Surprises Around the Corner
It's not necessary to travel underground in order to have an exciting or unusual day in your life. Sometimes the most ordinary day can turn out to be the most surprising. Write about a day in your life that turned out to be not so typical. Put your writing in your 🗂 **Working Portfolio.**

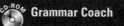 **Grammar Coach**

Choose the letter of the term that correctly identifies each underlined section.

<u>While her friends relax on weekends</u>, Davida works on her line
(1)
of fashion jeans and jackets. <u>Right now she is making an evening</u>
(2)
<u>jacket</u>. She is also working on a special order for a friend, <u>and she</u>
<u>is designing her first prom dress</u>. <u>Even though</u> these projects take
(3)   (4)
a lot of time, <u>each reflects a step toward Davida's dream</u>. <u>She</u>
(5)
<u>wants to be a fashion designer</u>. This dream, <u>which Davida has had</u>
(6)   (7)
<u>since childhood</u>, keeps her focused. Davida's friends encourage her,
<u>but</u> they wish she spent more time with them as well. <u>Whenever</u>
(8)
<u>she can, Davida invites her friends to go along with her to junk</u>
(9)
<u>shops, and together they hunt for buttons and fabrics that can be</u>
<u>used in Davida's designs</u>. Davida searches the shops <u>until she</u>
(10)
<u>finds just the right materials for her creations</u>.

1. A. independent clause
   B. dependent clause
   C. compound sentence
   D. simple sentence

2. A. simple sentence
   B. dependent clause
   C. compound sentence
   D. complex sentence

3. A. part of a compound sentence
   B. sentence fragment
   C. part of a complex sentence
   D. simple sentence

4. A. coordinating conjunction
   B. subordinating conjunction
   C. noun clause
   D. relative pronoun

5. A. independent clause
   B. dependent clause
   C. compound sentence
   D. simple sentence

6. A. simple sentence
   B. compound sentence
   C. complex sentence
   D. compound-complex sentence

7. A. noun clause
   B. adjective clause
   C. adverb clause
   D. independent clause

8. A. coordinating conjunction
   B. subordinating conjunction
   C. relative pronoun
   D. clause

9. A. simple sentence
   B. compound sentence
   C. complex sentence
   D. compound-complex sentence

10. A. noun clause
    B. adjective clause
    C. adverb clause
    D. independent clause

What Is a Clause?

❶ Here's the Idea

▶ **A clause is a group of words that contains a subject and a verb.** For example, the following sentence contains two clauses.

SUBJECT VERB
**Kate noted the day's events in her journal
before she went to bed.**
SUBJECT   VERB

There are two kinds of clauses: independent and dependent.

Independent and Dependent Clauses

▶ **An independent clause expresses a complete thought and can stand alone as a sentence.**

| Kate noted the day's events in her journal. |
INDEPENDENT CLAUSE

▶ **A dependent clause does not express a complete thought and cannot stand alone as a sentence.**

Most dependent clauses are introduced by words like *although, before, because, so that, when, while,* and *that.*

| before she went to bed |
DEPENDENT CLAUSE

A dependent clause can be joined to an independent clause to add to the complete thought that the independent clause expresses.

| Kate noted the day's events in her journal | before she went to bed. |

| Some writers keep journals | so that they can remember details about events. |

Dependent clauses are also known as subordinate clauses. These clauses cannot stand alone and are dependent on main clauses.

❷ Why It Matters in Writing

When you write, pay special attention to sentences that start with words such as *because, when, so that,* or other words that signal a dependent clause. Be sure you have not accidentally created a fragment. Notice how connecting the dependent clause to the preceding sentence in the model below makes a sentence that expresses a complete thought.

STUDENT MODEL

Kate and her horse Scarlet are one of the best teams in the junior rodeo. Because they practice together every day.

INDEPENDENT CLAUSE

DEPENDENT CLAUSE

❸ Practice and Apply

A. CONCEPT CHECK: What Is a Clause?

Identify each underlined group of words as an independent clause or a dependent clause.

A Day in the Life of a Junior Rodeo Competitor

1. Thirteen-year-old Kate is devoted to her horse Scarlet.
2. They won their first competition together when Kate was only nine years old.
3. While her brothers sleep, Kate slips out to the stable.
4. After she feeds Scarlet, Kate brushes her coat and mane.
5. She does this so that Scarlet's coat stays shiny.
6. Because Scarlet needs exercise, Kate rides her daily.
7. Kate and Scarlet entered a barrel-racing competition, which was very competitive.
8. Entrants raced around barrels that were put in the ring.
9. Kate and Scarlet's performance brought cheers from the crowd because they put everything they had into the race.
10. Now Kate and Scarlet have more than a dozen ribbons, and Kate plans to keep competing in the rodeo.

➡ **For a SELF-CHECK and more practice, see the EXERCISE BANK, p. 628.**

B. EDITING: Fixing Fragments

Read the following first draft of a student's paragraph. Rewrite the paragraph to eliminate any sentence fragments.

STUDENT MODEL

My friend Derrick is a butterfly collector. He invited me to join him on Saturday. So that I could help him catch butterflies for his collection. We hunkered down in our back field and waited quietly. Because we didn't want to frighten away the butterflies. Derrick pointed toward the tall pink flowers nearby. We watched the flowers sway in the breeze. While a beautiful orange and black monarch hovered over them. Now I want to collect butterflies too.

C. WRITING: Creating a Caption

This photograph shows a junior rodeo contestant barrel-racing. On a separate sheet of paper, write a caption for the picture, describing what is happening. Use at least one independent clause and one dependent clause.

① Here's the Idea

Simple Sentences

▶ **A simple sentence contains one independent clause and no dependent clauses.** Remember that even a simple sentence can include many details. Each of the following sentences has only a single independent clause.

Malika sings.
INDEPENDENT CLAUSE

Ben competes at chess every day after school.

Compound Sentences

▶ **A compound sentence contains two or more independent clauses and no dependent clauses.** The clauses in a compound sentence must be closely related.

Malika sings every day, and she practices with the choir.
INDEPENDENT CLAUSE   INDEPENDENT CLAUSE

Independent clauses can be joined by a comma and a coordinating conjunction or by a semicolon.

The choir rehearsed late on Tuesday, and the director praised their hard work.

The choir rehearsed late on Tuesday; the director praised their hard work.

Coordinating Conjunctions
for and nor or but so yet

Don't mistake a simple sentence with a compound verb for a compound sentence. No punctuation should separate the parts of a compound verb.

Ben planned a chess tournament for interested students×and promoted it.

SENTENCES

❷ Why It Matters in Writing

Too many short sentences can make your writing choppy. You can avoid this problem by using compound sentences. Notice how the writer of the model below combined related ideas to form compound sentences.

STUDENT MODEL

My grandfather enjoys listening to me
sing. He has many favorite songs, *and* I sing
them for him every night. He still has a
pretty strong voice, *so* He sometimes joins
in for a few verses.

> Related thoughts combined

❸ Practice and Apply

A. CONCEPT CHECK: Simple and Compound Sentences

Identify each sentence as simple or compound.

A Day in the Life of a Young Writer

1. Eighth-grader Max Marciano is working hard on his first mystery novel.
2. Max loves mysteries, and he has read every story about the detective Sherlock Holmes.
3. Max's older brother Tony and two friends are also fans of the famous detective.
4. Tony encourages Max with his novel.
5. Max writes a full page of text on most mornings, but sometimes he isn't inspired.
6. Max's friend Sophie made a suggestion.
7. She formed a small writing group, and now they meet once a week.
8. The writing group has motivated Max, and he now meets his writing goal each morning.

9. The main character in Max's story is named De Soto, and he is a master of disguise.

10. Max read his latest chapter to Sophie and Tony, and they loved it.

→ **For a SELF-CHECK and more practice, see the EXERCISE BANK, p. 628.**

B. REVISING: Combining Sentences

Combine each pair of sentences to form a compound sentence, using one of the coordinating conjunctions *and, but, for, or, nor, so,* and *yet.* Remember to use a comma before the coordinating conjunction.

Meeting Challenges Daily

1. Fourteen-year-old Marisha was born with both of her legs broken. No one noticed anything was wrong at first.

2. She has a rare bone disease. Her bones are brittle and soft.

3. Marisha has already had seven operations. She may need more in the future.

4. After an operation, physical therapy is a big part of Marisha's rehabilitation. She has four sessions of physical therapy a day.

5. A typical day in physical therapy always includes swimming. It also can include bike riding.

6. Sheri is Marisha's physical therapist. She is also Marisha's friend.

7. Together they work on exercises like sit-ups and leg lifts. They talk about Marisha's progress.

8. Sometimes Marisha feels a lot of pain. She doesn't like to show it.

9. Marisha works hard on her school work. She still has time for fun.

10. Marisha isn't sure of her future career. She thinks of becoming a pediatrician.

📁 **Working Portfolio: Revising** Reread what you wrote for the **Write Away** paragraph on page 184. Check to see if any short sentences can be combined to form compound sentences.

Complex Sentences

❶ Here's the Idea

▶ **A complex sentence contains one independent clause and one or more dependent clauses.**

INDEPENDENT CLAUSE   DEPENDENT CLAUSE

Mr. Hernandez, who is a professional storyteller, performs at many different festivals.

When Mr. Hernandez performs, he enchants the audience.

Young people love the way he tells stories because he changes his voice and wears costumes.

Most dependent clauses are introduced by subordinating conjunctions. A **subordinating conjunction** relates the dependent clause to the independent clause. The following is a list of the most common subordinating conjunctions.

Commonly Used Subordinating Conjunctions

after	as though	so that	whenever
although	because	than	where
as	before	though	wherever
as if	even though	unless	while
as long as	if	until	
as soon as	since	when	

❷ Why It Matters in Writing

You can use complex sentences to clarify relationships between ideas. Notice how the writer of the model on the next page used dependent clauses to convey details of character and plot.

LITERARY MODEL

"When the merchant arrived, he asked her if she could spin. "Spin?" answered the old woman, while the poor embarrassed girl stood by with bowed head. "Spin! The hanks [of linen fibers] disappear so fast you would think she was drinking them like water."

—"The Souls in Purgatory," retold by Guadalupe Baca-Vaughn

TELLS THE TIME OF THE EVENT

PROVIDES A DETAIL OF THE PLOT

TELLS HOW THE GIRL FEELS

❸ Practice and Apply

CONCEPT CHECK: Complex Sentences

Write these sentences on a sheet of paper. Underline each independent clause once and each dependent clause twice.

A Day in the Life of a Storyteller
1. Rick and José Hernandez enjoy hearing their father's stories because he performs them so cleverly.
2. When Mr. Hernandez performed on Saturday, he told the story "Aunty Misery."
3. Since the main character is a very old woman, Mr. Hernandez crumpled his face and walked with a stoop.
4. Aunty Misery, who lives alone, is teased by children.
5. When these children yell insults at the old woman, Mr. Hernandez makes his voice squeaky and high-pitched.
6. After she is kind to a stranger, she is given one wish.
7. Mr. Hernandez pulls a cape across his face so that the stranger looks mysterious.
8. Because her wish comes true, the children stick to a tree.
9. She ignores their cries until the children promise not to bother her.
10. The audience laughs when Mr. Hernandez portrays the naughty children stuck to the pear tree.

➜ For a SELF-CHECK and more practice, see the EXERCISE BANK, p. 629.

Kinds of Dependent Clauses

❶ Here's the Idea

Adjective Clauses

▶ **An adjective clause is a dependent clause used as an adjective.** An adjective clause modifies a noun or a pronoun. It tells what kind, which one, how many, or how much.

MODIFIES NOUN

Devon Kim is a climber who likes challenges.

ADJECTIVE CLAUSE

Adjective clauses are usually introduced by relative pronouns.

Relative Pronouns

who   whom   whose   that   which

His hardest climb, which took him three days, was Mount Whitney.

Notice that a clause that begins with *which* is set off with commas. Use commas when the clause isn't necessary to understand the meaning of a sentence.

Adverb Clauses

▶ **An adverb clause is a dependent clause used as an adverb.** It modifies a verb, an adjective, or an adverb. An adverb clause might tell where, when, how, why, to what extent, or under what conditions.

Adverb clauses are introduced by subordinating conjunctions such as *if, because, before, than, as, even though, than, so that, while, where, when, as if,* and *since.*

MODIFIES VERB

They checked their gear before they started the climb.

ADVERB CLAUSE

MODIFIES ADJECTIVE

They were cautious because ice made the trails slippery.

MODIFIES ADVERB

Devon worries about the weather more than Andy does.

When Devon started his climb, **the weather was good.**

ADVERB CLAUSE

An adverb clause should be followed by a comma when it comes before an independent clause. When an adverb clause comes after an independent clause, a comma may or may not be needed before it.

Because the weather was bad, **Devon canceled the climb.**

Devon canceled the climb because the weather was bad.

For more about adjectives and adverbs, see pages 126–136.

Noun Clauses

▶ **A noun clause is a dependent clause used as a noun.**
Like a noun, a noun clause can serve as a subject, a direct object, an indirect object, an object of a preposition, or a predicate noun.

NOUN CLAUSE SERVING AS SUBJECT

That the dedicated actor practiced her role every day
surprised no one.

NOUN CLAUSE SERVING AS DIRECT OBJECT

The director determined who would design the set.

NOUN CLAUSE SERVING AS AN INDIRECT OBJECT

The set designer gave whoever helped a bonus.

NOUN CLAUSE SERVING AS A PREDICATE NOUN

A love of theater is what motivates her.

NOUN CLAUSE SERVING AS AN OBJECT OF A PREPOSITION

She takes great satisfaction in whatever they perform.

Noun clauses are often introduced by words such as those shown in the following chart.

Words That Introduce Noun Clauses

that, how, when, where, whether, why, what, whatever, who, whom, whoever, whomever, which, whichever

If you can substitute the word *something* or *someone* for a clause in a sentence, it is a noun clause.

The director determined who would design the set.

The director determined something.

❷ Why It Matters in Writing

You can use dependent clauses to add detail and to provide explanations. Notice how the writer of the model below used adverb clauses to add information about the characters.

LITERARY MODEL

Because Annie was home for a semester break from college, we had decided to make a special Saturday visit. Now Annie was in bed, groaning theatrically—she's a drama major—but I told my mother I'd go, anyway. I hadn't seen my grandmother since she'd been admitted to Lawnrest.

—Robert Cormier, "The Moustache"

Adverb clause
tells why they decided to visit.

Adverb clause
tells when the narrator last saw his grandmother.

❸ Practice and Apply

A. CONCEPT CHECK: Kinds of Dependent Clauses

Write these sentences on a sheet of paper. Underline each dependent clause, and identify it as an adjective clause, an adverb clause, or a noun clause.

A Dog's Life

1. Rex is a yellow Labrador retriever who loves to chase squirrels.
2. As soon as he sees a squirrel, he yelps with delight.
3. After he has an exciting squirrel chase, Rex usually needs to take a very long nap.
4. That Rex is a swift runner is obvious to everyone.
5. Rachel and Jake have photos that show Rex as a puppy at the animal shelter.
6. He looks as if he wanted a good home.
7. Although Rex behaves well, they take him to obedience class.

8. Whoever meets Rex is impressed by his good nature.
9. Rex eagerly eats whatever dog food he is given, but he really likes lasagna and raw carrots.
10. Tonight Rachel and Jake will take Rex for a long walk because they have no homework.

➡ For a SELF-CHECK and more practice, see the EXERCISE BANK, p. 629.

B. WRITING: Using Clauses

Complete the sentences below by adding clauses of the types indicated in parentheses.

(1) Many dogs (adjective clause) _____ live long, healthy lives. (2) Dogs can help people live healthier lives (adverb clause) _____ . (3) Love and kindness are (noun clause) _____ .

Compound-Complex Sentences

LESSON 5

❶ Here's the Idea

▶ A compound-complex sentence contains two or more independent clauses and one or more dependent clauses.

DEPENDENT CLAUSE   INDEPENDENT CLAUSE

While she was fishing, Amy saw many deer, and she tried not to disturb them.

INDEPENDENT CLAUSE

Amy unhooked the salmon from the line, and she threw it back into the stream so that it could live.

❷ Why It Matters in Writing

A rich, detailed description is hard to create with only simple sentences. Notice how Marjorie Kinnan Rawlings used compound-complex sentences in a detailed description of a day in the life of a boy.

LITERARY MODEL

When I left my bed in the cool morning, the boy had come and gone, and a stack of kindling was neat against the cabin wall. He came again after school in the afternoon and worked until time to return to the orphanage. His name was Jerry; he was twelve years old, and he had been at the orphanage since he was four.

        —Marjorie Kinnan Rawlings,
        "A Mother in Mannville"

DEPENDENT CLAUSE

INDEPENDENT CLAUSE

❸ Practice and Apply

A. MIXED REVIEW: Compound, Complex, or Compound-Complex

Identify each sentence as compound, complex, or compound-complex.

Daily Life in the Middle Ages

1. Most young people in the Middle Ages spent their time on farm work, and they never learned reading and writing.
2. Boys and girls harvested grain, and they picked fruit.
3. Young boys in prosperous families were sent to school, where they studied grammar, rhetoric, and arithmetic.
4. Girls from wealthy families also learned reading and arithmetic so that they could manage households.
5. All girls were taught spinning when they were quite young, and they also learned weaving.
6. Wealthy families apprenticed their sons so that they could learn banking, business, and law.
7. If a young boy lived in a city, he could work for an artisan, and he could receive on-the-job training.
8. City life centered on the marketplace, where country people came to buy and sell; the shops offered all sorts of wares and services.
9. While housewives were at the marketplace, they met at the public fountain, and young people played games.
10. Although it was crowded and cramped, daily life in a medieval city could be lively and exciting.

➡ **For a SELF-CHECK and more practice, see the EXERCISE BANK, p. 630.**

B. WRITING: Creating Compound-Complex Sentences

Combine the following sentences to create a compound-complex sentence. Use *but* and *so that* in your new sentence.

Most young people in the Middle Ages worked. Today young people go to school. They learn reading and writing.

Grammar in Literature

Using Dependent Clauses to Enrich Writing

When you write descriptions of powerful memories, you will probably use complex sentences. All complex sentences are made up of independent and dependent clauses. In the passage below, notice how author Jewell Parker Rhodes weaves dependent clauses into her sentences as she shares her memories of what it was like to grow up in Pittsburgh, Pennsylvania, in the 1950s.

BLOCK PARTY

by Jewell Parker Rhodes

We lived in the dark green hills of Pittsburgh where the smoke from J.L. Steel dusted our clothes gray and blanketed the sky, causing sunsets to streak bright pink and orange. Streetcar wires crisscrossed overhead, making perches for the hungry crows who flew high when the lumbering cars came, spewing electric sparks. Sometimes we'd put pennies in the metal tracks and wait for them to be squashed flat as the streetcars rumbled over them, carrying passengers down the hills into the heart of the city that rested by the three rivers: Ohio, Monongahela, and Allegheny.

But what I remember most about growing up in Pittsburgh was living in a neighborhood where everyone acted like a relative—an aunt, an uncle, a brother, or a sister. Lots of women acted like my mother, bossing me, feeding me. Many would hold me on their laps and tell me stories about High John the Conqueror or John Henry. Some felt no shame about whipping out a comb and fixing my hair when they thought I looked too raggedy. And days when I was lucky, one of my neighborhood mothers would jump in the circle and join me in a waist-twisting, hip-rolling hula-hoop.

Practice and Apply

WRITING: Using Dependent Clauses

The notebook below contains a list of dependent clauses. Rewrite the following passage, using dependent clauses from the list. Follow the directions in parentheses to add noun clauses, adverb clauses, and adjective clauses. If you'd like to, make up your own dependent clauses.

We loved to use our hula-hoops *(adverb clause)*. Hula-hoops were circular tubes of plastic *(adjective clause)*. The challenge was to keep the hoops spinning *(adverb clause)*. We practiced *(adverb clause)* and *(adverb clause)*. Sometimes our older brothers and sisters *(adjective clause)* joined in the fun. Once my aunt *(adjective clause)* tried it herself *(adverb clause)*. *(Noun clause)* was the champion spinner. *(Adverb clause)*, we looked like we were doing the Hawaiian hula dance.

wherever there was enough room to play

as long as you could

when we really got going

when we had parties outside

who never played

whoever kept the hoop spinning the longest

whenever we had time

that you spun around your waist

who thought they were too old for toys

when we challenged her

Mixed Review

A. Simple, Compound, and Complex Sentences Read this excerpt about a young Chinese-American chess champion. Then answer the questions below it.

(1) A man who watched me play in the park suggested that my mother allow me to play in local chess tournaments. **(2)** My mother smiled graciously, an answer that meant nothing. **(3)** I desperately wanted to go, but I bit back my tongue. **(4)** I knew she would not let me play among strangers. **(5)** So as we walked home I said in a small voice that I didn't want to play in the local tournament. **(6)** They would have American rules. **(7)** If I lost, I would bring shame on my family.

—Amy Tan, "Rules of the Game"

1. Is sentence 1 simple or complex?
2. What is the adjective clause in sentence 1?
3. What is the noun clause in sentence 1?
4. Is sentence 3 complex or compound?
5. What is the coordinating conjunction in sentence 3?
6. What is the noun clause in sentence 5?
7. What is the independent clause in sentence 6?
8. What kind of sentence is sentence 6?
9. What is the dependent clause in sentence 7?
10. What is the subordinating conjunction in sentence 7?

B. Combining Clauses Rewrite the following paragraph, combining clauses to eliminate sentence fragments and to connect related ideas.

Learning the Yo-Yo
Jennifer Baybrook is a champion yo-yo player. Who began performing. When she was six. She was the first female ever to win national and world titles. Another American champion is Ed Giulietti. Who started when he was 11 years old. After he had practiced for only two years. He knew more than 500 tricks.

Choose the letter of the term that correctly identifies each underlined section.

> Rob steps backstage, and he senses the electric atmosphere
> (1)
> among the actors as they prepare for the opening night of *My Fair*
> (2)
> *Lady.* Rob has been cast in the role of Professor Henry Higgins.
> The role, which has always been one of Rob's favorites, calls for
> (3)
> wit, charm, and a touch of snobbery. As soon as Rob sees Angela
> and James, the actors who are playing Eliza and Colonel
> (4)
> Pickering, he wishes them luck. Rob, Angela, and James have only
> five minutes before the curtain rises, and they try to relax. That
> (5)
> the actors are a little nervous is understandable. Rob straightens
> (6)   (7)
> his bow tie and hat, which are supposed to make him look like a
> professor, and he clears his throat. Rob watches for his cue.
> (8)   (9)
> Whatever happens onstage, he is ready.
> (10)

1. A. independent clause
   B. dependent clause
   C. compound sentence
   D. simple sentence

2. A. adjective clause
   B. adverb clause
   C. noun clause
   D. independent clause

3. A. simple sentence
   B. compound sentence
   C. complex sentence
   D. noun clause

4. A. adjective clause
   B. adverb clause
   C. noun clause
   D. independent clause

5. A. adjective clause
   B. adverb clause
   C. noun clause
   D. independent clause

6. A. adjective clause
   B. adverb clause
   C. noun clause
   D. independent clause

7. A. independent clause
   B. dependent clause
   C. noun clause
   D. simple sentence

8. A. coordinating conjunction
   B. subordinating conjunction
   C. relative pronoun
   D. clause

9. A. simple sentence
   B. compound sentence
   C. complex sentence
   D. compound-complex sentence

10. A. independent clause
    B. dependent clause
    C. noun clause
    D. simple sentence

Student Help Desk

Sentence Structure at a Glance

SIMPLE SENTENCE = ⟦independent clause⟧
Jamal practices his saxophone every day.

COMPOUND SENTENCE = ⟦independent clause⟧ + ⟦independent clause(s)⟧
⟦He plays in the marching band,⟧ and ⟦he also plays in a jazz quartet.⟧

COMPLEX SENTENCE = ⟦independent clause⟧ + dependent clause(s)
Before the band practiced, ⟦they tuned their instruments.⟧

COMPOUND–COMPLEX SENTENCE =
⟦independent clauses⟧ + dependent clauses
⟦Jamal played a solo,⟧ and ⟦Christine joined in for a duet⟧ while they were
waiting for band practice to begin.

Punctuating Compound and Complex Sentences

Everyday Choices

Use Commas	Example
to join independent clauses with coordinating conjunctions	Christine plays the clarinet, **and** she also plays the piano.
after adverb clauses that begin sentences	After the band finished the practice, they rested.
to set off adjective clauses that begin with *which*	Jamal appreciates his dad's knowledge of jazz, **which he played as a young man,** and Jamal has learned much from him.
Use Semicolons	
to join independent clauses without conjunctions	Christine learned her music from her uncle; he is a piano teacher.

Avoiding Clause Confusion · Job Options

Dependent Clause	Function	Example
Adjective clause	• modifies noun or pronoun • tells what kind, which one, how many, or how much	The **students who attended the game** enjoyed the half-time performance.
Adverb clause	• modifies verb, adjective, or adverb • tells where, when, how, why, to what extent, or under what conditions	**Because it was raining,** the band got soaked.
Noun clause	• acts as subject, direct object, indirect object, object of a preposition, or predicate noun	**That Jamal and Christine won music scholarships** surprised no one.

The Bottom Line

Checklist for Sentence Structure

Have I improved my writing by . . .

____ eliminating sentence fragments?

____ creating compound sentences to link closely related ideas?

____ using dependent clauses to show how ideas are related?

____ using dependent clauses to add details?

____ punctuating compound and complex sentences correctly?

Subject-Verb Agreement

Are You a Drummer?

Our band are looking for you!
Does you have good rhythm? Can you
play up-beat music? Give us a call! We
needs a responsible team player with a
good sense of humor. Show-offs needs
not apply.

We has these drums
for you to use!

Theme: Elements of Personality

Agreeable People

These band members need to get their act together! They need
a drummer who'll fit their music style and whose personality will
fit well with their own. They want someone who will come to
rehearsals, someone who will share ideas—someone agreeable.

In addition to all this, they need to work on the agreement
of their subjects and verbs. Can you find the errors in their
poster? Subject-verb agreement is important for communication in writing. Mistakes in agreement may confuse, frustrate,
or annoy your readers. This chapter will help you use subjects
and verbs correctly.

Write Away: Celebrity Profile
Write a biographical sketch about a musician you admire,
whether it's someone famous or someone you know. Focus on
the elements of this musician's personality and how they
contribute to his or her music. Then save your writing in your
📁 **Working Portfolio.**

CD-ROM Grammar Coach

Diagnostic Test: What Do You Know?

For each numbered item, choose the letter of the best revision.

Who are you? <u>You doesn't seem</u> exactly like anyone else. Your
(1)
personality is the particular pattern of how you think, feel, and
act. <u>Heredity and environment shapes</u> your personality from the
(2)
time you are born. <u>Both influence</u> whether you are shy, good-
(3)
natured, or aggressive. <u>Scientists studying human behavior</u>
(4)
<u>believes</u> you inherit certain traits. However, your <u>surroundings</u>
(5)
<u>also affect</u> the kind of person you are. <u>Your family play</u> an
(6)
important role in your personality development, for instance, as do
your school, your community, and your cultural heritage. From
this combination of influences <u>result your unique personality</u>. <u>No</u>
(7)
<u>one else are quite like you.</u>
(8)

1. A. You doesn't seemed
   B. You don't seems
   C. You don't seem
   D. Correct as is

2. A. Heredity and environment
      is shaping
   B. Heredity and environment
      shape
   C. Heredity and environment
      has shaped
   D. Correct as is

3. A. Both influences
   B. Both has influenced
   C. Both is influencing
   D. Correct as is

4. A. Scientists studying human
      behavior are believing
   B. Scientists studying human
      behavior has believed
   C. Scientists studying human
      behavior believe
   D. Correct as is

5. A. surroundings also affects
   B. surroundings also does affect
   C. surroundings also has
      affected
   D. Correct as is

6. A. Your family plays
   B. Your family are playing
   C. Your family have been
      playing
   D. Correct as is

7. A. results your unique
      personality
   B. have resulted your unique
      personality
   C. are resulting your unique
      personality
   D. Correct as is

8. A. No one else was quite
      like you.
   B. No one else is quite like you.
   C. No one else are being quite
      like you.
   D. Correct as is

Agreement in Number

❶ Here's the Idea

▶ **A verb must agree with its subject in number.**

Number refers to whether a word is singular or plural. A word that refers to one person, place, thing, idea, action, or condition is singular. A word that refers to more than one is plural.

Singular and Plural Subjects

▶ **Singular subjects take singular verbs.**

AGREE ↙ SINGULAR VERB
Marla works cooperatively with her classmates.
↑ SINGULAR SUBJECT

She listens carefully to their suggestions.

▶ **Plural subjects take plural verbs.**

AGREE ↙ PLURAL VERB
The players work together well as a team.
↑ PLURAL SUBJECT

They listen carefully to the coach.

 Most nouns that end in s or es are plural. For example, *players* is a plural noun. However, most verbs that end in s are singular. *Works* is a singular verb form.

Verb Phrases

▶ **In a verb phrase, it is the first helping verb that agrees with the subject.** A verb phrase is made up of a main verb and one or more helping verbs.

AGREE
Lou has volunteered for the teen hotline.
↑ SINGULAR HELPING VERB

AGREE
He is answering calls from troubled kids.

AGREE

Callers have asked **for help.**
↖ PLURAL VERB

AGREE

They have been seeking **advice from their peers.**

Contractions *Doesn't* and *Don't*

Two contractions we often use are *doesn't* and *don't*. Use *doesn't* with all singular subjects except *I* and *you*. Use *don't* with all plural subjects and with the pronouns *I* and *you*.

Tiffany doesn't attend **folk concerts.**
SINGULAR VERB: does + not = doesn't

You don't like **to shop.**
WITH PRONOUN *YOU:* do + not = don't

They don't enjoy **noisy, crowded malls.**
PLURAL VERB: do + not = don't

❷ Why It Matters in Writing

When you revise your writing, you sometimes change a subject from singular to plural, or vice versa. When you revise, errors in subject-verb agreement can occur. Check your final draft carefully to make sure that the verb agrees with the new subject.

STUDENT MODEL

DRAFT

Tomorrow's tryout is not just a popularity contest. The **cheerleaders** need upbeat students with school spirit and athletic ability.

REVISION

Tomorrow's tryout is not just a popularity contest. The cheerleading **squad** needs upbeat students with school spirit and athletic ability.

➌ Practice and Apply

A. CONCEPT CHECK: Agreement in Number

For each sentence, write the verb that agrees with the subject.

Birds of a Feather

1. A popular saying (is, are) "Opposites attract."
2. On the contrary, we (doesn't, don't) often seek relationships with people who hold values and attitudes different from our own.
3. Personality clashes (spoils, spoil) relationships.
4. Differences (creates, create) tension.
5. Typically, a talkative person (prefers, prefer) the company of other sociable people.
6. A quiet individual sometimes (feels, feel) more comfortable with fellow introverts.
7. Teens usually (selects, select) friends who are most like them.
8. They sometimes (forms, form) tight-knit groups called cliques.
9. Still, friendships (has, have) developed among those with different personalities.
10. Open communication (helps, help) all kinds of friends to get along.

→ For a SELF-CHECK and more practice, see the EXERCISE BANK, p. 631.

B. PROOFREADING: Checking Subject-Verb Agreement

The following paragraph has five errors in subject-verb agreement. Rewrite the paragraph, correcting the errors.

Sometimes the best friends is the ones you least expect. More than once I has met someone I didn't grow to like for several years. When I met my friend Kelli two years ago, she were obnoxious and I couldn't stand her. Now we hangs out almost every day! She don't seem like the same person I once met.

C. REVISING: Using Correct Subject-Verb Agreement

Return to the **Write Away** you completed on page 206. If it is written in the past tense, revise it to be in the present tense. Then make sure that your subjects and verbs agree in number.

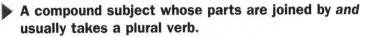

Compound Subjects

LESSON 2

❶ Here's the Idea

A **compound subject** is made up of two or more subjects joined by a conjunction such as *and, or,* or *nor.*

Subjects Joined by *And*

▶ **A compound subject whose parts are joined by *and* usually takes a plural verb.**

Career counselors and employers match **people with the right jobs.**

Sometimes a compound subject joined by *and* refers to a single thing or idea, so a singular verb is used.

Law and order appeals **strongly to Veronica.**

Subjects Joined by *Or* or *Nor*

▶ **When the parts of a compound subject are joined by *or* or *nor,* the verb should agree with the part closest to it.**

AGREE

Neither outdoor work nor office tasks suit **Matt very well.**

AGREE

Neither office tasks nor outdoor work suits **Matt very well.**

❷ Why It Matters in Writing

When revising their work, writers sometimes reverse the order of compound subjects. When you do this in your own writing, you may need to change the verb so that it agrees with the nearer part of the subject.

Babysitting or odd jobs are **what I like.**

Odd jobs or babysitting is **what I like.**

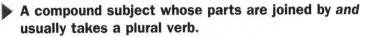S-V AGREEMENT

❸ Practice and Apply

A. CONCEPT CHECK: Compound Subjects

Proofread each of the following sentences to find the mistakes in subject-verb agreement. Then rewrite the sentence correctly. If a sentence contains no error, write *Correct*.

Working Ways

1. Psychologists and guidance counselors have linked personality types to occupations.
2. For example, carpentry or engineering sometimes attract introverted people.
3. Paramedics and police officers seeks adventure and risk.
4. On the other hand, structure and order suits those with good organizational ability.
5. Bookkeepers or office managers typically has stable, practical personalities.
6. Problem-solving skills and strong verbal communication is useful for judges and businesspeople.
7. Generally, neither lawyers nor the head of a company like to be told what to do.
8. Logic or good spatial perception is needed for jobs in engineering and mechanics.
9. Trial and error are one way to find the right job.
10. Neither your teacher nor your parents want to see you in a job that doesn't suit you.

➔ For a SELF-CHECK and more practice, see the EXERCISE BANK, p. 631.

B. REVISING: Making Compound Subjects and Verbs Agree

Revise the following announcement by reversing the order of the compound subjects. Make sure that the verbs agree with the new order. There are four compound subjects.

Calling All Theatrical Types

Auditions for *Hello, Dolly!* will be held on Thursday at 3 P.M. The musical score or scripts are available from Mr. Testaverde, Room 202. Actors and the lighting director report to the auditorium. Sound-effects creators and musicians come to the music room. Neither props nor a costume is needed to audition.

Agreement Problems in Sentences

❶ Here's the Idea

Some sentences can be tricky, such as those with subjects in unusual positions, those containing predicate nouns, or those in which prepositional phrases separate subjects and verbs. Here are some tips for choosing the correct verb forms in these situations.

Subjects in Unusual Positions

A subject can follow a verb or part of a verb phrase in a question, a sentence beginning with *here* or *there*, or a sentence in which an adjective, an adverb, or a phrase is placed first.

Madeline Albright is a first-born.

Subjects in Unusual Positions

Type of Sentence	Examples
Question	Does birth **order** shape personality?
Sentence beginning with *here* or *there*	Here **are** some famous **first-borns** with successful careers.
Sentence beginning with phrase	From years of study **come** our **ideas** about birth order.

The following tips can help you find the subject in one of these kinds of sentences.

Here's How) Choosing the Correct Verb

(Is, Are) last-borns more rebellious than middle children?

1. Turn the sentence around, putting the subject before the verb.
   Last-borns (is, are) more rebellious than middle children.

Is Robin Williams a last-born?

2. Determine whether the subject is singular or plural.
   Last-borns (plural)

3. Make sure the subject and verb agree.
   Last-borns are more rebellious than middle children.

Predicate Nouns

In a sentence containing a predicate noun, the verb should agree with the subject, not the predicate noun.

AGREE

One interesting topic is dreams and their meaning.

AGREE

Dreams are the voice of the subconscious.

Prepositional Phrases

The subject of a verb is never found in a prepositional phrase. Don't be fooled by words that come between a subject and a verb. Mentally block out those words. Then it will be easy to tell whether the subject is singular or plural.

AGREE

This book by two psychologists describes personality traits.

AGREE

Some theories of personality development are complex.

❷ Why It Matters in Writing

Writers often use prepositional phrases to paint visual pictures. When you use a prepositional phrase between a subject and a verb, make sure that the verb agrees with the subject, not the object of the preposition.

LITERARY MODEL

At one o'clock in the morning I walked down through the same section [of San Francisco]. Everything still stood intact. There was no fire. And yet there was a change. A **rain** of ashes was falling.

PREPOSITIONAL PHRASE

—Jack London, "The Story of an Eyewitness"

➌ Practice and Apply

A. CONCEPT CHECK: Agreement Problems in Sentences

Correct problems with subject-verb agreement in the sentences below. If a sentence contains no error, write *Correct*.

Pet Personality
1. Does pets have personalities?
2. Studies of animal behavior suggest differences in temperament.
3. There is many cats and dogs with distinctive traits.
4. For example, pit bulls is an aggressive breed of terrier.
5. On the other hand, a chihuahua is a very timid dog.
6. From careful observation comes new insights into pet behavior.
7. Heredity is one factor in determining what your pet is like.
8. There is some pets with serious behavioral problems.
9. Has you ever seen a cat chew wool?
10. On local radio stations play a popular call-in show for pet owners.

➜ For a SELF-CHECK and more practice, see the EXERCISE BANK, p. 632.

B. PROOFREADING AND EDITING: Correcting Agreement Errors

Find the four errors in subject verb agreement in this paragraph. Then change the verbs to agree with the subjects.

Twin Traits
Does you know any identical twins? Then you can probably observe their obvious physical similarities. Although people commonly believe that identical twins raised apart will develop different personalities, the opposite appears to be true. From studies at the University of Minnesota have been gathered information comparing the personality traits of twins separated after birth. There are evidence that separated twins still develop similar traits. Apparently, genes is an important factor in personality development.

Indefinite Pronouns as Subjects

❶ Here's the Idea

Some pronouns do not refer to a definite, or specific, person, place, thing, or idea. These pronouns are called **indefinite pronouns**.

▶ **When used as subjects, some indefinite pronouns are always singular, some are always plural, and others can be singular or plural, depending on how they're used.**

Indefinite Pronouns			
Singular	another	anybody	anyone
	anything	each	either
	everybody	everyone	everything
	neither	nobody	no one
	nothing	one	somebody
	someone	something	
Plural	both few many several		
Singular or Plural	all any most none some		

Singular indefinite pronouns take singular verbs.

Everyone wonders **how twins get along.**

Anything about twins fascinates **me.**

Plural indefinite pronouns take plural verbs.

Many of my friends know **a pair of twins.**

Several are **twins themselves.**

Both of the twins are wearing **red robes.**
Each of the twins is wearing **sunglasses.**

Singular or Plural?

The indefinite pronouns *all, any, most, none,* and *some* can be either singular or plural. When you use one of these words as a subject, think about the noun it refers to. If the noun is singular, use a singular verb; if it is plural, use a plural verb.

REFERS TO

Most of this book deals with twin research.

REFERS TO

All of the studies have been conducted by scientists.

WATCH OUT

Sometimes an indefinite pronoun refers to a noun in a previous sentence.

Sometimes Myla and Melissa coincidentally buy the same outfit. Both are surprised to find out.
INDEFINITE PRONOUN 🢂   🢁 PLURAL VERB

S-V AGREEMENT

❷ Why It Matters in Writing

When you write about the results of a classroom survey, you may use a number of indefinite pronouns as subjects. Using correct subject-verb agreement makes it easier for readers to understand your writing.

STUDENT MODEL

Many of the students surveyed know at least one pair of identical twins. Some feel that they cannot tell the twins apart, and a few have close friends who are twins. Of those students, all find that it gets easier to tell twins apart once they know them better.

SUBJECT

VERB

❸ Practice and Apply

A. CONCEPT CHECK: Indefinite Pronouns as Subjects

Proofread each of the following sentences. Then rewrite the sentences in which the verb does not agree with its subject. If a sentence is correct, write *Correct*.

Like Peas in a Pod

1. Some of my relatives has twins in their families.
2. Several have volunteered for twin research projects.
3. No one have explained why identical twins behave so similarly.
4. Many of the researchers believes that these twins act alike because they have the same genes.
5. Some feels that the similarities are due to a common upbringing.
6. Among twins, many have strange stories to tell.
7. Ask Royce and Brett; none of their friends likes to play certain games with them.
8. Each of the boys know what the other is thinking, so they have a competitive advantage.
9. Do anyone know how to explain this? At summer camp, twin sisters start singing in their sleep.
10. Both sing the same song!

➜ For a SELF-CHECK and more practice, see the EXERCISE BANK, p. 632.

B: WRITING: Agreement with Indefinite Pronouns

Have you seen these twins? Marian and Vivian Brown live in San Francisco. Write a caption for this photograph using indefinite pronouns. Then proofread your caption, checking for correct subject-verb agreement.

Problem Subjects

❶ Here's the Idea

When collective nouns, nouns ending in s, titles, and numerical expressions are used as subjects, it can be difficult to tell whether they take singular or plural verbs.

Collective Nouns

Collective nouns name groups of people or things.

Common Collective Nouns
group   class   team   staff   jury   family   committee

▶ **Many collective nouns can take singular or plural verbs, depending on how they are used.** When a collective noun refers to people or things acting as a group, it takes a singular verb.

> **The choir performs each year in the talent show.**
> (THE CHOIR MEMBERS ARE ACTING TOGETHER.)

When a collective noun refers to people or things acting as individuals, it takes a plural verb.

> **The choir come from three different schools.**
> (THE CHOIR MEMBERS ARE ACTING AS INDIVIDUALS.)

Singular Nouns Ending in *s*

▶ **Some nouns that end in s or *ics* look plural but are actually singular.** When used as subjects, they take singular verbs.

Singular Nouns with Plural Forms
measles   news   politics   mathematics
physics   economics   ceramics   molasses

AGREE

> **Politics attracts people with strong leadership qualities.**

> **The weekend news features local personalities.**

Titles

▶ **Titles of works of art, literature, and music are singular.**
Even a title consisting of a plural noun takes a singular verb.

The Outsiders is a popular young-adult novel.

Measures and Amounts

▶ **Words and phrases that express weights, measures, numbers, and lengths of time are often treated as singular.** They take singular verbs when they refer to amounts rather than numbers of individual items.

Measures and Amounts		
Measures	three cups forty miles	**Three pounds is** the approximate weight of an adult human's brain.
Amounts	two hours eight dollars	**Five hours is** a long time to wait for lunch.

A fraction can take a singular or plural verb, depending on whether it refers to a single part or to a number of items.

One-tenth of the brain's cells are lost during a lifetime.
(THE FRACTION REFERS TO A NUMBER OF CELLS.)

One-half of the cerebrum controls the body's left side.
(THE FRACTION REFERS TO ONE PART OF THE CEREBRUM.)

❷ Why It Matters in Writing

When you write about science or the history of science, you often need to use collective nouns, singular nouns that end in *s*, titles, weights, measures, and numbers. Be sure that your verbs agree with these problem subjects.

> **PROFESSIONAL MODEL**
>
> **Genetics,** or the study of heredity, was developed by an Austrian monk named Gregor Mendel. The **1860s** was the decade when he discovered the principles of genetics by observing that garden peas inherited traits in a way that he could predict.
>
> —Kathryn Strickland

➌ Practice and Apply

A. CONCEPT CHECK: Problem Subjects

Correct problems with subject-verb agreement in the sentences below. If a sentence contains no error, write *Correct*.

The Notion of Emotion

1. Pediatrics are the branch of medicine dealing with infants and children.
2. Our class learns the four emotions that newborns experience: excitement, surprise, relaxation, and distress.
3. Six weeks are the age when infants first express joy.
4. Twelve months is when babies first experience sadness.
5. Linguistics indicate that babies begin to imitate speech sounds at the age of eight months.
6. Two-thirds of the daycare group are absent today.
7. Five minutes seem a long time until parents arrive.
8. The family reacts to a child's different responses.
9. The public often seek advice about raising a child.
10. *Dr. Spock's Baby and Child Care* is a classic book.

➡ **For a SELF-CHECK and more practice, see the EXERCISE BANK, p. 633.**

B. WRITING: Agreement with Problem Subjects

Choose the correct verb forms to complete the sentences that interpret the bar graph.

1. Four-fifths of the children in Evansville (attends, attend) daycare.
2. One-fifth of the children (stays, stay) at home.
3. Six hours a day (is, are) the length of time two-fifths of the children spend at daycare.

Child Care in Evansville

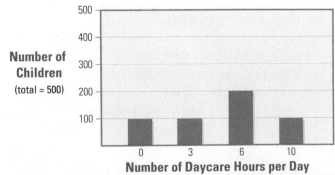

Grammar in Literature

Creative Writing and Subject-Verb Agreement

As you write, you may change from one tense to another. For example, you may choose to write descriptions or dialogues in the present tense. You may choose to write about past events in the past tense. When you choose to write in the present tense, you need to pay special attention to subject-verb agreement. As you read the passage from "A Mother in Mannville," notice the subjects and the verbs. Some verbs are in the present tense, others are past, but all of them agree with their subjects.

A MOTHER in MANNVILLE

by Marjorie Kinnan Rawlings

The orphanage is high in the Carolina mountains. Sometimes in winter the snowdrifts are so deep that the institution is cut off from the village below, from all the world. Fog hides the mountain peaks, the snow swirls down the valleys, and a wind blows so bitterly that the orphanage boys who take the milk twice daily to the baby cottage reach the door with fingers stiff in an agony of numbness.

"Or when we carry trays from the cook house for the ones that are sick," Jerry said, "we get our faces frostbit, because we can't put our hands over them. I have gloves," he added. "Some of the boys don't have any."

He liked the late spring, he said. The rhododendron was in bloom, a carpet of color, across the mountainsides, soft as the May winds that stirred the hemlocks. He called it laurel.

> **SINGULAR SUBJECTS AND VERBS**
>
> **PLURAL SUBJECTS AND VERBS**

Practice and Apply

A. DRAFTING: Using Different Tenses

The following passage from "A Mother in Mannville" is written in the past and past perfect tenses.

> He sat by the fire with me, with no other light, and told me of their two days together. The dog lay close to him and found a comfort there that I did not have for him. And it seemed to me that being with my dog, and caring for him, had brought the boy and me, too, together, so that he felt that he belonged to me as well as to the animal.

Imagine that as an author you are experimenting with the most effective tense to use for a scene like the one above. Write a version of the scene in the present tense. Notice that you need to pay attention to the subjects in order to choose the correct forms of the verbs. Check your subject-verb agreement.

S-V AGREEMENT

B. WRITING: Description

Think of a place you know well. Write a few characteristics of that place and the people, animals, or things that you find there. Then name the actions that people, animals, or things might do. Write a description of this place in the present tense. Watch out for subject-verb agreement. Put your description in your ☐ **Working Portfolio.**

After the Chase (1965), Andrew Wyeth. Wichita (Kansas) Art Museum.

223

A. Agreement in Number, Compound Subjects, and Indefinite Pronouns
Write the form of the verb that agrees with the subject of each sentence.

1. Everybody (has, have) a favorite character in a book or play.
2. Novelists and playwrights (creates, create) memorable portraits based on real or imaginary people.
3. A writer (uses, use) vivid description to bring characters to life.
4. Character traits such as honesty or shyness (is, are) developed through characterization.
5. For example, a character's own words or behavior (conveys, convey) his or her personality.
6. The words and actions of other characters also (reveals, reveal) character traits.
7. A main character usually (experiences, experience) the most development and growth.
8. Some of the most interesting characters (acts, act) courageously.
9. Many (changes, change) during the course of a novel or play.
10. A story with well-developed characters (entertains, entertain) readers.

B. Additional Agreement Problems Read the following newspaper help-wanted ad, identify the subject and verb in each sentence, and then correct the five errors in subject-verb agreement.

Section

.e
A-
s.
re
ey
ree
car
nd

se-
ub-
any
ar-

Do you like animals? Is you outgoing and well-spoken? Our demonstration team have a position for you.

The Pretty Pet Company seeks responsible, energetic individuals to demonstrate our exciting line of pet products. The company offer free training and flexible, part-time hours. Ten dollars are the hourly rate. Travel to pet stores throughout the tri-state area are required. For more information, please contact Mr. Finley, Ext. 315.

Choose the letter of the best revision for each underlined section.

The business world is highly competitive. Small businesses and
(1)   (2)
large corporations wants the right person for a job. Many gives
(3)
personality tests to evaluate the attitudes, behavior, and skills of
potential employees. Ten dollars are the average fee for a
(4)
personality test. A test for high-level executives costs $2,000. Since
(5)
personality tests help match applicants with jobs, many companies
use them to help in hiring. Some of these companies lose fewer
(6)
employees and increase productivity. There is concerns, however,
(7)
about the tests' accuracy and fairness. Critics questions whether
(8)
these tests discriminate against qualified workers.

S-V AGREEMENT

1. A. The business world are
   B. The business worlds are
   C. The business world was
   D. Correct as is

2. A. Small businesses and large
      corporations has wanted
   B. Small businesses and large
      corporations want
   C. Small businesses and large
      corporations is wanting
   D. Correct as is

3. A. Many is giving personality
      tests
   B. Many has given personality
      tests
   C. Many give personality tests
   D. Correct as is

4. A. Ten dollars is the average
      fee
   B. Ten dollars have been the
      average fee
   C. Ten dollars were the
      average fee
   D. Correct as is

5. A. A test for high-level
      executives cost
   B. A test for high-level
      executives are costing
   C. A test for high-level
      executives have cost
   D. Correct as is

6. A. Some of these company
      loses
   B. Some of these companies
      loses
   C. Some of these companies
      is losing
   D. Correct as is

7. A. There has been concerns
   B. There are concerns
   C. There was concerns
   D. Correct as is

8. A. Critics question
   B. Critics has questioned
   C. Critics is questioning
   D. Correct as is

Student Help Desk

Subject-Verb Agreement at a Glance

A singular subject takes a singular verb.

A plural subject takes a plural verb.

An extrovert likes social activities.

Introverts prefer being alone.

Subjects and Verbs	Tricky Cases
Verb phrase The first helping verb should agree with the subject.	**Jo** is playing darts. My **friends** are playing chess.
Prepositional phrase between subject and verb The subject of a verb is never in a prepositional phrase.	The **boys** down the street are shy.
Compound subject containing *and* Always use a plural verb.	**Soo** and **Meg** talk all the time.
Compound subject containing *or* **or** *nor* The verb should agree with the part of the subject closest to it.	Neither my **parents** nor my **sister** enjoys music.
Indefinite pronoun as subject Singular pronouns take singular verbs; plural pronouns take plural verbs. Some pronouns can be singular or plural.	**Everyone** thinks about the brain. **Few** understand it. **Most** of the research focuses on disorders. **Most** of the studies focus on disorders.
Collective noun Use a singular verb if it refers to a whole, a plural verb if it refers to individuals.	The **group** meets on Saturday. The **group** argue about the meeting time.
Singular noun ending in *s* Use a singular verb.	**Genetics** deals with inherited traits.
Title or amount Usually use a singular verb.	***Strange Personalities*** is my favorite book.

Other Agreement Problems

How to Deal with *Slippery* Subjects

Predicate noun Make sure the verb agrees with the subject.	**Teenagers** are the population with many identity questions. The **population** with many identity questions is teenagers.
Question Change the question to a statement to find the subject.	(Is, Are) personality tests a useful tool? Personality **tests** are a useful tool.
Sentence beginning with • *Here or There* • **phrase** Turn the sentence around to find the subject.	Here (is, are) a popular psychology course. A popular psychology **course** is here. On the shelf (is, are) stacked textbooks. **Textbooks** are stacked on the shelf.

S-V AGREEMENT

The Bottom Line

Checklist for Subject-Verb Agreement

Have I . . .

____ used a singular verb with a singular subject?

____ used a plural verb with a plural subject?

____ made the helping verb in a verb phrase agree with the subject?

____ used a plural verb with compound subjects joined by *and?*

____ made the verb agree with the closest part of a compound subject joined by *or* or *nor?*

____ checked whether indefinite-pronoun subjects are singular or plural?

____ used singular verbs with subjects that are titles, measures, or amounts?

____ made verbs agree with subjects in unusual positions?

Capitalization

| Back | Forward | Reload | Home | Images | Print | Security | Stop |

Location:

Wonders of the World Virtual Tour

learn more about the taj mahal by clicking on the pictures.

taj mahal

princess Mumtaz mahal

emperor shah jahan

Shah Jahan holding a turban jewel (detail), Victoria & Albert Museum, London/Art Resource, N.Y.

Theme: Wonders of the World

Passport to the Wonders

If you were writing a report on man-made wonders, would you use the Web page shown on this page as a reliable source? Most people would probably not trust it because there are too many capitalization errors on the page. The rules of capitalization are just as important as spelling and grammar rules.

Write Away: Just Wonder
The Taj Mahal is considered one of the world's most beautiful and famous tombs. In a short paragraph, describe a place that you find amazing. It could be an interesting public building, a breathtaking natural area, or an unusual amusement park. Save your paragraph in your 🗀 **Working Portfolio.**

CD-ROM **Grammar Coach**

For each underlined passage, choose the letter of the correct revision.

The Taj mahal, considered a man-made wonder, symbolizes the
(1)   (2)
country of india. It was built by Shah jahan, Mogul emperor of
(3)   (4)
India, in memory of his wife Mumtaz Mahal. He had vowed to
(5)
build her the most beautiful tomb ever imagined. He chose a site

by the Jumna river in agra, India, and consulted with craftsmen
(6)   (7)
from All over central Asia and european experts from France and
(8)   (9)
Italy. With its slender towers and onion-shaped dome, an islamic

symbol of both womanhood and paradise, the Taj Mahal has a
(10)
fairytale quality. The white marble of the monument seems to take

on different personalities at different times of the day. The inside

of the tomb is decorated with carved marble screens inlaid with

precious and semiprecious stones.

1. A. taj mahal
   B. taj Mahal
   C. Taj Mahal
   D. Correct as is

2. A. Symbolizes
   B. Country
   C. India
   D. Correct as is

3. A. Shah Jahan
   B. shah jahan
   C. shah Jahan
   D. Correct as is

4. A. Emperor of India
   B. Emperor of india
   C. emperor of india
   D. Correct as is

5. A. wife mumtaz mahal
   B. Wife Mumtaz mahal
   C. Wife Mumtaz Mahal
   D. Correct as is

6. A. The Jumna River
   B. the Jumna River
   C. the jumna river
   D. Correct as is

7. A. Agra, India, and Consulted
   B. Agra, India, and consulted
   C. Agra, India, And consulted
   D. Correct as is

8. A. all Over Central Asia
   B. all over central asia
   C. all over central Asia
   D. Correct as is

9. A. European Experts
   B. france and italy
   C. European experts
   D. Correct as is

10. A. Islamic Symbol
    B. Islamic symbol
    C. Womanhood and Paradise
    D. Correct as is

LESSON 1 People and Cultures

❶ Here's the Idea

Names and Initials

▶ **Capitalize people's names and initials.**

Cleopatra   **J.R.R.** Tolkien

Maria **T**heresa   Yasunari **K**awabata

Personal Titles and Abbreviations

▶ **Capitalize titles and abbreviations of titles that are used before names and in direct address.**

Professor Anita Jones   **D**r. Celia Brammer

Cardinal Richelieu   **G**eneral Dwight D. Eisenhower

Mr. and **M**s. Romer wrote a book entitled *The Seven Wonders of the World*.

Capitalize abbreviations of some titles when they follow names.

Ted Stein, **Jr.**   Sonia Rodriguez, **M.D.**

Mary Witt, **Ph.D.**   Meridyth Palmer, **D.D.S.**

▶ **Capitalize titles of heads of state, royalty, or nobility only when they are used before persons' names or in place of persons' names.**

Queen Marie Antoinette   **S**ir Thomas Browne

Chief **J**ustice William H. Rehnquist

The temple of Artemis at Ephesus was built by **K**ing Croesus.

Do not capitalize titles when they are used without proper names.

The **k**ing will be remembered for his contributions to great architecture.

The Ruins at Ephesus

Family Relationships

▶ **Capitalize words indicating family relationships only when they are used as names or before names.**

Aunt Paula   Cousin Sue   Grandpa Klein

Dad and Mom would like to see the Great Pyramid in Egypt.

In general, do not capitalize a word indicating a family relationship when it follows the person's name or is used without a proper name.

Maria Tellez, my cousin, saw the Great Pyramid.

My aunt and uncle will see the Leaning Tower of Pisa.

The Pronoun *I*

▶ **Always capitalize the pronoun *I*.**

Grandpa and I read all about Stonehenge.

Religious Terms

▶ **Capitalize the names of religions, sacred days, sacred writings, and deities.**

Religions and Religious Terms	
Religions	Christianity, Hinduism, Judaism
Sacred days	Ramadan, Good Friday, Purim
Sacred writings	Bible, Koran, Torah
Deities	God, Yahweh, Allah

Do not capitalize the words *god* and *goddess* when they refer to gods of ancient mythology.

The statue of Zeus at Olympia honored the Greek god Zeus.

Nationalities, Languages, and Races

▶ **Capitalize the names of nationalities, languages, races, and most ethnic groups, as well as the adjectives formed from these names.**

Romans	**M**asai	**G**reek
Incan	**A**frican-**A**merican	**E**gyptian

❷ Practice and Apply

CONCEPT CHECK: People and Cultures

Write the words, abbreviations, and initials that should be capitalized in the paragraph below, and capitalize each correctly. If a sentence has no errors, write the word *Correct.*

Vanished Wonders

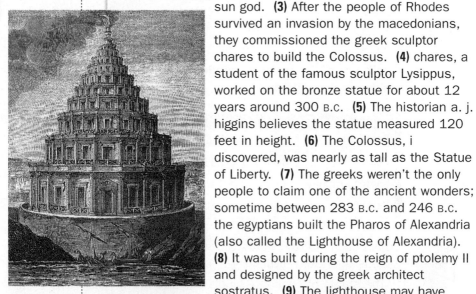

(1) In the book *Wonders of the World*, giovanni caselli gives a history of the Colossus of Rhodes. **(2)** The Colossus of Rhodes was a huge statue of helios, the Greek sun god. **(3)** After the people of Rhodes survived an invasion by the macedonians, they commissioned the greek sculptor chares to build the Colossus. **(4)** chares, a student of the famous sculptor Lysippus, worked on the bronze statue for about 12 years around 300 B.C. **(5)** The historian a. j. higgins believes the statue measured 120 feet in height. **(6)** The Colossus, i discovered, was nearly as tall as the Statue of Liberty. **(7)** The greeks weren't the only people to claim one of the ancient wonders; sometime between 283 B.C. and 246 B.C. the egyptians built the Pharos of Alexandria (also called the Lighthouse of Alexandria). **(8)** It was built during the reign of ptolemy II and designed by the greek architect sostratus. **(9)** The lighthouse may have been nearly 400 feet tall (larger than the Colossus and the Statue of Liberty), but an earthquake destroyed it after it had stood for almost 1,500 years.

Lighthouse of Alexandria

➡ For a SELF-CHECK and more practice, see the EXERCISE BANK, p. 633.

First Words and Titles

❶ Here's the Idea

Sentences and Poetry

▶ **Capitalize the first word of every sentence.**

The "seven wonders of the medieval world" date back to the Middle Ages.

▶ **In traditional poetry capitalize the first word of every line.**

LITERARY MODEL

The willow is like an etching,
Fine-lined against the sky.
The ginkgo is like a crude sketch,
Hardly worthy to be signed.
                    —Eve Merriam, "Simile: Willow and Ginkgo"

Modern poets sometimes choose not to begin each line of their poems with capital letters. If you make this choice in your own writing, make sure the meaning of your work is still clear.

Quotations

▶ **Capitalize the first word of a direct quotation if it begins a complete sentence.**

My teacher asked, "**H**as anyone read about the Colosseum?"

▶ **In a divided quotation, do not capitalize the first word of the second part unless it starts a new sentence.**

"I hear you're going to Italy," Theresa said. "**M**ake sure you see the Leaning Tower of Pisa."

"Did you know," asked Theresa, "**t**hat the Leaning Tower has been tilting for 800 years?"

Outlines

▶ **Capitalize the first word of each entry in an outline and the letters that introduce major subsections.**

I. **F**amous buildings of the Middle Ages
   A. The Leaning Tower of Pisa
      1. **C**onstruction of bell tower
      2. **R**epairs to tower foundation
   B. The Tower of London
      1. **C**onstruction of royal fortress
      2. **A**dditions to original site

Parts of a Letter

▶ **Capitalize the first word in the greeting and in the closing of a letter.**

Dear Ms. Song: **Y**ours truly,

Leaning Tower of Pisa

Titles

▶ **Capitalize the first word, the last word, and all other important words in a title. Don't capitalize articles, coordinating conjunctions, or prepositions of fewer than five letters.**

Type of Media	Examples
Books	*The House of Dies Drear, A Wrinkle in Time*
Plays and musicals	*The Phantom of the Opera, The Miracle Worker*
Short stories	"The Tell-Tale Heart," "The Bet"
Poems	"Legacies," "Jazz Fantasia"
Magazines and newspapers	*YM, Next Generation, The New York Times*
Musical compositions	Beethoven's Fifth Symphony," Jingle Bells"
Movies	*The Lion King, The Wizard of Oz, Home Alone*
Television shows	*The Practice, Dateline NBC, Total Request Live*
Works of art	*Starry Night, Venus de Milo*
Games	Warzone, TV Trivia, Brain Busters

❷ Practice and Apply

A. CONCEPT CHECK: First Words and Titles

Write the words that should be capitalized in each sentence.
Do not write words that are already capitalized.

The Secrets of Stonehenge

1. Kendra asked the tour guide, "what is Stonehenge?"

2. The tour guide responded, "it is an ancient monument on a plain in England, composed of huge rough-cut stones set in a circle."

3. "why are the stones there?" she continued. "what is their purpose?"

4. the guide answered, "that's something that no one knows."

5. "we do know that the ancient people who built Stonehenge were building something of great importance," she added. "It was probably used as a tribal gathering place."

6. She continued, "there is also evidence that the stones were used as some sort of huge astronomical calendar."

7. The meaning of Stonehenge was first discussed around 1139 in the book *history of the kings of Britain*.

8. A modern book titled *stonehenge complete* covers every detail concerning the ancient monument.

9. Writer Henry James once wrote about Stonehenge, "you may put a hundred questions to these rough-hewn giants as they bend in grim contemplation of their fallen companions."

10. An outline for stone circles in England might begin like this:

    I. stone circles in England

        A. stonehenge

        B. Avebury

➜ **For a SELF-CHECK and more practice, see the EXERCISE BANK, p. 634.**

Stonehenge

B. WRITING: A Trip to the Stones

Write a letter to a travel agency, inquiring if its tours of England go to any stone-circle sites, such as Stonehenge. Remember to capitalize the first word in the greeting and in the closing of your letter.

Places and Transportation

❶ Here's the Idea

Geographical Names

▶ In geographical names, capitalize each word except articles and prepositions.

Geographical Names	
Divisions of the world	Southern Hemisphere, Continental Divide, Tropic of Cancer
Continents	Africa, North America, Australia
Bodies of water	Mediterranean Sea, Gulf of Mexico, Indian Ocean
Islands	Java, Bahamas, Easter Island
Mountains	Mount Everest, Sierra Nevada, Mount Olympus
Other landforms	Victoria Falls, Grand Canyon, Gobi Desert
Regions	Latin America, Southeast Asia, New England
Countries/nations	Greece, Italy, China, England
States	North Carolina, Maine, Colorado, Texas
Cities/towns	San Francisco, Miami, Fort Wayne, Austin
Roads and streets	Interstate 90, North Street, Prairie Road

Bodies of the Universe

▶ Capitalize the names of planets and other specific objects in the universe.

Big Dipper   Pluto   North Star

WATCH OUT

Do not capitalize *sun* and *moon*. Do not capitalize *earth* when it is preceded by *the* and when it does not refer to the planet Earth.

Ants and earwigs tunneled through the earth under the porch.

Venus is called Earth's twin.

CHAPTER 10

Regions and Sections

▶ **Capitalize the words *north, south, east,* and *west* when they name particular regions of the United States or the world or when they are parts of proper names.**

The Golden Gate Bridge, the Empire State Building, and the Houston Astrodome are all modern wonders found in **N**orth America.

The Grand Canyon is one of the most popular tourist attractions in the **W**est.

Do not capitalize these words when they indicate general directions or locations.

The Statue of Liberty is **s**outh of the Empire State Building in New York City.

Buildings, Bridges, and Other Landmarks

▶ **Capitalize the names of specific buildings, bridges, monuments, and other landmarks.**

Sears **T**ower   **G**reat **W**all of **C**hina

Big **B**en   **T**acoma **N**arrows **B**ridge

Many people consider the **S**ydney **O**pera **H**ouse in Sydney, Australia, to be a modern wonder.

Planes, Trains, and Other Vehicles

▶ **Capitalize the names of specific airplanes, trains, ships, cars, and spacecraft.**

Vehicle Names	
Airplanes	*Air Force One, Memphis Belle*
Trains	*Orient Express, City of New Orleans*
Ships	*Mayflower, Niña, Seawise Giant*
Cars	*Cavalier, Taurus, Grand Prix*
Spacecraft	*Sputnik, Challenger, Voyager 2*

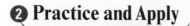

❷ Practice and Apply

A. CONCEPT CHECK: Places and Transportation

Write the words that should be capitalized in the paragraph below and capitalize them correctly. Do not write words that are already capitalized.

The Wonders of France

(1) As the plane flew over the atlantic ocean, I read a book about the modern wonders that can be found in France. **(2)** Of course, I knew about the eiffel tower, which attracts more than 6 million visitors each year. **(3)** I also knew about versailles, which is 4 miles southwest of Paris. **(4)** Versailles is the home of the Grand palace of versailles, which was the creation of King Louis XIV, the Sun King. **(5)** However, back in Paris, the Sacré-coeur (Church of the Sacred heart) is also considered by many to be a modern wonder. **(6)** On the bank of the seine river, in downtown Paris, lies a controversial building. **(7)** Completed in 1977, the pompidou center is a famous example of high-tech architecture. **(8)** Finally, the fifth modern wonder is the pyramid-shaped entrance of the louvre Museum, which was constructed in the 1980s.

➔ **For a SELF-CHECK and more practice, see the EXERCISE BANK, p. 634.**

B. WRITING: Description

Write a short paragraph in which you use the facts below and the picture of the Hall of Mirrors to describe the Palace of Versailles.

Palace of Versailles
- about 1,300 rooms
- about 1,400 fountains
- 250 acres of gardens, lawns, and woods
- contains a royal chapel and a private theater
- took more than 40 years to complete

CHAPTER 10

Organizations and Other Subjects

❶ Here's the Idea

Organizations and Institutions

▶ **Capitalize all important words in the names of organizations, institutions, stores, and companies.**

Muir Middle School	Dave's Hardware
Peace Corps	National Park Service
Niagara Falls Hospital	Sierra Club

Do not capitalize words such as *hospital, school, company, church,* and *college* when they are not used as parts of names.

The renovations in our church are now complete.

Organization and Business Abbreviations

▶ **Capitalize abbreviations of names of organizations, businesses, and institutions. Notice that these abbreviations are formed from the initial letters of the complete names and that the letters are usually not followed by periods.**

NFL (National Football League)

MADD (Mothers Against Drunk Driving)

NASA (National Aeronautics and Space Administration)

USMC (United States Marine Corps)

Historical Events, Periods, and Documents

▶ **Capitalize the names of historical events, periods, and documents.**

Historical Events, Periods, and Documents	
Events	Revolutionary War, Trail of Tears, Boston Massacre
Periods	Great Awakening, Roaring Twenties, Renaissance
Documents	National Environmental Policy Act, Treaty of Versailles

Thomas Jefferson wrote the Declaration of Independence.

Time Abbreviations and Calendar Items

▶ **Capitalize the abbreviations B.C., A.D., A.M., and P.M.**

Niagara Falls, one of the natural wonders of the world, was probably formed around 10,000 B.C.

▶ **Capitalize the names of months, days, and holidays but not the names of seasons.**

April	Saturday	Arbor Day
May	Tuesday	spring

Mexico's Paricutín volcano appeared from a crack in the earth in a cornfield on February 20, 1943.

 When a season is used in the title of a festival or celebration (Grove Fall Festival), capitalize all important words, including the season.

School Subjects and Class Names

▶ **Capitalize the names of school subjects only when they are names of languages, when they are followed by course numbers, or when they contain proper adjectives.**

algebra	German Literature
Spanish	Biology II

▶ **Capitalize the words *freshman, sophomore, junior,* or *senior* only when they are used as parts of titles.**

The freshmen will attend Freshman Orientation Week the last week in August.

Special Events, Awards, and Brand Names

▶ **Capitalize the names of special events and awards.**

Academy Awards	Pulitzer Prize
Nobel Prize	World Cup

Ray and Abby are planning to watch the Super Bowl.

▶ **Capitalize the brand names of products but not common nouns that follow brand names.**

Fiji compasses	Staton tents

❷ Practice and Apply

A. CONCEPT CHECK: Organizations and Other Subjects

For each sentence, write the words that should be capitalized.

Saving National Forests and Parks

1. Preservation of forests and parks has become an important issue for students at springhill middle school.
2. September is preservation awareness month.
3. Students who belong to the forest and park preservation society (fpps) hold annual fundraisers and give presentations about the organization.
4. Last year troy's auto shop donated $1,000.
5. On saturday, september 27, we will hold our first autumn day fest; we hope to raise $10,000.

➡ **For a SELF-CHECK and more practice, see the EXERCISE BANK, p. 635.**

B. PROOFREADING: The Great Outdoors

Find and correct the errors in capitalization in the event calendar page below.

Grand Canyon National Park

July 2	Monday	9:00 a.m. hike at Bright Angel Point 7:00 P.M. sierra club presentation
July 3	Tuesday	7:00 P.M. flagstaff Middle School Independence day celebration
July 4	Wednesday	Independence day 9:00 p.m. fireworks
July 5	thursday	9:00 A.M. Audubon society hike at South Kaibab
July 6	Friday	7:00 p.m. National park service presentation at amphitheater
July 7	Saturday	1:00 p.m. national wildlife federation presentation at Desert View
July 8	Sunday	10:00 a.m. Izaak Walton league hike at Hermit's Rest

Grammar in Math

Using Correct Capitalization

When you write about the geometry of famous architecture, remember that correct capitalization helps clearly identify specific people, places, and things. Notice the capitalization highlighted in the following exercise.

Section 4 Circles and Circumference

The CIRCUS Maximus

Setting the Stage •

One of the wonders of the **R**oman **E**mpire was the **C**ircus **M**aximus. This enormous arena was the largest gathering place in ancient **R**ome, seating 250,000 screaming spectators. As many as 20 four-horse chariots raced around the low wall which ran down the middle of the arena.

Think About It

1 Describe the shape of the track where the chariots raced.

2 How can you estimate the perimeter of the **C**ircus **M**aximus? How can you estimate the length of the curved part of the building?

3 The **A**strodome in **H**ouston, **T**exas, holds 60,000 people. About how many times as many people did the **C**ircus **M**aximus hold?

Practice and Apply

A. CAPITALIZING CORRECTLY

A **scale** is the ratio of a measurement on a model or a drawing to the corresponding measurement on the actual object. Study the diagram on page 242. Then use the scale 1 in. : 200 ft and your ruler and compass to make a scale drawing of the Circus Maximus. Label your drawing with the actual measurements, and write a brief caption based on the information on page 242.

B. WRITING: Using Capitalization in Math

With a small group of classmates, do some research and create a scale drawing or a scale model of one of the following structures:

• an architectural wonder in your community or state

• the Great Wall of China

• the Taj Mahal

• the Great Pyramid at Giza

Using correct capitalization, write a brief caption for your drawing or model. Include the location of the structure, its measurements, and other important information.

Save your drawings and captions in your 📁 **Working Portfolio.**

The Great Wall of China

The Taj Mahal

The Great Pyramid at Giza

A. Proofreading: Capitalization Identify and correct the 11 capitalization errors in the following paragraph.

STUDENT MODEL

The Channel Tunnel, which many people consider a modern wonder, was opened in may 1994. It links the towns of folkestone, England, and coquelles, France, via a tunnel that is 31 miles long—24 miles of which are 130 feet under the seabed of the english channel! Cars, buses, and trucks drive onto high-speed electric trains for the trip through the Channel Tunnel. Passengers also ride on high-speed electric trains. The company that operates the Channel Tunnel is called eurotunnel, so the Channel Tunnel is called the eurotunnel, too. Although the shore-to-shore part of the trip takes only 35 minutes, the trip east from london to Paris is three hours long. If you left London at 9:00 a.m., you would be in paris by lunchtime.

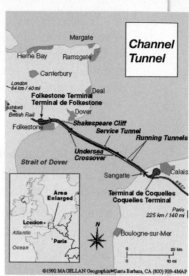

B. Capitalization of Book Titles Capitalize the following book titles correctly.

Wonders of the World Books
1. *the seven wonders of the ancient world*
2. *the stonehenge people*
3. *the world of the pharaohs*
4. *the empire state building*
5. *the great wall of china*

C. Revising: Capitalizing Important Words Look at the Web page on page 228. Using the capitalization rules in this chapter, identify and correct the ten capitalization errors. Each incorrect letter counts as one error.

For each underlined passage, choose the letter of the correct revision.

the first reference to making a list of notable places to visit was
(1)
written by herodotus in the fifth century b.c. About a century later,
(2)   (3)
when alexander the Great conquered most of the known world,
(4)
several greek writers, including antipater of Sidon, began
(5)   (6)
compiling lists of places that no traveler should miss. These lists
were eventually combined to make a list of the seven wonders of
the ancient world. Of these seven, all but the Great pyramid are
(7)
now gone. At some point during the middle Ages, another list
(8)
appeared, of the seven wonders of the medieval world, which
included some of the ancient marvels and some from the Middle
Ages, such as the Leaning Tower of pisa and the Great Wall of
(9)   (10)
China.

1. A. The first Reference
   B. The first reference
   C. The First Reference
   D. Correct as is

2. A. Was written by Herodotus
   B. was written by Herodotus
   C. was written By Herodotus
   D. Correct as is

3. A. Fifth Century B.C.
   B. fifth Century b.c.
   C. fifth century B.C.
   D. Correct as is

4. A. Alexander the great
   B. Alexander The Great
   C. Alexander the Great
   D. Correct as is

5. A. several Greek Writers
   B. several greek Writers
   C. several Greek writers
   D. Correct as is

6. A. Antipater of Sidon,
   B. Antipater of sidon,
   C. Antipater Of Sidon,
   D. Correct as is

7. A. The Great Pyramid
   B. the Great Pyramid
   C. the great Pyramid
   D. Correct as is

8. A. the Middle Ages
   B. the Middle ages
   C. The Middle ages
   D. Correct as is

9. A. Leaning tower of pisa
   B. leaning tower of pisa
   C. Leaning Tower of Pisa
   D. Correct as is

10. A. Great wall of China
    B. great wall of china
    C. great wall of China
    D. Correct as is

CAPITALIZATION

Student Help Desk

Capitalization at a Glance

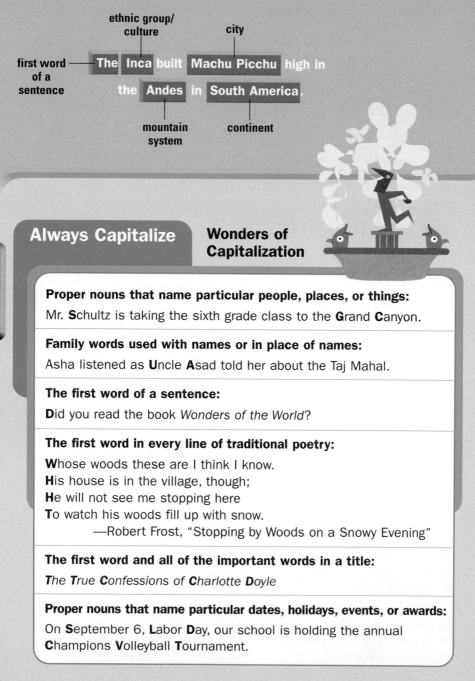

first word of a sentence — ethnic group/culture — city — mountain system — continent

The Inca built Machu Picchu high in the Andes in South America.

Always Capitalize

Wonders of Capitalization

Proper nouns that name particular people, places, or things:
Mr. **S**chultz is taking the sixth grade class to the **G**rand **C**anyon.

Family words used with names or in place of names:
Asha listened as **U**ncle **A**sad told her about the Taj Mahal.

The first word of a sentence:
Did you read the book *Wonders of the World*?

The first word in every line of traditional poetry:
Whose woods these are I think I know.
His house is in the village, though;
He will not see me stopping here
To watch his woods fill up with snow.
　　　　　—Robert Frost, "Stopping by Woods on a Snowy Evening"

The first word and all of the important words in a title:
The **T**rue **C**onfessions of **C**harlotte **D**oyle

Proper nouns that name particular dates, holidays, events, or awards:
On **S**eptember 6, **L**abor **D**ay, our school is holding the annual **C**hampions **V**olleyball **T**ournament.

Never Capitalize — Ruins of Capitalization

Common nouns that name people, places, or things:
Our coach is taking us on a tour of the park.

Family words used as common nouns:
My aunt bought a souvenir at a shop in the Empire State Building.

Word(s) after the first word of a closing in a letter:
Yours truly,   Sincerely yours,

Articles, conjunctions, and short prepositions:
"How to Paint the Most Captivating Portrait of a Bird"

Calendar items if they name a season:
Every winter our school has a skiing contest on the slopes.

The Bottom Line

Checklist for Capitalization

Have I capitalized . . .

_____ people's names and initials?

_____ personal titles and religious terms?

_____ names of ethnic groups, languages, cultures, and races?

_____ names of bodies of the universe?

_____ names of monuments, bridges, and other landmarks?

_____ names of particular planes, trains, and other vehicles?

_____ names of historical events, eras, and documents?

_____ names of special events, awards, and product brands?

_____ names of organizations, institutions, businesses, and their abbreviations?

_____ names of school subjects when they contain a proper noun or proper adjective and class names when they are used as proper nouns?

Punctuation

What did you get Celia?

Theme: A History of Communication
Birthday Messages

Is the brother asking his sister what kind of present she bought Celia? Or is he asking Celia what kind of present she just opened?

If you heard the brother speaking, you could probably tell what he meant; however, to communicate clearly in writing, you need punctuation. A comma after the word *get* would tell you that the brother is talking to Celia.

Write Away: What's Your Point?
What kind of communication do you use? You might dash off a quick e-mail message for a friend's birthday, or you might write a birthday song or a poem. Write a birthday message to a friend or family member. Put your writing into your **Working Portfolio.**

CD-ROM Grammar Coach

For each numbered item, choose the letter of the best revision.

Historians are not sure when the first books appeared, but evidence shows that they were written as early as 2700 B.C. in Egypt? These ancient books, however were made differently from
(1)   (2)
the books we use today. For instance Egyptians recorded facts
(3)
of their daily lives on scrolls made of papyrus (a material crafted
(4)
from papyrus stems). In Babylonia, people made marks on soft clay
(5)
tablets to document personal and cultural events. The Babylonian's
(6)
tablets relate information in the following areas; business, law,
(7)
government, and family life. Experts indicate that "during A.D. 300,
(8)
people made bound texts that resemble our own modern books. By
the Middle Ages, some books, such as a copy of "The Canterbury
(9)
Tales" now in London, England included rich decorations.
(10)

1. A. Egypt!
   B. Egypt,
   C. Egypt.
   D. Correct as is

2. A. books however
   B. books, however,
   C. books however,
   D. Correct as is

3. A. instance, Egyptians
   B. instance, Egyptians,
   C. instance; Egyptians
   D. Correct as is

4. A. papyrus—a
   B. papyrus-a
   C. papyrus: a
   D. Correct as is

5. A. soft, clay, tablets
   B. soft, clay tablets
   C. soft, clay, tablets,
   D. Correct as is

6. A. Babylonians'
   B. Babylonians's
   C. Babylonians
   D. Correct as is

7. A. areas' business
   B. area's business
   C. areas: business
   D. Correct as is

8. A. that during
   B. "that during
   C. "that, during
   D. Correct as is

9. A. *"The Canterbury Tales"*
   B. *The Canterbury Tales*
   C. The Canterbury Tales
   D. Correct as is

10. A. London, England,
    B. London England
    C. London England,
    D. Correct as is

Periods and Other End Marks

❶ Here's the Idea

Periods, question marks, and exclamation points are known as **end marks** because they are used to indicate the end of a sentence. Periods have other uses as well.

Periods

▶ **Use a period at the end of a declarative sentence.** A declarative sentence makes a statement.

The general wrote a message to the president **.**

▶ **Use a period at the end of almost every imperative sentence.** An imperative sentence gives a command. Some imperative sentences express excitement or emotion and therefore end with exclamation points.

Take this message to the president **.**

Wait **!** Use the faster horse **!**

▶ **Use a period at the end of an indirect question.**

An indirect question reports what a person asked without using the person's exact words.

DIRECT The aide asked, "Which route should I take, sir **?** "

INDIRECT The aide asked the general which route to take **.**

Question Marks

▶ **Use a question mark at the end of an interrogative sentence.** An interrogative sentence asks a question.

Where are the maps **?**

How soon can you pack and be ready to go **?**

Exclamation Points

▶ **Use an exclamation point to end an exclamatory sentence.** An exclamatory sentence expresses strong feeling.

The maps are missing**!** We're in trouble now**!**

▶ **Use an exclamation point after an interjection or any other exclamatory expression.**

What**!** Where could they be?

Quick**!** Search the woods for spies**!**

Other Uses of Periods

▶ **Use a period at the end of most abbreviations and initials.**

Common Abbreviations and Initials

Abbreviations

sec. second	**Dr.** Doctor	**Jr.** Junior	**tsp.** teaspoon
min. minute	**Oct.** October	**N.** North	**in.** inch
hr. hour	**Mon.** Monday	**Ave.** Avenue	**Co.** Company

Initials

P.O. post office	**A.M.** *ante meridiem* (before noon)
M.D. doctor of medicine	**U.S.A.** United States of America
B.A. bachelor of arts	**A.E.S.** Ann Elizabeth Stevens

Abbreviations Without Periods

CD compact disc	**TV** television
ER emergency room	**mph** miles per hour
MN Minnesota	**km** kilometer

▶ **Use a period after each number or letter in an outline or a list.**

Outline

Early Communication
I. Visual
  A. Sign language
  B. Writing
II. Oral
  A. Speech
  B. Song

List

Methods of Communication
1. Writing
2. Speaking
3. Sign language
4. Semaphores
5. Codes
6. Body language

❷ Practice and Apply

A. CONCEPT CHECK: Periods and Other End Marks

Write the words from the paragraph that should be followed by periods, question marks, or exclamation points. Include these punctuation marks in your answers.

Run till You Drop

Did you know that the modern marathon comes from ancient Greek history In 490 B.C., Greek military leaders ordered a young soldier, Pheidippides, to carry the news of their conquest of Persian armies The poor fellow He had to run from the city of Marathon to Athens, nearly 40 km (about twenty-six miles) Can you imagine running that distance When he finally arrived in Athens, Pheidippides shouted to the people, "Rejoice, we conquer" Unfortunately, he was unable to give more information because he immediately collapsed and died. How awful Aren't you glad that we have easier ways of sending messages

→ For a SELF-CHECK and more practice, see the EXERCISE BANK, p. 636.

B. REVISING: A Message from a Machine

The computer below has written a message. Unfortunately, the message doesn't contain any end marks. Rewrite it, adding periods, question marks, and exclamation points where needed.

Hello, I'm 7220 Jr, a portable computer Have you ever wondered how a computer operates Well, it involves really hard work Can you believe I send and receive countless numbers, words, pictures, sounds, and calculations every day It's amazing The next time you feel you have too much to do, think of me

Commas in Sentences

❶ Here's the Idea

Commas are used to separate certain parts of sentences.

Commas in Compound Sentences

▶ **Use a comma before a conjunction that joins independent clauses in a compound sentence.**

Most people know Thomas Edison for his creation of the light bulb **,** **but** he also developed many communication devices.

Edison's inventions were completely new **,** **or** they were refined versions of older works.

Alexander Graham Bell devised the modern telephone **,** **and** Edison improved it by adding a stronger vocal transmitter.

Sometimes a sentence has a compound verb but is not a compound sentence. Do not use a comma in this kind of sentence.

Edison also **constructed a model** and **tested the first phonograph.**

Commas with Items in a Series

▶ **Use a comma after every item in a series except the last one.** A series consists of three or more items.

Curiosity , **ingenuity ,** and **determination** were qualities that helped shape Edison's career.

Edison's phonograph mainly consisted of **a metal disk , a steel needle ,** and **a rotating cylinder.**

In time, Edison's recording mechanism generated other inventions: **dictation machines , musical records ,** and **talking dolls.**

Thomas Edison in his famous laboratory.

▶ **Use commas between two or more adjectives of equal rank that modify the same noun.**

Inventors are creative **,** practical people.

To decide whether to use a comma between two adjectives modifying the same noun, try the following tests.

> **Here's How** Adding Commas Between Adjectives
>
> In his youth, Edison was a likable clever prankster.
>
> 1. Place the word *and* between the adjectives.
>   In his youth, Edison was a likable and clever prankster.
>
> 2. If the sentence still makes sense, replace *and* with a comma.
>   In his youth, Edison was a likable **,** clever prankster.
>
> 3. Another test is to reverse the order of the adjectives.
>   In his youth, Edison was a clever likable prankster.
>
> 4. If the meaning of the sentence hasn't changed, use a comma.
>   In his youth, Edison was a likable **,** clever prankster.

Commas with Introductory Words and Phrases

▶ **Use a comma after an introductory word or phrase to separate it from the rest of the sentence.**

Slowly, Edison learned to use the telegraph.

Hampered by poor hearing, he invented the repeating telegraph.

Commas with Interrupters

▶ **Use commas to set off words or phrases that interrupt, or break, the flow of thought in a sentence.**

Edison, **at last,** could pick up whole telegraph messages.

Commas with Nouns of Direct Address

▶ **Use commas to set off nouns of direct address.** A noun of direct address names the person or group being spoken to.

Tell us, **Kyla,** how Edison helped the movie industry.

Commas with Appositives

An **appositive** is a word or phrase that identifies or renames a noun or pronoun that comes right before it. Use commas when the appositive adds extra information; do not use commas when the appositive is needed to make the meaning clear.

Thomas Edison**, an American inventor,** is responsible for many patents. (The phrase *an American inventor* adds extra information.)

The American inventor **Thomas Edison** had patents for 1,093 inventions. (The phrase *Thomas Edison* tells which inventor and makes the sentence clear and complete.)

Commas to Avoid Confusion

▶ **Use a comma whenever the reader might otherwise be confused.**

UNCLEAR Edison built a huge laboratory for inventing his life's work.

CLEAR Edison built a huge laboratory for inventing, his life's work.

❷ Practice and Apply

CONCEPT CHECK: Commas in Sentences

Write the words and numbers from the paragraph that should be followed by commas.

Messages over the Air

Radio waves were discovered in 1888 and Guglielmo Marconi first used them to send messages in the 1890s. Although many claimed the credit, the first voice heard on the radio belonged to Reginald Fessendens. In 1906 Fessenden a physicist born in Canada spoke from Massachusetts to ships offshore. Generally speaking radio communication was most useful in rescues. The "wireless" was used for ship-to-ship and ship-to-shore messages. By 1930 radio was being used by airline pilots the police and military personnel. Commercial broadcasting began according to experts when a Pittsburgh station aired the 1920 presidential election results.

➡ **For a SELF-CHECK and more practice, see the EXERCISE BANK, p. 636.**

Commas: Dates, Addresses, and Letters

❶ Here's the Idea

See these rules used in the letter below.

Commas in Dates, Addresses, and Letters	
Commas in dates	In dates, use a comma between the day and the year. (Use a comma after the year if the sentence continues.)
Commas in addresses	Use a comma between the city or town and the state or country. (Use a comma after the state or country if the sentence continues.)
Commas in letters	Use a comma after the greeting of a casual letter and after the closing of a casual or business letter.

1   1810 Peach Tree Ln.

2   Charleston, SC 29423

3   June 28, 2000

Line 2: comma between city and state

Line 3: comma between day and year

4 Dear Samira,

5   I heard the most incredible story today.
6 Holley Anderson, who lived in Preston,
7 Connecticut, put a message into a bottle.
8 She then threw it into the Atlantic Ocean,
9 off the coast of Maine. She was eleven at
10 the time. Five years later, she got a letter
11 from a boy who lived in Järna, Sweden,
12 and who had found the bottle. It had
13 traveled nearly 5,000 miles!

Line 4: comma after greeting

Lines 6–7: commas after town and state

Line 11: commas after city and country

14   I'm going to try to send a bottle
15 message tomorrow. Maybe I'll hear about
16 it by June 29, 2005, five years from now.
17 Wouldn't that be cool? Let me know if
18 you decide to send your own bottle
19 message.

Line 16: commas after day and year

20   Your pal,
21   Cindy

Line 20: comma after closing

WATCH OUT

Do not use a comma between the state and the ZIP code.

➋ Practice and Apply

A. CONCEPT CHECK: Commas: Dates, Addresses, and Letters

Write the words and numbers from the letter that should be followed by commas.

688 Waveland Ave.
Providence RI 02904
May 22 2000

Dear Thad
   Ricardo and I were playing last week on the beach. While digging in the sand, Ricardo found a large, worn shell. At first, we didn't think it was anything special, but then I looked closer. On its side were some carved words and an old anchor. Ricardo and I immediately showed it to my mom. It reminded her of valuable examples of scrimshaw she had seen in Mystic Connecticut at a naval museum.
   I'm hoping to find more shells when my family visits San Juan Puerto Rico to see relatives. I should be back by June 10 2000 my fourteenth birthday.
                                             Your friend
                                             Rosa

➡ **For a SELF-CHECK and more practice, see the EXERCISE BANK, p. 636.**

B. WRITING: Dear Friend

Choose one of the notes written in this cartoon and rewrite it as a complete letter. Be sure to include all the elements of a letter.

Zits by Jerry Scott & Jim Borgman

Punctuating Quotations

① Here's the Idea

To punctuate quotations, you need to know where to put quotation marks, commas, and end marks.

Direct Quotations

A direct quotation is a report of a speaker's exact words.

▶ **Use quotation marks at the beginning and end of a direct quotation.**

"In the mid-1800s, Ada, countess of Lovelace, created the first computer program," explained Carla.

▶ **Use commas to set off explanatory words used with direct quotations (whether they occur at the beginning, in the middle, or at the end of the sentence).**

Mark said, "She also wrote about an early computer."

"She also," said Mark, "wrote about an early computer."

"She also wrote about an early computer," said Mark.

▶ **If a quotation is a question or an exclamation, place the question mark or exclamation point inside the closing quotation marks.**

"Who could deny her remarkable contributions?" asked Carla.

▶ **If quoted words are part of a question or exclamation, place the question mark or exclamation point outside the closing quotation marks.**

Did Mark say, "A computer language was named in her honor"?

HOT TIP

Commas and periods always go inside closing quotation marks. They're too little to stay outside.

Lady Lovelace, a computer science pioneer.

Indirect Quotations

▶ **Do not use quotation marks to set off an indirect quotation.** An indirect quotation is a restatement, in different words, of what someone said. An indirect quotation is often introduced by the word *that*. It does not require a comma.

DIRECT   Todd said, "The name of one of the first electronic computers was ENIAC."

INDIRECT   Todd said **that** one of the first electronic computers was named ENIAC.

Divided Quotations

A divided quotation is a direct quotation that is separated into two parts, with explanatory words such as *he said* or *she said* between the parts.

▶ **Use quotation marks to enclose both parts of a divided quotation.**

"ENIAC," said Todd, "was constructed of 18,000 vacuum tubes and nearly filled an entire building."

▶ **Do not capitalize the first word of the second part of a divided quotation unless it begins a new sentence.**

"If we still used vacuum tubes," explained James, "we would need whole houses for our computers."

"Hmm, that's interesting," answered Todd. "My brother would have no place to put all his CDs."

▶ **Use commas to set off the explanatory words used with a divided quotation.**

"Well," exclaimed James, "he could always give them to me!"

Quotation Marks in Dialogue

▶ **In dialogue, a new paragraph and a new set of quotation marks signal a change in speakers.**

A dialogue is a conversation between two or more speakers.

LITERARY MODEL

The boy was probably twelve years old, but undersized. He wore overalls and a torn shirt, and was barefooted.

He said, "I can chop some wood today."

I said, "But I have a boy coming from the orphanage."

"I'm the boy."

"You? But you're small."

"Size don't matter, chopping wood," he said.

—Marjorie Kinnan Rawlings, "A Mother in Mannville"

❷ Practice and Apply

CONCEPT CHECK: Punctuating Quotations

Rewrite each sentence, adding quotation marks and other punctuation where needed. If a sentence is correct, write *Correct*.

How Intelligent Is a Robot?

"I've been reading an article about artificial intelligence said Lashawna. "Scientists use it in robots and other computers."

"You mean a robot or a computer can be intelligent? laughed Stacy

"Well, yes, if humans teach it," said Lashawna. For example, they can teach a robot to pick up an egg without breaking it."

"That's fantastic agreed Stacy. What else can robots do?

Scientists are teaching robots to move their heads in response to sounds and to wave their arms to get attention.

"It's amazing!"

➡ **For a SELF-CHECK and more practice, see the EXERCISE BANK, p. 637.**

A. End Marks and Commas Write the words and numbers from the postcard below that should be followed by end marks or commas. Include these punctuation marks in your answers.

Nov 14 2000

Dear Tisha
My family and I are here in Chicago
Illinois visiting my aunt In a little while
we're going to the Museum of
Broadcast Communications I can't wait
Do you believe that it has more than
30,000 television and radio programs in
its library I'm not lying Now I might at
last see the final episode of <u>Samantha</u>
See you later
   Julia

Tisha Reynolds
155 Sparrow St
Tulsa OK 74103

Q

B. Punctuation in Dialogue Have you ever written a dialogue with a partner? If not, here's your chance. At the top of a piece of paper, write the following question: How will communication be different in the future?

Write your first response; then let your partner write a response. Continue to take turns, with each partner writing four responses. Make sure to use correct punctuation throughout your dialogue. The example below will help you get started.

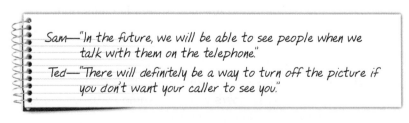

Sam—"In the future, we will be able to see people when we
        talk with them on the telephone."
Ted—"There will definitely be a way to turn off the picture if
        you don't want your caller to see you."

Semicolons and Colons

LESSON 5

① Here's the Idea

A **semicolon** separates elements in a sentence. It is stronger than a comma but not as strong as a period. A **colon** indicates that a list follows. Colons are also used after greetings in business letters and in expressions of time.

Semicolons in Compound Sentences

▶ **Use a semicolon to join parts of a compound sentence without a coordinating conjunction.**

The Pony Express Company was formed in 1860**;** it carried mail between St. Joseph, Missouri, and Sacramento, California.

▶ **Use a semicolon between parts of a compound sentence when the clauses are long and complicated or when they contain commas.**

Pony Express riders were young, strong men**;** and they rode for many hours at a stretch, persisted in bad weather, and avoided fights with settlers.

Semicolons with Items in a Series

▶ **When there are commas within parts of a series, use semicolons to separate the parts.**

The riders were expected to treat the horses, oxen, and other animals well**;** to carry horns to sound their arrival**;** and, above all, to reach their destinations on time.

Colons

▶ **Use a colon to introduce a list of items.**

Pony Express riders wore the same clothing**:** red shirts, slouch hats, jeans, and boots.

Avoid using a colon directly after a verb or a preposition.

INCORRECT   The clothing was **:** red shirts and jeans.

INCORRECT   At one time, mail was delivered to California by **:** steamships, trains, and stagecoaches.

▶ **Use a colon after the formal greeting in a business letter.**

Dear Dr. Russell**:**   Dear Ms. Wells**:**

For models, see the business letters in the Model Bank.

▶ **Use a colon between hours and minutes in expressions of time.**

The exhausted rider arrived at 11**:**35 A.M. He threw the mail pouch to the waiting rider, who galloped off at 11**:**36 A.M.

② Practice and Apply

CONCEPT CHECK: Semicolons and Colons

Write the words and numbers from the paragraph that should be followed by semicolons or colons. Include these punctuation marks in your answers.

Not Just Ponies

Many animals have carried the mail pigeons, mules, camels, and reindeer are among them. Pigeons are good postal carriers moreover, one of these winged messengers was awarded a medal during World War I. Camels have also carried some U.S. mail they were used on desert routes in the Southwest. Unfortunately, people had several complaints about the camels they smelled, they got angry, and they spit! In Alaska, before airplanes delivered mail, dogsleds often carried letters reindeer were also used. The Havasupai Indian reservation is in Arizona it sits deep in the Grand Canyon. There are only three ways in and out of the canyon on foot, by horseback, or on a mule. Mules make the trip five days each week the journey takes three to five hours each way. Your postal carrier is actually very lucky he or she may get off work by 330 P.M.

➡ **For a SELF-CHECK and more practice, see the EXERCISE BANK, p. 638.**

MAIL

MAIL

LESSON 6 Hyphens, Dashes, and Parentheses

❶ Here's the Idea

Hyphens, dashes, and parentheses help make your writing clear by separating or setting off words or parts of words.

Hyphens

▶ **Use a hyphen if part of a word must be carried over from one line to the next.**

1. The word must have at least two syllables to be broken.
RIGHT: com - puter   WRONG: dis - k

2. Separate the word between syllables.
RIGHT: broad - cast   WRONG: broadc - ast

3. You must leave at least two letters on each line.
RIGHT: sig - nal   WRONG: a - bout

▶ **Use hyphens in certain compound words.**

vice - president   self - reliance

▶ **Use hyphens in compound numbers from twenty-one through ninety-nine.**

thirty - three   forty - nine

▶ **Use hyphens in spelled-out fractions.**

three - eighths of an inch   one - third of a cup

Dashes

▶ **Use dashes to show an abrupt break in thought.**

Clara Barton — whose nickname was Angel of the Battlefield — founded the Red Cross.

Parentheses

▶ **Use parentheses to set off material that is loosely related to the rest of the sentence.**

During the Civil War (1861–1865) she helped keep track of dead soldiers in order to help their families.

❷ Practice and Apply

A. CONCEPT CHECK: Hyphens, Dashes, and Parentheses

Read the following paragraphs. Then indicate where hyphens, dashes, and parentheses are needed in each underlined passage. If the underlined text is correct, write *Correct.*

Women's Work

Clara Barton was born during a period **(1)** the early 1800s when women did not live independent lives. She is best remembered for founding the Red Cross when she was about **(2)** fifty nine. During the Civil War **(3)** 1861–1865, however, Barton performed another important national service.

First, she started an ambitious project to help **(4)** in-jured soldiers and their families. More soldiers died of disease **(5)** measles, smallpox, and typhoid than died of hostile gunfire. Barton was a rare sight on the battlefield because **(6)** I'm not kidding women were not supposed to travel on their own. She began recording the names of wounded and dead soldiers **(7)** she had nursed many of them to publish in newspapers. Pressure on the U.S. War Department **(8)** including a letter to President Lincoln led to her being given an office for her work. Over time she and her staff were able to find about 22,000 missing soldiers, **(9)** including many in a famous prison. Barton's communication skills served her well in her relief efforts. Today, the Red Cross continues Barton's work, successfully responding to people **(10)** victims of hurricanes, floods, fires, and wars in emergencies.

➜ For a SELF-CHECK and more practice, see the EXERCISE BANK, p. 638.

B. REVISING: Adding Hyphens

Rewrite the following phrases, adding hyphens where needed. If the phrase is correct, write *Correct.*

three hundred points   fourth quarter of the game
tonight's half moon   one half the weight

PUNCTUATION

Apostrophes

❶ Here's the Idea

Apostrophes are used in possessive nouns, contractions, and some plurals.

Apostrophes in Possessives

▶ **Use an apostrophe to form the possessive of any noun, whether singular or plural.**

For a singular noun, add 's even if the word ends in s.

Jenny **'s** e-mail   Russ **'s** computer

For plural nouns that end in s, add only an apostrophe.

the robot **s'** programs   the prisoner **s'** escape

For plural nouns that do not end in s, add 's.

the men **'s** conversation   the women **'s** relay

Apostrophes in Contractions

▶ **Use apostrophes in contractions.**

In a contraction, words are joined and letters are left out. An apostrophe replaces the letter or letters that are missing.

Commonly Used Contractions					
I am	Æ I'm	you are	Æ you're	you will	Æ you'll
she is	Æ she's	they have	Æ they've	it is	Æ it's
cannot	Æ can't	they are	Æ they're	was not	Æ wasn't

Don't confuse contractions with possessive pronouns, which do not contain apostrophes.

Contractions versus Possessive Pronouns	
Contraction	**Possessive Pronoun**
it's (*it is* or *it has*)	its (belonging to it—*its claws*)
who's (*who is*)	whose (belonging to whom—*whose home*)
you're (*you are*)	your (belonging to you—*your letter*)
they're (*they are*)	their (belonging to them—*their addresses*)

Apostrophes in Plurals

▶ **Use an apostrophe and *s* to form the plural of a letter, a numeral, or a word referred to as a word.**

Dot your *i* **'s**.

He scored 9**'s** and 10**'s** in competition.

Replace some of your *said* **'s** with stronger verbs.

❷ Practice and Apply

A. CONCEPT CHECK: Apostrophes

Find and correct the errors in the use of apostrophes.

Calling All Hams

Teenager Richard Paczkowski has a neat job; hes a ham operator and the assistant emergency coordinator of the Amateur Radio Emergency Service. He likes to hear his friend's voices over his two-way radio. Sometimes Richards' job is fun. But occasionally its' involved with danger. Richard lives in Florida; the states' hot summer of 1998 caused an outbreak of wildfires. After the firefighters's work had controlled the fires, many started up again. The Red Cross' shelters needed ham operators. Richard and his 75-member crew worked for many days getting victim's messages to and from shelters. He remembers that the job was'nt easy, especially when a fire approached his own home. Luckily, Richard's home didnt burn.

➡ For a SELF-CHECK and more practice, see the EXERCISE BANK, p. 639.

B. WRITING: Using Possessives and Contractions

Write the correct forms from the choices in parentheses.

(Whose, Who's) going to help me make signs for the game tonight? We want to let the other team know (they're, their) going to lose badly. We also have to support (Jeannie's, Jeannies') comeback and encourage the team to do (its, it's) best. Come on, folks! (You're, Your) not artists, but you can write cheers!

PUNCTUATION

Punctuating Titles

LESSON 8

❶ Here's the Idea

Use quotation marks and italics correctly in titles to show what kind of work or selection you are writing about.

Quotation Marks

▶ **Use quotation marks to set off the titles of short works.**

Quotation Marks for Titles	
Book chapter	"Into the Primitive" from *The Call of the Wild*
Story	"Block Party"
Essay	"Reprise"
Article	"Do Try This at Home"
TV episode	"The City on the Edge of Forever" from *Star Trek*
Song	"America the Beautiful"
Poem	"Speech to the Young/Speech to the Progress-Toward"

Italics and Underlining

▶ **Use italics for titles of longer works and for the names of ships, trains, spacecraft, and airplanes (but not for types of planes).** In handwriting, you show that something should be in italic type by **underlining** it.

Italics or Underlines for Titles and Names			
Book	*Roughing It*	Epic poem	*Iliad*
Play	*Ragtime*	Painting	*Starry Night*
Magazine	*Life*	Ship	U.S.S. *Constitution*
Movie	*The Phantom Menace*	Train	*Broadway Limited*
TV series	*Dateline NBC*	Spacecraft	*Voyager 1*
Long musical work	*Music for the Royal Fireworks*	Airplane	*Flyer*

❷ Practice and Apply

A. CONCEPT CHECK: Punctuating Titles

Read the paragraph and rewrite the titles and vehicle names, using either quotation marks or underlining as appropriate.

He Reached for the Stars

Astronomer Carl Sagan was a scientist, writer, and teacher who died in 1996. The magazine Odyssey published an entire issue on his life and work. Sagan grew up reading

science fiction, such as Edgar Rice Burroughs's novel Gods of Mars. He worked on the project that sent the spacecraft Voyager 1 and Voyager 2 to explore the outer solar system. Recordings of Earth songs were sent on the spacecraft, including Chuck Berry's Johnny B. Goode and Louis Armstrong's Melancholy Blues. Sagan produced a television series about the universe, called Cosmos. He wrote the book Pale Blue Dot to teach readers about Earth and other planets and the novel Contact about a human encounter with aliens. Sagan's appearances on Johnny

Carl Sagan and co-workers busy at work.

Carson's Tonight Show thrilled many viewers with the wonders that surround us.

➡ **For a SELF-CHECK and more practice, see the EXERCISE BANK, p. 639.**

B. MIXED REVIEW: The Critic's Corner

Write a short review of your favorite book, short story, movie, TV show, or magazine article. Include the title of your choice and a few sentences explaining why you enjoy it. At the end, write a quotation from your selection that you find memorable. Make sure to use correct punctuation throughout your review.

Grammar in Fine Arts

Punctuation and Writing About Art

Even when you write about great pieces of fine art, details like punctuation matter. Punctuation is especially important when you refer to titles of works of art, books, or articles. Notice the punctuation in the student model.

Communication, 1995, by Diane Ong

The Letter, 1891, by Mary Cassatt

Art often reflects the lifestyles and technology of its time period. The Letter, by Mary Cassatt, and Communication, by Diane Ong, were created over a hundred years apart. Each shows a woman in the act of communicating; one is writing a letter, and the other is talking on the phone.

In her article about the two paintings, "Letters and Phone Calls in Art," student Marie Moore writes that the two paintings are "different in style, but similar in content." While they show very different moods and very different kinds of communication, the fact is that both show people sharing ideas.

Practice and Apply

WRITING: Using Punctuation

For a fine-arts project, you might be asked to write a short essay about an artist. Below are examples of typical notes a student might take. Write two or three paragraphs about Cassatt, taking care to correctly punctuate the titles of books, magazines, and works of art. Save your work in your 📁 **Working Portfolio.**

BOOK: Mary Cassatt: Impressionist at Home
AUTHOR: Barbara Stern Shapiro
PUBLISHER: Universe
DATE: 1998
—mostly private, indoor settings
—famous paintings:
   Mother and Child, The Boating Party, Woman Bathing,
   Lady at the Tea Table, The Letter

BOOK: Mary Cassatt, Modern Woman
AUTHOR: Judith A. Barter, et al.
PUBLISHER: Art Institute of Chicago and Harry
         N. Abrams
DATE: 1998
—born 1844 in Pittsburgh, U.S.A.
—died 1926 in Paris, France
—studied at Pennsylvania Academy of Fine
   Arts in Philadelphia, where she met other
   important artists

Contains information about exhibitions of Cassatt's works.
Also contains information about criticism of Cassatt's works

PUNCTUATION

Mixed Review

A. Punctuation Write the words from the following paragraph that should be followed by commas, semicolons, or colons. Include these punctuation marks in your answers.

Fourteen-year-old Chelsea Hernandez of Austin Texas is already a top-notch communicator. Every Sunday morning viewers tune in to watch her on *Kids' Ideas* a program she helped create. Chelsea holds three important positions co-director writer, and star. Her show focuses on kids and their hobbies, talents and concerns. She says "Kids listen to me because I'm a kid." Good preparation is also important it kept her from being too nervous when she interviewed members of Congress. Chelsea is something of a celebrity in her hometown. She is often asked to sign autographs at the mall and this pleases her. She wants *Kids' Ideas* to be the best show it can be.

B. Punctuation Proofread the following passage and correct errors in the use of punctuation.

Ramon and Sal met on the library steps after school! Sal asked Ramon if "he had finished his research on communication?"

"I'm only half done," sighed Ramon, because there's just so much to find out. Did you know there are almost 4,000 languages spoken today?" He added, "About 845 of those are spoken in India."

Sal broke in, I know that Chinese is the most common language and is spoken by more than a billion people.

Right, said Ramon. "So what else did you find out?"

Sal told his friend that "several African languages use clicks for some of the sounds." Sal also said that "Canary Islands people use whistles to communicate with their neighbors.

For each numbered item, choose the letter of the best revision.

Television was invented in the <u>early 1900s; but</u> it became
(1)
popular only after World War II. The quality of early television was
not <u>very good, in fact</u>, it was dreadful. The picture <u>skipped; rolled</u>
(2)   (3)
<u>over and</u>, created ghost images. Often a <u>sets'</u> picture and sound
(3)   (4)
disappeared altogether. Early TV producers <u>did'nt</u> want to spend
(5)
money, so production values suffered. Stages had to be well <u>lighted</u>
<u>and hot lights</u> caused problems. Actors sweated so much that they
(6)
dripped sweated into their <u>shoes?</u> <u>Still</u>, there were popular shows,
(7)   (8)
including *The Lone Ranger* and <u>"The Texaco Star Theater."</u> When
(9)
asked what he liked about his invention, Vladimir Zworykin
replied, <u>The off switch.</u>
(10)

1. A. early 1900s but
   B. early 1900s, but
   C. early, 1900s, but
   D. Correct as is

2. A. very good: in fact,
   B. very good. in fact,
   C. very good; in fact,
   D. Correct as is

3. A. skipped, rolled over, and
   B. skipped: rolled over; and
   C. skipped (rolled over) and
   D. Correct as is

4. A. sets
   B. set's
   C. sets's
   D. Correct as is

5. A. didnt'
   B. didn't
   C. did'not
   D. Correct as is

6. A. lighted, and hot lights
   B. lighted — and hot lights
   C. lighted (and hot lights)
   D. Correct as is

7. A. shoes,
   B. shoes;
   C. shoes!
   D. Correct as is

8. A. Still;
   B. Still:
   C. Still-
   D. Correct as is

9. A. *"The Texaco Star Theater"*
   B. The Texaco Star Theater
   C. *The Texaco Star Theater*
   D. Correct as is

10. A. The off switch.
    B. "The off switch."
    C. — The off switch —.
    D. Correct as is

PUNCTUATION

Student Help Desk

Punctuation at a Glance

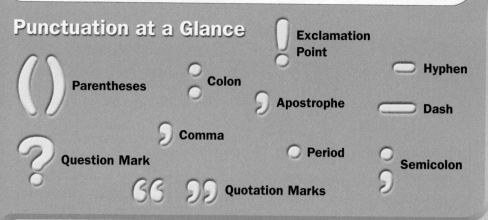

( ) **Parentheses**

Colon

! **Exclamation Point**

Hyphen

, **Apostrophe**

Dash

, **Comma**

? **Question Mark**

Period

Semicolon

" " **Quotation Marks**

Punctuating Titles   Long and Short

Italics (longer works)

books, movies, magazines, plays, TV series, paintings, long musical works, epic poems

Quotation Marks (shorter works)

stories, essays, songs, poems, book chapters, episodes of TV series, magazine articles

Punctuation with Commas   Breaks and Interruptions

	Use commas . . .	Examples
Items in a series	to separate items in a series	Do you enjoy watching TV comedies, dramas, or sports?
Adjectives	to separate adjectives	I really like old, funny shows.
Introductory words	after introductory words	In winter, Adam watches football games.
Interrupters	to set off interrupters	Mom and Dad, however, prefer to see documentaries.
Nouns of direct address	to set off nouns of direct address	What's your favorite show, Jenna?

Punctuation with Quotation Marks   The Inside Scoop

Always Inside (no matter what)

Period   Alanna said, "I didn't like that movie**.**"

Comma   "I liked the special effects**,**" said Harry.

Sometimes Inside (if they punctuate the part within the quote marks)

Question mark   "Do you have to make a speech **?**" asked Delia.

Exclamation point   "Oh, no, everyone will leave **!**" moaned Sue.

Sometimes Outside (if they punctuate the overall sentence, not just the quote)

Question mark   Did you read Nikki Giovanni's poem "Choices **"?**

Exclamation point   I was surprised by the ending of "A Mother in Mannville **"!**

The Bottom Line

Checklist for Punctuation

Have I . . .

___ ended every sentence with the appropriate end mark?

___ used a comma before the conjunction in a compound sentence?

___ used commas to separate items in a series?

___ used commas correctly in dates, addresses, and letters?

___ used quotation marks before and after a speaker's exact words?

___ used apostrophes correctly?

___ used italics and quotation marks correctly to set off titles?

Diagramming: Sentence Parts

Here's the Idea

Diagramming is a way of showing the structure of a sentence. Drawing a diagram can help you see how the parts of a sentence work together to form a complete thought.

Watch me for diagramming tips!

Simple Subjects and Verbs

Write the simple subject and verb on one line. Separate them with a vertical line that crosses the main line.

Journalists investigate.

Journalists | investigate

Compound Subjects and Verbs

For a compound subject or verb, split the main line. Put the conjunction on a dotted line connecting the compound parts.

Compound Subject

Journalists and reporters investigate.

Because there are two subjects, the left side of the main line is split into two parts.

Compound Verb

Journalists investigate and inform.

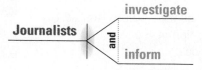

Compound Subject and Compound Verb

Journalists and reporters investigate and inform.

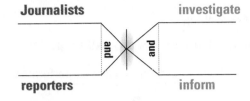

Because there are two subjects and two verbs, both sides of the main line are split into two parts.

A. CONCEPT CHECK: Subjects and Verbs

Diagram these sentences, using what you have learned.

1. News breaks.
2. Reporters and photographers scramble.
3. Editors and copyeditors read and revise.

Adjectives and Adverbs

Write adjectives and adverbs on slanted lines below the words they modify.

Busy reporters scribble very rapidly.

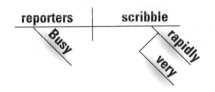

B. CONCEPT CHECK: Adjectives and Adverbs

Diagram these sentences, using what you have learned.

1. Television anchors speak clearly.
2. Anxious directors watch and worry.
3. Successful news broadcasts end very promptly.

Subject Complements

- Write a predicate noun or a predicate adjective on the main line after the verb.
- Separate the subject complement from the verb with a slanted line that does not cross the main line.

Predicate Noun

Television anchors are skillful performers.

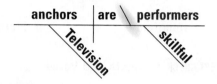

Predicate Adjective

They are usually very articulate.

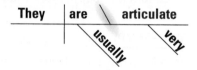

C. CONCEPT CHECK: Subject Complements

Diagram these sentences, using what you have learned.

1. Journalism is not always easy.
2. A journalist must be a forceful person.

Direct Objects

Write a direct object on the main line after the verb.

Many anchors write their own stories.

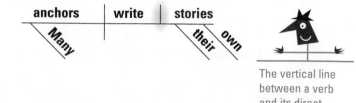

The vertical line between a verb and its direct object does not cross the main line.

Sometimes a sentence has a compound direct object. Write the direct objects on parallel horizontal lines that branch from the main line.

The news director selects the stories and the visual images.

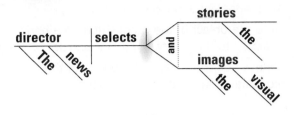

Indirect Objects

Write an indirect object below the verb, on a horizontal line connected to the verb by a slanted line.

The director may give the reporters their assignments.

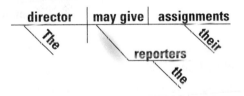

D. CONCEPT CHECK: Direct and Indirect Objects

Diagram these sentences, using what you have learned.

1. A reporter gets a tip.
2. The reporter tells the news director the idea.
3. The director gives the reporter her approval.

E. MIXED REVIEW: Diagramming

Diagram the following sentences.

1. A fierce warehouse fire starts quickly.
2. Reporters and photographers are soon busy.
3. The reporters ask witnesses numerous questions.
4. Camera operators bring their bulky equipment.
5. They rapidly shoot dramatic video footage.
6. They send the station their sensational images.
7. The warehouse soon becomes a ruin.
8. The witnesses remain quite anxious.
9. Later they watch the TV news.
10. They see their own faces!

Diagramming: Phrases

Prepositional Phrases

- Write the preposition on a slanted line below the word that the prepositional phrase modifies.
- Write the object of the preposition on a horizontal line attached to the slanted line and parallel to the main line.
- Write words that modify the object of the preposition on slanted lines below it.

Adjective Prepositional Phrase

The climbers reached the camp at the base of the mountain.

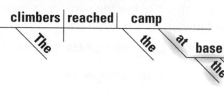
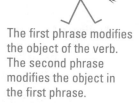

The first phrase modifies the object of the verb. The second phrase modifies the object in the first phrase.

Adverb Prepositional Phrase

They pitched their tents in twenty minutes.

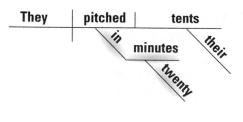

This adverb phrase modifies a verb. Adverb phrases can also modify adjectives and adverbs.

F. CONCEPT CHECK: Prepositional Phrases

Diagram these sentences using, what you have learned.

1. The heavy clouds lifted during the night.
2. The climbers could see to the top of the peak.
3. They began the climb of their lives.

Participles and Participial Phrases

- The participle curves along a bent line below the word it modifies.
- For a participial phrase, diagram direct and indirect objects after the participle in the usual way.
- Diagram any prepositional phrases as usual.
- Write modifiers, such as adverbs and adjectives, on slanted lines below the words they modify.

Fascinated tourists watched the erupting volcano.

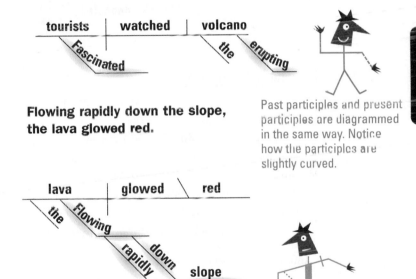

Flowing rapidly down the slope, the lava glowed red.

Past participles and present participles are diagrammed in the same way. Notice how the participles are slightly curved.

G. CONCEPT CHECK: Participles and Participial Phrases

Diagram these sentences, using what you have learned.

1. Glowing lava flowed swiftly.
2. The lava cooled, hardening into solid rock.
3. Built by many eruptions, the volcano was immense.

Gerunds and Gerund Phrases

- The gerund curves over a line that looks like a step.
- Use a vertical forked line to connect the step to the part of the diagram that corresponds to the role of the phrase in the sentence.
- Diagram the other parts of the sentence in the usual way.

Standing too close could be dangerous.

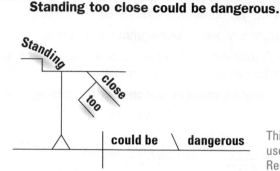

This gerund phrase is used as a subject. Remember that a gerund phrase can be used in any way a noun can.

Infinitives and Infinitive Phrases

- Write the infinitive on a bent line, with the word *to* on the slanted part and the verb on the horizontal part.
- If the infinitive or infinitive phrase functions as a noun, use a vertical forked line to connect the bent line to the part of the diagram that corresponds to its role in the sentence.
- If the infinitive or infinitive phrase functions as a modifier, place the bent line below the word it modifies.
- Diagram the other parts of the sentence in the usual way.

Infinitive Phrase as a Noun

The explorers decided to visit the distant island.

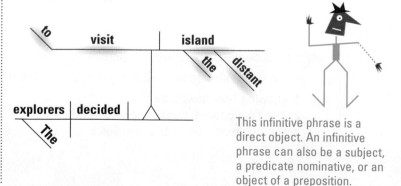

This infinitive phrase is a direct object. An infinitive phrase can also be a subject, a predicate nominative, or an object of a preposition.

Infinitive Phrase as a Modifier

Their decision to sail there was courageous.

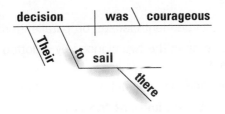

This infinitive phrase acts as an adjective modifying *decision*. An infinitive phrase can also act as an adverb.

H. CONCEPT CHECK: Gerund and Infinitive Phrases

Diagram these sentences, using what you have learned.

1. Their aim was to reach the distant island.
2. They would need to cross dangerous waters.
3. Sailing against the current posed a problem.
4. To cross the inlet would be difficult.
5. They considered abandoning their plans.

I. MIXED REVIEW: Diagramming

Diagram the following sentences.

1. People of all ages enjoy fishing.
2. Catching fish is not always easy.
3. First, you need to find a likely pond.
4. You may find fish hiding under rocks.
5. Hidden fish are not easily seen.
6. Your plan to catch a fish requires the right bait.
7. Some fish like wriggling worms or squirming minnows.
8. The challenge is to find the best lure.
9. Some people like to use flies.
10. They enjoy tying their own flies.

Diagramming: Clauses

Compound Sentences

- Diagram the independent clauses on parallel horizontal lines.
- Connect the verbs in the two clauses by a dotted line with a solid step in it.
- Write the coordinating conjunction on the step.

**Visitors talk to the lions at the zoo,
but the large cats typically ignore them.**

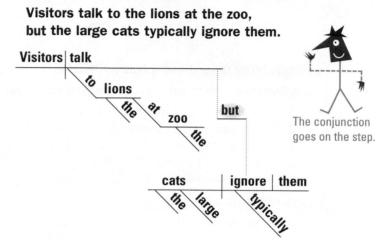

The conjunction goes on the step.

J. CONCEPT CHECK: Compound Sentences

Diagram these sentences, using what you have learned.

1. The lions are in their habitats, and the visitors are safely outside.
2. You can watch the lions eating, but you should not feed them.
3. The animals are not behind bars, yet they do not escape.

Complex Sentences

Adjective and Adverb Clauses

- Diagram the main clause first, and then diagram the dependent clause on its own horizontal line below the main line.
- Use a dotted line to connect the word introducing the clause to the word that it modifies.

Adjective Clauses

The polar bear is a creature that swims very well.

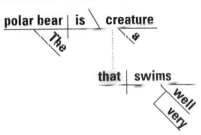

Here the pronoun introducing the clause is the subject of the clause.

Polar bear cubs have faces that people like.

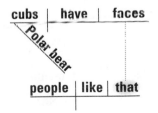

Here the pronoun introducing the clause is the direct object of the verb in the clause.

Adverb Clause

After they took the complete tour, the visitors returned to the bears.

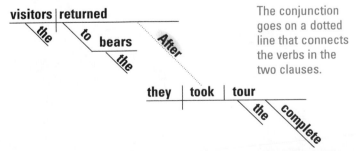

The conjunction goes on a dotted line that connects the verbs in the two clauses.

Noun Clauses

- Diagram the main clause first.
- Figure out what role the dependent clause plays in the sentence.
- Diagram the dependent clause on a separate line that is attached to the main line with a vertical forked line.
- Place the forked line in the diagram according to the role of the noun clause in the sentence.
- Diagram the word introducing the noun clause according to its function in the clause.

Noun Clause Used as a Direct Object

The zookeepers decide what the animals eat.

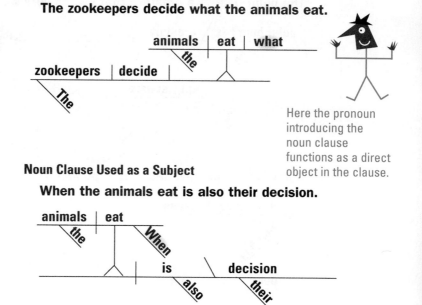

Here the pronoun introducing the noun clause functions as a direct object in the clause.

Noun Clause Used as a Subject

When the animals eat is also their decision.

K. CONCEPT CHECK: Complex Sentences

Diagram these sentences, using what you have learned.

1. The habitats include places where the animals can hide.
2. You can guess why the animals hide.
3. After they have had visitors throughout the day, the pandas become shy.

L. MIXED REVIEW: Diagramming

Diagram the following sentences.

1. Modern zoos keep animals in settings that resemble their original homes.
2. Because they offer safe environments, zoos have saved animal lives.
3. A zoo is safe, but it can also be a dull place for animals.
4. Zoos provide whatever amuses the animals.
5. They give apes poles that resemble trees.
6. Polar bears are given chunks of ice, which they can push around.
7. Chimpanzees, who are very smart, poke artificial anthills for food.
8. Zoos even provide waterfalls for animals who like them
9. You can go with a guide, or you can tour on your own.
10. Whatever you see will probably be worthwhile.

QUICK FIX

Quick-Fix Editing Machine

You've worked hard on your assignment. Don't let misplaced commas, sentence fragments, and missing details lower your grade. Use this Quick-Fix Editing Guide to help you detect grammatical errors and make your writing more precise.

Fixing Errors

Improving Style

1 Sentence Fragments

What's the problem? Part of a sentence has been left out.

Why does it matter? A fragment doesn't convey a complete thought.

What should you do about it? Find out what is missing and add it.

What's the Problem?

Quick Fix

A. A subject is missing.

Practiced for a whole week.

Add a subject.

My friends and I practiced for a whole week.

B. A predicate is missing.

Auditions in the school auditorium.

Add a predicate.

Auditions **were held** in the school auditorium.

C. Both a subject and a predicate are missing.

For almost a month.

Add a subject and a predicate to make an independent clause.

We rehearsed for almost a month.

D. A dependent clause is treated as if it were a sentence.

Because we all wore costumes.

Combine the fragment with an independent clause.

The performance was exciting because we all wore costumes.

OR

Delete the conjunction.

~~Because~~ **W**e all wore costumes.

For more help, see Chapter 1, pp. 25–27.

Run-On Sentences

What's the problem? Two or more sentences have been written as though they were a single sentence.

Why does it matter? A run-on sentence doesn't show where one idea ends and another begins.

What should you do about it? Find the best way to separate ideas or to show the proper relationship between them.

What's the Problem?

Quick Fix	

A. The end mark separating two sentences is missing.

Dolapo raced up the court her defender closed in.

> Add an end mark to divide the run-on into two sentences.
>
> Dolapo raced up the court. **H**er defender closed in.

B. Two sentences are separated only by a comma.

Dolapo faked a shot, her defender wasn't fooled.

> Add a coordinating conjunction.
>
> Dolapo faked a shot, **but** her defender wasn't fooled.
>
> **OR**
>
> Change the comma to a semicolon.
>
> Dolapo faked a shot; her defender wasn't fooled.
>
> **OR**
>
> Replace the comma with an end mark and start a new sentence.
>
> Dolapo faked a shot. **H**er defender wasn't fooled.
>
> **OR**
>
> Change one of the independent clauses to a dependent clause by adding a subordinating conjunction.
>
> **Although Dolapo faked a shot,** her defender wasn't fooled.

For more help, see Chapter 1, pp. 25–27.

③ Subject-Verb Agreement

What's the problem? A verb does not agree with its subject in number.

Why does it matter? Readers may think your work is careless.

What should you do about it? Identify the subject and use a verb that matches it in number.

What's the Problem?

Quick Fix

What's the Problem?	Quick Fix
A. The first helping verb in a verb phrase does not agree with the subject. **We has** been enjoying tea during our stay in London.	Decide whether the subject is singular or plural, and make the helping verb agree with it. **We have** been enjoying tea during our stay in London.
B. The contraction doesn't agree with its subject. Many **Britons doesn't** work at 4:00 P.M. because of teatime.	Use a contraction that agrees with the subject. Many **Britons don't** work at 4:00 P.M. because of teatime.
C. A singular verb is used with a compound subject that contains *and*. Many **natives and** an **occasional tourist visits** this fancy tearoom.	Use a plural verb. Many **natives and** an occasional **tourist visit** this fancy tearoom.
D. A verb doesn't agree with the nearer part of a compound subject containing *or* or *nor*. Neither the waiters nor the **owner want** any unhappy customers.	Make the verb agree with the nearer part. Neither the waiters nor the **owner wants** any unhappy customers.
E. A verb doesn't agree with an indefinite-pronoun subject. **Each** of the servers **give** customers undivided attention.	Decide whether the pronoun is singular or plural, and make the verb agree with it. **Each** of the servers **gives** patrons undivided attention.

For more help, see Chapter 9, pp. 208–221.

What's the Problem?

Quick Fix

F. A collective noun referring to individuals is treated as singular.

The **staff dresses** in formal attire.

Use a plural verb if the collective noun refers to individuals.

The **staff dress** in formal attire.

G. A singular subject ending in *s* or *ics* is mistaken for a plural.

Politics are often discussed in the tearoom.

Watch out for these nouns and use singular verbs with them.

Politics is often discussed in the tearoom.

H. A verb doesn't agree with the true subject of a sentence beginning with *here* or *there*.

There is tea, finger sandwiches, and cakes on the menu.

Mentally turn the sentence around so that the subject comes first, and make the verb agree with it.

There **are tea, finger sandwiches, and cakes** on the menu.

I. A verb agrees with the object of a preposition rather than with its subject.

A tea in some **areas tend** to be a meal.

Mentally block out the prepositional phrase, and make the verb agree with the subject.

A **tea** ~~in some areas~~ **tends** to be a meal.

J. A plural verb is used with a period of time or an amount.

Two hours are all the time we had to enjoy our tea.

Use a singular verb.

Two hours is all the time we had to enjoy our tea.

For more help, see Chapter 9, pp. 208–221.

QUICK FIX

④ **Pronoun Reference Problems**

What's the problem? A pronoun does not agree in number, person, or gender with its antecedent, or an antecedent is unclear.

Why does it matter? Lack of agreement or unclear antecedents can confuse your readers.

What should you do about it? Find the antecedent and make the pronoun agree with it, or rewrite the sentence to make the antecedent clear.

What's the Problem?	Quick Fix
A. A pronoun doesn't agree in number with its antecedent. A computer user **group** has **their** advantages.	**Make the pronoun agree in number with the antecedent.** A computer user **group** has **its** advantages.
B. A pronoun doesn't agree in person or in gender with its antecedent. **Ernesto** has discovered **you** can learn valuable tips from others.	**Make the pronoun agree with its antecedent.** **Ernesto** has discovered **he** can learn valuable tips from others.
C. A pronoun doesn't agree with an indefinite-pronoun antecedent. **Anyone** who owns a computer can increase **their** knowledge by sharing with a group.	**Decide whether the indefinite pronoun is singular or plural, and make the pronoun agree with it.** **Anyone** who owns a computer can increase **his or her** knowledge by sharing with a group.
D. A pronoun could refer to more than one noun. **Irma** and **Kira** attended a meeting. **She** learned a lot.	**Substitute a noun for the pronoun to make the reference clear.** **Irma** and **Kira** attended a meeting. **Kira** learned a lot.
E. A pronoun agrees with a word or a phrase that comes between it and its antecedent. **Kira,** like many **people,** may not know a lot about **their** computer.	**Mentally block out the word or phrase and change the pronoun so that it agrees with its antecedent.** **Kira,** ~~like many people,~~ may not know a lot about **her** computer.

For more help, see Chapter 3, pp. 73–83.

⑤ Incorrect Pronoun Case

What's the problem? A pronoun is in the wrong case.

Why does it matter? Readers may think your work is careless, especially if you are writing a school paper or formal letter.

What should you do about it? Identify how the pronoun is being used, and replace it with the correct form.

What's the Problem?	Quick Fix
A. A pronoun that follows a linking verb is in the wrong case. The most experienced computer user **is her.**	Always use the subject case after a linking verb. The most experienced computer user **is she.**
B. A pronoun used as an object is in the wrong case. Kira **showed** Kent and **I** some shortcuts.	Always use an object pronoun as a direct object, an indirect object, or the object of a preposition. Kira **showed** Kent and **me** some shortcuts.
C. A contraction is used instead of a possessive pronoun. **You're** computer skills have really improved.	Use a possessive pronoun. **Your** computer skills have really improved.
D. A pronoun in a compound subject is in the wrong case. A few members and **me** talked about software problems.	Always use the subject case when a pronoun is used as part of a compound subject. A few members and **I** talked about software problems.
E. A pronoun followed by an identifying noun is in the wrong case. A software company asked **we members** to test a new game.	Mentally block out the identifying noun to test for the correct case. A software company asked **us** ~~members~~ to test a new game.

For more help, see Chapter 3, pp. 61–83.

6 *Who* and *Whom*

What's the problem? The pronoun *who* or *whom* is used incorrectly.

Why does it matter? When writers use *who* or *whom* correctly, readers are more likely to take their ideas seriously.

What should you do about it? Decide how the pronoun functions in the sentence, and then choose the correct form.

What's the Problem?

Quick Fix

What's the Problem?	Quick Fix
A. ***Whom*** **is incorrectly used as a subject pronoun.** **Whom knows** the origin of origami?	Use *who* as a subject pronoun. **Who knows** the origin of origami?
B. ***Whom*** **is incorrectly used as a predicate pronoun.** The expert on origami **is whom?**	Use *who* as a predicate pronoun. The expert on origami **is who?**
C. ***Who*** **is incorrectly used as a direct object.** **Who can** we **ask** about these paper sculptures?	Use *whom* as a direct object. **Whom can** we **ask** about these paper sculptures?
D. ***Who*** **is incorrectly used as the object of a preposition.** These instructions are **for who?**	Use *whom* as the object of a preposition. These instructions are **for whom?**
E. ***Who*** **is incorrectly used as an indirect object.** You **asked who** these questions?	Use *whom* as an indirect object. You **asked whom** these questions?
F. ***Who's*** **is incorrectly used as the possessive pronoun *whose*.** **Who's sculpture** is most likely to win first prize?	Use *whose* to show possession. **Whose sculpture** is most likely to win first prize?

For more help, see Chapter 3, pp. 70–72.

7 Confusing Comparisons

What's the problem? The wrong form of an adjective or adverb is used in making a comparison.

Why does it matter? Comparisons that are not worded correctly can be confusing.

What should you do about it? Use a form that makes the comparison clear.

What's the Problem?

Quick Fix

A. Both -er and more or -est and most are used in making a comparison.

Long ago, chariot races in Rome were **more dangerouser** than any modern auto race.

The best driver was not the one who raced **most fastest**.

Delete one of the forms from the sentence.

Long ago, chariot races in Rome were **more dangerouser** than any modern auto race.

The best driver was not the one who raced **most fastest**.

B. A comparative form is used where a superlative form is needed.

The best driver was the one who was **more** successful at forcing other drivers to crash.

Use the superlative form when comparing more than two things.

The best driver was the one who was **most** successful at forcing other drivers to crash.

C. A superlative form is used where a comparative form is needed.

However, crowds cheered **most** loudly for land battles than for chariot races.

Use the comparative form when comparing two things.

However, crowds cheered **more** loudly for land battles than for chariot races.

For more help, see Chapter 5, pp. 137–139.

8 Verb Forms and Tenses

What's the problem? The wrong form or tense of a verb is used.

Why does it matter? Readers may regard your work as careless or find it confusing.

What should you do about it? Change the verb to the correct form or tense.

QUICK FIX

What's the Problem?

Quick Fix

What's the Problem?	Quick Fix
A. The wrong form of a verb is used with a helping verb. Many towns **have grew** with the expansion of railroads.	Always use a participle form with a helping verb. Many towns **have grown** with the expansion of railroads.
B. A helping verb is missing. In the late 1800s, herds of cattle **raised** in Texas.	Add a helping verb. In the late 1800s, herds of cattle **were raised** in Texas.
C. A past participle is used incorrectly. Cowhands **gone** to the end of the rail lines with their cattle.	To write about the past, use the past form of a verb. Cowhands **went** to the end of the rail lines with their cattle. **OR** Change the verb to the past perfect form by adding a helping verb. Cowhands **had gone** to the end of the rail lines with their cattle.
D. Different tenses are used in the same sentence even though no change in time has occurred. Cow towns **sprang** up around the rail lines, and more **appear** farther west as the railroads **did.**	Use the same tense throughout the sentence. Cow towns **sprang** up around the rail lines, and more **appeared** farther west as the railroads **did.**

For more help, see Chapter 4, pp. 100–114.

⑨ Missing or Misplaced Commas

What's the problem? Commas are missing or are used incorrectly.

Why does it matter? Incorrect use of commas can make sentences difficult to follow.

What should you do about it? Figure out where commas are needed, and add or omit them as necessary.

What's the Problem?

Quick Fix

What's the Problem?	Quick Fix
A. A comma is missing from a compound sentence. The cover of this book is torn and the pages are missing.	**Add a comma before the coordinating conjunction.** The cover of this book is torn, and the pages are missing.
B. A comma is incorrectly placed after a closing quotation mark. "I'll have to take this book back to the library", said Tristan.	**Always put a comma before a closing quotation mark.** "I'll have to take this book back to the library," said Tristan.
C. A comma is missing before the conjunction in a series. Ivan, LaToya and Keiko will meet him there after school.	**Add a comma.** Ivan, LaToya, and Keiko will meet him there after school.
D. A comma is missing after an introductory word, phrase, or clause. Fortunately Tristan proved that he did not damage the book.	**Add a comma after an introductory word, phrase, or clause.** Fortunately, Tristan proved that he did not damage the book.
E. Commas are missing around an appositive or a clause that is not essential to the meaning of the sentence. The librarian Tristan's aunt assured us that the book will be repaired immediately.	**Add commas to set off the appositive or clause.** The librarian, Tristan's aunt, assured us that the book will be repaired immediately.

For more help, see Chapter 11, pp. 253–255.

10 Improving Weak Sentences

What's the problem? A sentence repeats ideas or contains too many ideas.

Why does it matter? Repetitive or overloaded sentences can bore readers and weaken the message.

What should you do about it? Make sure that every sentence contains a clearly focused idea.

What's the Problem?	Quick Fix
A. An idea is repeated. Thursday was garbage collection day, **so the garbage would be picked up.**	**Eliminate the repeated idea.** Thursday was garbage collection day. ~~so the garbage would be picked up.~~
B. A single sentence contains too many loosely connected ideas. I heard a strange noise and looked outside, and the wind was so strong, and many garbage cans toppled over, and the whole block was covered with debris.	**Divide the sentence into two or more sentences, using conjunctions such as _and, but,_ or _when_ to show relationships between ideas.** I looked outside **when** I heard a strange noise. The strong wind had toppled many garbage cans, **and** the whole block was covered with debris.
C. Too much information is crammed into one sentence. Luckily, it was a holiday and many people were at home so everyone cleaned up the mess, and Ms. Ramirez made hot chocolate for all the neighbors, who really had fun working together.	**Divide the sentence into two or more sentences, using conjunctions such as _and, but, when, although,_ and _because_ to show relationships between ideas.** Luckily, many people were at home **because** it was a holiday. **While** everyone cleaned up the mess, Ms. Ramirez made hot chocolate for all the neighbors. We really had fun working together.

For more help, see Chapter 18, pp. 396–401.

Avoiding Wordiness

What's the problem? A sentence contains unnecessary words.

Why does it matter? The meaning of wordy sentences can be unclear to readers.

What should you do about it? Use words that are precise and eliminate extra words.

What's the Problem?

Quick Fix

A. An idea is unnecessarily expressed in two ways.

At 3:00 P.M. **in the afternoon,** the townspeople discovered that their worst fear was true.

Delete the unnecessary words.

At 3:00 P.M. ~~In the afternoon~~, the townspeople discovered that their worst fear was true.

B. A simple idea is expressed in too many words.

Because of the fact that there had been little snow that winter, the water level in the reservoir was low.

Simplify the expression.

~~Because of the fact that~~ there had been little snow that winter, the water level in the reservoir was low.

C. A sentence contains words that do not add to its meaning.

The point is that young people were upset because the pool, **which was** a source of jobs for teenagers, had to be closed.

Delete the unnecessary words.

~~The point is that~~ Young people were upset because the pool, ~~which was~~ a source of jobs for teenagers, had to be closed.

For more help, see Chapter 18, pp. 396–401.

12 Varying Sentence Structure

What's the problem? Too many sentences begin in the same way, or one type of sentence is overused.

Why does it matter? Lack of variety in sentences makes writing dull and choppy.

What should you do about it? Rearrange the phrases in some of the sentences, and use different types of sentences for variety and impact.

What's the Problem?

Quick Fix

A. Too many sentences in a paragraph start the same way.

The microprocessor was developed in 1971. **The microprocessor** is a tiny computer chip. It has had a big impact on the computer industry. **Video games** appeared when smaller computers became possible. **Video games** became popular quickly, especially among teenagers.

Rearrange words or phrases in some of the sentences.

Developed in 1971, the microprocessor is a tiny computer chip. It has had a big impact on the computer industry. Video games appeared when smaller computers became possible. **Especially among teenagers,** video games became popular quickly.

B. Too many declarative sentences are used.

Video games are fun because they have realistic graphics and interesting sound effects. Winning requires certain skills. A player must have good coordina-tion and quick reflexes; however, a player's greatest challenge is concentration.

Add variety by rewriting one sentence as a command, a question, or an exclamation.

Video games are fun because they have realistic graphics and interesting sound effects. **What skills does a player need to win?** Good coordination and quick reflexes are important; however, a player's greatest challenge is concentration.

For more help, see Chapter 18, pp. 402–403.

13 Varying Sentence Length

What's the problem? A piece of writing contains too many short, repetitive sentences.

Why does it matter? The use of too many short, repetitive sentences makes writing choppy and monotonous.

What should you do about it? Combine or reword sentences to create sentences of varying lengths.

What's the Problem?

Too many short sentences are used.

The National Weather Service issued a warning. The warning was about a storm. Torrential rains had struck towns. The towns were along the coast. Now the storm was turning. Its turn was sudden. It was turning inland. Many travelers were stranded. This happened when the airport had to close. The closing was temporary. The National Weather Service urged people to evacuate the area. Many people stayed at home. It rained for several days. There was flooding. People had to be rescued.

For more help, see Chapter 8, pp. 192–199 and Chapter 18, pp. 404–405.

Quick Fix

Combine sentences that add only one detail about the subject with other sentences.

The National Weather Service issued a **storm** warning. Torrential rains had struck towns **along the coast. Suddenly** the storm turned **inland.**

OR

Use conjunctions such as *or, and,* **or** *but* **to combine related sentences.**

The airport had to close temporarily, **and** many travelers were stranded.

OR

Use words such as *while* **or** *although* **to form a complex sentence.**

Although the National Weather Service urged people to evacuate the area, many people stayed at home.

OR

Combine the sentences to form a compound-complex sentence.

After it rained for several days, there was flooding, **and** people had to be rescued.

14 Adding Supporting Details

What's the problem? Not enough details are given for readers to fully understand the topic.

Why does it matter? Unexplained terms and unsupported claims can weaken a piece of writing.

What should you do about it? Add information and details that will make statements clear.

What's the Problem?

Quick Fix

A. An important word is not explained or defined.

Computer **chips** are made from quartz rock.

Engineers can now fit computer circuitry into tiny squares called chips, composed of material that comes from quartz rock.

B. No details are given.

An early electronic digital computer was built in 1946.

Add details that will help readers understand the significance of the topic.

An early electronic digital computer was built in 1946. **It was huge compared with computers of today. At first, only scientists used computers, but now people use them at home, school, and work.**

C. No supporting facts are given.

Computer chips are used in many things.

Add supporting facts.

Computer chips are used in **watches, cars, games, telephones, and many household appliances.**

D. No reason is given for an opinion.

Our lives would be quite different without computer chips.

Add a reason.

Our lives would be quite different without computer chips. **Computer chips have helped us automate processes and achieve other technological gains.**

For more help, see Chapter 17, pp. 386–389.

15 Avoiding Clichés and Slang

What's the problem? A piece of formal writing contains clichés or slang expressions.

Why does it matter? Clichés do not convey fresh images to readers. Slang is not appropriate in formal writing.

What should you do about it? Replace the clichés and slang with clear, fresh expressions.

What's the Problem?

Quick Fix

A. A sentence contains a cliché.

After their tournament victory, the members of the women's volleyball team **were as happy as larks.**

Replace the cliché with a fresh description or explanation.

After their tournament victory, the members of the women's volleyball team **frantically cheered, laughed, and hugged one another. They were like students on graduation day, full of joy and relief all at once.**

B. A sentence contains inappropriate slang.

The explanation he gave is **whack.**

Replace the slang with more appropriate language.

The explanation he gave is **not acceptable.**

For more help, see Chapter 19, pp. 412–417.

QUICK FIX

16 Using Precise Words

What's the problem? Nouns, modifiers, and verbs are not precise.

Why does it matter? Writers who use vague or general words don't give readers an accurate picture of their topic.

What should you do about it? Replace vague words with precise and vivid ones.

What's the Problem?

Quick Fix

A. Nouns and pronouns are too general.

The **people** walked into that **passageway during the day** without **some supplies.**

Use specific words.

The **hikers** walked into that **canyon at noon** without **water.**

B. Modifiers are too general.

As they marched, the **hot** sun actually felt **good** on their backs. **Later,** the **hot** weather felt **bad.**

Use vivid adjectives and adverbs.

As they marched, the **radiant** sun actually felt **comforting** on their backs. **Two hours later,** the **steamy** weather felt **oppressive.**

C. Verbs tell about the action rather than show it.

The group **sat** on some rocks to rest. Without water, their throats **were** full of dry, dusty canyon air. They **got nervous** when a thunderstorm **came.**

Use vivid verbs to show the action.

The group **sprawled** on some rocks to rest. Without water, their throats **were parched** from dry, dusty canyon air. They **panicked** when a thunderstorm **approached.**

For more help, see Chapter 19, pp. 414–415.

17 Using Figurative Language

What's the problem? A piece of writing is dull or unimaginative.

Why does it matter? Dull writing bores readers because it doesn't help them form mental pictures of what is being described.

What should you do about it? Add figures of speech to make writing lively and to create pictures in readers' minds.

What's the Problem?

A description is dull and lifeless.

The principal was the first one to get the message about a movie. She flashed the news to the teachers. However, a student must have overheard the teachers talking about the announcement, because by the afternoon, everyone seemed to have the information.

Of course, by then the story was exaggerated.

There were so many different stories. Were we really going to be in a movie?

For more help, see Chapter 19, pp. 416–417.

Quick Fix

Add a simile.

The principal was the first one to get the message about a movie. **Like a child waving a new toy,** she flashed the news to the teachers. However, a student must have overheard the teachers talking about the announcement, because by the afternoon, everyone seemed to have the information.

OR

Add a metaphor.

Of course, by then the story was **a wildfire that could not be contained.**

OR

Use personification.

The burning excitement fueled **rumors that skipped and darted down the hallways and into the classrooms.** Were we really going to be in a movie?

QUICK FIX

18 Paragraphing

What's the problem? A paragraph contains too many ideas.

Why does it matter? A long paragraph discourages readers from continuing.

What should you do about it? Break the paragraph into shorter paragraphs. Start a new paragraph whenever a new idea is presented or the time, place, or speaker changes.

What's the Problem?

Too many ideas are contained in one paragraph.

I'll never forget the first time I saw a rattlesnake. Willie and I were camping in the mountains when we decided to go for a hike on a trail heading up the rocky side of a hill. As I stepped across a rock along the trail, I noticed something in the way. I leaped into the air and jumped backward in one fluid motion. "Arrgh!," I cried. "I think it's a snake." "Ha! I bet this is one of your tricks," Willie snickered. After the longest moment of my life, we heard a hiss and a rattling sound at the same time. We froze as we watched the snake slither into the bushes. We were more cautious about where we stepped after that harrowing experience.

Quick Fix

I'll never forget the first time I saw a rattlesnake. Willie and I were camping in the mountains when we decided to go for a hike on a trail heading up the rocky side of a hill.

Start a new paragraph to introduce a new idea.

As I stepped across a rock along the trail, I noticed something in the way. I leaped into the air and jumped backward in one fluid motion.

Start a new paragraph whenever the speaker changes.

"Arrgh!," I cried. "I think it's a snake."

"Ha! I bet this is one of your tricks," Willie snickered.

Start a new paragraph when the time or place changes.

After the longest moment of my life, we heard a hiss and a rattling sound at the same time. We froze as we watched the snake slither into the bushes. We were more cautious about where we stepped after that harrowing experience.

For more help, see Chapter 16, pp. 372–373.

What's the Problem?

An essay is treated as one long paragraph.

To stay up to date on what's happening in the world of technology, computer users need to know about laptop computers and how they compare with desktop models. Both types have their own strengths and weaknesses. Desktops generally have larger and clearer screens and larger keyboards than laptops have. Some desktops have more memory capacity and can do jobs more quickly. Laptops generally run on batteries and come with adapters for household current, so users can take them anywhere. Some laptops weigh as little as five pounds. As their name implies, laptops are small enough to be used on a person's lap. However, because of their small size, their screens are often fuzzier and their keyboards more cramped than desktop models. For years the desktop model has been the more popular of the two models. However, people are beginning to choose laptops as their main computers because of their flexibility.

For more help, see Chapter 16, pp. 372–373.

Quick Fix

To stay up to date on what's happening in the world of technology, computer users need to know about laptop computers and how they compare with desktop models. Both types have their own strengths and weaknesses.

Start a new paragraph to introduce the first main idea.

Desktops generally have larger and clearer screens and larger keyboards than laptops have. Some desktops have more memory capacity and can do jobs more quickly.

Start a new paragraph to introduce a new idea.

Laptops generally run on batteries and come with adapters for household current, so users can take them anywhere. Some laptops weigh as little as five pounds. As their name implies, laptops are small enough to be used on a person's lap. However, because of their small size, their screens are often fuzzier and their keyboards more cramped than desktop models.

Set off the conclusion in its own paragraph.

For years the desktop model has been the more popular of the two models. However, people are beginning to choose laptops as their main computers because of their flexibility.

Essential Writing Skills

In Focus

Writing allows you to look closely at an idea. Picking the right word or most interesting detail helps you focus your thinking and your writing. Sharpen your skills and develop your own style.

Power Words
Vocabulary for Precise Writing

Inventive Words

Use these words to describe your inventive process and the marvelous things you could invent.

An Original Thought

It's tough trying to **think up** something no one has ever **dreamed of** before. **Devising** a new game, **coining** a new word, **concocting** a recipe, **hatching** a clever plan—these are not easy things to do. You'll have to **start from the ground up** by **developing** your idea, **tinkering** with it, and then **perfecting** it.

Creative Genius

If your invention or idea is **original, fresh,** and **novel** enough, if it is completely **ingenious** and **innovative,** people will praise it as **unique** and **matchless.** They'll say you have made a **creative** masterpiece, a work **without equal.** You will feel proud to have done something so **extraordinary.**

But don't be discouraged if the **gadget** or **gizmo** you think up isn't the greatest **invention** or **contrivance** ever. Whatever the **contraption,** it can still be fun for you!

▷ **Your Turn** Put Your Heads Together

In a small group, dream up a new invention that would make your life easier. Have someone in the group draw a sketch of the invention, and then write a five sentence description of your group's inventive process.

Writing Process

Writing assignment:
Describe an invention
that is important in your life.
Explain <u>how</u> it is important.

2 pages

Mission Impossible?

Imagine that your teacher has asked you to complete the writing assignment above. You could be thinking, "Great! Another writing assignment! I can't wait to get started!" However, you're not alone if your thoughts are closer to this: "Oh, no. Another writing assignment. What will I write about? Where should I begin?"

Writing isn't something you can do in one giant step. Instead, writing is a process, or a series of smaller steps. These include prewriting, drafting, revising, editing, and publishing. If you focus on completing these individual activities, writing will become much easier for you.

Write Away: You Can Do It!
Use this chapter to guide you through your current writing assignment or your next assignment. Right now, answer these questions: Is there any part of writing assignments that is especially difficult for you? Which kinds of assignments are most fun? Why? Save your answers to these questions in your 🗂 **Working Portfolio.**

Prewriting

The first part of the writing process involves more thinking than writing. During prewriting, you decide what you will write about, why you are writing, and for whom you are writing.

❶ Finding a Topic

How do you decide what to write about? Sometimes your teacher assigns you a topic, and sometimes you get to choose your own. Try one of the following techniques when you need help coming up with a writing topic.

Freewriting

Think of a subject that interests you. For 10 minutes, write down whatever comes to mind about it. Don't stop to read what you've written or to make corrections. When the time is up, look at what you've written and circle the most interesting ideas. Choose one of these ideas as your topic.

STUDENT MODEL

Mom showed me a box of her old clothes and stuff. I can't believe her roller skates fit me! They're really different from the skates kids have today — they have weird wheels!

Self-Inventory

Ask yourself open-ended questions about your interests and hobbies (What are my hobbies? What do I want to know more about? What do I do in my free time? Who are my heroes?). Your answers can give you topic ideas.

Brainstorming

Get together with some classmates. Choose one person to take notes. Begin by suggesting a subject to talk about. Then take turns tossing out ideas and thoughts about it. Come up with as many ideas as you can without stopping to talk about them. Pick a writing topic from the list.

❷ Thinking about Purpose, Audience, and Form

Writing about your topic will be easier if you know why you are writing (your **purpose**) and for whom you are writing (your **audience**). Use the questions below to make decisions about your purpose and your audience.

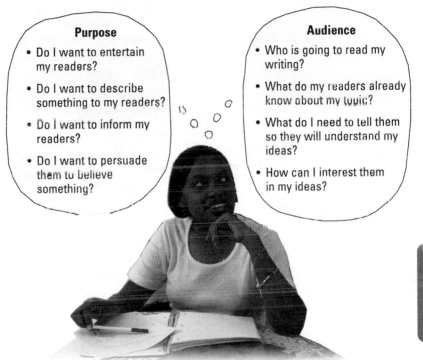

Purpose

- Do I want to entertain my readers?

- Do I want to describe something to my readers?

- Do I want to inform my readers?

- Do I want to persuade them to believe something?

Audience

- Who is going to read my writing?

- What do my readers already know about my topic?

- What do I need to tell them so they will understand my ideas?

- How can I interest them in my ideas?

You might want to write a statement that helps you think about your purpose and your audience as you work on your writing assignment. Below are examples of purpose/audience statements you might write.

- I want to inform my classmates about in-line skating.
- I want to entertain my neighbors with stories about my family vacation.

Form Often you'll be told what form of writing to use. Some common forms are essay, short story, poem, letter, and report. If you're told to choose a form, think about which one will work best with your topic, purpose, and audience.

❸ Exploring and Limiting a Topic

If your teacher told you to write a report on in-line skating, you might think, "That's a big topic. What part of in-line skating should I write about?" Here are two ways to limit your topic.

Create a Cluster Diagram

Begin by writing down the big topic and drawing a circle around it. Then write down things you know or want to know about the topic. Circle each of these ideas and questions and draw lines connecting them to the topic. Continue to do this until you run out of ideas. Then choose one to write about.

Ask Specific Questions

Another way to limit a topic is to write questions about it that begin with *who, what, when, where, why,* and *how.* Choose the most interesting question to write about.

• When were in-line skates invented?

• How are in-line skates and roller skates different?

If you don't have enough information about your topic, you can read magazine and encyclopedia articles to find out more about it. Then use the techniques above.

❹ Organizing Ideas

At some point, you need to organize your writing so readers can follow your ideas. One way to organize is to make a list of all the important ideas you want to cover. Once you've done this, you can decide in which order you should write about them. Spend some time thinking about the order, and try out different arrangements of ideas to see which one works best.

Drafting

Drafting means writing down your ideas. There's no one right way to do this. You can start writing right away or plan out what you want to write before you begin drafting. The important part of drafting is getting your ideas on paper.

❶ Drafting to Discover

You may have many ideas about your topic and still not know exactly how to begin writing. At times like this, you might find it helpful to just start writing about one of your ideas and see what happens. You may find new ideas or decide not to use the idea you started with. This is called **discovery drafting** because writers usually discover new ideas during this process. Don't worry if your ideas change as you write—that's what discovery drafting is all about.

❷ Drafting from a Plan

For some kinds of writing, you may want to make a plan that you can follow as you write. This way of drafting is often helpful with essays and research reports. The list below is one kind of plan. It shows the main ideas and key facts about a topic in the order they will be presented in the paper.

> **STUDENT MODEL**
>
> 1. Joseph Merlin creates the first pair of roller skates (1760)
> 2. Problems with early versions of skates
> 3. James Plimpton's design improvements (1863)
> 4. Today's in-line skates

Using a plan doesn't mean there's no room for changes. If a new idea occurs to you as you draft, you can revise your plan to include it.

❸ Using Peer Response

What is peer response? It's the comments your classmates make about your writing. This feedback can help you make your writing clearer and more interesting. As a writer, you need to know how to ask your classmates for feedback. When you are asked to be a peer reader, you need to know how to give feedback to the writer.

As the writer, you should . . .	As the reader, you should . . .
• give the reader enough time to read through the piece	• carefully read the writer's work
• ask the reader to be open and honest about your work	• be respectful and positive when you talk about the writer's work
• ask specific questions that will help you solve problems in your writing	• think carefully about the writer's questions and give specific feedback
• listen politely to the reader's comments and ideas	• not give feedback that wasn't asked for

Sample Questions

Getting yes or no answers to your questions about your writing is not as helpful as getting detailed comments and suggestions. Here are some questions you might ask to get more useful feedback from your peer readers.

• How would you restate my main idea in your own words?

• What parts of my draft do you especially like? Why?

• Which parts of my draft seemed confusing? Why?

You don't have to use the comments and suggestions you get from your classmates. It's up to you to decide what changes to make to your writing.

For more about getting and giving feedback, see p. 327.

HOT TIP

Your peer-response session can be with just one reader or with a small group of readers. You can even e-mail your draft and a list of questions to a partner.

Revising

When you revise, you look for ways to improve your writing. You may need to change the order of your sentences or paragraphs. You may also need to use different words to express your ideas.

Six Traits of Good Writing

The following chart shows six traits that are usually found in good writing. Use these traits to help you improve your work.

Six Traits of Good Writing

1. Ideas and Content	Ideas are clear, focused, and well-supported with relevant details.
2. Organization	Ideas are arranged in a logical order that moves the reader through the text.
3. Voice	The writing shows individual style and personality.
4. Word Choice	Language is precise, powerful, and engaging.
5. Sentence Fluency	Writing has a pleasing rhythm and flow, and shows varied sentence length and structure.
6. Conventions	Grammar, spelling, and punctuation errors are eliminated.

Checking Ideas and Content

Use the questions below to test whether your ideas are clear and supported with details. If you answer no to any of these questions, you need to revise your ideas and content.

> **Here's How** **Checking Ideas and Content**
>
> - Are my main ideas clearly stated?
> - Do my details explain and support my ideas?
> - Is my purpose easy to identify?
> - Have I deleted all unrelated information?

Checking Organization

Make sure your ideas are organized in a way that will help readers understand them. Change the organization if you answer no to any of the following questions.

> **Here's How** **Checking Organization**
>
> - Is there a clear beginning, middle, and end?
> - Is the beginning of my paper interesting enough to make readers want to keep reading?
> - Do my ideas follow one another logically?
> - Does my ending bring together my final thoughts on the topic?

Checking Voice, Word Choice, and Sentence Fluency

The way you write about your ideas is called your style. Check the style of your writing by looking closely at your voice, word choice, and sentence fluency.

Voice

Your writing has a special sound that makes it different from anyone else's writing. This sound is called your voice. Your voice should

- sound natural (Don't try to sound like someone else.)
- show your true feelings about the topic
- speak to your audience

Word Choice

Why use the same old words all the time when there are so many other powerful and interesting ones? The words you choose should

- include strong verbs, precise nouns, and interesting adjectives
- make your ideas clear
- match your purpose for writing (Don't use big words just to impress your readers.)
- create pictures in the reader's mind

Sentence fluency is the rhythm and flow of your sentences. If all your sentences begin the same way (for example, with the word *I*) and are the same length, your writing will seem dull. Make sure your sentences

- are of different lengths (some short, some long)
- have different beginnings
- flow together nicely and sound smooth when you read them

The writer of the following model paid attention to her voice, word choice, and sentence fluency. She used strong verbs, precise nouns, and interesting adjectives. Her sentences flow together smoothly, and they begin in different ways.

PROFESSIONAL MODEL

The first pair of roller skates made their appearance in 1760 at a masked ball in London, attached to the feet of their Belgian inventor, Joseph Merlin. Sure that his new invention would be a stunning success, Merlin made a grand entrance by gliding into the ballroom while sawing out a tune on a violin. Because he couldn't turn or stop on his skates, Merlin rolled helplessly across the floor and crashed into a massive mirror. He shattered the mirror, splintered the violin, and suffered major injuries himself.

—Jane Birdsall

VARIED SENTENCE BEGINNINGS

PRECISE NOUNS

STRONG VERBS

INTERESTING ADJECTIVES

WRITING PROCESS

Try reading your writing out loud to check sentence fluency. If your writing sounds flat or choppy, you probably need to change the length and beginnings of some of your sentences.

Peanuts by Charles Schulz

Editing and Proofreading

After you've finished revising your work, you need to edit and proofread your draft. This step will help you find and correct errors in grammar, punctuation, and spelling.

❶ Checking Conventions

Your readers will be frustrated if your writing is full of careless errors. Some of the most common errors writers make are on the checklist below. Be sure to correct these errors in your writing.

> **Common Errors Checklist**
> ____ Did I capitalize the first word of every sentence?
> ____ Did I use correct verb tenses?
> ____ Have I created any run-on sentences or sentence fragments?
> ____ Is any punctuation mark missing or unnecessary?
> ____ Have I spelled all of my words correctly?

Use the tips below as you focus on editing and proofreading your work.

> **Here's How** **Editing and Proofreading Your Work**
>
> • Read your work slowly—one sentence at a time.
> • Look for mistakes you know you make often, as well as other errors.
> • Use a dictionary to check the spelling of unfamiliar words and words that often give you trouble.
> • Ask a friend or relative to read your work, looking for errors you might have missed.

Don't rely on computer spell checkers to find all errors. Spell checkers can catch misspellings, but they won't catch usage errors. These errors happen when you use a correctly spelled word in the wrong way. **Example:** Its to hot out hear.

❷ Using Proofreading Symbols

Proofreading symbols are a handy way to mark mistakes that need to be fixed. The chart below shows some of the most commonly used symbols.

Proofreading Symbols

∧	Add a letter or word.	⌷	Take out letters or words.
⊙	Add a period.	◡	Close up.
∧	Add a comma.	≡	Capitalize a letter.
#	Add a space.	¶	Begin a new paragraph.
∩	Switch the positions of letters or words.	⫽	Make a capital letter lowercase.

STUDENT MODEL

¶In 1863, an American, inventor named James Plimpton made a better four-wheel skate. The skate was called a quad, and it had two weels at the front of the skate and two wheels at the back. the skatewheels were attached to a rubber cushion, which made it easy for skaters to turn by leaning in one direction or an other. Plimpton's new designe made roller skating unbelievably popular.

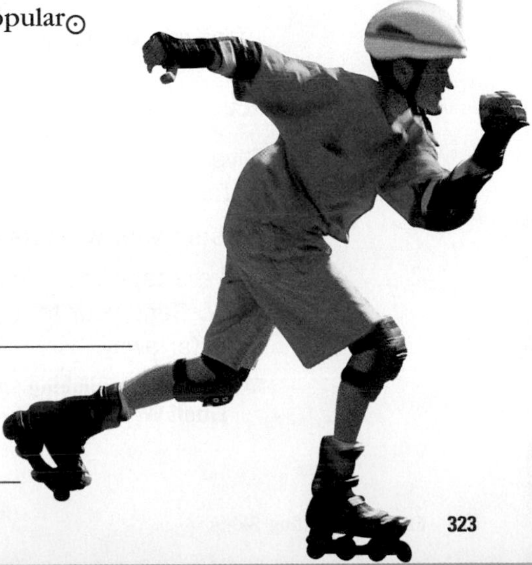

Publishing and Reflecting

You've worked hard to make your writing the best it can be. Now it's time to share your work with your audience. You can do this in any number of interesting ways.

❶ Sharing Your Writing

Print

- Submit your work to your school newspaper or literary magazine.
- Make a poster by taping your work onto a big piece of paper. Create a collage or drawings around the border of the poster. Display the poster in your school.
- Create a magazine that contains your best writing. Add illustrations and a cover. Display the magazine in your classroom.

Electronic Media

- E-mail your work to a relative or friend.
- Post your work on your school's Web site.
- Submit your work to an online magazine of student writing.

Check out the
new student writing
on our site!

Performance

- Give a dramatic reading of your work to friends or family members.
- Present your work as a speech.
- Make a tape recording of yourself reading your work. Send your tape to a friend or relative who lives far away.

➡ **For more publishing options, go to the McDougal Littell Web site: mcdougallittell.com**

❷ Reflecting on Your Writing

After you've presented your work, take some time to think about the writing process. Does your process work for you, or do you need to change it? Answer the following questions to find out how you can make writing go more smoothly.

Questions for Reflection

- What parts of the process were the easiest? the most difficult?
- What were the most useful suggestions I got from my peers?
- What would I do differently next time?
- What did I learn about my topic from writing about it?

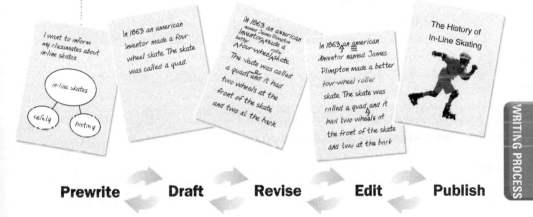

Prewrite **Draft** **Revise** **Edit** **Publish**

Using Portfolios

You can save all your writing in folders called portfolios.

Working Portfolio
This is where you'll store most of your writing assignments—including the ones you're still working on. Even if you're not crazy about the way some assignments turned out, you should hold on to them. Look through this portfolio from time to time to understand how your writing skills have improved.

Presentation Portfolio
Put your best writing in your Presentation Portfolio. The pieces in this portfolio should be the ones you are proud to share with others. When you want to show someone an example of your skill as a writer, select a piece from this portfolio.

Student Help Desk

Writing Process at a Glance

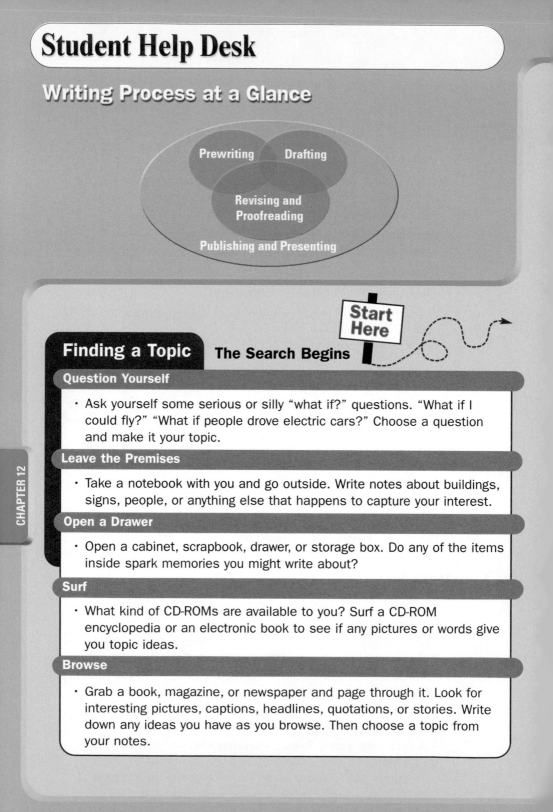

Prewriting

Drafting

Revising and Proofreading

Publishing and Presenting

Finding a Topic   The Search Begins

Start Here

Question Yourself

- Ask yourself some serious or silly "what if?" questions. "What if I could fly?" "What if people drove electric cars?" Choose a question and make it your topic.

Leave the Premises

- Take a notebook with you and go outside. Write notes about buildings, signs, people, or anything else that happens to capture your interest.

Open a Drawer

- Open a cabinet, scrapbook, drawer, or storage box. Do any of the items inside spark memories you might write about?

Surf

- What kind of CD-ROMs are available to you? Surf a CD-ROM encyclopedia or an electronic book to see if any pictures or words give you topic ideas.

Browse

- Grab a book, magazine, or newspaper and page through it. Look for interesting pictures, captions, headlines, quotations, or stories. Write down any ideas you have as you browse. Then choose a topic from your notes.

"Which details seemed confusing or unnecessary?"
"Most of your details were very interesting. I was confused by the part about the design of the first roller skates."

"Which words or phrases did you especially like?"
"I loved the phrase 'independent as a hog on ice.' Many of the words you used helped me picture what you were describing."

"How could I make my introduction more interesting?"
"The quotation you used was great! Can you tie it into the rest of your introduction more clearly?"

Six Traits of Good Writing The Big Six!

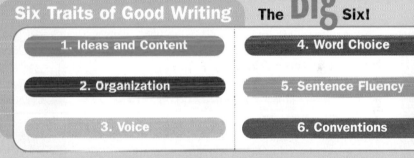

1. Ideas and Content
2. Organization
3. Voice
4. Word Choice
5. Sentence Fluency
6. Conventions

The Bottom Line

Checklist for Writing Process

Have I . . .

____ presented my ideas clearly and used details to support them?

____ organized my ideas logically?

____ expressed my ideas in my own voice?

____ used precise, powerful, and interesting words?

____ made my sentences flow smoothly?

____ corrected all spelling, grammar, and punctuation mistakes?

Power Words
Vocabulary for Precise Writing

rare

unusual

extraordinary

amazing

astounding

From Dashing to Dull

Use these words to help you describe things you rarely see and things you might see every day.

Look at That Weird Sky

If the sun came up one day and the sky looked orange and fiery, we would say it is not just **unusual,** but more like **amazing** and **astounding** to look at, even **extraordinary.** But if the sun came up and the sky looked green, it would be more than **rare,** it would be **shocking** and **unique.** The media would really play up such an **oddball** and **exceptional** story, saying it was absolutely **stupendous.** Scientists would call a green sky **curious, irregular,** and **anomalous,** and nothing less than **peculiar.**

Nothing Strange About This Sky

On the other hand, suppose we saw only a gray, cloudy sky. That would indicate **nothing special**—just a **run-of-the-mill** dull day. We get used to such **average, familiar, so-so** weather because everything about it is **unremarkable.** An overcast sky is **commonplace,** an **everyday** occurrence—it happens all the time. A **plain vanilla** day, you might call it, **unexceptional** and **routine.**

exceptional

▷ **Your Turn** Did You See That?

In a small group, brainstorm some of the unusual, peculiar, or amazing things you've seen. Pick the most interesting one, and make a list of 15 words that best describe this particular thing. Tell the rest of the class what it is, and read the list of words that describe it.

unique

stupendous

Crafting Sentences

> Hi Everyone!
> It's the third day of our vacation. We saw a big fish and a few other things.
>
> Kevin

> The Fremonts
> 524 Main Street
> Topeka, KS 66601

A big attraction at the National Freshwater Fishing Hall of Fame in Hayward, Wisconsin, this four-story-high muskie is made of fiberglass. It stands 143 feet long and weighs 500 tons.

A Fish Story

What's wrong with the sentences on this postcard? Each one is complete. Each one is factual. But are they interesting sentences? Do they tell the whole story? If you didn't have the picture to go by, would you be able to imagine what the writer saw? A good writer could improve these sentences by using precise words, inserting rich details, and varying sentence structure.

If your family traveled to Hayward, Wisconsin, to visit the National Freshwater Fishing Hall of Fame and climb into the mouth of the giant fiberglass muskie, could you write a more interesting, descriptive postcard?

Write Away: What's Your Hobby?

Do you like to paint? Do you collect things? Do you assemble models? Do you stargaze? Write a paragraph describing a hobby you enjoy or would like to find out more about. Save this paragraph in your 📁 **Working Portfolio.**

Expanding Sentences

A sentence may be grammatically perfect and complete, but if it doesn't tell you what you need to know, it hasn't done its job. Look at this sentence: **She went.** It raises more questions than it answers. Where did she go? Who is she, anyway? Precise nouns, verbs, and modifiers could expand this basic sentence into one that is clear and informative.

❶ Using Precise Words

A good writer chooses words carefully, selecting precise nouns and verbs that express exactly what the writer wants to say. Notice how the bland, unclear sentence below becomes more meaningful when general nouns and verbs are replaced with precise ones.

She looked at the fish.

Esme stared at the muskie.

Good writers also use modifiers—adjectives and adverbs—to add details to their sentences. Notice how the sentence is transformed by the use of modifiers.

Esme stared wide-eyed at the four-story fiberglass muskie.

To choose precise modifiers, read your sentence and ask yourself the questions *why, what, where, when, who,* and *how.* Use modifiers that answer these questions to expand your sentence.

PRACTICE A Spice It Up

Improve these sentences by following the directions in parentheses.

1. We took a trip. (Use precise words.)
2. We saw a barn. (Add modifiers.)
3. It was old. (Use precise words.)
4. The barn had a sign on the side. (Add modifiers.)
5. It was hard to read. (Use precise words.)

Now, look in your 🗀 **Working Portfolio** and find the paragraph you wrote for the **Write Away** exercise on page 329. Revise the paragraph by replacing general words with precise words and adding modifiers.

❷ Adding Phrases

Phrases add focus and detail to your writing. Like a single-word modifier, a phrase changes or clarifies parts of a sentence. A prepositional phrase, for example, can tell where or when the action took place. You can add phrases to the beginning, middle, or end of a sentence. The examples below show how different phrases can change the same sentence.

Dan's family rented a cabin.

In the Rocky Mountains, Dan's family rented a cabin.
PREPOSITIONAL PHRASE

Dan's family, three kids and their parents, rented a cabin.
APPOSITIVE PHRASE

Dan's family rented a cabin shaped like a tepee.
PARTICIPIAL PHRASE

 Make sure your sentence is complete before you try to expand it. If it doesn't have a subject and a predicate, it's a fragment.

PRACTICE B Liven Up This Family's Vacation

To improve these simple sentences, add a phrase to each by following the directions in parentheses. Then add precise words or modifiers where you think they will improve each sentence.

1. My family went on vacation. (Add a phrase to the end.)
2. We saw a display of dinosaur replicas. (Add a phrase to the beginning.)
3. My sister and I dug for fossils. (Add a phrase in the middle.)
4. She found a tiny jawbone. (Add a phrase to the end.)
5. The guide said it was from an ancient mammal. (Add a phrase in the middle.)

Combining Complete Sentences

Sometimes a simple sentence is all you need, but a series of short, choppy sentences can be boring to read. For variety, use conjunctions to combine simple sentences into compound or complex sentences.

❶ Forming Compound Sentences

Sometimes joining sentences makes the relationship between them clearer. When you use a conjunction such as *and, but, or, so,* or *nor* to join two short, related sentences, you make a **compound sentence.** This chart shows when to use each of these conjunctions.

Conjunctions for Compound Sentences		
In order to	**Use this conjunction**	**Example**
Join sentences with similar ideas	**and**	My mother is a chemist, **and** my father invents computer games.
Join sentences with contrasting ideas	**but**	I like water ballet, **but** my friend prefers swimming laps.
Join sentences to offer a choice	**or**	We can hike to the lake, **or** Mom can drive us to the water slides.
Join sentences to show cause and effect	**so**	I sprained my ankle, **so** I can't go skating for two weeks.
Join two sentences that express negatives	**nor**	Douglas won't eat asparagus, **nor** will he eat liver.

WATCH OUT

Remember to use a comma when you use a conjunction such as *and, but, or, so,* or *nor* to join two sentences. Put the comma before the conjunction.

CHAPTER 13

❷ Forming Complex Sentences

Sometimes the idea in one sentence helps explain or clarify the idea in another sentence. You can use a conjunction such as *although, since, if, as, until,* or *because* to join these sentences and make a **complex sentence.**

> **Al is worried about his science project. It smells awful.**
>
> **Al is worried about his science project because it smells awful.**

> **Ann likes ice cream. She's buying it for our party.**
>
> **Since Ann likes ice cream, she's buying it for our party.**

> **Sonya lost the race. She tied the record in the mile run.**
>
> **Although Sonya lost the race, she tied the record in the mile run.**

HOT TIP

You can also combine sentences by using pairs of conjunctions such as *either/or, neither/nor, both/and,* and *whether/or.*

> **We go to the Thai restaurant. We eat at home.**
>
> **Either we can go to the Thai restaurant, or we can eat at home.**

PRACTICE Combining with Conjunctions

Combine each pair of short sentences below, using the conjunction in parentheses.

1. Lila complains too much. Erika puts up with it. *(but)*
2. Our plane leaves tomorrow. We'd better pack today. *(so)*
3. Every day is an adventure. We don't enjoy every one. *(although)*
4. You're 48 inches tall. You can ride the Cliffhanger. *(if)*
5. That was a boring party. There was no entertainment. *(because)*
6. You can run track. You can join the swim team. *(either/or)*
7. The snow is deep. Put on some high boots. *(since)*
8. The ship docks. Stay on this deck. *(until)*
9. Eva writes poetry. Eva reads stories. *(and)*
10. Ed likes to read mysteries. Vi enjoys biographies. *(and)*

Combining Sentence Parts

You can take information from two or more sentences and combine it into one sentence to add variety and keep your writing crisp and to the point.

① Inserting Words

Sometimes two sentences contain similar information. Often you can combine these sentences by moving a word or words from one sentence into the other.

Katya plays guitar. Rachel plays guitar too.

Katya and Rachel play guitar.

Emilio writes songs for his band. Emilio also arranges songs for his band.

Emilio writes and arranges songs for his band.

Sometimes when you move a word from one sentence to another, you must change the form of the word.

Greg pounds the drums. He is a vigorous drummer.

Greg pounds the drums vigorously.

Ingrid sang into the microphone. She smiled.

Smiling, Ingrid sang into the microphone.

PRACTICE Combining Sentence Parts

Combine each pair of sentences by moving an important word or words from one sentence to the other. If necessary, change the form of the word or words you add.

1. John Adams lived to be 90. Herbert Hoover did too.
2. Grandma posed for a portrait. The pose was glamorous.
3. Mr. Clay makes math seem easy. He makes science seem easy too.
4. We stumbled along the path. The path was rough and rocky.
5. The door fell off its hinges. The hinges were rusty.

❷ Inserting Phrases

Another way to combine two sentences is to make one into a phrase and insert it into the other sentence.

Kofi found an old letter. It was in the attic.

Kofi found an old letter in the attic.

It was addressed to Juan. Juan is Kofi's uncle.

It was addressed to Juan, Kofi's uncle.

Kofi wanted to find out more. She looked at the return address.

To find out more, Kofi looked at the return address.

As you read the model below, notice how much information the writer includes in only two smoothly written sentences. The use of phrases makes this possible.

LITERARY MODEL

According to tradition, the idea of the Frankenstein monster was first put into words in Switzerland on a stormy evening in 1816. A group of friends decided to pass the evening by telling stories based on supernatural events.

—Daniel Cohen, "Man-Made Monsters"

PREPOSITIONAL PHRASES

GERUND PHRASE

PARTICIPIAL PHRASE

PRACTICE B Phrase It

Combine each pair of sentences by turning one into a phrase and inserting it into the other.

1. Maria's family is moving. They are going to Denver.
2. Her mom works for Acme, Inc. She is an accountant.
3. Denver is in Colorado. It is located at the foot of the Rockies.
4. Maria wants to ski down a mountain. She will need some instruction.
5. Mr. Lopez gave a farewell party for Maria. He is her teacher.

Using *Who, That,* **and** *Which*

You can use the word *who* to combine sentences about people. To combine sentences about places or things, you can use the word *that* or *which.*

❶ Adding Details About People

Sometimes one sentence contains details about a person who is mentioned in another sentence. You can use the word *who* to combine these sentences.

> **The woman brought us a crazy tin-can sculpture. She said someone left it at her door by mistake.**

> **The woman who brought us a crazy tin-can sculpture said someone left it at her door by mistake.**

If the information you are adding is not essential to the meaning of the sentence, set it off with commas.

> **Howard Finster exhibits his folk art all over the world. He lives in Summerville, Georgia.**

> **Howard Finster, who lives in Summerville, Georgia, exhibits his folk art all over the world.**

Information is considered essential if it is necessary to the meaning of the sentence. If you can take out the information and not change the meaning of the sentence, the information is nonessential.

PRACTICE A ▸ Who Did It?

Combine each pair of sentences using the word *who.* Remember to use commas to set off nonessential information.

1. My teacher exhibited her paintings at a gallery. She is a talented artist.
2. That woman is very rude. She is blocking my view of the stage.
3. Zeke is saving money to buy a computer. He works part-time.
4. That boy should get a reward. He found the lost documents.
5. Dana owns a chameleon. He won the weird pet contest.

❷ Adding Details About Places and Things

If you have one sentence that introduces a place or thing and another sentence that provides more details about that place or thing, you can use the word *that* or *which* to combine the sentences. If the information you are adding is essential to the meaning of the sentence, use the word *that.*

My friend has a carved box. The box is a good example of tramp art.

My friend has a carved box that is a good example of tramp art.

If you are adding details that make the sentence more interesting but don't affect its meaning, use the word *which.*

This unusual throne is constructed of thousands of bottle caps. It was crafted by Mr. Imagination.

This unusual throne, which was crafted by Mr. Imagination, is constructed of thousands of bottle caps.

Use commas when you add *which* to combine sentences. Don't use commas when you combine sentences with *that.*

PRACTICE B *That or Which?*

Combine the two sentences in each item below by using the word *that* or *which.*

1. This is the sandpaper. You need it to finish the project.
2. Tyrone read his paper to the class. It earned an A.
3. Maples are deciduous trees. They lose their leaves each autumn.
4. An abstract painting won the contest. It was hung upside down.
5. Marla's drawing did not attract much attention. It was not her best.

Using Active and Passive Voice

What is the difference between these two sentences?

Zoe hit the ball over the fence.

The ball was hit over the fence by Zoe.

In the first sentence the verb is in the **active voice;** the subject (Zoe) is performing the action. The verb in the second sentence is in the **passive voice;** the subject (the ball) is receiving the action, or being acted upon.

❶ Using Active Voice

Active voice lends strength and confidence to writing. In the model below, notice how the writer uses active voice to convey the excitement of a baseball game.

LITERARY MODEL

...Sandy Amoros, fleet of foot, gallant of will, raced to within inches of the concrete left-field wall, stretched out his gloved hand, and snatched the ball ... then ... wheeled and rocketed the ball to Reese, the cutoff man, who, in turn, threw to first to double up McDougald.

—Doris Kearns Goodwin, *Wait Till Next Year: A Memoir*

Why Writers Use Active Voice	
Reason	**Example**
To emphasize who or what is doing the action	**Hank blasted that ball out of the park.** (emphasizes Hank) **The ball was blasted out of the park by Hank.** (emphasizes the ball)
To capture the reader's attention	**Bill plucked the ball from the air.** (creates sense of action) **The ball was plucked from the air by Bill.** (slows the action)
To be more concise	**Amanda tagged the runner out at third.** (concise) **The runner was tagged out at third by Amanda.** (wordy)

❷ Using Passive Voice for Effect

To emphasize the receiver of the action or the action itself, use passive voice. You can also use passive voice when the person performing the action is unknown or unimportant, the way passive voice is used in the model below.

> **LITERARY MODEL**
>
> When the lineups were announced, I was dismayed to learn that Jackie Robinson was not starting. Hobbled by a strained Achilles tendon, he was replaced by rookie Don Hoak.
>
> —Doris Kearns Goodwin, *Wait Till Next Year: A Memoir*

Why Writers Use Passive Voice

Reason	Example
To emphasize the receiver of the action or the action itself	**Our star batter was benched for a week.** (The benching of the player is most important to the fans.)
To convey that the performer of the action is unknown or unimportant	**The pitcher and shortstop were tapped for the All Star game.** (The people who decided they were All Stars aren't important to the sentence.)
To create a passive, timeless mood or tone	**For more than a century, these bases have been pounded by cleat-clad feet.**

 HOT TIP Use passive voice in a science lab report to emphasize the data and results rather than the person conducting the experiment.

PRACTICE Active vs. Passive

Decide whether active or passive voice is used in each of the following sentences. Then change the voice.

1. The bat was swung by Lana with great force.
2. Someone took Matt off the roster today.
3. Mom's meatloaf was eaten by the dog.
4. New rules for detention were announced by Ms. Casey.
5. The room was painted red by Frank.

Student Help Desk

Crafting Sentences at a Glance

Begin with a simple, complete sentence.

> I made a whatsit.

Expand it.

> In my workshop, I invented an amazing whatsit.

Combine it with another sentence.

> In my workshop, I invented an amazing whatsit that can fly and play music.

Combining Sentences — Weld Those Words

Technique	Example
Combine complete sentences.	Rachel designed the model rocket, **and** Lamar shot it high into the sky.
Add words and phrases.	Akira **expertly** constructed a house of cards.
	Greg assembled models **of a ship and a car.**
Add details about people.	Mauricio, **who wants to be a lawyer,** studied how to patent an invention.
Add details about places or things.	My invention, **which is a device that counts swimming strokes,** won a ribbon at the Young Designer's Fair.

Expanding Sentences Fine-Tune with Precision

Technique	Base Sentence	Expanded Sentence
Use precise words.	Tran made something.	Tran **assembled** a **periscope**.
Add modifiers.	He used cardboard and mirrors.	He used **sturdy** cardboard and **well-polished** mirrors.
Add phrases.	It worked well.	**When used by Tran to see around the corner of his house,** it worked well.

Conjunctions

Use this memory device to remember conjunctions that make compound sentences.

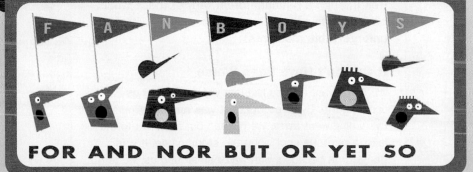

FOR AND NOR BUT OR YET SO

SENTENCES

The Bottom Line

Checklist for Crafting Sentences

Have I . . .

___ made sure my sentence is complete?

___ used precise words?

___ added words or phrases to make my sentences stronger and more varied?

___ combined similar sentences to eliminate unneeded repetition?

___ added details about people, places, and things?

___ used active or passive voice to achieve the best effect?

abandoned

thrilling

unforgettable

MOMENTOUS

excitin

awry

Power Words
Vocabulary for Precise Writing

A Trip to Remember

These words can help you separate fun experiences from the ones you'd rather forget!

How Could It Be Better?

This year, wouldn't it be great to do something **special** and **fun** and really **noteworthy** for our vacation? What if we could do some **exciting** white water rafting out west, or take a **thrilling** ride on Brazil's Amazon River? A **memorable** visit to a foreign city would be great, or a **momentous** trek through a national forest. Any of these would be a **once-in-a-lifetime** experience, filled with **unforgettable** moments.

It Couldn't Have Been Worse

We don't want it to be like last year's **disastrous** camping trip. By all accounts, it was **appalling.** Everything went **awry.** We pitched our tent next to the lake, a **perilous** spot when the storm came. It was **dangerous** because, with water all around us, we felt **stranded** and **marooned,** wondering how long we might be **abandoned** in the tent! Luckily, the sun came out the next day and our **miserable** trip finally ended.

▷ **Your Turn** Dream Vacation

What would be the ideal vacation spot for you? Would it be a real place or one you dream up? Perhaps it's even a place you've been before. Design a travel brochure advertising this spot. Describe the setting, the weather, the food, and explain why someone would want to travel there. Use a computer graphics program to design your travel brochure.

MAROONED

disastrou

Building Paragraphs

"I hope you realize that I'm the one who has to write about this stupid vacation next fall."

© The New Yorker Collection 1999 Peter Steiner from cartoonbank.com.

Virtual Vacation

A good writer can turn even a bad vacation into a memorable well-written paragraph. By organizing events in an interesting way and including descriptive details, a writer can create a paragraph that brings the story—good or bad—to life.

Write Away: The Perfect Vacation
Write a paragraph explaining your idea of the perfect vacation. You might describe a vacation that you or a friend took, or you could write about a real or an imaginary place you'd like to visit. Save your paragraph in your 🗂 **Working Portfolio.**

Types of Paragraphs

A **paragraph** is a group of related sentences that work together to develop a single idea. There are four types of paragraphs: descriptive, narrative, informative, and persuasive. They are used for different purposes and have different characteristics. When writing is logically divided into paragraphs, it is easier for the reader to understand.

❶ Paragraphs That Describe

A **descriptive** paragraph helps the reader to re-create a person, a place, a thing, or an experience. In the paragraph below, notice how the writer includes many details that help you to understand something about the president.

> **LITERARY MODEL**
>
> The morning he died, Lincoln had in his pockets a pair of small spectacles folded into a silver case; a small velvet eyeglass cleaner; a large linen handkerchief with *A. Lincoln* stitched in red; an ivory pocketknife trimmed with silver; and a brown leather wallet lined with purple silk.
>
> —Russell Freedman, *Lincoln: A Photobiography*

Details help the reader focus on Lincoln's possessions.

Here's How **Writing a Descriptive Paragraph**

- Create a list or cluster diagram of descriptive details, including sensory items: sights, sounds, textures, smells, and tastes.
- Choose details that will create a particular impression on the reader.

❷ Paragraphs That Tell a Story

A **narrative** paragraph tells a story or relates an incident. It must have a definite beginning, middle, and end. Narrative paragraphs are often used to tell **anecdotes**—short and amusing accounts of incidents, such as the one on the next page.

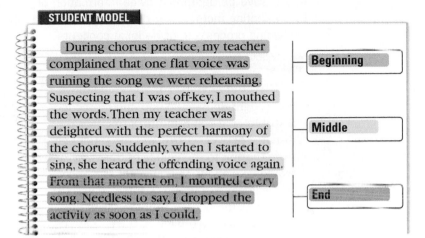

During chorus practice, my teacher complained that one flat voice was ruining the song we were rehearsing. Suspecting that I was off-key, I mouthed the words. Then my teacher was delighted with the perfect harmony of the chorus. Suddenly, when I started to sing, she heard the offending voice again. From that moment on, I mouthed every song. Needless to say, I dropped the activity as soon as I could.

Beginning

Middle

End

Here's How **Writing a Narrative Paragraph**

- List events in sequence.
- Add details that answer the questions *who, what, when, where, why,* and *how.*
- Use transition words— such as *then* and *suddenly*—to help readers follow the sequence.

PRACTICE A **As If You're There**

Write a paragraph describing this photo of a ballpark. Describe what you might see, hear, smell, taste, or feel by using sensory details.

For more transition words, see p. 353.

PRACTICE B **Tell All About It**

Write a narrative paragraph about something that happened to you. Here are some possibilities: an embarrassing incident, something you did for the first time, a funny experience, or a special sports victory.

PARAGRAPHS 1

❸ Paragraphs That Inform

Informative paragraphs provide information or explanation by presenting facts, giving directions, analyzing situations, explaining processes, or defining concepts.

PROFESSIONAL MODEL

How big is space? If you could move as fast as light does—186,000 miles a second—it would take you 8 minutes to cover the distance between Earth and the sun. To go from the sun to the center of the Milky Way would take about 33,000 years. The Milky Way belongs to a group of some 20 galaxies known as the Local Group. To cross the Local Group you'd have to travel for 2 million years.

—"Exploring Galaxies," *National Geographic World*

> **Topic sentence** gives the focus of the paragraph

> Explains main idea with facts

Here's How ▸ Writing an Informative Paragraph

- Compose a topic sentence that gives interesting key information about the subject.
- Present additional facts, definitions, and explanations as support.
- Use examples and descriptions to illustrate facts.

PRACTICE C ▸ Writing an Informative Paragraph

Look at the diagram of the water cycle below. Then write an informative paragraph that explains it.

Evaporation

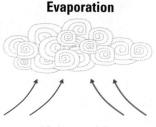

Moisture rising

Precipitation

Moisture falling

❹ Paragraphs That Persuade

A **persuasive** paragraph presents a point of view and tries to make readers agree with it. To be convincing, a good argument depends on sound reasoning and factual support.

STUDENT MODEL

Middle school students should be allowed to vote in political elections. We are exposed to politics on television and in the newspapers every day of our lives. We have our own opinions. Why not let us cast ballots? Eighth graders study United States history and take the Constitution Test. Because of these requirements, we know more than many adults. If we could vote, we would pay more attention to politics and the government. Some of us might even work to get our candidates elected. Many decisions that affect students are made by politicians. We should have a voice in these decisions. Let us vote!

Topic sentence states the opinion.

REASON 1

REASON 2

REASON 3

Here's How Writing a Persuasive Paragraph

- State your opinion in the topic sentence.
- Give clear reasons to persuade readers to agree.
- Support your opinion with facts and/or examples.

PRACTICE D Trust Me, I'm Right!

Write a letter to the editor of your student newspaper concerning one of the following proposed issues:

1. Requiring uniforms to be worn in school
2. Scheduling all students for a mandatory daily study hall
3. Abolishing cheerleading as a sport

Pick one issue and write a topic sentence that states whether you agree or disagree with the issue. Then finish the paragraph; support your opinion and persuade others to agree with you.

Unity in Paragraphs

All good paragraphs share two characteristics: unity and coherence. **Unity** in a paragraph means that all the sentences work together to support a central idea. **Coherence** means that all the sentences flow smoothly and logically from one to another.

❶ Topic Sentence: The Most Valuable Player

The key sentence in a unified paragraph is the topic sentence. A **topic sentence** states the main idea of the paragraph.

STUDENT MODEL

> Many claim that Michael Jordan is the greatest basketball player of all time, but he wasn't always a superstar. At the University of North Carolina, Jordan played well, but wasn't chosen college player of the year until his last season. He turned pro in 1984 when he joined the Chicago Bulls. Yet it wasn't until the late 1980s that Jordan dominated the NBA by being the scoring leader year after year.

Topic sentence states a fact that the rest of the sentences support.

Avoid topic sentences that are vague or too general. Get straight to the point and state the important idea first.

Here's How Composing a Topic Sentence

1. Decide on the main point of your paragraph.
2. State your main point and related information in a sentence.
3. Rewrite your sentence until it is interesting and engaging.

Weak Bill Gates is both successful and talented. *(doesn't state important idea or interest the reader)*

Better Bill Gates, the computer genius, has affected the way we live as much as Thomas Edison did. *(tells who he is and what the paragraph will be about)*

❷ Implied Topic Sentence: The Implied Main Idea

Sometimes the topic sentence in a good paragraph is **implied,** or suggested, rather than directly stated. The main idea of the paragraph is still clear because all the sentences directly relate to it.

STUDENT MODEL

Five days a week students have to get up early to get to school on time. Many of us have school activities that require us to arrive at 6:30 or 7:00 A.M. Then, we have a full day of classes with barely enough time for lunch, much less a rest. After school, many students play sports or are busy with clubs or organizations. When we finally arrive home, dinner is often a rushed meal, followed by homework. Many teens hold down part-time jobs. By the time these obligations are fulfilled, it is 10:00 or 11:00 P.M.

> **Implied Topic Sentence:** Teenagers do not have enough free time.

Here is another model with an implied main idea.

PROFESSIONAL MODEL

Does anybody remember tiddlywinks? Kids these days seem to crave electronic games.... They're not just for kids, of course—much ... new software is geared toward adults. But the software, hardware, and portables still appeal most to youthful buyers, who could push U.S. retail sales in this industry as high as $7 billion this year.

> **Implied Topic Sentence:** Kids are the major consumers of electronic games.

—"Video Games," *Business Week*

To make sure that you have included a topic sentence, compose a sentence that summarizes your main point, and make sure something similar to it appears in your paragraph.

❸ Understanding Unity: Paring Down the Details

You don't bring a tennis racket to the library—it doesn't belong there. The same holds true for irrelevant information in a paragraph. Keep only what relates to the main idea and throw out the rest.

STUDENT MODEL

Exercise is so important to good health that it should be part of every teenager's life. ~~Eating the right foods is also good for you.~~ Team sports are great exercise, but you have to have enough people to play. If you're home alone, you have to be more creative. One way to get exercise is to jump rope or do jumping jacks. You can also buy a small trampoline at a sporting goods store and use it to jump on. ~~Some people are lucky enough to have a big trampoline in their backyard.~~

Topic sentence states the main idea.

Irrelevant information distracts from the main idea.

Here's How Revising for Unity

- Make sure that every sentence relates to the main idea.
- Remove all unrelated sentences or details.

PRACTICE A Spotting Irrelevant Detail

Identify the topic sentence in the following paragraph, and state which unrelated sentence or sentences should be removed.

Be sure to drink water before, during, and after exercise. I happen to prefer orange juice. Exercise causes your body to lose water by sweating, so you need to constantly replace what you've lost. Sweating is absolutely disgusting! Your body is more than 90 percent water. Although ads claim that sports drinks restore vital nutrients lost during exercise, experts say the best thing to drink is water.

PRACTICE B Making Repairs

In your 🗐 **Working Portfolio,** find your **Write Away** paragraph. Revise your paragraph, using what you have learned about unity.

Coherence in Paragraphs

While unity involves a paragraph as a whole, coherence depends on the connections between the individual ideas in a paragraph.

Understanding Coherence: Connect the Sentences

A paragraph has coherence when all its sentences are arranged in a logical order, so that readers can follow the flow of ideas. Transition words make connections between sentences easier to follow and establish order in a paragraph.

DRAFT

I believe that students at our school should continue to wear uniforms. Wearing uniforms saves money. If we didn't have uniforms we would have to buy new clothes. Putting on a uniform saves time in the morning. You don't have to decide what to wear. The school does allow us to wear our own shoes. Most students feel better about wearing the rest of the uniform.

> Sentences are not linked by transition words.

REVISION

I believe that students at our school should continue to wear uniforms. **First of all,** wearing uniforms saves money. If we didn't have uniforms we would have to buy new clothes. **Second,** putting on a uniform saves time in the morning **because** you don't have to decide what to wear. **Finally,** the school does allow us to wear different kinds of shoes now, **so** most students feel better about wearing the rest of the uniform.

> Sentences are in logical order and build on one another.

> **Transition words** help readers follow the argument.

Student Help Desk

Building Paragraphs at a Glance

Building Blocks of Prime Paragraphs

UNITY:
Teamwork
All sentences support the main idea.

TOPIC SENTENCE:
Most Valuable Player
One sentence expresses the main idea.

COHERENCE:
Connections
Each sentence flows logically into the next.

Types of Paragraphs   Paragraph Profiles

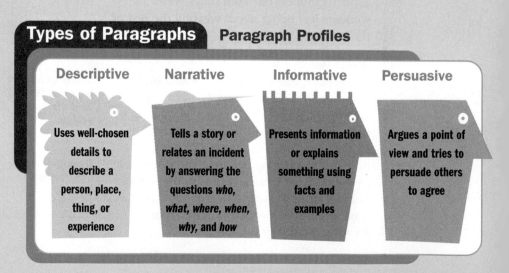

Descriptive

Uses well-chosen details to describe a person, place, thing, or experience

Narrative

Tells a story or relates an incident by answering the questions *who, what, where, when, why,* and *how*

Informative

Presents information or explains something using facts and examples

Persuasive

Argues a point of view and tries to persuade others to agree

Test for Paragraph Unity Does It Make the Grade?

✓ Check that each sentence relates to the main idea. *A+*

✓ Revise or remove sentences that distract from the main idea. *A+*

✓ Save interesting but distracting sentences for another paragraph. *A+*

Bridge the Gap

Transition Words

Descriptive	Narrative	Informative	Persuasive
above	first	also	beyond
across	later	instead	outside
behind	eventually	as a result	in between
below	next	similarly	then
inside	suddenly	although	finally
around	after	because	meanwhile
beyond	then	for example	for example
outside	finally	likewise	since
between	meanwhile	for this reason	in conclusion

The Bottom Line

Checklist for Building Paragraphs

Have I . . .

____ expressed the main idea in a stated or implied topic sentence?

____ checked to see that all sentences support the main idea?

____ added transition words where needed?

____ included vivid details in my descriptive paragraph?

____ answered important questions in my narrative paragraph?

____ used facts and examples in my informative paragraph?

____ used logical reasoning in my persuasive paragraph?

puzzle

incoherent

Power Words
Vocabulary for Precise Writing

illogical

senseless

Get the Story Straight

Use these words to describe what is confusing and what is clear.

What Do You Mean?

If you were a reporter for your city's newspaper, first you'd want to get the facts of your story straight. A **mixed-up, muddled** reporter may write **incoherent, senseless** stories that **puzzle** readers, and seem to be **without rhyme or reason.** You wouldn't want **disorganized, disjointed, illogical** writing to **mislead** or **confuse** your audience. Then your readers would be too **befuddled** to tell what happened or when.

The Facts, Please

Organizing your information before writing will help your readers **understand, comprehend,** and **make sense** of your article. When readers can **digest** the facts, **grasp** the concepts, **fathom** the ideas, and **perceive** your meaning, you've done a good job of communicating the information. **Apprehending** a topic always helps you write an **intelligible** article.

▷ **Your Turn** What's Happening?

Find a newspaper article and clip out the first two paragraphs. Rewrite it, moving the sentences around so the story no longer makes any sense. Ask a classmate to figure out what is happening in the story, and try to put it in order.

misle

confuse

mudd

di jointed

befuddl

Organizing Paragraphs

The Gold Nugget News

Thursday, March 18, 1849

Forty-Niner Loses Fortune in Rough and Ready

Jack Meade is currently in a Rough and Ready boarding house tending to his wounds. The men jumped him, beat him, stole his gold and his mule. Little did he know, that six outlaws were lying in wait in the mountains between the American River and Rough and Ready. Meade, fresh from Ireland, loaded twenty bags onto a mule and began his journey west, back to Rough and Ready. He is currently staying in Rough and Ready, California. Last week, twenty-year-old miner Jack Meade discovered gold nuggets at his claim on the American River.

The center of California Gold Rush Country

Out of Order

What really happened at Rough and Ready in 1849? It seems the writer of this story got the facts out of order. A paragraph like this is hard to read and even harder to understand. Can you organize the sentences so that the events of the story make sense?

Write Away: Getting Organized

Think of a recent newsworthy event that you experienced firsthand. Maybe you saw a music group in concert, or perhaps your favorite school politician was elected to the student board. Write a short paragraph as if you were a reporter covering a news story. Save the paragraph in your **Working Portfolio.**

PARAGRAPHS 2

Sequential Order

Using Sequence and Time

Use **sequential order** when you want to show the order in which events occur. Sequential order can be used to give directions or to show steps in a process. **Chronological order** is a special type of sequential order. It can be used to tell a story or to show the order in which events happen over time.

The model below uses sequential order to describe a medical procedure.

LITERARY MODEL

I did a craniectomy. **First** I opened her head and took off the front portion of her skull. The skull bone was put in a sterile solution. **Then** I opened up the covering of her brain—the dura. Between the two halves of the brain is an area called the falx. By splitting the falx, the two halves could communicate together and equalize the pressure between her hemispheres. Using cadaveric dura (dura from a dead person), I sewed it over her brain. . . . **Once** I covered the area, I closed the scalp. The surgery took about two hours.

—Ben Carson, M.D., *Gifted Hands*

> **Transition words** help readers follow the sequence of events.

Here's How   Planning to Write in Sequential Order

1. List the events or steps you want to describe.

2. Arrange the events or steps in order of occurrence.

3. Use transition words such as *first, next,* and *after* to link the events.

PRACTICE   How Did It Go?

Have you ever dissected an animal? made a tiny hair braid? built a house of cards? Think of a time you had to use your hands to perform a task that took a great deal of concentration. Re-create the process in your mind, and then write a paragraph that describes the sequence of steps you went through in trying to get the job done.

Spatial Order

Describing Objects and People

Spatial order shows how people and objects are arranged in a space or scene. A description can be organized spatially in several ways: from top to bottom, outside to inside, left to right, near to far, or the reverse of any of these.

To help the reader form a picture of the Bighorn Medicine Wheel, the writer of this model describes the structure from the center outward.

PROFESSIONAL MODEL

High on a bare, windswept mountaintop in northern Wyoming lies an unusual circle of stones, about eighty feet across. **In the center,** more rocks are gathered into a pile called a *cairn*. Twenty-eight lines of stones lead **from the center** cairn **to the edge** of the circle, like spokes of a wheel. **Just outside** the circle stand six smaller cairns.

—Elsa Marston,
Mysteries in American Archeology

> **Direction words** help readers understand the arrangement of objects in this space.

Bighorn Medicine Wheel

When you are organizing information spatially, using directional words and phrases such as *above, beneath, to the right, next to,* and *overhead* can help you craft a successful paragraph.

Here's How **Planning to Write in Spatial Order**

1. Picture the person, place, thing, or experience you want to describe.
2. Decide how much of the scene you want to include.
3. Choose the best way to approach your description—for example, top to bottom or side to side.
4. As you write the scene, move from one object or person to the next, using directional words and phrases to describe the spatial relationships.

PARAGRAPHS 2

Cause-and-Effect Order

Explaining How or Why

Cause-and-effect order is often the best way to organize a description of the reasons certain events happen. A **cause** is what makes something happen. An **effect** is what results from a cause. For example,

Because Trixy left the birdcage door open,	CAUSE
Bizby the parakeet got loose in the house,	EFFECT
and then he flew out the front door.	EFFECT

Historical and scientific writing often contains paragraphs arranged in cause-and-effect order. In the example below, each effect becomes the cause of another effect.

PROFESSIONAL MODEL

A flash flood is triggered when a large amount of rain falls in a very short time over a mountainous area. Little or no water seeps into the soil as it rushes down the steep slopes. So the water level in a mountain stream rises very quickly, sending a flood wave roaring down the valley battering anything in its path.

—Derek Elsom, *Weather Explained*

First sentence introduces the subject.

Supporting sentences describe the chain of causes and effects.

Here's How Using Cause-and-Effect Order

- Use your topic sentence to state the cause-and-effect relationship.
- Clearly explain how the causes are connected to the effects.
- Use transition words and phrases such as *so, because, when,* and *as a result* to link the causes and effects to one another.

You can use cause-and-effect order to explain how one cause leads to one or more effects or how several causes contribute to one effect. Transition words and phrases help make the relationships clear.

On October 29, 1929, later known as Black Tuesday, the stock market crashed in the United States. **Because of** the public panic created by the crash, long lines formed at banks as people waited to withdraw all their money. Most banks ran out of funds, and many people lost their savings. **As a result,** millions of Americans ended up living in the streets.

> First sentence sets up cause.

> Transition phrases alert reader to a cause-and-effect relationship.

Just because one event comes after another does not mean they have a cause-and-effect relationship. For example, "I forgot to wear my lucky necklace, so I didn't get a role in the play" is faulty cause-and-effect reasoning.

PRACTICE Not-So-Special Effects

Imagine you are writing a paper about the damaging effects of the Great Long Island Hurricane of 1938. You have listed its cause and effects on notecards. Now write a paragraph explaining how the cause and the effects are related.

Cause

In 1938, an unpredicted Category-3 hurricane with winds up to 186 mph strikes Long Island, New York.

Effects

• More than 6 feet of water flood Westhampton's main streets.
• 20,000 miles of electrical power and telephone lines are downed.
• 63,000 people are left homeless.

PARAGRAPHS 2

Compare-and-Contrast Order

Showing Similarities and Differences

Compare-and-contrast order is often used in science and social studies writing. There are two ways to compare and contrast things: by subjects or by features. The **feature-by-feature** approach used in the model below focuses on the features, or characteristics, of blimps and airships.

PROFESSIONAL MODEL

The Navy's ZMC-2 airship of the 1930s, the "Tin Balloon," may look similar to an advertising blimp of today, but the differences are many. **Like** a modern blimp, the ZMC-2 was bullet-shaped and filled with helium. However, **unlike** a modern blimp, which is covered with tough polyester fabric, the ZMC-2 had an outer skin that was all metal. **Another difference** involves the comfort of the crew. **Instead** of cruising smoothly like modern blimps, the ZMC-2 gave its crew such a rough ride that they often got sick!

—Alex Task

> Topic sentence sets up the comparison.

> **Transition words and phrases** help set up a feature-by-feature discussion.

During prewriting, you can use a Venn diagram like the one below to make the similarities and differences clear.

Navy airship only:
• metal covering
• rough ride

Both:
• bullet-shaped
• full of helium

Modern blimp only:
• polyester covering
• cruises smoothly

Similarities

 HOT TIP

Remember that when you **compare,** you discuss similarities. When you **contrast,** you discuss differences.

When you use a **subject-by-subject** organization, first describe one of the items and then the other.

What is a wetland? To qualify, the area must have standing water either at the surface of the land or near the roots of plants. Contrary to popular belief, all wetlands are not murky swamps. A frozen landscape like the Arctic is also a wetland. The Arctic has standing water at the surface of the land. The water in this case is frozen. In contrast, the water in a swamp sits at the roots of the plants and rarely gets cold enough to freeze. The Florida Everglades are a good example of swampland.

—Anne Boehm

Topic sentence introduces both subjects: types of wetlands

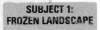

SUBJECT 1:
FROZEN LANDSCAPE

SUBJECT 2:
SWAMP

Here's How Using Compare-and-Contrast Order

- Use a Venn diagram to identify major similarities and differences.
- Decide whether the information would be better presented subject-by-subject or feature-by-feature.
- Use transition words and phrases such as *both, like, unlike,* and *on the other hand.*

PARAGRAPHS 2

PRACTICE What's the Difference?

An igloo is built of snow blocks and is about ten feet in diameter. A geodesic dome is made of aluminum, steel, and plastic triangles and usually is the size of a small house. Using this information and the photographs above, write a paragraph in which you compare and contrast these structures.

Order of Degree

Organizing by Degree

You can use **order of degree** to present information in order of increasing or decreasing importance, usefulness, or familiarity. Order of degree is often used in persuasive paragraphs. In an effort to persuade people not to smoke, the author of the model below describes the effects of carbon monoxide (CO) on cigarette smokers in order of increasing severity.

PROFESSIONAL MODEL

The first symptoms of CO poisoning experienced by cigarette smokers are the inability to perform strenuous activity and a shortness of breath. If the level of CO in the blood reaches around 30 percent, the smoker may become nauseous, dizzy, and suffer from headaches. At a level of 60 percent or higher, damage to the brain and heart occurs, and death can follow in just a few minutes.

LEAST SERIOUS

MORE SERIOUS

MOST SERIOUS

—Gilda Berger, *Smoking Not Allowed*

Three degrees of severity, from least serious to most serious, are described in the professional model:

- inability to perform strenuous activity, shortness of breath
- nausea and dizziness, headaches
- brain and heart damage, death

Here's How **Using Order of Degree**

- Rank details according to their importance, usefulness, or familiarity, or according to some other quality.
- Choose a most-to-least pattern or a least-to-most pattern.
- Use transition words such as *least, more,* and *most* to show the relative importance of each detail.

Notice how comparative and superlative adjectives serve as transition words in this student's paragraph.

When you go to the store to buy something, do you really need to bring it home in a plastic bag that will end up in the huge collection under your kitchen sink? The people who are **MOST HELPFUL** most committed to conserving natural resources buy fewer items and carry them home in a backpack. Sometimes, however, that's not practical. But you can still help save **MORE HELPFUL** resources by investing in a reusable cloth bag that will last for years. At the very least, you **LEAST HELPFUL** can take one of those plastic bags from under the sink to the store and reuse it.

PRACTICE Test Your Persuasive Powers

Do you believe that students should study a foreign language in school? Write a persuasive paragraph stating your opinion. Rank the reasons in order of the least to the most important factors. Try to convince your readers to agree with you.

Calvin and Hobbes by Bill Watterson

Calvin imagines the worst possible consequences of holding a library book past its due date. But are the consequences written in order of degree? Reorder the consequences from the most severe to the least severe.

PARAGRAPHS 2

Student Help Desk

Organizing Paragraphs at a Glance

Sequential Order First (Event 1) ➔ Next (Event 2) ➔ Final (Event 3)

Spatial Order Beside ➔ ◻ ⬅ Next to

Cause-and-Effect Order Cause ➔ Effect 1 ➔ Effect 2 ➔ Effect 3

Compare-and-Contrast Order Subject 1 Both Subject 2

Order of Degree Least ➔ More ➔ Most

Transition Tool Box — Words and Phrases That Link

COMPARE
as
also
in the same
way
like
likewise
similarly

CONTRAST
but
however
in contrast
instead
on the other
hand
unlike

SEQUENTIAL ORDER
next
then
during
last
later
once

SPATIAL ORDER
around
below
center
in front of
outside
surrounding
to the left
to the right

CAUSE-AND-EFFECT ORDER
as a result
because
caused by
consequently
due to
for this reason
if . . . then

ORDER OF DEGREE
even less
even more
finally
first
from . . . to
furthermore
least
most
to

Organizing a Paragraph

Sequential Order

Used in short stories, news reports, "how-to" manuals, biographies, science and history writing
Example: To make a print from a mushroom spore, **first** cut off the mushroom's cap. **Then** place the cap on a piece of paper for two hours.

Spatial Order

Used in science writing, mysteries, eyewitness accounts, short stories
Example: The cauliflower fungus grows **on** the roots of pine trees, **very close to** the base of the tree's trunk.

Cause-and-Effect Order

Used in science and history writing, editorials, persuasive writing
Example: As a result of the increased use of pesticides and fertilizers, field mushrooms have become much less common.

Compare-and-Contrast Order

Used in book reviews, encyclopedias, consumer guides
Example: The dirty trich and the sticky gray trich mushrooms are members of the **same** species. They are **similar** in size. The sticky gray trich can be eaten, **but** the dirty trich is poisonous.

Order of Degree

Used in persuasive writing, editorials, reference books, advertisements
Example: The lawn mower's mushroom is a **familiar** mushroom. The giant puffball is **more unusual.** However, the stinky squid is **very** rare.

The Bottom Line

Checklist for Organizing Paragraphs

Have I . . .

____ chosen a pattern of organization that fits my purpose?

____ used appropriate transition words and phrases?

____ verified any cause-and-effect relationships?

____ established a point of comparison before making a contrast?

Power Words
Vocabulary for Precise Writing

Turn Up the Volume

Some say music is a universal language. Here are some words to add to your "worldly" vocabulary.

Does That Sound Good?

Do songs you like make you want to nod your head to their **pulsing, driving** beat? Or maybe you want to belt out some **harmonious, melodious** verse from the rooftop? Perhaps you like a simple **lilting** rhythm to tap your foot to. Chances are you cringe when you hear something **out of tune,** or **discordant.** Most ears are sensitive to **strident, atonal** sounds because they can be **grating** and sound **off-key.** However, what some consider **harsh, raucous** "noise" is popular, and many say that it's here to stay.

Music Makes the Mood

Do you know a child who falls asleep to a **lullaby?** Has a **symphony** ever filled you with wonder? A **polka** or a **rumba,** a **salsa** or a bit of **swing,** makes some people want to jump up and dance. A school band's **march** or the **musical score** from a movie can make your pulse race. Older people sometimes get nostalgic listening to the **oldies** of their youth or to their favorites, the **golden oldies.**

▶ **Your Turn** Call Your Own Tune

Pick out a piece of music you really enjoy listening to. Using some of the words above, write a review describing the kind of music it is, the qualities it has, and why it appeals to you.

Building Compositions

Jelly Roll Morton, Dizzy Gillespie, and Billie Holiday were "household" names in the 1930s and 1940s. Today, many consider these jazz musicians legendary.

COMPOSITIONS

Note by Note

The history of jazz music is packed with interesting characters and creative melodies. Over the years, jazz musicians have developed many different sounds, like swing, bebop, and jazz fusion. If you decided to write a paper about jazz music, or any other subject with such a long history, how would you go about it?

When you write a composition, it can be difficult even knowing where to begin. A good first step is to get your thoughts organized. This chapter will help you understand how to arrange all of your "notable" ideas into a clear and interesting composition.

Write Away: Meaning in the Music
Find the lyrics to a song you like, and jot them down. Try to figure out what main idea the writer is trying to communicate. Write a paragraph on what you think the song is about and why. Save the paragraph in your 🗂 **Working Portfolio.**

The Parts of a Composition

❶ What Is a Composition?

A **composition** is a piece of writing made up of several paragraphs. You can think of paragraphs as the building blocks of a composition. Writing strong paragraphs can help you put together a successful composition. The chart below shows some of the features paragraphs and compositions share.

Paragraphs and Compositions	
A paragraph has	**A composition has**
A topic sentence	An introduction containing a thesis statement (main idea)
Sentences that offer supporting details	Body paragraphs that develop the topic, or "main idea"
	A concluding paragraph
Unity and coherence among sentences	Unity and coherence within and between paragraphs

Unity in a composition means that the ideas in each paragraph support and explain the thesis statement. **Coherence** means that sentences and paragraphs in a composition connect logically and smoothly to each other.

❷ The Three Parts of a Composition

A composition has three parts: an introduction, a body, and a conclusion.

The **introduction** is the first part of a composition; it introduces the topic. The introduction contains a thesis statement, a sentence that states the main idea and purpose of the composition.

The **body** comes after the introduction and usually consists of at least three paragraphs. Each body paragraph should support, develop, or help explain the idea presented in the thesis statement.

The **conclusion** is the last part of the composition. The conclusion rounds out the composition and brings it to a close.

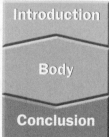

When he was only 22, trumpeter Wynton Marsalis released a jazz recording and a classical recording. Both won Grammy Awards. This was quite amazing because no musician had ever won in those two categories at the same time before. However, performing is just one of his achievements. Marsalis is also a talented composer. **Many of Marsalis's musical compositions are based on his experiences growing up in the South.**

Some of Marsalis's musical compositions reflect his religious upbringing. For example, in his piece *In This House, on This Morning,* one musician plays a melody and another "responds" to it. Marsalis meant for this to remind listeners of the call and response between a minister and a congregation in some African-American churches.

Marsalis also wrote a jazz opera called *Blood on the Fields.* The work deals with the history of slavery in the South. It was highly praised and became the first jazz piece ever to win a Pulitzer Prize.

His childhood experiences also led him to create one unique soundtrack. When Marsalis was young, the only jazz he ever heard on television was the soundtracks of *Peanuts* TV specials. Eventually, he composed the score of the *Peanuts* special "The Wright Brothers at Kitty Hawk." By writing it, he hoped to introduce other children to jazz.

As a performer and a composer Marsalis has gained worldwide fame. Before he had even turned 40, *Time* magazine named him one of "America's 25 Most Influential People." Let's hope Marsalis will continue to develop and share his talents for many years.

—Donald Wymoth

INTRODUCTION
Captures reader's attention with an interesting statement about Marsalis

Thesis statement

BODY
Each body paragraph develops the thesis statement. Each **topic sentence** introduces a new key idea.

CONCLUSION
Restates the main idea and leaves readers with something to think about

COMPOSITIONS

The Introduction

A good **introduction** includes a thesis statement that tells readers what your composition is about. An introduction should also grab your readers' attention and make them want to read more.

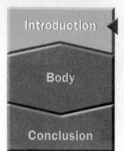

Introduction

Body

Conclusion

❶ The Thesis Statement

An effective **thesis statement** clearly introduces your main idea and your purpose for writing the composition. Your thesis statement should state exactly what the composition is about. If it is too general at first, revise it until it is specific.

> **DRAFT (too general)**
> Oscar Peterson and the late Art Tatum are famous jazz pianists.

> **REVISION (specific and effective)**
> Oscar Peterson and the late Art Tatum are both known as famous jazz pianists, but their playing styles differ greatly.

❷ Types of Introductions

You can start your introduction with a strong description, an anecdote (a brief story), or an interesting statement.

Use a Strong Description

PROFESSIONAL MODEL

Deep in the forest, a blob of glistening yellow slime creeps slowly over the surface of a damp, rotting log. This weird organism isn't an alien life form—it's a slime mold. **Brightly colored, jelly-like slime molds are among the oddest members of the fungus family, and the only ones that can move.**

—Elaine Pascoe, *Slime Molds and Fungi*

The writer uses **vivid description** to lead up to her thesis statement.

The **thesis statement** introduces the main idea in a specific way.

Start with an Anecdote

An anecdote is a brief story that is interesting or funny.

LITERARY MODEL

I first heard of Grace Wiley when Dr. William Mann, former director of the National Zoological Park in Washington, D.C., handed me a picture of a tiny woman with a gigantic king cobra draped over her shoulders like a garden hose. The snake had partly spread his hood and was looking intently into the camera while his mistress stroked his head to quiet him.

> The writer uses a surprising story in his introduction.

—Daniel P. Mannix,
"A Running Brook of Horror"

Make an Interesting Statement

An unusual statement catches the reader's attention.

PROFESSIONAL MODEL

It's strange that Nature isn't nicer. It sure deals in a lot of death. The animals around our summer place don't have much of a life and what they do have doesn't last that long. The flowers don't have it much better, with either too much or too little rain, too much or too little sun and always a killer weed after them.

> The writer opens with an **interesting statement** that makes the reader want to know more.

> The **thesis statement** tells what the composition will be about.

—Andrew A. Rooney, *Not That You Asked . . .*

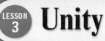
Unity

The **body** of a composition is usually at least three paragraphs long. The paragraphs in the body should have **unity,** which means that they should all relate to and support the thesis statement with facts, details, and related information.

Introduction

Body

Conclusion

❶ Creating Unity

A good way to make sure a composition has unity is to sketch out an informal outline that includes the topic sentence of each body paragraph. If all the topic sentences are related to the thesis statement, the composition is unified.

Informal Outline: Two Jazz Piano Legends

Introduction Thesis Statement:
Oscar Peterson and Art Tatum are both famous jazz pianists, but their playing styles differ greatly.

Body:
1st paragraph: Both Peterson and Tatum are known as awe-inspiring soloists.
~~2nd paragraph: Duke Ellington was also a jazz pianist.~~
3rd paragraph: Tatum was strictly a swing player, while Peterson plays in both the swing and bebop styles.
4th paragraph: Tatum preferred to play alone, but Peterson plays both as a soloist and with groups.
~~5th paragraph: Thelonious Monk's style was not like Tatum's or Peterson's.~~

Oscar Peterson
1925–

Art Tatum
1910–1956

Conclusion:
Despite their differing approaches, both Oscar Peterson and Art Tatum will be remembered for the huge contributions they made to jazz.

CHAPTER 16

❷ Paragraphing

Often you'll find that a long paragraph really addresses more than one idea. Breaking the paragraph into two and using transition words or phrases to link the two paragraphs can make your composition more readable and more unified.

STUDENT MODEL

Art Tatum was famous for his piano solos. He was best known for his ability to play a difficult series of notes very quickly, ⌐, on the other hand, delighting his listeners. He was strictly a swing player, though, and rarely strayed far from the main melody. Oscar Peterson plays two styles of jazz—swing and bebop. He is known for experimenting with the melody during his solos. Peterson's style is "improvisational," meaning he can compose music as he plays it.

> Adding a **transition** connects the first paragraph to the second one.

PRACTICE Creating Unity

The following long paragraph lacks unity. Rewrite it, deleting ideas that are not related to the topic sentence and breaking the paragraph into two.

Kids are supposed to lead carefree lives, but, according to one study, students today spend about eight more hours in school each week than students did in 1981. Today's students also spend more time playing team sports such as soccer and softball. This leaves very little time for students to develop their own interests. I am very interested in women's tennis, for example. The study also reports that, on average, students still manage to watch one and a half hours of TV each weekday. There are also studies about how snacking on too much junk food is bad for you. Maybe kids watch so much TV because after putting in time at school, playing sports, and doing homework, they just don't have the energy to do anything else.

Coherence

LESSON 4

To give your composition **coherence,** you need to organize it logically and show how ideas are connected. You can use transitions and repeated words and phrases to make those connections clear.

Before you begin writing, it is helpful to choose an organizational pattern. Using a pattern of organization such as sequential order (used in the model below) can help you achieve coherence. Other organizational patterns include

- spatial order
- compare-and-contrast order
- cause-and-effect order
- order of degree

❶ Transition Words and Phrases

You can use transition words and phrases to help guide readers from one idea to the next.

PROFESSIONAL MODEL

Mariner 10's **first** encounter with Mercury took place 146 days **after** it was launched from Earth. Reaching Mercury was a remarkable feat of accuracy. It was like tossing a baseball into the glove of a person standing 100 miles (160 kilometers) away.

After its first encounter with Mercury, *Mariner 10* sped away in a large looping orbit of the sun. Its orbit was perfectly shaped, and 176 days **later,** *Mariner 10* and Mercury passed by each other a **second** time. A **third** encounter took place six months **later.**

—Gregory L. Vogt, *Mercury*

Transition words and phrases within and between the paragraphs help readers chart *Mariner 10*'s voyage across the solar system.

Mercury as seen from *Mariner 10*

❷ Repeated Words and Phrases

You can use repeated words and phrases to tie paragraphs together.

LITERARY MODEL

He [Otto Lilienthal] was at the height of his fame when one of his gliders stalled during a Sunday afternoon flight on August 9, 1896. It plunged 50 feet, breaking Lilienthal's spine. He died the next day in a Berlin hospital. His last words: "**Sacrifices** must be made."

Lilienthal wasn't the first to **sacrifice** his life in an effort to fly. Since the earliest times, earthbound humans had envied the freedom of birds and dreamed of imitating them.

—Russell Freedman,
*The Wright Brothers:
How They Invented the Airplane*

> A **repeated word** links the first paragraph to the second.

PRACTICE **Could You Rephrase That?**

Improve the coherence between these two paragraphs. Rewrite the boldface sentence, repeating a word or phrase from the first paragraph or adding a transition.

Before space missions, many thought there was life on the moon. People reasoned that if the Earth could sustain life, why not other planets? When Neil Armstrong first set foot on the moon's surface, what he saw, or rather, what he didn't see, confirmed that there was no life there.

It doesn't have any plant life or water. The two things needed to sustain life as we know it are oxygen and water, and plant life depends on both. The moon is made up of frozen rock, and the temperatures are either too hot or too cold for anything to live there.

LESSON 5 · The Conclusion

The **conclusion** is your final chance to get your point across, so you want to leave readers with something to think about. The models below show three strategies for creating a strong conclusion.

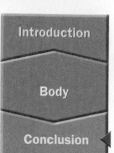
Introduction
Body
Conclusion

Types of Conclusions

Restate the Main Idea

When writing a conclusion, you can "sum up" the composition, as the following model does. Be careful not to add any new information.

> **STUDENT MODEL**
>
> Despite their different styles, both Oscar Peterson and Art Tatum will be remembered for their huge contributions to jazz. Bebop and swing music have gone through many changes since the 1930s, and the talent of men like Peterson and Tatum helped shape the sound of jazz throughout the 1950s. Both will be remembered for their unique abilities as pioneers of jazz piano techniques.

Making a Call to Action

In this conclusion, the writer gives a call to action based on her opinion of Anne Frank's diary.

> **LITERARY MODEL**
>
> This is the legacy she left us, the understanding of things all of us take for granted. Through understanding, let us assure that all people everywhere can live in freedom so that a book like "The Diary of Anne Frank" will never be written again as a true story.
>
> —Gerda Weissmann Klein,
> "A Diary from Another World"

Stating the Significance

In this conclusion of a speech promoting the cause of the Americans with Disabilities Act, the actor Christopher Reeve urges his audience to learn from a former president.

PROFESSIONAL MODEL

President Roosevelt showed us that a man who could barely lift himself out of a wheelchair could still lift a nation out of despair. And I believe—and so does this administration—in the most important principle FDR taught us: **America does not let its needy citizens fend for themselves. America is stronger when all of us take care of all of us.** Giving new life to that ideal is the challenge before us tonight.

—Christopher Reeve, speech at the Democratic National Convention, August 26, 1996

> The writer ties in the **significance** of FDR's message with that of his own.

Here's How Writing the Conclusion

- Restate the main idea given in the thesis statement.
- Sum up the body paragraphs by touching on their major points.
- Leave your readers with a final thought on the topic by offering a call to action or a statement of significance.

HOT TIP

Several good concluding ideas may occur to you as you are drafting the body. Stop and jot them down. That way you'll have a head start when it comes time to work on your conclusion.

COMPOSITIONS

Student Help Desk

Building Compositions at a Glance

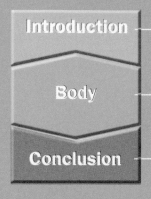

Introduction — Presents the composition's main idea in a focused thesis statement and captures the reader's interest.

Body — All paragraphs support and develop the thesis statement. Paragraphs flow smoothly from one to another.

Conclusion — Brings the composition to a close, leaving the reader with something to ponder.

Types of Introductions A Snappy Start

Use these techniques to get your reader's attention.

Technique	Example
Strong description	Taking the stage, Dizzy Gillespie raised his trumpet to his lips. He filled his cheeks with air until they looked like balloons ready to explode.
Anecdote (brief story)	In 1953 someone accidentally sat on Gillespie's horn, which bent the bell upward. Gillespie tried playing it anyway. To his surprise, he liked the way it sounded and never played a "regular" trumpet again.
Interesting statement	For most of his career Dizzy Gillespie played a squashed trumpet.

Types of Conclusions   A Lasting Impression

You can use these techniques as part of your conclusion.

Technique	Example
Restate the main idea	In his long career, Dizzy Gillespie played a role in the popularization of jazz around the world and the creation of new jazz styles.
Call to action	Without a doubt, Dizzy Gillespie should be considered by all to be one of the great legends in jazz history.
Statement of significance	Dizzy Gillespie made important contributions to the development of jazz and was an inspiration to many young musicians.

The Bottom Line

Checklist for Building Compositions

Have I . . .

____ written a thesis statement that clearly describes my main idea?

____ used an attention-getting technique in the introduction?

____ checked for unity by making sure that my paragraphs' topic sentences support my thesis statement?

____ organized my paragraphs in a way that is logical and easy to follow?

____ made sure my paragraphs flow smoothly from one to another?

____ written a strong conclusion that leaves my readers with something to think about?

COMPOSITIONS

Power Words
Vocabulary for Precise Writing

Why Me?

Often it seems words aren't enough to describe being embarrassed. Do any of these words fit?

Did I Do That?

There are all sorts of **mishaps** and **mistakes** we can make. We can make an **error** or a **fumble** on the playing field. We can have a **lapse** in memory or make a **misstep** in evaluating a situation. A **goof** or a **boo-boo** can happen when you least expect it.

All Eyes Are on You!

Why is your face so red? Are you a little **embarrassed?** Perhaps you are **humiliated** or **mortified** because you are wearing two shoes that don't match. Being put **on the spot** can make you feel **ill-at-ease, perturbed,** and even **rattled** inside. What do you do when you have **egg on your face?**

Make a Quick Recovery

If you are **quick on your feet,** you can **regain composure, recoup,** and **reset** yourself by just laughing it off. Simply **resume** a natural pose and **rally** from the setback. You might even want to **downplay** the mishap so that others will **discount** and **minimize** it. Whatever you do, don't **belittle** yourself. Everyone gets embarrassed!

▷ **Your Turn** Swap Stories

With a small group, talk about a time you felt embarrassed. Use some of the words above to help you tell the story.

Elaboration

That's Not What I Meant!

What would you do to prevent something like this from happening to you? You would probably use **elaboration,** providing more information and details, when asking for a haircut. For instance, you could explain the length you wanted, or you might show the stylist a photo of a hairstyle you liked.

You might already have used elaboration when writing an essay or short story. Elaboration can make the ideas and images in your writing clearer and prevent readers from misunderstanding you.

Write Away: See What I Mean?
Write a paragraph describing a haircut that is popular at your school, or imagine a new hairstyle and describe that. Make sure you add enough supporting details for a reader to picture the style you're describing. Save your writing in your ⬚ **Working Portfolio.**

Understanding Elaboration

❶ What Is Elaboration?

Close to Home by John McPherson

• NO TALKING • NO SMILING • NO WEARING WEIRD CLOTHES
• NO RUNNING • NO EATING • NO DUMB QUESTIONS
• NO KICKING • NO SWEATING • NO COMING IN LATE
• NO BITING • NO SWEARING • NO COMING IN EARLY
• NO LAUGHING • NO BURPING • NO LOOKING AT THE CLOCK
• NO TICKL... • NO SNEEZING • NO LOOKING OUT THE WINDOW
• NO HO... • NO COUGHING • NO SMART-ALECKY REMARKS
• NO S... • ...ROOLING • NO MAKING STUPID FACES
• NO ... • ...SCREAMING • NO CRYING DURING TESTS
• NO ... • ...GIGGLING • NO GOOFY HAIRSTYLES

Mrs. Mutner liked to go over a few of her rules
on the first day of school.

Instead of saying simply, "Behave in class," Mrs. Mutner elaborates, or adds information, to make sure students know exactly what she means. In writing, the purpose of elaboration is to answer important questions that readers might have about your topic, such as *who, what, when, where, why,* or *how.* Without this kind of elaboration, your ideas may seem dull, confusing, or incomplete.

Notice how one writer used elaboration to revise the draft below.

STUDENT MODEL

DRAFT

There are many unspoken rules in our culture. One of them is how far away you should stand from someone else. Most of us need a certain amount of physical space between ourselves and others to feel comfortable.

> This draft needs to answer such questions as *How much space? What happens without that space?*

REVISION

One of the unspoken rules in our culture is how far away you should stand from someone else if you wish to be polite. For instance, in the United States, people tend to prefer 4 to 10 feet between themselves and strangers. If anyone invades this space, a person may grow anxious and back away to get more distance.

> This writer adds specific examples to revise the draft.

❷ Methods of Elaboration

The chart below lists some of the techniques you can use to elaborate in your writing.

Elaboration Techniques	Examples
Support opinions Give reasons, examples, and facts to back up your opinions.	Some cities have odd laws. For instance, in Pacific Grove, California, threatening a butterfly is illegal.
Provide evidence Give supporting details, examples, facts, and quotations.	The chance of being arrested for threatening a butterfly is slim. Even Pacific Grove does not have a single case entered in its records.
Describe Describe how your topic looks, tastes, feels, sounds, or smells. Add similes or metaphors to make comparisons.	One breezy spring day, I saw a man trying to catch a small cloud of butterflies that had landed on a park bench.
Show, don't tell Instead of telling readers, "The man was sad," show his sadness through his actions or dialogue. You can also use visuals— charts and graphs—to show your ideas.	When the butterflies flew out of his reach, the man looked like he might cry. "I almost had them," he said, sighing.

PRACTICE Claiming Your Space

Use any one of the techniques described above to elaborate on one of the ideas below.

- People often use body language to tell each other to back off or come closer.
- When waiting for a bus or train, most people observe a common social etiquette.
- Sharing a bedroom or locker can bring out different space preferences between two people.
- People standing in an elevator behave in very similar ways.

ELABORATION

Using Description

❶ Appealing to the Senses

Sensory details—descriptions of how things look, sound, smell, taste, and feel—can help you *show* rather than *tell* your readers more about a topic. Notice how sensory details make the following description more vivid.

LITERARY MODEL

I am looking at a [bear's] head that is bigger around than my steering wheel, a pair of paws, awash in river bubbles, that could cover half my windshield. . . .   **SIGHT**

While she is occupied devouring the fish—I can hear her teeth clacking together . . . .   **SOUND**

With a bear at your side, it is not the simplest thing to play a fish properly, but the presence of this huge animal, and especially her long snout, thick as my thigh, wonderfully concentrates the mind. She smells like the forest floor, like crushed moss and damp leaves, and she is as warm as a radiator back in my Massachusetts home. . . .   **SMELL** **TOUCH**

—Robert H. Abel, "Appetizer"

Be careful not to overload your writing with details. This sentence contains too much of a good thing:

I could feel the bear's warm, salmon-smelling breath on my icy, bare, goosebump-covered neck.

❷ Making Comparisons

Sometimes the most effective way to describe something is to compare it to something else. You can use comparative or superlative forms of modifiers to describe how things differ ("The bear was four feet *taller* than I was"). Or you can convey how things are alike by using comparisons such as similes and metaphors.

Creating Similes and Metaphors

Similes compare two things using the word *like* or *as*.	The bear's fur was thick and plush, **like a cloak** wrapped tightly around her.
Metaphors describe a thing as if it were something else, without using the word *like* or *as*.	The bear's fur **was a thick, plush cloak** wrapped tightly around her.

Notice the way the writer of this passage makes comparisons using similes and metaphors to describe a nature scene.

LITERARY MODEL

After two days of gentle winter rains, the small pond behind my house is lapping at its banks, content as a well-fed kitten. . . . Two or three times **SIMILE** a year when the rain kept up for more than a day, water would run past in a hurry on its way to flood the road. . . . All the rest of the time this little valley lay empty, a toasted rock patch pierced **METAPHOR** with cactus.

—Barbara Kingsolver, *High Tide in Tucson*

ELABORATION

PRACTICE ➤ **Nature Writing**

Write a paragraph comparing the two plants in these photos. How are the plants alike? How are they different? Use your imagination to include sensory details and other descriptions in your comparisons.

CHALLENGE Rewrite the sentence in the **Watch Out** on page 384 so that the sentence provides clear details, but not too many.

Providing Evidence

❶ Using Examples

When you make general statements in your writing, readers may not understand what you mean. Adding specific examples can clarify your ideas. The author of the model below provides specific examples to explain what he means when he says the world seems to be shrinking.

PROFESSIONAL MODEL

The world seems to be shrinking at an incredible rate. Countries such as England and Brazil that, two generations ago, took weeks of boat travel to reach from the U.S. are now accessible in less than a day via airplanes. Faxes, cell phones, pagers, and the Internet make it possible to reach someone within seconds, no matter where he or she may be. Meanwhile, satellites send the same TV shows to homes in Los Angeles, California, and Shanghai, China, so that—except for the different languages the programs use—families all over the world can share similar viewing experiences. The result is, no matter where we live, the rest of the world can seem like it's just outside our own front door.

> **TOPIC SENTENCE**
>
> Example
>
> Example
>
> Example

PRACTICE A — Global Versus Specific Statements

Write a paragraph for one of the topic sentences below. Make sure you include examples in your paragraph.

Topic Sentence: Some people—especially athletes, performers, and politicians—seem to be known throughout the world.

Topic Sentence: Music from many countries and cultures plays on American radio every day.

❷ Including Facts and Statistics

Using facts or statistics can impress readers and help support the general statements you make when writing. **Facts** are statements that can be proved. **Statistics** are facts expressed using numbers.

PROFESSIONAL MODEL

If it seems that life in the West has become a fast-forward blur, consider China. In just 20 years,... life for many urban Chinese has changed drastically. A recent survey of 12 major cities showed that 97 percent of the respondents had televisions, and 88 percent had refrigerators and washing machines. Another study revealed that farmers are eating 48 percent more meat each year and 400 percent more fruit.

—Erla Zwingle, "A World Together"

> Writer presents general idea: life is changing quickly all over the world.

> Provides statistics to support general idea

PRACTICE B Facts Make the Difference

Write a paragraph presenting your ideas about how cultures from around the world may or may not be changing. Include some of the facts, statistics, and examples below. You may also want to include examples from your own experience.

- In one California school 32 different languages are spoken by the student body.
- More than one-fifth of the world's population speaks English.
- Television took 13 years to acquire 50 million users; however, within five years, the Internet had 50 million users.
- Russia, China, and India now have some of the same fast-food restaurant chains that the U.S. has.
- Some immigrants to new countries retain their language and customs at home.

Supporting Your Opinions

❶ Using Reasons

When you write a persuasive argument, readers will want to know why they should agree with your opinions. To tell them why your opinion is valid, you need to elaborate your argument with **reasons.** The writer of the following argument gives reasons to support her opinion that people don't get enough sleep.

PROFESSIONAL MODEL

Lack of sleep has become a growing problem in the U.S. Once upon a time, before light bulbs and 24-hour stores, the sun set, the world went dark, and people got a full night's rest. In fact, according to experts, a century ago, people usually slept an average of 8 or 9 hours each night. However, research shows that nowadays most people are lucky to sleep 6 to 8 hours each night, and everyone is suffering for it. Sleepy people have more accidents, don't do as well at school or at work, and are grouchy, experts say. That affects everyone.

TOPIC SENTENCE

FACT

REASON

REASON

If you're not sure what reasons might support your opinions, try brainstorming. Organize your ideas using a cluster like the one below. Then decide what kind of research you need to support each idea.

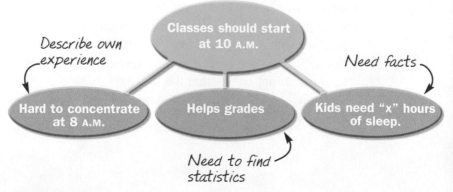

Describe own experience

Classes should start at 10 A.M.

Need facts

Hard to concentrate at 8 A.M.

Helps grades

Kids need "x" hours of sleep.

Need to find statistics

❷ Adding Quotations

In your writing, you may want to quote experts or other people who have experience with your topic. A **quotation** reproduces the exact words spoken or written by another person. A quotation must be surrounded by quotation marks so that your readers will know that the words came from another person, not from you.

STUDENT MODEL

DRAFT

Starting school at 7:45 A.M. is too early and does not allow students to get enough rest. Going to bed earlier won't help the problem, either, because some teens need at least nine hours of sleep each night.

> Why can't teens just go to bed earlier? Who says they need this much sleep?

REVISION

Starting school at 7:45 A.M. is too early and does not allow students to get enough rest. A recent University of Minnesota study showed that some students need at least nine hours of sleep a night. Some people say students should just go to bed earlier. However, this may not help many students. The Minnesota study showed that teens naturally fall asleep later than adults do. "What people don't get is you can send them [teens] to bed any time you want, but they can't fall asleep," said Mark Mahowald, director of a sleep disorders clinic. The best solution is for schools to start later.

> The writer cites a study for support.

> Quoting an expert also adds support to the writer's ideas.

ELABORATION

PRACTICE ▸ What Do You Think?

"Students need more rest, so schools should eliminate sports and other extracurricular activities. Then classes could start later in the morning and continue into late afternoon." Do you agree or disagree with this proposal? Write a paragraph explaining your opinion. Be sure to give at least one reason supporting your opinion.

Using Visuals

Sometimes adding a visual is the best way to explain or support an idea in your writing. Diagrams, charts, and graphs are types of visuals that can be especially helpful when you're preparing research reports and multimedia presentations.

❶ Diagrams Make It Clear

Diagrams are drawings that give information about an object or a process. Labeled drawings, time lines, and flow charts are all types of diagrams.

STUDENT MODEL

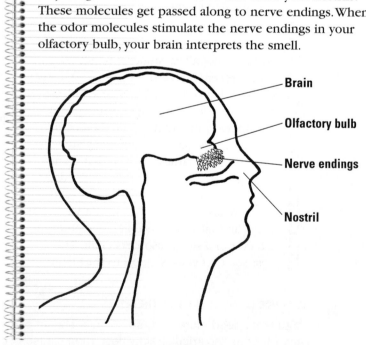

How Smell Works

Objects give off odor molecules that enter your nostrils. These molecules get passed along to nerve endings. When the odor molecules stimulate the nerve endings in your olfactory bulb, your brain interprets the smell.

Sources: Carl M. Raab, *Life Sciences;* www.InnerBody.com

If you use data or a visual that already exists, remember to credit your source in your work. Not crediting a source, or plagiarizing, can get you in trouble.

❷ Charts and Graphs Add Information

Charts can show facts and statistics visually in your research reports and other writing. The chart below is a pie chart, but you could also make a traditional chart with rows and columns.

STUDENT MODEL

A recent poll at Glenn Middle School showed that only 17 percent of the student body does homework or studies in silence. Many students say they prefer to play music while they study.

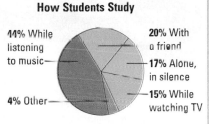

How Students Study

- **11%** While listening to music
- **4%** Other
- **20%** With a friend
- **17%** Alone, in silence
- **15%** While watching TV

You can also use **graphs** to present statistics. Line graphs are useful for showing change over time. Bar graphs like the one below are useful for making comparisons.

STUDENT MODEL

Although 9 out of 10 of my friends say they save money, experts say that teens are spending more money than ever. Experts expect teen spending to continue to rise through the early 2000s.

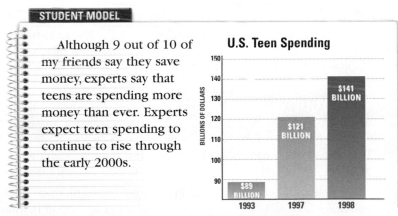

U.S. Teen Spending

BILLIONS OF DOLLARS

- 1993: **$89 BILLION**
- 1997: **$121 BILLION**
- 1998: **$141 BILLION**

Sources: 12th Annual Teen Survey, *USA Weekend*; Teenage Research Unlimited, Inc.

PRACTICE › **Money Talk**

Collect data about your classmates' spending and saving habits. For instance, you might ask students to explain what they would be most likely to do with a $100 bill. After you collect and tally your data, create a visual to show the results.

Student Help Desk

Elaboration at a Glance

Describe: use sensory details, comparisons, similes, metaphors

Provide Evidence: give examples, facts, statistics

To Elaborate

Support Opinions: provide reasons, quotes

Visualize: add diagrams, charts, graphs

Show, Don't Tell Creating Specific Details

Examples	Telling	Showing
Actions	The dog was mean.	The dog growled at us.
Emotions	She was mad.	She slammed the door as she left.
Dialogue	He told me not to leave.	"Don't leave," he said.
Sensory details	The soup was awful.	The soup tasted like cold, sour milk.

Make Your Words Count

Vague Statements	Adding Facts
The human brain can detect a lot of odors.	The human brain can detect up to 10,000 different odors.
The sense of smell peaks early in humans.	The sense of smell peaks at around age 20 in humans.
Your tongue has more taste buds than you might think.	Your tongue is covered with about 9,000 taste buds.
Taste buds respond to different kinds of food.	Taste buds distinguish four tastes: sweet, salty, sour, and bitter.

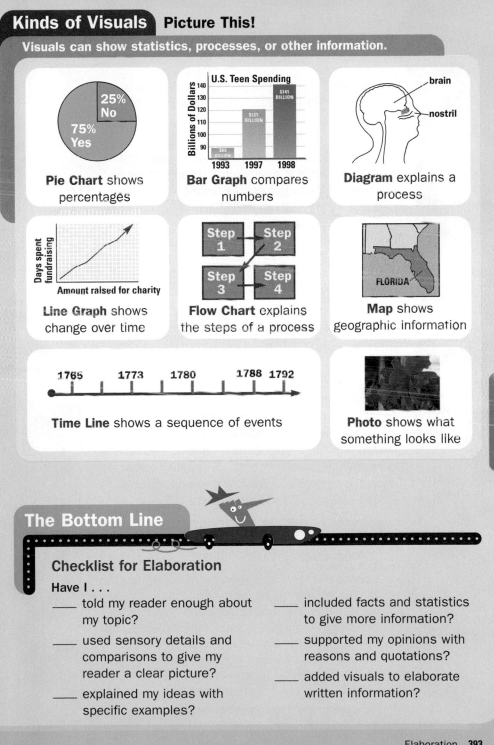

Kinds of Visuals Picture This!

Visuals can show statistics, processes, or other information.

Pie Chart shows percentages

25% No
75% Yes

Bar Graph compares numbers

U.S. Teen Spending
Billions of Dollars
140
130
120
110
100
90
$88 BILLION — 1993
$121 BILLION — 1997
$141 BILLION — 1998

Diagram explains a process

brain
nostril

Line Graph shows change over time

Days spent fundraising
Amount raised for charity

Flow Chart explains the steps of a process

Step 1 → Step 2
Step 3 → Step 4

Map shows geographic information

FLORIDA

Time Line shows a sequence of events

1765 1773 1780 1788 1792

Photo shows what something looks like

The Bottom Line

Checklist for Elaboration

Have I . . .

_____ told my reader enough about my topic?

_____ used sensory details and comparisons to give my reader a clear picture?

_____ explained my ideas with specific examples?

_____ included facts and statistics to give more information?

_____ supported my opinions with reasons and quotations?

_____ added visuals to elaborate written information?

Power Words
Vocabulary for Precise Writing

EMPHASIZ

Storytelling

The way you tell a story is as important as the story itself. Use these words to talk about telling tales.

A Tale Well Told

It takes practice to **tell** a story well, to **spin** a yarn so your audience is spellbound. If you just **recite** or **state** dull facts but don't **recount** interesting details, people will be bored. **Narrate** your tale energetically, **describe** what you see in your mind's eye, and **elaborate** on interesting characters.

Use Your Full Voice

You can add interest to a story by the **expressive** way you tell it. Put some **enthusiasm** in your tone! When you use a **colorful, lively** voice, your audience will want to hear more of your **dynamic** storytelling, with all its **vivid, larger-than-life** descriptions.

What to Listen for

An **interesting** tale will be **engrossing, suspenseful,** and **fascinating** to the listener. A **boring** tale will be **dreary, tedious,** and **tiresome.** Remember, you can **embellish** the facts a bit—it's OK to **emphasize** and **underline** some parts. But don't **overdo**—people will get suspicious if you **exaggerate** too much.

vivi

CHAPTER 18

expressive

▷ **Your Turn** Speak Up!

Choose the first few sentences of a story or novel to present dramatically to a small group of class-mates. After everyone in the group has read his or her selection aloud, go around again. Before your next turn, have members of the group call out a storytelling-related word from this page, such as "lively" or "dreary." Read your line again, altering your voice or tone to match the called-out word.

exaggerate

tell

ENGROSSING   dynamic

Revising Sentences

... and then we went to the Grand Canyon and it was so incredibly enormous you just wouldn't believe it and my mom and dad and brother and I hiked down the Bright Angel Trail to this place called Indian Gardens where there is a stream and trees and we had a picnic there but then we had to start back up and it took us SO long because it takes you twice as long to cover the same distance when you are climbing out of the canyon as when you are hiking down into it and we were grumbling about all the water we. had to [illegible] e way down but we really were glad [illegible] n the. way back up because we [illegible] but anyway about half [illegible] he trail we saw [illegible] phs which [illegible] ns made [illegible] e [illegible] and [illegible] eally [illegible] ng [illegible] use

The Tedious Travel Tale

This nonstop narrative makes the Grand Canyon seem like one big yawn instead of the immense and beautiful chasm that it is. If you read carefully, you'll see that this traveler's vacation was filled with interesting things to see and do. Stringing sentences together like this, however, can make a fascinating story seem dull. How would you revise this babbler's long-winded tale? Could you make it brilliant instead of boring?

Write Away: Dream Vacation
Write a paragraph about a trip you've always wanted to take. Where do you want to go? Why? How would you get there? What would you do there? Save your paragraph in your
📁 **Working Portfolio**.

Empty and Padded Sentences

If you don't know much about a topic, or if you don't have a lot to say about it, you may write sentences that don't say anything at all, or you may pad sentences with unnecessary words. As you revise, check for padded or empty sentences. Use the techniques listed here to fix them.

❶ Filling Empty Sentences

Some empty sentences repeat the same idea, while others make statements without supporting them. If you need to know more about your topic, do additional research.

DRAFT

A freight train is a train that carries freight.

only repeats an idea

REVISION

Freight trains carry grain, coal, and other goods.

gives specific examples

DRAFT

Trains are a good way to transport goods.

Why?

REVISION

Rail transport is efficient because freight trains don't get delayed in traffic as trucks might.

gives a reason

Notice how this writer improved the sentences in this model.

STUDENT MODEL

DRAFT

The Grand Canyon Railway is a railroad that goes to the Grand Canyon. There is a lot to see and do on this train.

REPETITIVE SENTENCE

EMPTY SENTENCE

REVISION

The Grand Canyon Railway transports tourists from Williams, Arizona, to Grand Canyon National Park. The train passes through beautiful desert scenery, and actors in costumes mix with passengers to make it seem like the Old West.

CLEAR INFORMATION

BETTER DESCRIPTION

❷ Streamlining Padded Sentences

A padded sentence contains too many words—words that don't add anything to the sentence but more words. How many unnecessary words can you find in this example?

When my family went on vacation, my family went to visit this cave in Arizona where bandits who held up a train hid the loot, which was thousands of dollars of gold coins and other gold.

That writer used more than 35 words to say what could be said more clearly in less than 20 words.

On our vacation my family visited a cave in Arizona where train robbers hid thousands of dollars of gold.

Notice how the revision below eliminates repetitive words and streamlines long phrases.

STUDENT MODEL

DRAFT	REVISION
Colossal Cave is a cave in Arizona near Tucson in the southern part of Arizona in the desert. Long ago it was once a hideout where a bunch of local guys who were thieves and bandits hid things they robbed from trains, such as gold and silver and jewelry and other expensive stuff.	Colossal Cave is located in the southern Arizona desert, near Tucson. It was once a hideout for local train robbers. They stashed their loot in the cave.

REVISING

1. Think about the ideas you want to express.
2. Look for unnecessary words and phrases to take out.
3. Look for long phrases that don't tell your reader much. Replace each of those phrases with one or two words.

Unnecessary Phrase	Replacement
• in spite of the fact that	• although
• is of the belief that	• believes *or* thinks
• the reason why is because	• the reason is *or* because
• the fact of the matter is that	• (Just say it!)
• what I want to say is	• (Just say it!)

Don't deliberately pad a sentence just to meet a composition's required word count. If you need more words, find more facts or details to add.

PRACTICE **Get to the Point**

Revise these sentences using the directions in parentheses.

1. Train travel is better than car travel. (Add a reason or fact.)
2. Commuter trains ease urban traffic congestion on account of the fact that they can transport so many people. (Eliminate unnecessary words.)
3. Everyone should travel by train. (Add a reason or fact.)
4. Open-top rail cars don't have tops and carry coal, iron ore, and other minerals. (Eliminate the repeated idea.)
5. Train travel is faster than bus travel because it is speedier. (Eliminate the repeated idea; add a reason or fact.)
6. You'll like the food that is served on a train. (Add a reason or fact.)
7. The dining car, where most of the passengers eat, offers many different meals and a variety of food. (Eliminate repeated ideas.)
8. From the windows, you can see scenery. (Add details.)
9. Many people are travelers who like to ride the train because of the fact that they are scared and frightened of flying. (Eliminate unnecessary words.)
10. Trains are safer than cars. (Add a reason or fact.)

Stringy and Overloaded Sentences

Both stringy and overloaded sentences present too many ideas at once.
It's hard to figure out how the ideas in the sentence are related.

❶ Untangling Stringy Sentences

A stringy sentence contains too many ideas loosely connected
by the word *and*. In the draft below, the writer has strung
together too many ideas. The sentence is long and confusing.

STUDENT MODEL

DRAFT

The komondor's hair is long
and white **and** it grows into
long mats **and** the mats have to
be groomed **and** they must be
carefully separated into cords
and it takes several hours **and**
this has to be done each time the
dog sheds its undercoat **and** this
happens twice a year.

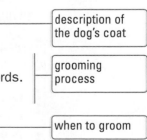

Start untangling this stringy sentence by listing each idea.
Then, think of the relationships among the ideas. Do they
belong in a certain order? Are there any causes and effects?

- The komondor has long white hair.
- It grows into long mats.

  description of the dog's coat

- The mats must be groomed.
- They must be carefully separated into cords.
- It takes several hours to do this.

  grooming process

- It has to be done each time the dog sheds its undercoat.
- This happens twice a year.

  when to groom

Examine your list and decide which ideas can be combined
and which should remain separate.

For more about combining sentences, see pp. 332–337.

Read the revision below. Notice which sentences the writer chose to combine. Can you tell why?

STUDENT MODEL

REVISION

The komondor has long white hair that grows into mats. To groom the komondor, the owner must carefully separate the mats into cords. This takes several hours. It must be done twice a year, each time the dog sheds its undercoat.

Here's How Revising Stringy Sentences

1. List each idea separately.
2. Think of the relationships between ideas.
3. Decide which ideas to combine and which to keep separate.
4. Combine ideas and rewrite sentences.
5. Read your new sentences to make sure they are grammatical.

❷ Unloading Overloaded Sentences

An overloaded sentence is long and confusing, like a stringy sentence. Unlike a stringy sentence, an overloaded sentence simply contains too much information. To revise this kind of sentence, first divide it into smaller parts, as the writer of the draft below has done.

STUDENT MODEL

DRAFT

The vet said that my fat cat, who weighed 18 pounds, needed to lose a bit of weight, / so I started his reducing diet by cutting out his many snacks, / serving him three small meals a day, because I used to serve him one big one / and playing with him more so that he would get enough exercise instead of just sleeping all day.

Next, rewrite the parts as complete sentences. It's all right to combine two ideas in one sentence for clarity or variety. You can also take out repetitive or unnecessary words.

REVISION

   The vet said that my 18-pound cat needed to lose weight. I started his diet by cutting out snacks and serving him three small meals a day. I also played with him more so he would get enough exercise.

Here's How **Revising Overloaded Sentences**

1. Divide the sentence into smaller parts, each containing one idea.
2. Rewrite the sentence parts as complete sentences.
3. Combine two ideas into one sentence if it adds clarity.
4. Delete unnecessary words, phrases, or ideas.
5. Read your new sentences to make sure they are grammatical.

PRACTICE   **Where Does It End?**

Rewrite the following stringy and overloaded sentences as clear paragraphs.

1. My grandmother's dog is very helpful and every morning he goes down the driveway and picks up the newspaper and brings it to her and he can carry things from her to my grandfather if she tells him to.
2. An iguana can be an interesting pet, but it may be difficult to raise because of supplying special equipment like a heat lamp to make sure the temperature is warm enough, replacing the glass tank with a larger one when the iguana grows, and making sure it has the right kind of food.
3. Rabbits make good house pets and can be trained to use a litter box, but if you keep one in your home you must "bunny-proof" by hiding or covering electrical cords, protecting the furniture, and giving the rabbit lots of teething toys because rabbits must nibble on things to wear down their teeth, which are always growing.
4. I really want to get a puffer fish because they are so cute and they are very smart, friendly fish and they have big eyes and puff way up when they are frightened or angry and the way they puff up is by breathing in air or water and they can have poison on their skin and so you have to be careful if you put them in a tank with other fish.

REVISING

Varying Sentence Structure

❶ Rearranging Phrases

Good writers often experiment with different versions of their sentences. One way to vary a sentence is to rearrange phrases—shifting them to the beginning or end of a sentence to see which version will have the best effect on the reader. Which sentence below sounds best to you?

Thousands of bats fly in a spiral from the mouth of Carlsbad Caverns at sunset.

At sunset, thousands of bats fly in a spiral from the mouth of Carlsbad Caverns.

From the mouth of Carlsbad Caverns, at sunset, thousands of bats fly in a spiral.

Each of the sentences is correct. The first is very straightforward. The second sets the sunset scene by mentioning it first. Because the two prepositional phrases come before the subject and predicate, the third sentence seems more formal than the other two. Which do you prefer?

PRACTICE A It's All in the Arrangement

Rewrite each sentence in two ways, as shown in the examples above.

1. The librarian heard a snicker in the middle aisle near the books by Mark Twain.
2. The old, vacant house on the hill stands above the bustling town of Mount Pleasant.

❷ Varying Types of Sentences

In any piece of writing, most sentences are declarative. So adding a question, a command, or an exclamation can be a good way to emphasize a point or catch the reader's interest. Notice how the variety of sentences lends a conversational air to a passage about scientific research.

Where on Earth can you find clues to life on Mars? Go underground! Since evidence suggests that Mars was once much more like Earth, some scientists think there may be caves beneath the red planet's surface. If that is true, the caves of Mars may contain microbes similar to those discovered deep in New Mexico's Lechuguilla Cave— microbes that feed on manganese, iron, and sulfur. All three minerals are present on Mars. Should we send a caver along on the first Mars expedition?

Question draws reader in.

Exclamatory command grabs attention.

Gypsum chandeliers in Lechuguilla Cave

Question involves the reader.

Even though variety can spice up your writing, you don't want to overdo it. Too many questions, exclamations, or commands can be worse than none at all.

For more on types of sentences, see pp. 16–17.

PRACTICE B   Add Some Variety

Revise the paragraph below by turning some of the sentences into questions, exclamations, or commands.

You may be interested in time travel or in life on other planets. If you read science fiction, you can explore these ideas. Science fiction writers often combine scientific information and imaginary characters to create a story. Often writers use a futuristic setting to discuss current issues, such as pollution or the use of computers. If science fiction appeals to you, it's a good idea to try a story by Isaac Asimov, Anne McCaffrey, or another science fiction writer. Their visions of the future may surprise you.

Varying Sentence Length

❶ Smoothing Choppy Sentences

Have you ever been on a road that had a traffic light at every intersection? You start and stop, and it takes a long time to get anywhere. Reading a string of choppy sentences is a similar experience. You spend your time stopping at periods, and it takes too long to get to the point. By combining some of your sentences, you eliminate some of those stops and starts. Notice how the revision below smooths out the choppy sentences of the draft.

STUDENT MODEL

DRAFT

    The cobra was in the basket. The snake charmer opened the lid. The snake rose up. The snake charmer started playing his flute. He started swaying. The snake couldn't hear the music. It looked at the flute going back and forth. It swayed, too. Then it was the end of the show. The snake charmer kissed the snake. He bent down over the snake's head to kiss it.

REVISION

    As the snake charmer opened the lid of the cobra's basket, the snake rose up. The snake charmer began playing his flute **and** swaying. **Although** the snake couldn't hear the music, it swayed along with the motions of the flute. **Then,** at the end of the show, the snake charmer bent down over the snake's head **and** kissed it.

Here's How **Revising Choppy Sentences**

- To combine related sentences, use conjunctions such as *and, but,* or *although.*
- To show time connections, use sequence words such as *first, then, next,* or *last.*
- To show how sentences relate to each other, use transitions such as *also, indeed,* or *for example.*

❷ Establishing Rhythm

Using sentences of different lengths establishes a sense of rhythm that makes your writing flow more smoothly. Your reader will find the going easy and will want to keep on reading. Notice how the rhythm of the sentences in this model draws the reader in.

LITERARY MODEL

Grace deliberately tried to touch the rigid, quivering hood. The cobra struck at her hand. He missed. Quietly, Grace presented her open palm. The cobra hesitated a split second, his reared body quivering like a plucked banjo string. Then he struck.

> The short sentences reflect action

> The long sentence creates suspense.

I felt sick as I saw his head hit Grace's hand, but the cobra did not bite. He struck with his mouth closed.

—Daniel P. Mannix, "A Running Brook of Horror"

PRACTICE A Add Some Rhythm

Revise these choppy sentences into a smoothly written paragraph. Combine some of the sentences, and provide transitions if they are needed. Be sure to vary the lengths of your sentences.

Garter snakes are yellow and black. Some are yellow and brown. They live along streams. They live in forests. They live in many neighborhoods. They bask on rocks. They bask on swimming pool decks. You might see one near your home. Don't try to catch it. They can bite. They are not poisonous. Their bite can cause a rash. It can also cause swelling.

PRACTICE B Where in the World?

In your 🗀 **Working Portfolio,** find your **Write Away** paragraph from page 395. Use the concepts you learned in this chapter to revise your paragraph and make your sentences more interesting. Then, trade papers with a partner and discuss each other's work.

Student Help Desk

Revising Sentences at a Glance

Watch for unrevised sentences

- Fill empty sentences.
- Streamline overloaded sentences.

Danger– no variety

- Rearrange phrases.
- Vary types of sentences.

Beware of choppy sentences

- Combine related sentences.
- Add some rhythm.

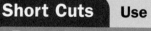

Short Cuts Use the Direct Route

Too wordy	Replace it with
am of the opinion that	believe or think
last but not least	finally
the reason why	the reason
in this day and age	now
in our modern world	
at the present time	
due to the fact that	because or since
on account of the fact that	
in spite of the fact that	although
what I want to say is	(Just say it!)
the fact is that	

A ⟰ B

Sentence Variety Punctuation Points of Interest

Types of Sentences	Example
Statements give information.	The view from the Royal Gorge Bridge in Colorado will take your breath away.
Questions help your reader relate the topic to his or her life.	Have you ever gone surfing in Hawaii?
Commands urge your reader to take action.	Stay on the trails when you walk through the wildlife preserve so you don't disturb the animals.
Exclamations show strong feelings.	The Slithering Cobra of Doom is the most thrilling roller coaster I have ever ridden!

The Bottom Line

Checklist for Revising Sentences

Can I improve my sentences by . . .

____ dropping unnecessary words from padded sentences?

____ taking out empty sentences, or adding facts or reasons to make them meaningful?

____ dividing stringy sentences into shorter, clearer ones?

____ rephrasing to add emphasis?

____ changing sentence structure and length to add variety?

____ making choppy sentences easier to understand?

____ dividing overloaded sentences?

Power Words
Vocabulary for Precise Writing

dignified

SUPERFICIAL

Show Your Style

It's not just what you say; it's how you say it. Use these words when you describe style.

Nothing to Hide

When you want your readers to believe what you write, you probably use an **honest** and **truthful** style. The best way to convince readers is to be **frank, open,** and **candid** about everything. Some of the best writers tell it **straight from the heart** in a **forthright, genuine,** and **sincere** style.

Holding Back

Writing that tries to avoid the truth can sound **empty** and **hollow**. Readers may find it **dishonest** and **false**. Writing that expresses **insincere** emotion often sounds **shallow** and **superficial**.

Who's on the Other End?

If you were writing a letter to your state senator, you might choose **proper, precise** language that sounds **formal** and **dignified** because your audience is **serious** and **reserved**. When writing to your friends, you might be more **informal** and **laid-back**. It's natural to feel **easy going, colloquial,** and **casual** with friends.

HONEST

easy going

genuine

▷ **Your Turn** How Would You Say It?

Imagine you are going to write a letter to your favorite musician, and one to your state senator. Use a Venn diagram to list words that describe the style of writing you would use in each letter.

shallow

408 *sincere*

informal

Style and Effective Language

DEAR JESSICA
YAY! WE GOT TO BE IN
HOMEROOM AND SOCIAL
STUDIES CLASS THIS YEAR!
I COULDN'T HAVE
SURVIVED WITHOUT YOU.
BEST FRIENDS 4-EVER.
LOVE, TRISH

Dear Jessica ~ I'll
never forget your
story about the train
station. You're a fine
writer. Keep it up and
I know you'll go far!
Good luck next year.
~ Ms. Jones

Hey Jess! Do you actually expect me to write
something mushy in here? I think Trish covered
that—ha ha! Well, this year rocked, but it's on to
bigger and better things in high school!
Danny

STYLE

It's All in the Words

What does each of the above yearbook messages tell you
about the person who wrote it? How is it possible to learn
about people through their writing?

Every writer has a unique **style,** which might be formal or
informal, plain or fancy, serious or funny. Successful writers
use styles that reflect their personalities, ideas, and attitudes.
In this chapter, you'll learn how to recognize various writing
styles. You'll also discover why different situations sometimes
call for different kinds of language.

Write Away: Signature Style
Write a mock yearbook message to a friend. Keep it in your
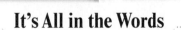 **Working Portfolio.**

What Is Style?

Your own writing **style** is expressed by the words you choose and the way you use them. Your style reflects your personality as well as your attitude toward whatever you're writing. Your readers will react not only to what you say but also to how you say it.

❶ Recognizing Style

You see different styles of writing all the time: in letters, e-mails, books, and magazines. Recognizing the differences between them takes a bit of training and plenty of practice. How do the writing styles differ in the models below?

LITERARY MODEL

The kid was a boy of ten, with ... freckles and **hair the color of the cover of the magazine you buy at the newsstand when you want to catch a train.** Bill and me figured that Ebenezer would melt down for a ransom of two thousand dollars to a cent. **But wait till I tell you.**

—O. Henry, "The Ransom of Red Chief"

> Colorful, informal description

> Nonstandard English and slang

> Conversational, everyday tone

LITERARY MODEL

I have had the applause of the crowd and the **satisfaction that comes of being approved by the multitude,** while the most that you have done has been **witnessed by a few trembling, scarred, and footsore bondmen and women,** whom you have led out of the house of bondage, and whose heartfelt *"God Bless you"* has been your only reward. The midnight sky and the silent stars have been the witnesses of your ... heroism.

—Frederick Douglass, letter to Harriet Tubman

> Formal tone

> Longer, detailed sentences

Frederick Douglass

❷ Describing Style

Here are some of the terms used to describe the various elements of style. You will learn more about them in the rest of the chapter.

Levels of Language

Writers use formal or informal language depending on their audience and purpose.

Formal She cradled a small, mixed-breed dog.

Informal She held a cute little mutt.

Word Choice

Choose your words carefully to say exactly what you mean. Don't leave your reader guessing.

Vague wording The boy took the dog upstairs.

Precise wording The toddler dragged the squirming puppy up four flights of stairs.

Figurative Language

Figures of speech can describe things by comparing them to other things.

Simile The puppy growled like a motorcycle waiting at a red light.

Metaphor A motorcycle rumbled in the puppy's throat.

Tone

Tone is a writer's attitude toward the subject matter.

Positive tone The stately old mansion overflowed with young pups of every size and shape.

Negative tone The huge barn of a house was crawling with little mongrels.

STYLE

Levels of Language

Think of the language you use when telling a funny story to a group of friends. Would you use the same kind of language to give a book report in class? Of course you wouldn't. It's important to realize that different kinds of language are appropriate for different audiences and purposes.

❶ Formal and Informal Language

Formal language has a serious, polite tone and is grammatically correct. **Informal language** is casual, everyday language. It may contain contractions or slang.

When deciding whether to write formally or informally, consider your audience. Use formal language for school and business. Use informal language for personal writing or writing that's aimed at an audience of peers, friends, or family. Note the differing language levels in the following model.

STUDENT MODEL

INFORMAL
Hi Chris!
I hope my sister gives you this note. Guess what? Bad news—no field trip for me tomorrow. I have the flu, so I'm stuck in bed till it's over.
　　　　　　　—Eric

FORMAL
Dear Mrs. Juarez,
I will be unable to attend tomorrow's field trip, as I have the flu. I'll be sorry to miss it.

　　　　　　　Sincerely,
　　　　　　　Eric

❷ Idioms and Slang

Idioms and slang can spice up your writing and give your reader a clear picture. However, they are appropriate for informal audiences only.

Idioms

An **idiom** is a commonly used expression whose intended meaning is different from its literal meaning. Make sure your audience understands idioms before you use them. Read the cartoon on the next page. What does the father really mean?

Color Blind by Orrin Brewster

Compare the literal meanings of these idioms with their intended meanings. How do you think these expressions came about?

Idioms	
Idiom	**Meaning**
Drop me a line.	Write me a letter.
Let's call it a day.	Let's say we're finished for today.

Slang

Slang describes the expressions used in casual communication, often among members of a particular group. New slang is constantly being invented and quickly goes out of use.

Here are two sets of different expressions that mean the same thing. What other expressions might you use in their place?

Slang Expressions	
Meaning	**Expressions**
It's a good idea.	I'm all over it. It's all good. Sounds like a plan.
Don't get upset.	Chill. Hold your horses. Don't have a cow.

Notice how some of these expressions are outdated. Slang becomes outdated very quickly; this is one reason it is not well suited to formal writing.

PRACTICE ▶ **Make It Proper**

Rewrite the following note using formal language.

Dear Mr. Jones,
Dude—thanks for giving me the science award. That made me feel really smart and good. I was pumped! You're the best.

Later, *Rachel*

STYLE

Word Choice

As a writer, it is your job to choose the words you put on the page. The more precise you are about choosing words and their meanings, the stronger the impression you'll make on your readers.

❶ Using Precise Language

If you have a choice between a general word and a more specific one, choose the specific one. A well-chosen noun, verb, or modifier will give your writing punch and clarity.

She put the book down and looked at me.

She threw the dictionary on the floor and glared at me.

Notice how the strong verbs and precise modifiers add life to the model on the right as written by the author.

	LITERARY MODEL
The dogs **pulled** against the straps, and the sled **moved quickly** away, almost throwing him off. Then it **went** into the creek, **tilting** on one runner. He was **worried** until it **straightened** itself out and **moved forward** again.	The dogs **sprang** against the yoke straps, and the sled **jerked** under way so **suddenly** as to almost throw him off. Then it **curved** into the creek, **poising perilously** on the runner. He was almost **breathless** with suspense, when it finally **righted** with a bound and **sprang** ahead again. —Jack London, "The King of Mazy May"

Verbs

Modifiers

PRACTICE A Revising

Rewrite the paragraph below, using specific nouns, verbs, and modifiers in place of general ones.

> The woman came around the corner, holding the precious object in her hand. Behind her was a group of children, calling her name and running. Heat rose from the ground as rain began to fall from the sky. It looked like they might catch her.

❷ Connotation and Denotation

Every word has a **denotation,** which is simply its literal dictionary definition. Words also have particular **connotations**—sets of thoughts, feelings, and emotions that the words bring to people's minds. A word's connotation may be positive, negative, or neutral.

Positive	**Neutral**	**Negative**
What an **aroma**!	What a **smell**!	What a **stench**!
He's so **slender**.	He's so **thin**.	He's so **scrawny**.
She's **charming**.	She's **polite**.	She's **slick**.

When choosing your words, pay close attention to their connotations—these shades of meaning will help you say exactly what you want to say. A dictionary definition will sometimes include tips about a word's connotation.

PRACTICE B Recognizing Connotations

Replace the boldface words in the following sentences with words that have different connotations.

1. We **chatted** every day over lunch.
2. That is a **competitive** bunch of athletes.
3. The cat **perched** on the front stoop.
4. I'm feeling very **relaxed** today.
5. She has a **unique** way of dressing.

STYLE

Figurative Language

❶ Figures of Speech

Figurative language is descriptive language that is not intended to be taken literally. A **figure of speech** often describes something by comparing it directly or indirectly with something else. Use figures of speech to make your writing vivid and memorable.

Simile

In a **simile** the word *like* or *as* is used to compare two things.

> **LITERARY MODEL**
>
> I looked at him, actually, for the first time. His hair was the color of the corn shocks, and **his eyes, very direct, were like the mountain sky when rain is pending—** gray, with a shadowing of that miraculous blue.
>
> —Marjorie Kinnan Rawlings, "A Mother in Mannville"

Metaphor

In a **metaphor** one thing is presented as if it were another thing, without the use of the word *like* or *as*.

> **LITERARY MODEL**
>
> While I tried to slaughter Josh, I rooted for him to win. **The game became a quicksand of passion for us.** After an emotional loss, he would pretend not to care, but his lower lip would tremble. Dejected, he'd go off to his room and my heart would be broken.
>
> —Fred Waitzkin, *Searching for Bobby Fischer*

Hyperbole

Hyperbole is exaggeration for the purpose of emphasis or humor. In the model above, the slaughter and the broken heart are two examples that exaggerate the emotions involved.

Personification

Personification is the giving of human qualities to ideas, objects, or animals.

> **LITERARY MODEL**
>
> Last May, I saw a dragonfly as long as my hand— longer than an average-sized songbird. She circled and circled, flexing her body, **trying to decide if my little lake was worthy of her precious eggs.**
>
> —Barbara Kingsolver, from *High Tide in Tucson*

PRACTICE Using Figurative Language

Rewrite each sentence, using one of the types of figurative language. Be sure to use all four types in your revision.

1. It was dark, and they couldn't see a thing.
2. From the noises, she knew that her car was out of gas.
3. The telephone rang loudly.
4. The crowd made a lot of noise at the touchdown.

❷ Avoiding Clichés

A **cliché** is an overused expression that you should avoid in writing. Many clichés are old, familiar figures of speech. While these expressions were once new, they've run out of zip by now. When tempted to use a cliché, try for a fresher way to express yourself.

Cliché-Away!	
Stale Expression	**Fresh Replacement**
quiet as a mouse	quiet as a bug on cotton
pretty as a picture	pretty as a spring morning
come rain or shine	even if the sky shatters
big as a house	makes the *Titanic* look small
it's a piece of cake	it's as easy as dreaming

❶ Tone

A writer's **tone** expresses his or her attitude toward a subject. It is shown in the writer's choice of words and images. The writers below have very different attitudes toward the same topic.

PROFESSIONAL MODEL

Lake Palowell has come a long way in the past few years; the old weedy pond is now a **lovely** recreation spot. All summer long, **children splash in the shallows, boats dot the lake's surface, and families picnic** in the surrounding park. **Charming** restaurants and boutiques have opened nearby, paving the way to a **thriving** business district.

—Anthony Williams

Positive modifiers

Quiet, pretty images

Positive, sincere tone

PROFESSIONAL MODEL

The mayor has turned Lake Palowell into a **crowded, noisy tourist trap.** What a **nightmare! You can't walk two feet down there without running smack into a screaming child or stepping on someone's mayonnaise sandwich. Whining motorboats have driven away the birds,** although the tourists don't care. **(Most of them wouldn't know the difference between a duck and a dodo.)**

—Juliana Davis

Negative nouns and modifiers

Unpleasant images

Insulting remark

Sarcastic, negative tone

Your choice of tone will greatly affect your readers' perception of you and what you have to say. Before you write, consider the attitude you'd like to convey and adjust your tone to match it.

PRACTICE A ▷ **Changing Tone**

Pull the yearbook inscription from your 🗀 **Working Portfolio.** Write it again, this time using a different tone.

❷ Voice

A writer's **voice** refers to the personality a reader "hears" while reading. Read the following models aloud and listen to the differences between the two voices.

LITERARY MODEL

> Now some people like to act like things come easy to them, won't let on that they practice. Not me. I'll high-prance down 34th Street like a rodeo pony to keep my knees strong even if it does get my mother uptight so that she walks ahead like she's not with me, don't know me, is all by herself on a shopping trip, and I am somebody else's crazy child.
>
> —Toni Cade Bambara, "Raymond's Run"

Conversational language

Colorful, humorous simile

Everyday subject matter

Long, rambling sentence sounds like a young person.

LITERARY MODEL

> Presently I heard a slight groan, and I knew it was the groan of mortal terror. It was not a groan of pain or grief—oh, no!—it was the low, stifled sound that arises from the bottom of the soul when overcharged with awe. I knew the sound well. Many a night, just at midnight, when all the world slept, it has welled up from my own bosom, deepening, with its dreadful echo, the terrors that distracted me.
>
> —Edgar Allan Poe, "The Tell-Tale Heart"

Formal language

Forceful interjection

Dramatic images

Long sentence with many pauses builds suspense.

STYLE

A writer's voice grows and develops over years. You can develop your own voice by writing naturally and honestly.

PRACTICE B ▸ **Recognizing Voice**

Take one or two pieces from your 🗀 **Working Portfolio.** Read your writing out loud and revise passages that sound forced or unnatural.

Student Help Desk

Style and Effective Language at a Glance

Language Levels — Know your audience, and use appropriate language.

Word Choice — Be precise, clear, and accurate.

Figurative Language — Be creative with comparisons, and avoid clichés.

Tone and Voice — Consider your attitude and the way your writing "sounds."

FORMAL	Informal
The language of school and business	**The language of everyday conversation**
May I be excused?	Can I go?
Unfortunately, we will not be able to attend.	Looks like we won't be able to make it.
The book was interesting and well written.	The book was great! I really got into it.

Connotation and Denotation — Watch Your Words!

Positive	Neutral	Negative
inquisitive	curious	nosy
challenging	complex	confusing
unique	unusual	weird
confident	assertive	pushy
playful	lively	rowdy

Figurative Language · Creative Comparisons

Simile (uses *like* or *as*)	The house was **as cold as a grave.**
Metaphor (does not use *like* or *as*)	The house was **a giant meat locker.**
Hyperbole (exaggeration)	Inside the house, it was **a hundred degrees below zero.**
Personification (gives human qualities to nonhuman things)	The house **shivered miserably, crying out** with every bitter gust of wind.

Word Bank · Using Precise Language

When you want to say	Do you really mean . . . ?
walk	saunter
say	protest
look at	examine
think	worry
show	movie
nice	friendly

STYLE

The Bottom Line

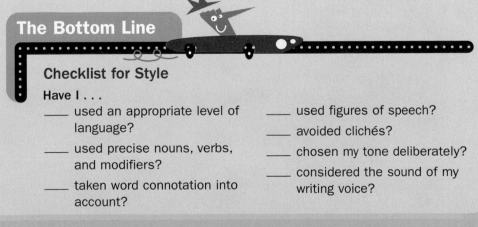

Checklist for Style

Have I . . .

____ used an appropriate level of language?

____ used precise nouns, verbs, and modifiers?

____ taken word connotation into account?

____ used figures of speech?

____ avoided clichés?

____ chosen my tone deliberately?

____ considered the sound of my writing voice?

Style and Effective Language **421**

Writing Workshops

Windows of Opportunity

The sky is limitless. But look how beautiful it is when framed by a window. You can use the structure of different writing forms to bring out the beauty in your own writing.

Autobiographical Incident

Learn What It Is

Certain moments of your life stand out in your memory. Writing about those special moments can help you understand their meaning. Such a first-hand account is an **autobiographical incident.** Writing about the experience can help you realize why the incident is so important to you.

Basics in a Box

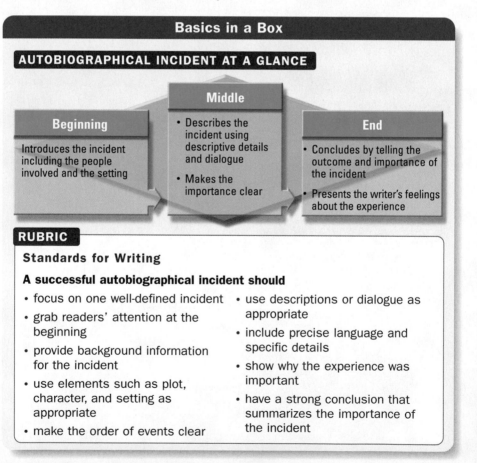

AUTOBIOGRAPHICAL INCIDENT AT A GLANCE

Beginning

Introduces the incident including the people involved and the setting

Middle

• Describes the incident using descriptive details and dialogue

• Makes the importance clear

End

• Concludes by telling the outcome and importance of the incident

• Presents the writer's feelings about the experience

RUBRIC

Standards for Writing

A successful autobiographical incident should

- focus on one well-defined incident
- grab readers' attention at the beginning
- provide background information for the incident
- use elements such as plot, character, and setting as appropriate
- make the order of events clear
- use descriptions or dialogue as appropriate
- include precise language and specific details
- show why the experience was important
- have a strong conclusion that summarizes the importance of the incident

See How It's Done: *Autobiographical Incident*

RUBRIC
IN ACTION

My Performance

As the auditorium went dark, I seemed to pass through a time tunnel back to a place where nerves were left at the door and everyone applauded even if someone did horribly. Unfortunately, I was not at that forgiving place. I was at the Thomas variety show, where I would soon be performing.

❶ Grabs the reader's attention

I had attended the night before to watch. Then, it seemed to me that everyone who performed went up on that black tile stage and calmly did what they did best. I had no thought that those brave souls were even slightly nervous. But, now that I've been through the horror myself, I know the truth.

❷ Focuses on one well-defined incident

❸ Provides background information for the incident

I was ninth in the Saturday night performance, three acts after a ten-minute intermission. I tried to be cool and collected as I thought to myself, "Jess, you have a beautiful voice and you'll do great." But that just didn't make this situation any more comfortable. I watched as the other acts went on wonderfully. I hoped and prayed that would be the same for me.

Finally, it was my turn. I reluctantly took the stage with Kate at my side, Amy on the piano, and butterflies in my stomach. I whispered my last good-byes to friends in the wing of the stage as the stage lights went dark. The curtains opened slowly to reveal the three of us. A bright stream of light flooded the once–pitch-black stage. My palms began to sweat. I could see shadows of familiar people in the audience, but I couldn't make out any faces. I quivered a little, and the song began.

❹ Makes the order of events clear

AUTOBIO. INCIDENT

Kate started the song with her solo. Her voice was crystal clear. She put all she had into her singing, and it was perfect. Her solo was coming to an end, and it was my turn. I inched forward to center stage to accept the spotlight and began to sing. To my surprise, I sounded almost as good as my talented partner. I was becoming more and more confident when all of a sudden, the sweet sound of the piano music stopped. I heard the ruffling of sheet music and whispers in the audience. My confidence took a blow. Fortunately, after a few painful seconds, the melodious song began once more and I continued.

❺ Uses precise language and specific details

Although I was a little less sure of myself now, I did keep going. Finally, the song ended and Kate and I took our bows. We watched in awe as friends and others, too, stood up and applauded. As the curtains closed, I knew that I had faced my fear and conquered it.

❻ This writer describes the reaction of her friends.

Another option: Include dialogue relating the friends' comments.

After the entire show was over, Kate and I went out into the crowded auditorium. We were happy to be mobbed by all of our friends and their compliments. Each one said we had done a good job. I was extremely proud of the fact that I had gone up there and had done what I wanted most to do—sing well and enjoy it.

❼ Concludes by summarizing the importance of the incident

Do It Yourself

Writing Prompt Write an autobiographical incident about something important that happened to you.

Purpose To explain why an event was meaningful to you

Audience Family members, friends

❶ Prewriting

Identify an incident. Make a list of remembered moments that have meaning for you. For inspiration, you might look at photo albums or page through your journal. Post cards can remind you of vacations, and a file of programs can help you recall special occasions. Pick one of your memories to explore in more detail.

For more topic ideas, see the Idea Bank, p. 430.

Decide why this memory is important. Did you learn something from the incident? Did it change you? Are there other reasons for its importance?

Recall and organize the details. Say aloud to yourself or to another person all the details you remember. Describe the time of day, the people involved, and the place. You might want to make a time line so that you can put events in order.

❷ Drafting

Plan the beginning, middle, and end. Give your incident a clear beginning, middle, and end. Be sure to start in an appealing way. Use care in organizing details and making transitions in the middle. To leave readers with a lasting and positive impression, create a strong ending.

Add vivid words. Find ways to use words that appeal to the senses as you begin writing about the details. You can help readers experience the moment by using words that tell how things sounded or smelled or looked. If the audience was restless or noisy, make sure readers know.

Consider using dialogue. Quoting those involved can help make the incident come alive for readers.

For information about getting feedback from your peers, see p. 431.

AUTOBIO. INCIDENT

❸ Revising

TARGET SKILL ▶ Sensory Details Including details that appeal to the senses can make your essay livelier and more appealing than it would be without them. For more help with revising, review the rubric on page 424.

> stream of ~~flooded the once–pitch-black~~
> A bright light ~~covered the~~ stage. My palms began to sweat. I
> ~~shadows of familiar~~
> could see ~~that there were~~ people in the audience, but I
> ~~make out any faces~~ ~~quivered a little~~
> couldn't ~~tell who they were~~. I ~~stood in silence~~, and the
>
> song began.

❹ Editing and Proofreading

TARGET SKILL ▶ Misplaced Phrases Sometimes phrases are placed in sentences in ways that confuse readers. *Joe is known for his basketball skills by fans* is an example of a sentence containing a misplaced phrase. Not only can a misplaced phrase sound ridiculous, but it can also mislead.

> I whispered my last good-byes to friends as the stage lights
>
> went dark in the wing of the stage.

For more on misplaced phrases, see p. 156.

❺ Sharing and Reflecting

You could **share** your autobiographical incident by reading it to a partner or submitting it to your school newspaper or literary magazine.

For Your Working Portfolio Think of ways you could have made your autobiographical incident clearer as you **reflect** on the process of writing it. Would it have been helpful to add examples or dialogue? Keep your reflections with your autobiographical incident in your 📁 **Working Portfolio.**

CHAPTER 20

Speak for Yourself: *Monologue*

"I inched forward to center stage to accept the spotlight and began to sing."

Getting up in front of an audience and telling about something that happened to you can be a scary experience. But when you present your **autobiographical incident** as a monologue, you can mesmerize your audience with your experience and your skills as a storyteller.

Here's How | Creating a Monologue

- Pick a part of your autobiographical incident that has the most action or the most interesting characters.

- Change your more formal written language into everyday, conversational language.

- Practice your monologue in front of a friend. Ask for feedback on your delivery and on the story itself. Could your friend follow the story easily?

- When you present the monologue, use gestures and different voices for each character in your incident.

- Look at your audience. Don't read off a page.

- Be informal and friendly. You are just talking to your audience, telling them about something you experienced.

For more information on speaking skills, see pp. 563–565.

Student Help Desk

Autobiographical Incident at a Glance

Beginning

Introduces the incident including the people involved and the setting

Middle

• Describes the incident using descriptive details and dialogue

• Makes the importance clear

End

• Concludes by telling the outcome and importance of the incident

• Presents the writer's feelings about the experience

Idea Bank

Finding a Writing Idea

Check your diaries, scrapbooks, and letters.

Ask your family to recall stories that involve you.

Remember your proudest moment or most embarrassing moment.

Think about how something might have turned out in a different way if you had known what you know now.

Recall when something saved you from making a big mistake.

Read literature to find examples of autobiographical incidents. You might get ideas from reading *Wait Till Next Year* by Doris Kearns Goodwin or "The Great Rat Hunt" by Laurence Yep (*The Language of Literature,* Grade 8).

Including Dialogue

Quoting a speaker will make your writing more believable

• If you don't know or remember another person's exact words, you can always quote yourself: You might describe yourself asking the diving instructor, "Do you really expect me to jump off this precipice?"

• Give the quoted speaker strong emotions, but be wary of overusing exclamation marks.

• Quoting both speakers in a discussion or argument can provide exciting tension. Be sure to let the reader know which words belong to which speaker.

Friendly Feedback

Questions for Your Peer Reader

- What did you like best about my autobiographical incident?
- What evidence shows that the incident is important to me?
- What background information helped explain the incident?
- What other details or descriptions would have been helpful?
- Where could I have chosen more precise words?

Publishing Options

Print	With classmates, gather the class essays and organize them by theme. Make a booklet for the classroom library.
Oral Communication	Have a storytelling session in which several classmates relate their autobiographical incidents. Speakers should ask for feedback about the effectiveness of their presentations.
Online	Check out **mcdougallittell.com** for more publishing options.

The Bottom Line

Checklist for Autobiographical Incident

Have I . . .

- ___ kept the focus on one well-defined incident?
- ___ created an attention-grabbing beginning?
- ___ provided background information as needed?
- ___ used elements such as plot, character, and setting?
- ___ included dialogue as appropriate?
- ___ used precise language and specific details?
- ___ shown clearly why the incident is meaningful to me?
- ___ included a strong conclusion that summarizes the incident?

Eyewitness Report

Learn What It Is

If you are an eyewitness to an event, you have an advantage over anyone who just reads about the event. You were there. You saw it with your own eyes. In an **eyewitness report,** you write about an event you actually saw. You try to make it seem real to your readers, so that they can experience it almost as you did.

Basics in a Box

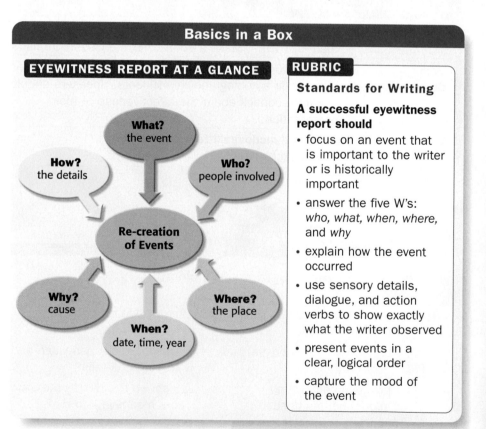

EYEWITNESS REPORT AT A GLANCE

- **What?** the event
- **How?** the details
- **Who?** people involved
- **Re-creation of Events**
- **Why?** cause
- **When?** date, time, year
- **Where?** the place

RUBRIC

Standards for Writing

A successful eyewitness report should

- focus on an event that is important to the writer or is historically important
- answer the five W's: *who, what, when, where,* and *why*
- explain how the event occurred
- use sensory details, dialogue, and action verbs to show exactly what the writer observed
- present events in a clear, logical order
- capture the mood of the event

See How It's Done: *Eyewitness Report*

RUBRIC
IN ACTION

The Perfect Performance

Only a few hours ago, I was inside the U.T. Tyler auditorium watching a wonderful presentation put on by the talented, exotic National Acrobats of China. The performance I saw included a man executing acrobatics on top of a 15-foot tower of chairs.

❶ Begins by telling when, where, who, and what about the event

At the beginning of the performance, a man brought out a tall, four-legged, stool-type platform. It had a blue cape around the perimeter that seemed to be made of crushed velvet and was decorated in blue and gold. Another man brought in four wine bottles, which he tapped to demonstrate that they were really made of glass. He then placed the bottles on each of the four corners of the stool, and on top of the bottles he placed a chair with its legs resting on the bottles. The men would place many other chairs on top of that chair throughout the course of the performance. These chairs were plain white with blue trim, and their backs were straight and vertical, with no curve.

❷ Uses sensory details of sight and sound

To the very tiptop of this lofty tower of chairs went an acrobat dressed in silken clothes of blue and white. Great suspense grew among the audience as the men on the stage thrust yet another chair into the air for him. The performer, however, knew exactly what he was doing. Though he laughed and smiled for the audience, he was dead serious. Catching the chair, he placed it on the top chair and tilted it diagonally, so that just two of its legs touched the rest of the tower. The audience was silent in awe as he did a handstand on the tilted chair and then spun around, using only one arm to hold his limber body in midair over the chair.

❸ Captures the mood of the event

EYEWITNESS

For a finale, the acrobat added three more chairs, and he stood on his head at the very top. As he was doing this, the chairs shook. I was secretly scared, but he came out all right. Last, as he climbed down, he threw the chairs down one by one to the three other performers on the stage. When the tower of chairs was completely demolished, he leaped into the air and did a dizzying somersault to the ground, landing perfectly.

❹ Presents events in a clear logical order

This was the most mind-blowing show I'd ever witnessed. Not only did the performer keep my attention, but he also pulled off the performance with style, grace, and perfection, deserving nothing less than a standing ovation.

❺ Ends by emphasizing the overall performance

Do It Yourself

Writing Prompt Write an eyewitness account of an event of personal or historical importance.

Purpose To inform or to entertain

Audience Anyone interested in you or the event

❶ Prewriting

Identify an event. Events suitable for eyewitness reports are everywhere. Remember, the event you describe does not have to be exciting or dramatic. Consider these approaches.

- **Be there.** Carry a notebook with you for several days and record any event you see that you think would make a good subject for an eyewitness account.

- **Search your memory.** Have you already witnessed something that stands out as a unique event?

For more topic ideas, see the Idea Bank, p. 438.

List the five W's. So that you will cover all the basics, complete a chart with the headings *Who, What, When, Where,* and *Why.*

Remember your five senses. Make notes about things you saw, heard, smelled, tasted, or touched during the event.

❷ Drafting

Get organized. One good way to organize an eyewitness report is to present events in the order they happened. Try filling in a flow chart like the one below. Use your notes as a basis.

First Event → Second Event → Third Event → Fourth Event

Begin writing. Your first aim is to get your reader's attention. Accordingly, you may want to begin with an interesting description or an exciting quotation. At some point near the beginning, however, you will need to provide some basic information, such as what happened, when it happened, and who was there.

Use descriptive details. Give enough details so that your reader can see, hear, and feel what is happening.

For information on getting feedback from your peers, see p. 439.

EYEWITNESS

❸ Revising

TARGET SKILL ▶**Sequencing** Present events in a logical sequence, so that your reader will understand what happened when. Use transition words and phrases to help make the sequence of events clear. For more help with revising, review the rubric on page 432.

> *For a finale,*
> ~~The~~ acrobat added three more chairs, and he stood on his
> ^   *As he was doing this,*
> head at the very top. ~~The~~ chairs shook.
>   ^

❹ Editing and Proofreading

TARGET SKILL ▶**Correcting Fragments** A sentence fragment does not express a complete thought. Sometimes you can correct a fragment by connecting it to another sentence.

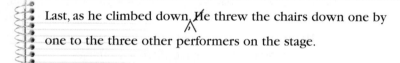

> Last, as he climbed down, ~~He~~ threw the chairs down one by
>   ^
> one to the three other performers on the stage.

For more on sentence fragments, see pp. 25–27.

❺ Sharing and Reflecting

Share your eyewitness report with an audience of friends or family members. Include photographs, drawings, or even a videotape to make your presentation lively.

For Your Working Portfolio As you **reflect** on your report, make notes about other ways you might have organized it. Note ideas from your friends' reports that you might have used to good effect. Save your comments along with your finished report in your 📁 **Working Portfolio.**

CHAPTER 21

Speak for Yourself: *News Report*

"The acrobat stood on his head on a shaking tower of chairs."

You've seen the evening news where a reporter at the scene of an event relays the facts of what he or she has just seen. You can play the role of reporter on assignment and present your own news account based on your **eyewitness report.**

Here's How | **Creating a News Report**

- Read over your eyewitness report and highlight all the facts. Make sure they are in sequential order.

- Rewrite your eyewitness report from the point of view of a reporter. You will need to start with answering the questions *what*, *when*, and *where*. Imagine that you are on camera, speaking to a television audience.

- Relate the facts as they happened, then include some of your own reactions as an eyewitness observer. Remember, it is your job to make the news report exciting for your imaginary TV viewers.

- When you give your presentation, wear clothes that make you look professional. Carry something to represent the microphone you would be speaking into.

For more information on speaking skills, see pp. 563–565.

EYEWITNESS

Student Help Desk

Eyewitness Report at a Glance

What? the event

How? the details

Who? people involved

Re-creation of Events

Why? cause

When? date, time, year

Where? the place

Idea Bank

Finding a topic

Look for puzzles. Think about something you have seen that puzzles you. You could describe what you saw and what it left you wondering.

What's new? Think about something new in your life. You might describe a day in the life of a new baby brother or sister or a new pet. You might describe your first outing in a new family car or your first experience with a new computer.

Take a walk. Describe something that catches your interest on a walk, either in your neighborhood or someplace unfamiliar.

Check your calendar. Does the future hold a sports event, club event, or family gathering? Plan to attend and take notes.

Including Quotations

"It happened right in front of me!"

- **Find another witness.** Quote another person who saw the same thing you did. The quotation might support your view or contrast with it.
- **Quote an expert.** Cite the words of an expert on the topic.
- **Be creative.** Provide a literary quotation or song lyrics to illustrate the point of your report.

Friendly Feedback

Questions for Your Peer Reader

- What did I describe and when did it take place?
- What mood did I create?
- What details helped you experience the event?
- How did I show the order of events?
- What did you like best about my report?

Publishing Options

Print	Submit your eyewitness report to a magazine or newspaper as a human interest story.
Oral Communication	Refine your eyewitness report for presentation as a radio report. You might want to add some simple sound effects, such as recorded applause or suspenseful music.
Online	Check out **mcdougallittell.com** for more publishing options.

The Bottom Line

Checklist for Eyewitness Report

Have I . . .

____ focused on an event that has personal or historical meaning?

____ answered the five W's: *who, what, when, where,* and *why?*

____ used precise language and sensory images?

____ presented what happened in a clear, logical order?

____ captured the mood of the event?

Analyzing a Story

Learn What It Is

Why does a story stick in your memory? Is it because of a certain character or a particular event? If you don't like a story, why is that? When you explore elements of a story in writing, you are **analyzing a story.** The process of creating your analysis will help you better understand both the story and your own reactions to it.

Basics in a Box

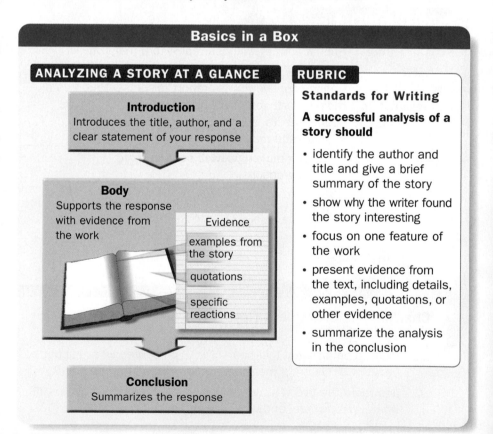

ANALYZING A STORY AT A GLANCE

Introduction
Introduces the title, author, and a clear statement of your response

Body
Supports the response with evidence from the work

Evidence

examples from the story

quotations

specific reactions

Conclusion
Summarizes the response

RUBRIC

Standards for Writing

A successful analysis of a story should

• identify the author and title and give a brief summary of the story

• show why the writer found the story interesting

• focus on one feature of the work

• present evidence from the text, including details, examples, quotations, or other evidence

• summarize the analysis in the conclusion

CHAPTER 22

See How It's Done: *Analyzing a Story*

Student Model
Julia Risk
Wood Oaks Junior High

RUBRIC
IN ACTION

"Raymond's Run"

Squeaky, the main character in Toni Cade Bambara's short story "Raymond's Run," has two priorities in life. The first is taking care of her mentally handicapped brother, Raymond, and the other is running. Squeaky is impressive because she knows herself.

The story opens one morning just before a big race as Squeaky and Raymond are out doing exercises. A popular girl named Gretchen teases Squeaky and says that she, Gretchen, will win the races this year. When Gretchen and her friends start to tease Raymond, Squeaky defends him. On the day of the big race, Squeaky looks over from the track to see Raymond running with her. After she wins the race, Squeaky sees how excited and happy Raymond is just to have run. She decides that winning is not the most important thing, and she realizes she is willing to give up winning so that she can coach Raymond. By showing us these two important parts of Squeaky's life, Raymond and running, Bambara lets us know the kind of person Squeaky is.

As Bambara shows in the story, Squeaky's relationship with her brother is not like most brother-sister relationships. She is a tough girl with no responsibility except her brother. Although this may seem like no big deal, events in the story make clear that it presents difficulties. Squeaky has to bring Raymond along everywhere—on her morning walks, on her training runs, to her races. But Squeaky doesn't mind, because she enjoys his company: "I'm jumping up and down so glad to see him—my brother Raymond, a great runner in the family tradition." She looks out for Raymond and won't let anybody bother him. When Squeaky bumps into Gretchen and her friends, who start talking to Raymond, she says, "You got anything to

❶ Clearly identifies the literary work

❷ Gives a clear statement of her overall analysis

❸ Gives a brief summary of the story so that readers can understand her response

❹ Supports statements with quotations

ANALYZING/STORY

Analyzing a Story **441**

say to my brother, you say it to me." Squeaky is not embarrassed by Raymond. She can see past another's disabilities and appreciate the person for who he or she is.

Bambara also shows us a lot about Squeaky through her running. It means a lot to Squeaky that she is a very good runner. She is not worried about winning, because she believes she is the best. Squeaky is competitive and determined to win. In the end, though, she realizes that winning isn't the most important thing. When she sees how happy Raymond is, she thinks, "I can always retire as a runner and begin a whole new career as a coach with Raymond as my champion. . . . I've got a roomful of ribbons and medals and awards. But what has Raymond got to call his own?" Squeaky is willing to make major changes to the most important thing in her life in order to include Raymond in it and make him happy.

❺ Focuses on one feature of the work, in this case the author's presentation of the main character

Squeaky is forgiving toward Gretchen. Although Gretchen was mean to Squeaky, Squeaky thinks, "Maybe she'd like to help me coach Raymond." Squeaky can make the big step of setting aside her differences with someone and finding the similarities.

Bambara depicts Squeaky as someone who cares deeply for her family as well as for herself. She has a good heart and lots of potential. I envy Squeaky's character and her relationships with people. I think everyone should learn from Squeaky and take life as it is and take others as they are.

In Squeaky's words, "Maybe we too busy being flowers or fairies or strawberries instead of something honest and worthy of respect . . . you know . . . like being people." We can all learn from Squeaky to be ourselves and let others be just what they are, too.

❻ Concludes with a quotation that captures the significance of the story

Do It Yourself

Writing Prompt   Write an analysis of a story you found interesting.

Purpose To share your reaction to a story

Audience Friends and classmates who may be interested in the story

❶ Prewriting

Choose a story that made an impact on you. Think about a story that you especially like—or one you think has problems. Jot down some ideas about why you feel as you do.

For more topic ideas, see the Idea Bank, p. 446.

Reread the story. Read the story several times. Take notes or make a chart that includes the main elements in the story: characters, plot, setting, and conflict. Describe each element. For example, a note about Squeaky might read, "Loves running; protects her handicapped brother."

Pick quotations. As you reread, find passages you might quote to support your analysis of the story. The writer of the model chose passages that show that Squeaky protects her brother.

❷ Drafting

Organize your draft. Include an introduction, body, and conclusion. Within each part, include the following elements:

Analyzing a Story		
Introduction	**Body**	**Conclusion**
• title and author	• step-by-step analysis	• summary of your response
• brief summary of the story	• supporting details	
	• supporting quotations	
• your response		

Maintain focus. It isn't necessary to tell everything about the story. As you write your draft, find the main point you want to make and stick to it.

For information about getting feedback from your peers, see p. 447.

ANALYZING/STORY

❸ Revising

TARGET SKILL ►Elaborating with Quotations Use exact words from the story to support your analysis. Enclose any exact wording in quotation marks. For more help with revising, review the rubric on page 440.

> When Squeaky bumps into Gretchen and her friends,
> who start talking to Raymond, she ~~stands up to the other~~ says, "You got anything to say to my brother, you say it to me."
> ~~girls and protects Raymond.~~

❹ Editing and Proofreading

TARGET SKILL ►Consistent Point of View Be sure to keep the same point of view throughout your analysis. If you are writing in the first person, using the pronouns *I* and *me,* for example, don't suddenly change to the second person.

> I
> ~~You~~ envy Squeaky's character and her relationships with
> people. I think everyone should learn from Squeaky and
> take life as it is and take others as they are.

❺ Sharing and Reflecting

You might want to **share** your analysis with someone who has read the story you analyzed. Ask your partner for feedback on your ideas.

For Your Working Portfolio As you think about your analysis, **reflect** on what you have learned. Did your opinion of the story change over the course of writing? What part of your analysis was the hardest to write? Write your responses and save them along with your finished analysis in your 📁 **Working Portfolio.**

Speak for Yourself: *Oral Interpretation*

If you've ever heard a public reading of a short story, you know how the reader's feelings about the story can be heard in his or her voice and manner. When presenting your **analysis of a story** as an oral interpretation, you will be able to convey your feelings about a story to your audience.

"You got anything to say to my brother, you say it to me . . ."

Here's How Creating an Oral Interpretation

- Choose one part of the story you wrote about. You may pick your favorite scene or one that you feel represents the larger story.

- Make notes to yourself on the page for things like tone of your voice, hand gestures, and anything else that will help you express your understanding of the story.

- Have your passage semi-memorized. Don't bury your nose in your paper. Look at the audience and command their attention.

- Exaggerate certain important words and phrases. Not only will it grab the attention of your audience, but it will make your interpretation clear.

- Briefly explain your interpretation of the story after your reading. You may want to take this opportunity to answer questions from the class.

For more information on speaking skills, see pp. 564–567.

ANALYZING/STORY

Then they all look at Raymond who has just brought *(wise tone)* his mule team to a standstill. And they're about to see what trouble they can get into through him.

"What grade you in now, Raymond?" *(sassy)*

"You got anything to say to my brother, you say it to me, Mary Louise Williams of Raggedy Town Baltimore." *(tough tone—hands on hips)*

Student Help Desk

Analyzing a Story at a Glance

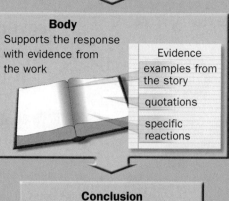

Introduction
Introduces the title, author, and a clear statement of your response

Body
Supports the response with evidence from the work

Evidence
- examples from the story
- quotations
- specific reactions

Conclusion
Summarizes the response

Idea Bank

Tips for Finding an Idea

Recall a favorite story from when you were younger. Maybe it's a story someone read to you.

Look for mysteries—or science fiction or scary stories. Analyze how the authors create the suspense, weird science, or fear.

Discuss with a classmate why the two of you disagree about a story.

Choose the story with the most unusual character, the most intriguing plot, or the most memorable setting.

Show, Don't Tell

- Use quotations from the story to show instead of tell. For example, don't describe a character's anger, show it with a quotation.

- Support your general statements with specific examples from the story. If you describe a character or setting, for example, follow your description with a short quotation that supports it.

- Use quotation marks around any direct quotation.

- Keep your quotation short and to the point.

CHAPTER 22

Friendly Feedback

Questions for Your Peer Reader

- What points in my analysis do you agree with?
- What points do you disagree with?
- What is the most interesting part of my analysis?
- What new ideas did my analysis give you?

Publishing Options

Print	Submit your essay to a student writing contest or to your school's literary journal.
Oral Communication	Gather a small group of students who have read the same story. Have each student read a part of the story aloud. Then share your responses and discuss how they differ.
Online	Check out **mcdougallittell.com** for more publishing options.

The Bottom Line

Checklist for Analyzing a Story

Have I . . .

___ clearly identified the story in my introduction?

___ presented my overall response in the introduction?

___ told enough of the story so that readers understand my response?

___ given specific reactions to the story?

___ supported my statements with quotations and details?

___ summarized my response in the conclusion?

Problem-Solution Essay

Learn What It Is

Problems are a regular part of life. Sometimes when you write about a problem, you can see it more clearly. You may even come up with a workable solution. Writing a **problem-solution essay** is a way to think through a problem, consider solutions, and propose one logical answer.

Basics in a Box

PROBLEM-SOLUTION ESSAY AT A GLANCE

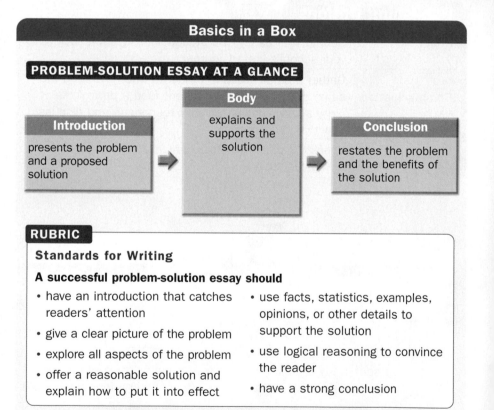

Introduction

presents the problem and a proposed solution

Body

explains and supports the solution

Conclusion

restates the problem and the benefits of the solution

RUBRIC

Standards for Writing

A successful problem-solution essay should

- have an introduction that catches readers' attention
- give a clear picture of the problem
- explore all aspects of the problem
- offer a reasonable solution and explain how to put it into effect
- use facts, statistics, examples, opinions, or other details to support the solution
- use logical reasoning to convince the reader
- have a strong conclusion

See How It's Done: *Problem-Solution Essay*

Student Model
Ann Marie Gasparro
Coppell Middle School
North

RUBRIC
IN ACTION

The Future Lies in Their Hands

Are you ever annoyed with the lengthy, seemingly meaningless bulletins that force you to miss the crucial ending to *Days of Our Lives* or *The Brady Bunch?* Well, these days the special news breaks are more disturbing than ever. Too often they are stories about violence in schools. It seems that all attempts to rid us of this problem have failed. Perhaps school violence will never go away completely. Still, there are some ideas that haven't been tried. One idea I strongly support is requiring mental-health classes.

❶ Catches the reader's attention with a question

I believe that the main cause of school violence is the poor mental health of many children and teens. In order to solve the problem, we must ensure the stable mental health of the students. Why do we require general health classes in our high schools but not offer a single mental-health course? Mental-health classes would simply teach right from wrong. Consider a young child who walks out of a store with a stuffed animal without paying for it, not knowing it is wrong to do so. Once reprimanded and told what he has done, he probably won't steal again. However, if he is not punished in any way, he will likely grow up not changing his ways and may even end his life in a jail cell.

❷ Gives a clear picture of the problem and proposes a solution

❸ Explores causes and effects of the problem

Not being taught right from wrong can also be the main cause of violence. A child who is told not to push, hit, or express anger in physical ways is not likely to grow up using violence to deal with her anger. Because some teenagers were not taught these valuable lessons as children, the school should take the responsibility to teach them now. It is an opportunity, and the school has the ability to do it.

PROB.-SOLUTION

Many solutions to eliminate violence in school simply address the symptoms of the problem rather than the core cause. One such attempted solution is the use of metal detectors. Metal detectors only keep weapons out of buildings; they don't prevent people from being harmed outside of the school. A better solution to prevent violence is the use of guidance counselors. They could have the same positive effect as a mental-health class, assuming that the students in question would ever go to a counseling session.

4 Addresses an opposing view

The most common solution attempted, though, is the threat of consequences whenever a student is caught in a violent act. However, if a child is depressed enough to feel the need to harm others, suspension from school or even spending time in jail is not very likely to stop his actions.

5 This writer negates the most common solution and offers a better one.

The best solution is a required mental-health class. I believe this would positively affect children's mental health in the same way that required general health classes have affected other health problems. Within two years of a health course being required for high school graduation, teen pregnancies went down from 27 percent to 14 percent, and teenage drug use went down from 46 percent to 31 percent, according to the Center for Healthy Living. We could expect similar positive results from a required mental-health class.

6 Uses statistics to support the solution

The incidence of violence in schools would surely be tremendously reduced if all students participated in a mental-health class. If we believe that the future rests in the hands of our children, shouldn't we make them good hands?

7 Strongly restates the argument in the conclusion

Do It Yourself

Writing Prompt Write a problem-solution essay about a problem that matters to you.

Purpose To persuade and inform

Audience Anyone interested in the problem

❶ Prewriting

Explore topics. To find a topic, try to remember talks with your family or friends about problems. Think about the special problems faced by such groups as minorities, teenagers, and the elderly.

For more topic ideas, see the Idea Bank, p. 454.

Brainstorm solutions. Make a list of ways to solve your chosen problem. Choose the solution that seems most workable.

Think about your audience. Who is interested in the problem? Why? With what points will your audience agree or disagree?

❷ Drafting

Begin writing. You may begin with any part of your essay. However, at some point you must organize your essay into an introduction, a body, and a conclusion.

Organizing Your Problem-Solution Essay	
Introduction	• Catch the reader's attention. • Identify the problem and your proposed solution.
Body	• Explain the problem's cause. • Give examples and facts to support your ideas. • Explain your solution and why it would work. • Describe how to put your solution into effect.
Conclusion	• Summarize the problem and your solution.

Use clear arguments. Don't jump to conclusions. Be sure you are making a clear, logical connection between the problem and your solution.

Watch your language. Don't use general words like *all*, *everyone*, *always*, and *never*. The statement "All teenagers are rowdy" is meaningless because it is impossible to prove.

For information about getting feedback from your peers, see p. 455.

PROB.-SOLUTION

❸ Revising

TARGET SKILL ▶Using Examples and Facts Whenever you make a general statement, be sure to back it up with supporting evidence. For more help with revising, review the rubric on page 448.

> Many solutions to eliminate violence in school simply
>
> address the symptoms of the problem rather than the core
> ~~cause.~~ *One such attempted solution is the use of metal detectors. Metal*
> ~~If schools just address the symptoms, they won't~~
> *detectors only keep weapons out of buildings; they don't prevent*
> ~~solve the problem. I could name several attempted~~
> *people from being harmed outside of the school.*
> ~~solutions.~~

❹ Editing and Proofreading

TARGET SKILL ▶Consistent Verb Tense Keep the verb tense consistent throughout your essay. Shift tense only when you need to show that an event happened at a different time than other events mentioned.

> Well, these days the special news breaks are more
>
> disturbing than ever. Too often they ~~were~~ *are* stories about
>
> violence in schools.

For more on verb tenses, see pp. 105–114.

❺ Sharing and Reflecting

Find other students who wrote about the same problem you did. **Share** your essays and compare your solutions.

For Your Working Portfolio After discussing your essay with peer readers, **reflect** on what you have learned. Were there other examples you could have used? What else could you have done differently? Place your answers and your finished essay in your 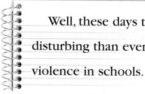 **Working Portfolio.**

Speak for Yourself: *Persuasive Speech*

Required Mental Health Class
- reduce violence in schools
- teach lawful behavior
- teach acceptable ways to express anger
- encourage positive attitudes

"To reduce school violence, every student should be required to take a mental health class."

Public speakers are often successful because they aim their speeches at the needs and interests of their audience. As you adapt your **problem-solution essay** into a persuasive speech, keep your audience in mind so that you can effectively persuade them.

Here's How   Creating a Persuasive Speech

- Choose the most important parts of your essay to emphasize. Condense your ideas; don't simply plan to read your essay aloud.

- Write out your speech. Give a brief overview of the problem, then a point-by- point explanation of your solution. Use examples to clarify and support your argument.

- As you sell your ideas, remember the entire package. Dress neatly and professionally and give a practiced presentation.

- Prepare some visuals such as a flip chart to clearly outline the problem and your solution, and perhaps a poster containing a slogan so people will remember your idea.

- Practice your speech in front of a friend. Use gestures, pacing (how quickly or slowly you speak), and tone of voice to get your meaning across and to convince your audience to agree with you.

For more information on speaking skills,
see pp. 563–565.

PROB.-SOLUTION

Student Help Desk

Problem-Solution Essay at a Glance

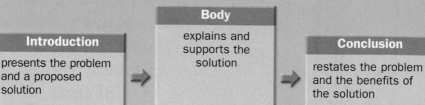

Introduction
presents the problem and a proposed solution

Body
explains and supports the solution

Conclusion
restates the problem and the benefits of the solution

Idea Bank

Solutions for Finding a Topic

Interview. Ask neighbors for their ideas about problems in the neighborhood.

Read. Check newspaper stories, advice columns, magazine articles, school bulletins. For example, how would you solve the problem of noise in the school hallways?

Talk with friends. What bugs your friends? What do they think can be done about it?

Read the literature. Get ideas from reading what others have written. For example, you might consider how the characters in "Raymond's Run" by Toni Cade Bambara deal with their problems (*The Language of Literature,* Grade 8).

Check Your Thinking

Logical Fallacies to Avoid

Circular reasoning—trying to prove your point by repeating it in different words ("A new pool is necessary because we need it.")

Overgeneralization—making a statement that is too broad to prove ("Everyone loves to swim.")

Either/or fallacy—saying there is only one solution when there is really more than one ("Either we build a new pool or no child will learn to swim.")

Cause-and-effect fallacy—arguing that because one event followed another, the first event caused the second ("Another town opened a new pool, and curfew violations declined.")

Friendly Feedback

Questions for Your Peer Reader

- What problem did I describe?
- What solution did I offer?
- What did you like about my solution?
- What aspects of my solution did you disagree with?
- How could I make my solution seem more workable?

Publishing Options

Print	Submit your work to your school or local newspaper for possible publication as an editorial or a letter to the editor.
Oral Communication	Present your work to your classmates. Use charts to illustrate your main point.
Online	Check out **mcdougallittell.com** for more publishing options.

The Bottom Line

Checklist for Problem-Solution Essay

Have I . . .

- ____ caught the reader's attention in the introduction?
- ____ given a clear picture of the problem?
- ____ described the causes and effects of the problem?
- ____ offered a reasonable solution?
- ____ explained how to put the solution into effect?
- ____ used facts, statistics, opinions, or other details to support the solution?
- ____ used logical reasoning?
- ____ ended with a strong conclusion?

Comparison-Contrast Essay

Learn What It Is

How is the eighth grade like the seventh grade? How is it different? If you and your friends made a list of similarities and differences between the two grades, you would have the beginnings of a comparison-contrast essay. A **comparison-contrast essay** evaluates two things or ideas by discussing the ways they are similar and the ways they are different.

Basics in a Box

COMPARISON-CONTRAST ESSAY AT A GLANCE

Introduction	Body	Conclusion
• introduces the **subjects** being compared	explains similarities and differences	• summarizes the comparison
• tells the **reason** for the comparison	Subject A only Both subjects Subject B only	• explains new understanding

RUBRIC

Standards for Writing

A successful comparison-contrast essay should

- introduce the subjects being compared
- give a clear purpose for the comparison
- include both similarities and differences and support each statement with examples and details

- follow a clear organizational pattern
- use transitional words and phrases to make the similarities and differences clear
- summarize the comparison in the conclusion

See How It's Done: *Comparison-Contrast Essay*

Student Model
Caitlyn Fox
Lake Forest Country
Day School

RUBRIC
IN ACTION

Books for Then and Now

"Look, look. I see a big yellow car. See the yellow car go."

This is an excerpt from the picture book *Fun with Dick and Jane*, by William S. Gray and May Hill Arbuthnot, published in 1946. Picture books have long been used to develop early reading skills. These books have developed over many years, and today's children's books catch young readers' attention and then teach a point that makes the child think. Modern books address real-life issues, are more challenging, and are more creatively executed than those of 50 years ago.

In the past, many stories centered around a white family living in a middle-class suburb with a boy, a girl, and two happily married parents. The truth is, many children today live in far different situations. Children's literature has changed drastically to address this. Aspects such as race, broken homes, and the environment are brought up commonly in today's stories.

Music, Music for Everyone by Vera B. Williams is a perfect example of this. The book is about a young girl who wants to help her single mother by earning money for the family money jar. She and her friends, all from various ethnic backgrounds, create the idea of playing their instruments to earn money. Books like this are popular because children like to learn about others more like themselves, not impossibly perfect people like Dick and Jane. Dick and Jane never had any serious problems and their life seemed very boring.

❶ This writer opens with a quotation to catch the reader's attention.
Another option: Open by identifying both subjects.

❷ Identifies the subjects being compared: picture books then and now

❸ Discusses the first feature: real life as shown in stories

❹ Uses a specific example to support the point about real life

COMPARISON

Using everyday events, picture books today treat children more intelligently. Modern authors expect children to notice the underlying themes. The book *Nappy Hair* is about an African-American named Brenda who had "the kinkiest, the nappiest, the fuzziest, the most screwed up, squeezed up, knotted up, tangled up, twisted up . . . the nappiest hair you've ever seen in your life." The author, Carolivia Herron, said, "Children understand right away that this book is about acceptance and celebration." There are no themes like this to be found in the "Dick and Jane" books.

❺ Identifies another feature—treating children intelligently—and gives an example

More advanced vocabulary is also used in today's books. "Listen to the story of Abu Kassem, the merchant, who was known throughout Baghdad not only for his riches and his parsimony but also for his slippers, which were the outward and visible sign of his miserliness." This is an excerpt from *Two Pairs of Shoes.* Obviously, the vocabulary used would be a challenge for most young readers. Challenging stories appeal to children. Older books had less challenging words and therefore required less from children.

❻ Discusses a third feature: vocabulary

Take yourself back to age six or seven. Dick and Jane? "We can go away in a boat. Away in a big blue boat." Or Abu Kassem? "But he counseled Abu saying, '. . . when a thing is no longer useful, that thing should be relinquished.'"

Simple, uninteresting picture books are a thing of the past and in their place are modern stories that attract and excite young minds.

❼ Ends with contrasting quotations and a clear statement summarizing the point of the comparison

Do It Yourself

Write an essay to show how how two subjects are alike and different.

Purpose To explain or clarify

Audience Anyone interested in the subjects

❶ Prewriting

Decide on a topic. Think of all the comparisons you make every day. You might compare two movies, two products, two types of sports, or practically anything.

For more topic ideas, see the Idea Bank, p. 462.

Decide on your purpose. Do you need to decide which movie to see? What product to buy? Which sport to choose? Your purpose will help guide what you write.

Choose a focus. Concentrate on the most important features, the ones that will help you achieve your purpose.

❷ Drafting

Organize your thoughts. Making a chart can help you choose an organization. Comparison-contrast essays are organized in one of two ways, a subject-by-subject pattern or a feature-by-feature pattern. After choosing an organization, begin writing.

Subject-by-Subject	
Subject A	**Older books (Dick & Jane)**
Feature 1	Unrealistic, perfect world
Feature 2	Simple language
Subject B	**Today's books**
Feature 1	Realistic, imperfect world
Feature 2	Challenging language

Feature-by-Feature	
Feature 1	**Realistic World**
Subject A	Older books like Dick & Jane
Subject B	Today's books
Feature 2	**Language**
Subject A	Simple language in Dick & Jane
Subject B	Challenging language in today's books

COMPARISON

For information about getting feedback from your peers, see p. 463.

❸ Revising

TARGET SKILL ▶Errors in Reasoning Express your ideas
accurately and clearly to convince your readers. Watch out for
common errors in reasoning, such as saying that *all* older books
are poorly written or that *every* child likes realistic stories. You
can correct such errors by using words like *some* and *many*. For
more help with revising, review the rubric on page 456.

>   *many*
> In the past, ˰stories centered around a white family living
>
> in a middle-class suburb with a boy, a girl, and two happily
>   *many*
> married parents. The truth is, ˰children today live in far
>
> different situations.

❹ Editing and Proofreading

TARGET SKILL ▶Subject-Verb Agreement If your subject is
singular, make sure your verb is singular. If the subject is
plural, the verb must be plural.

>   Aspects such as race, broken homes, and the
>   *are*
> environment ˰i̶s̶ brought up commonly in today's stories.

For more on subject-verb agreement, see pp. 206–221.

❺ Sharing and Reflecting

Find others who are interested in the topic of your comparison-
contrast essay, and **share** it with them. Ask them to give you
feedback on the clarity of your comparisons.

For Your Working Portfolio Consider what other points you
might have made or what points could have been deleted as
you **reflect** on your essay. Make notes on anything you would
have done differently. Save your notes along with your essay in
your **Working Portfolio.**

Speak for Yourself: *Oral Report*

Often in commercials two products are compared side-by-side to show how one is better. You can do the same thing in an oral report based on your **comparison-contrast essay**. You will show how two things are similar or different.

"Today's children's books show real-life issues, not the impossibly perfect family of older books."

For more information on speaking skills, see pp. 563–565.

Here's How   Creating an Oral Report

- Choose points from your essay to use in your oral report. Make some notes or write out what you plan to say. Don't simply read your essay out loud.

- Bring in things you are comparing, or bring in photographs of them. As you give your report you can refer to them and display them. That way the audience can see first hand what you are talking about.

- If you don't have items or photos, then use a flip chart, maps, or other visual ways to add to your presentation.

- Make a chart that lists the key comparisons you are making. This will help keep the information clear in the minds of your audience.

COMPARISON

Student Help Desk

Comparison-Contrast Essay at a Glance

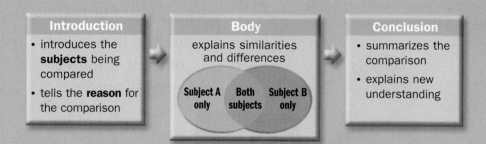

Introduction
- introduces the **subjects** being compared
- tells the **reason** for the comparison

Body
explains similarities and differences

Subject A only | Both subjects | Subject B only

Conclusion
- summarizes the comparison
- explains new understanding

Idea Bank

Think how you would compare and contrast . . .

- the advantages and disadvantages of certain pets
- two kinds of popular music
- a movie with the book it was based on
- two competing brands of food or clothes
- two school courses and which one you would benefit most from
- two popular movies
- a camping trip and a trip to a theme park
- two sports offered at the same time
- the advantages and disadvantages of a large family
- two characters in literature or a character at different points in life like the central character in "Flowers for Algernon" (*The Language of Literature*, Grade 8)

Friendly Feedback

Questions for Your Peer Reader

- How are the things I compared alike?
- How are they different?
- What was my purpose in comparing and contrasting these two things?
- In what areas did you agree with my conclusion? In what areas did you disagree?

Publishing Options

Print	Submit your essay to the school newspaper for consideration. If there are similar essays, see if they could be posted on the class bulletin board.
Oral Communication	Find classmates who have different viewpoints on related topics and set up a debate series.
Online	Check out **mcdougallittell.com** for more publishing options.

The Bottom Line

Checklist for Comparison-Contrast Essay

Have I . . .

____ identified the subjects being compared?

____ clearly shown my purpose for comparing them?

____ included both similarities and differences?

____ supported my statements with specific examples and details?

____ followed a clear organizational pattern?

____ used transitional words and phrases to make the relationships among ideas clear?

____ summarized the comparison in the conclusion?

Persuasive Essay

Learn What It Is

Is there an issue that you have strong feelings about? Would you like others to feel the same way you do? One way to convince others is to write a **persuasive essay**. In this essay, you will present your ideas and the reasons your audience should agree with you.

Basics in a Box

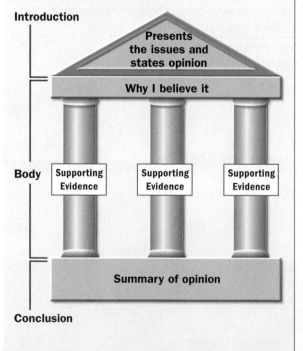

PERSUASIVE ESSAY AT A GLANCE

Introduction

Presents the issues and states opinion

Why I believe it

Body — Supporting Evidence | Supporting Evidence | Supporting Evidence

Summary of opinion

Conclusion

RUBRIC

Standards for Writing

A successful persuasive essay should

- clearly state the issue and your position on it in the introduction
- use language appropriate to the audience you are trying to convince
- support your position with facts, statistics, and reasons
- answer possible objections to your position
- show clear reasoning
- conclude with a summary of your position or a call to action

See How It's Done: *Persuasive Essay*

Student Model
Echo Bergquist
Oak Hill Middle School

Doing Dishes

From a grown-up's point of view, dinner is a pleasant time. First, the meal; then dessert perhaps; and afterwards, an hour in the easy chair with a good book. However, a kid's point of view is drastically different. Instead of spending dinnertime enjoying the food, children try to mentally force people not to dirty their knives, in hopes of lessening the horrible burden that faces the children after everyone has finished eating.

Doing the dishes is one of the most dreadful tasks put upon children. Many people think that doing the dishes is a short, simple task, but forcing children to do the dishes every night wastes a lot of time and energy. To rinse an average load of tableware and put it in the dishwasher, then wash all the things too large or delicate to wash in the machine takes about fifteen minutes. However, "doing dishes" no longer consists simply of washing dishes; parents have added to this great chore the clearing of leftovers, the wiping of the table and counter, and the getting rid of leftover water in the sink which has revolting bits of food still floating in it. This adds an extra five minutes, which brings us to a grand total of 20 minutes. By itself that isn't a large amount of time, but when a child does the dishes five nights per week, that adds up to approximately 87 hours of hard labor each year.

Children should be playing outside or doing homework in the evening, not scrubbing at the sink for almost four days a year. Those 87 hours could mean the difference between straight A's or straight C's. Those nightly 20 minutes are important for finishing homework. If homework has already been

RUBRIC
IN ACTION

❶ This writer uses the first paragraph to hook the reader with an interesting scene.

❷ This writer clearly states the issue and her position on it after a scene-setting introduction.

Another option: State the issue and your position on it immediately.

❸ Supports position with facts and statistics

PERSUASION

done, that time could be used for getting fresh air, which can prevent colds and fevers.

Doing dishes is physically harmful. When hands are constantly exposed to water, they become chapped and peel, or even blister. Rubber gloves don't work, since it is impossible to feel the pots and pans through them. This makes it easy for the pots to come out of the water greasy and with streaks of food still on them. Later, the child gets scolded for not producing "squeaky clean" pans. Also, the washer is required to constantly lean over the sink, which can cause temporary backaches, or long-term effects such as scoliosis, or a curved spine.

❹ Supports position with clear, humorous reasons

Last, washing dishes is a job only for people aged at least eighteen. Parents must realize that it is their responsibility to feed, clothe, educate, and clean up after their child. When they are old enough, children can be expected to clean their rooms or put away their toys. However, only a mean and contemptible parent would demand that an innocent child be put to work scrubbing not only the child's mess, but also the mess made by the parents. Of course, when the teenager goes to college or moves out, the job becomes the teenager's own, since he or she is making all the mess and is no longer under the parents' care. Until then, parents are obligated to clean up the dinner mess on their own.

❺ Gives answers to possible objections to her position

Dishes should not be washed by children. Parents should consider that the money they would spend on tutors and medical bills would greatly exceed the cost of a housekeeper.

❻ Concludes with a summary of her position and a call to action

Do It Yourself

Writing Prompt Choose an issue you feel strongly about, and write a persuasive essay about it.

Purpose To influence people's beliefs or actions

Audience Anyone who is interested in or affected by the issue

❶ Prewriting

Decide on your stand. If you don't already know what you want to write about, use some of the following suggestions to come up with ideas.

- **Check the newspaper.** Look through news stories, editorials, political cartoons, and letters to the editor. What grabs your attention? What is happening in the world that you feel strongly about? What ideas do you wish you could debate?

- **Conduct a survey.** Ask several people the following question: What do you think is the most important issue facing us today?

- **Recall arguments.** What are some things that you and a friend have debated in the past? Are these issues something that a larger audience would be affected by or interested in?

For more topic ideas, see the Idea Bank, p. 472.

Focus your options. Once you've come up with a few possible topics for your essay, pick one or two that you find most interesting. Then ask yourself the following questions about your choices.

- **Is the topic too big? too small?** Solving world poverty is too large to tackle in a short essay. However, you could focus your ideas on helping needy individuals in your own community.

- **Does it really matter to you?** How strongly do you feel about the issue? To convince others, you must be convinced yourself.

Consider your audience. To persuade your audience to see things your way or take a specific action, you need to know something about your readers. Ask yourself these questions:

- Who is my audience? Classmates? Family members? School administrators? Community leaders?
- What do they already know about the topic? What do they need to know?
- What are their opinions about the topic?
- What reasons might appeal to this audience?

Think about the tone of your essay. The writer of the model used humor as well as facts and figures to get her point across. Would your audience respond to humor, or would they want a more serious approach?

Strengthen your position. Once you decide on a topic, use these suggestions to help you put your opinions and ideas in writing:

- **Develop a pro and con list.** List arguments for your position in one column and arguments against it in another column.

Doing Dishes

Arguments Against Children Doing Dishes	Arguments in Favor of Children Doing Dishes
Waste of time and energy	Builds character
Can affect grades	Teaches responsibility
Could use extra time to do homework or play	Teaches a task the children will one day have to do
Causes physical harm	

- **Choose the most important arguments.** As you review your list, look for points that show what your basic position is. Then look for points that support your ideas.
- **Think about the opposing view.** What arguments in your list are people likely to use if they oppose your position? What points on your list can be used to counter these arguments?

❷ Drafting

Decide how to organize. The writer of the model chose to list all of her reasons and supporting evidence before giving answers to possible opposing arguments. Another option is to follow each reason and supporting evidence with answers to possible objections. Use the following to guide your writing.

- **Introduction:** State clearly what the issue is and where you stand on it.
- **Body: Support your arguments.** Give your reasons for your opinion, and back up your reasons with convincing evidence. You can use facts and figures, examples, or quotations from experts to make your case.
- **Conclusion:** Sum up what you have said in support of your stand. If appropriate, ask readers to take a specific action.

Be logical. Your arguments can't be exaggerated or misleading. Opponents will be looking for errors in reasoning. Here are some common errors to avoid.

Errors in Reasoning		
Circular reasoning	Trying to prove a statement by repeating it in different words	"Crime must be stopped so it won't happen anymore." (We haven't been told why crime must be stopped.)
Overgeneralization	Making a statement that is too broad to prove	"No one will ever like the new schedule." (There are probably a few people who will.)
Either/or fallacy	Claiming that there is only one possible solution when there are many	"Either we add more study halls, or grades will fall." (There are other ways to increase studying.)
Cause-and-effect fallacy	Assuming that because one event follows another, the second event is caused by the first	"Because the new school was built, more families moved into the area." (Education is just one of many reasons why families may choose to live in a particular community.)

For information about getting feedback from your peers, see p. 473.

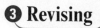
❸ Revising

> **TARGET SKILL ►Using Appropriate Language** If your audience is your friends, you might choose words that include some slang; but for parents, teachers, or community leaders, you'll want to choose words that are more dignified. For more help with revising, review the rubric on page 464.

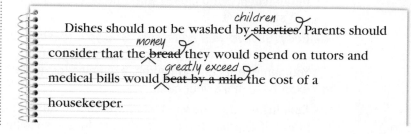

Dishes should not be washed by ~~shorties~~ *children*. Parents should consider that the ~~bread~~ *money* they would spend on tutors and medical bills would ~~beat by a mile~~ *greatly exceed* the cost of a housekeeper.

❹ Editing and Proofreading

> **TARGET SKILL ►Correcting Run-Ons** As you write your first draft, you might accidentally write two sentences as though they were a single sentence. One way to correct this mistake is to add a comma and conjunction between the two sentences.

Many people think that doing the dishes is a short, simple task *but* forcing children to do the dishes every night wastes a lot of time and energy.

For more on run-ons, see pp. 25–27.

❺ Sharing and Reflecting

Find some people from your target audience, and **share** your essay with them. Ask your readers to share their views and tell whether those views changed as a result of your essay.

For Your Working Portfolio Consider and **reflect** on the comments from your audience. Did your essay achieve its purpose? Did your readers react as you expected them to? Save your answers along with your essay in your
📁 **Working Portfolio.**

Speak for Yourself: *Public Service Commercial*

Commercials on television try to persuade people to change their thinking, to buy something, to act a certain way. You can turn the ideas in your **persuasive essay** into a public service commercial as a way to get your ideas across.

VIDEO	AUDIO
1. Family sitting at dinner table.	Girl (voiceover): *For your parents dinner is a pleasant time. But for you, It's simply a reminder that soon you'll be . . .*
2. Daughter standing at kitchen sink, which is filled with suds and dirty plates.	GIRL: *. . . forced to do the dishes. Doing the dishes is one of the most dreadful tasks put upon children. To completely wash an average mess like this takes about fifteen minutes. But that doesn't even include the time it takes to put everything away, wipe the table, wipe the counter, and then clean out the sink.*

1. *Family dinner table.*
2. *Daughter doing dishes.*
3. *Dishes stacked high.*

"**Doing the dishes is one of the most dreadful tasks put upon children.**"

Here's How **Creating a Commercial**

- Start by identifying a single strong idea from your essay that you can show visually.
- Create a script for your commercial. Decide if actors in the commercial will have lines to say or if an unseen narrator will convey the message.
- Begin making frame-by-frame sketches of what you want your commercial to look like. This process is called making a storyboard.
- Decide on the tone of your script. Will you be friendly? scornful? funny?
- Make a video of your commercial if you can. Otherwise, present your storyboard and script to your class.
- Come up with a slogan that sums up your message. "Dishwashing is a dirty business." Or "Don't tie your fate to dirty plates."

For more information on speaking skills, see pp. 563–565.

For more information on video production, see the 📼 **Media Focus video.**

PERSUASION

471

Student Help Desk

Persuasive Essay at a Glance

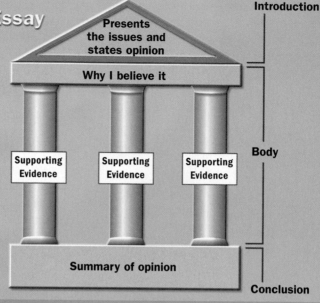

Presents the issues and states opinion — Introduction

Why I believe it

Supporting Evidence | Supporting Evidence | Supporting Evidence — Body

Summary of opinion — Conclusion

Idea Bank

Tips for finding a topic

Recommend a book and explain why you feel it is worth reading.

Read the teen news section of a newspaper. Write a letter to the editor about one of the articles.

Write an essay to answer this question: If you could do one thing to change the world, what would you do?

Think of a change that would improve your school, and come up with good reasons why the change should be made.

Choose a product such as the one recommended in the cartoon below, and write an essay explaining why you shouldn't use it.

Calvin and Hobbes by Bill Watterson

Friendly Feedback

Questions for Your Peer Reader

- What did you like best about my essay?
- Which of my reasons were most convincing?
- What evidence can you think of that would support my position?
- How would you argue against my position?
- What did you learn from reading my essay?

Publishing Options

Print	Give your essay to someone like a parent, teacher, or school principal who can work on the changes you suggest.
Oral Communication	Stage a debate, with one person presenting his or her essay and a volunteer rebutting it.
Online	Check out **mcdougallittell.com** for more publishing options.

The Bottom Line

Checklist for Persuasive Essay

Have I . . .

_____ stated the issue and my position on it clearly in my introduction?

_____ geared my essay to convince my intended audience?

_____ supported my position with facts, statistics, and reasons?

_____ answered possible objections to my position?

_____ shown clear reasoning?

_____ concluded with a summary of my position and added a call to action if a call is needed?

Short Story and Poem

Learn What It Is: *Short Story*

Stories and poems are ways for writers to capture the special meanings of experiences. In this workshop you will have the opportunity to try both forms of creative writing.

In a novel or a play, there is lots of time to develop characters, setting, and plot. In a **short story**, though, the story elements come together more quickly. Your original short story will introduce people, an event, and a place that will carry your readers quickly into a new experience.

Basics in a Box

SHORT STORY AT A GLANCE

Introduction

Sets the stage by
• introducing the **characters**
• describing the **setting**

Body

Develops the plot by
• introducing the conflict
• telling a sequence of **events**
• developing **characters** through words and actions
• building towards a **climax**

Conclusion

Finishes the story by
• resolving the **conflict**
• telling the **last event**

RUBRIC

Standards for Writing

A successful short story should

• have a strong beginning and ending
• use the elements of character, setting, and plot to create a convincing world
• use techniques such as vivid sensory language, concrete details, and dialogue to create believable characters and setting
• have a central conflict
• present a clear sequence of events
• maintain a consistent point of view

See How It's Done: *Short Story*

Student Model
Angela Tressler
Jane Addams Middle
School

RUBRIC
IN ACTION

The Trap

Panic! That's what I was feeling. My friend Jack
and I were riding bikes after school. When we're
riding, I never pay attention to where we're going,
but after about an hour I realized that nothing
looked familiar anymore.

❶ The strong
beginning sets up
the tension and
the mystery.

"Hey, Jack? . . . Any idea where we are?"

"Well," he answered, "it must be a new sub-
division or something."

"Must be. . . . Let's see if we can find our way out."

We kept riding. Soon it started getting dark.
"Maybe we better ask someone where we are."

The first person we saw was a guy about our
age. "Excuse me, how do we get out of this sub-
division?" Jack asked him.

"Sub-division?" he asked us. "Funny, I haven't
heard that one in a while." Then he started laughing
and making fun of us; calling us all these weird
names so we decided to find someone else to ask
for directions.

❷ Sets the scene
using details
to describe
the actions of
characters

Soon we came across this old lady sitting on her
front porch with her cats. "Ma'am," I called out,
"could you please tell us how to get out of here?"

"Child, you'll have to hurry. Once it gets dark,
there's no way of ever leaving."

Suddenly, all the pieces started falling into place.
Jack and I had ridden into the Time-To-Relive-
Actuality-Permanently area. Also called Time Trap
for short.

❸ Identifies and
explains the main
story element

I remember reading about this. As soon as you
cross the border of our town if you're going in the
right direction, and the sun is about half set, you'll end
up in the Time Trap. Once you're in, you can only get
out before the sun sets completely that same day.

SHORT STORY

. . ."No way, lady, this can't be happening."

"Hush up, child. Only your believing me can save you now. If you get out of here, and back to your neighborhood before the sun disappears in the sky you will have escaped the curse. . . . If you don't make it every day will be identical for the rest of your immortal life."

"So all we have to do is go back the way we came?" I asked.

"Not quite. You have to go back by going the exact opposite way you came. It sounds odd, I know, but trust me, it's your only way home."

"So what is the opposite way?" Jack asked. "In case you haven't noticed we're lost!"

"Come in, I'll show you on a map."

. . .We followed Yellow Mill to the creek just like she said, but we must have made a wrong turn after that, because we were nowhere near where we should've been. The sun had disappeared almost completely, and we knew that within a half-hour it would be dark. . . .

After quite a while we started to see some familiar things; like the lady's house. Sure enough, she was still sitting on her front porch.

. . ."Quick, just tell us what to do after the creek!"

"You turn right, then left at the next stop."

"Okay, we got it now. Come on, Jack, we can still make it!" I cried.

As we rode away, the old lady muttered under her breath, "The idiots, don't they realize they've been doing the same thing for fifteen years?"

❹ Presents the central conflict clearly

❺ Uses dialogue to present believable characters

❻ Gives a clear sequence of events

❼ This writer uses another character's words to provide the surprise ending.

Another option: Describe how the youngsters continue to ride, year after year.

Do It Yourself

Writing Prompt   Write a short story about something that happened or might have happened to you.

Purpose   To entertain

Audience   Your classmates or other readers who might find your story enjoyable

❶ Prewriting

Pick a moment. You might think of moments in your life that took an unexpected turn or moments that were especially exciting. Choose one that you would like to write about.

For more topic ideas, see the Idea Bank, p. 484.

Consider character, setting, and point of view. Who is involved in your story? How can each character stand out as unique? What is special about where your story takes place? Will you write the story using a first-person point of view, or will you refer to your characters in the third person (he/she)?

Make an outline of the plot. Every story needs a plot—a good beginning, a series of events that build toward a climax, and a sound conclusion. Outline the parts of the plot before you begin your first draft.

❷ Drafting

Gather your thoughts and begin. Begin to write even if you haven't decided yet exactly how your story will go. You might find that the very act of writing begins to give you ideas about how to organize your thoughts.

Show, don't tell. Find places to use dialogue so that the characters show what they are like in their own words. Use various ways of speaking for each character to show how they are different.

Include details. Describe the events with concrete words that appeal to the senses. Give details about how big, how fast, how frightening.

For information about getting feedback from your peers, see p. 485.

SHORT STORY

❸ Revising

TARGET SKILL ►Show Don't Tell Using characters' own words often shows more about the characters than does a description of what they are saying. For more help with revising, review the rubric on page 474.

Soon we came across this old lady sitting on her front
porch with her cats. ~~"Ma'am,"~~ ~~"could you please tell us how to get~~
~~out of here?"~~ I called out, ~~to ask how we could get~~ ~~out of here?"~~

~~"Child, you'll have to hurry. Once it gets dark, there's no~~
~~She said we would have to hurry because there was no~~
~~way of ever leaving."~~
~~way to leave after dark.~~

❹ Editing and Proofreading

TARGET SKILL ►Punctuating Dialogue Put a character's exact words in double quotation marks. Put end punctuation inside the quotation marks. Start a new paragraph each time the speaker changes.

"So what is the opposite way?" Jack asked. "In case you haven't noticed we're lost!" ¶ "Come in, I'll show you on a map."

For more on using quotation marks, see pp. 258–261.

❺ Sharing and Reflecting

You can **share** your story with several friends and observe whether the story had the effect you expected. Ask your listeners to explain their reactions to your story.

For Your Working Portfolio As you **reflect** on your story, write some of the reasons you organized the plot the way you did and how your readers reacted to it. Save your comments and your completed story in your **Working Portfolio.**

Learn What It Is: *Poem*

Poetry expresses a mood or a feeling. Usually, poetry uses fewer words than prose, but every word is chosen carefully so that each one carries a great deal of meaning. When you write a **poem**, you have a chance to share a special feeling through carefully chosen images.

Basics in a Box

POETRY AT A GLANCE

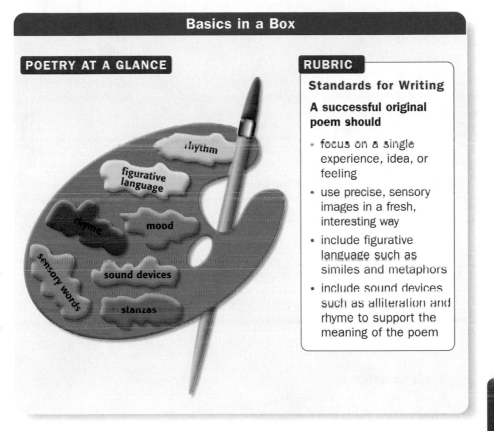

rhythm

figurative language

rhyme

mood

sensory words

sound devices

stanzas

RUBRIC

Standards for Writing

A successful original poem should

- focus on a single experience, idea, or feeling
- use precise, sensory images in a fresh, interesting way
- include figurative language such as similes and metaphors
- include sound devices such as alliteration and rhyme to support the meaning of the poem

POEM

See How It's Done: *Poem*

Sawdust
The smell of sawdust
drifts by,
and I remember Dad.
He was a logger
when I was younger.
He came home late
and walked in the door,
wearing the sweet smell of the trees
cut down hours before.
He left a trail of
wood chips all the way down
the basement stairs.

—Katelyn Peters, Target Range School

❶ Focuses on a single idea

❷ Uses alliteration

❸ Includes end rhyme

9 volt batteries
When I was five my dad carved
a homemade bat out of a pine tree
limb, bark still clinging
to the handle. As my brother
played golf on the coarse
dry lawn, I stood behind him
begging for a turn. He swung hard
and cracked me distracted, fillings
rattled like glass in my back
teeth. Pain tasted like a mouthful
of 9 volt batteries as the world
flipped over itself and grew bright.

—Danny Krantz, Charlo School

❹ Uses precise imagery in an interesting way

❺ Uses similes and a fresh sensory image

CHAPTER 26

Do It Yourself

Writing Prompt Write a poem about something that matters to you.

Purpose To write expressively

Audience Friends, family members

❶ Prewriting

Brainstorm topics. You might begin by writing as many ideas as you can—hobbies, events, feelings. Include a phrase for each item so you can explore how you might develop your poem.

For more topic ideas, see the Idea Bank, p. 484.

Add Images. Pick one of your ideas, and write as many images as you can connected with it. You might want to do this by making an observation chart. Such a chart will help you develop images for your poem.

Observation Chart	
Sight	bright reds and golds
Sound	crackling leaves
Touch	slimy pumpkin seeds
Taste	sweet cold cider
Smell	smoky burning leaves

❷ Drafting

Be moody. Decide on the effect you want—humor, sympathy, pensiveness, surprise. Use words that help create the mood.

Read your ideas aloud. When you hear the sound of your words, it will help you find the rhythm you want and the length of lines that seems right.

Be stingy with words. As you work with your poem, look for any words that you can do without. Be sure that every word is exactly the right word for the meaning you want to express.

For information about getting feedback from your peers, see p. 485.

POEM

3 Revising

TARGET SKILL ►Using Sensory Images When you revise, look for opportunities to use sensory images. Use words relating to the five senses, and also include similes and metaphors that will make your poem memorable. For more help with revising, review the rubric on page 479.

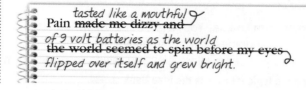

Pain ~~made me dizzy and~~ tasted like a mouthful of 9 volt batteries as the world ~~the world seemed to spin before my eyes~~ flipped over itself and grew bright.

4 Editing and Proofreading

TARGET SKILL ►Punctuating Poetry Poets can make their own decisions about how to punctuate their poems, but in general it is best to use standard rules for punctuating your poetry. Use end marks after full sentences and commas in the usual way.

He was a logger
when I was younger ⊙
He came home late,
and walked in the door,
wearing the sweet smell of the trees
cut down hours before ⊙

5 Sharing and Reflecting

Sharing and Reflecting You might invite classmates to join a reading aloud session in which you **share** your original poems. Give each other feedback about your presentations.

For Your Working Portfolio As you **reflect** on the process of writing your poem, make some notes about where your topic came from and how you went about developing it. Keep your notes with your finished poem in your 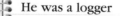 **Working Portfolio.**

Speak for Yourself: *Drama*

Many movies, plays, and TV shows are based on books and stories. The writer and director have to adapt the original piece so that it will work effectively in a new medium. Adapt your **short story** into a drama and take advantage of how that form helps you tell your story

Suddenly all the pieces started falling into place. Jack and I had ridden into the Time-To-Relive-Actuality-Permanently area. Also called Time Trap for short.

ANDY: The Time Trap? I've heard about this!

JACK: Me, too. The Time-To-Relive-Actuality-Permanently area!

Here's How ▸ Creating a Drama

- Write a script from your story. Look in your literature book to see what a printed drama looks like.

- Use existing dialogue and create dialogue for the unspoken parts of your story. Write notes to your actors telling them what the characters are doing. Remember, everything your audience knows will come from what the characters say and do.

- If there is important information given in your story that is not spoken or shown through action, have one of your characters say it.

- Get some friends to play the different roles and rehearse the drama with them.

- Bring in props, music and costumes to add some realism and mood to your drama.

For more information on speaking skills, see pp. 563–567.

"You boys are in the Time Trap!"

Student Help Desk

Short Story and Poem at a Glance

SHORT STORY

Introduction
Sets the stage by
• introducing the **characters**
• describing the **setting**

Body
Develops the plot by
• introducing the **conflict**
• telling a sequence of **events**
• developing **characters** through words and actions
• building towards a **climax**

Conclusion
Finishes the story by
• resolving the **conflict**
• telling the **last event**

POEM

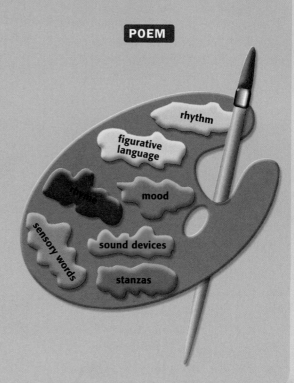

rhythm

figurative language

rhyme

mood

sensory words

sound devices

stanzas

Idea Bank

Finding a topic for a short story or poem

Make a list of alliterative names for story characters—Freddie the Frightened Firefighter, Mario the Merry Marionette Master.

Make up a myth for how an event of nature first began.

Write a piece that gives the story behind a favorite song.

Look hard at the world around you. What is the most significant blue thing you see? What does the wind taste like?

Examine your feelings. What makes you happy? sad? lonely? amused?

Think of the most important people in your life. Why are they important?

Friendly Feedback

Questions for Your Peer Reader

- What was the best part of my story or poem?
- How effective was the beginning of my story?
- How did I make the sequence of events in the story clear?
- What is your favorite line of my poem?
- Where in the poem could I have used more sensory images?

Publishing Options

Print	Enter your work in a literary contest. Also, submit it to your school's literary magazine.
Oral Communication	Organize a listening lounge in your classroom or elsewhere in your school and post times when you and other students can read your original works aloud.
Online	Check out **mcdougallittell.com** for more publishing options.

The Bottom Line

Checklist for Short Story

Have I . . .

____ provided a strong beginning and ending?

____ presented a convincing world through the characters, setting, and plot?

____ used vivid sensory language, concrete details, and dialogue effectively?

____ developed a main conflict?

____ made the sequence of events clear?

____ maintained a consistent point of view?

Checklist for Poem

Have I . . .

____ focused on one idea or feeling?

____ used precise words in an interesting way?

____ included fresh sensory words?

____ used figurative language, such as similes and metaphors?

____ included sound devices, such as alliteration and rhyme?

STORY/POEM

Research Report

Learn What It Is

Doing a **research report** can help you learn a lot more about a subject that interests you. It is also a good way to develop your research and writing skills.

Basics in a Box

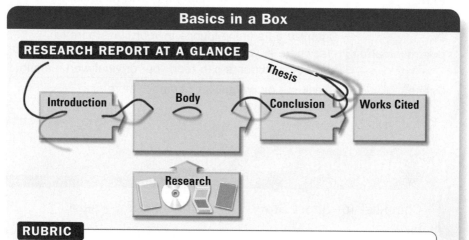

RUBRIC

Standards for Writing

A successful research report should

- include a strong introduction with a clear thesis statement
- contain evidence from sources that develops and supports the writer's ideas
- credit the sources of information
- have a logical pattern of organization, with transitions between ideas

- summarize the writer's ideas in the conclusion
- include information from more than one source
- include a correctly formatted Works Cited list at the end.

CHAPTER 27

See How It's Done: *Research Report*

Brown 1

Roger Brown

Mrs. Logan

English

30 April 2000

RUBRIC
IN ACTION

The Battle of the Little Bighorn

The Battle of the Little Bighorn, also known as "Custer's Last Stand," took place on June 25, 1876, at the Little Bighorn River in Montana. Lieutenant Colonel George A. Custer, leader of the Seventh Cavalry, and more than 200 of his men were killed in a fierce battle (Josephy 347). The battle has been called the "last major Indian victory in the Indian Wars of the American West" ("Little Bighorn"). I think it was not a victory at all. The Battle of the Little Bighorn was a battle that everyone lost.

❶ Includes a clear thesis statement

Since it was the last major Indian victory, it may seem strange to say that the Indians lost, but as Alvin Josephy says, "Crazy Horse and Sitting Bull lost by winning" (348). The country was stunned by Custer's defeat. As a result, the U.S. military poured even more effort into defeating the Indians.

❷ Credits source

Some of the men who died with Custer might have lived if Custer had not been so rash. Even though his troops were heavily outnumbered, he was sure that his men could defeat the Indians. He divided his men into three groups. Two of the groups suffered heavy losses; the group that Custer led was wiped out (Dippie).

Custer <u>not only</u> lost his life in the battle but <u>also</u> damaged his place in history. In Bernard DeVoto's view, "George Armstrong Custer's private blend of egotism and stupidity would get the Seventh Cavalry massacred" (125).

❸ Uses transitions in a logical organization

REPORT

Research Report **487**

As recently as 1998, Custer was the subject of a moot trial at the University of Indiana Law School. (A moot is an imaginary law case.) The mock court found Custer guilty of two of the three charges against him. He was found not guilty of disobeying orders but guilty of negligent conduct and neglect of duty (McIlveen).

Custer was not the only person whose reputation suffered. One of the other people was Major Marcus A. Reno, who was in command of one of the three groups that Custer created. Reno's troops were badly beaten, and Reno retreated to the other side of the river. People who supported Custer believed that Reno's retreat was cowardly. Reno was cleared of such a charge by a military court in 1879, but the following year he was dishonorably discharged from the army on other charges. It wasn't

❹ In this part of the report, the writer supports his thesis by focusing on losses suffered by individuals.

Another option: Focus only on military strategies and troop movements.

Works Cited

DeVoto, Bernard. Across the Wide Missouri. Boston: Houghton, 1947.

Dippie, Brian W. "Custer, George Armstrong." The World Book Encyclopedia. 1999 ed.

Josephy, Alvin M., Jr., ed. The American Heritage Book of Indians. New York: American Heritage, 1961.

"Little Bighorn, Battle of the." Grolier Multimedia Encyclopedia. CD-ROM. Deluxe ed. Danbury: Grolier, 1998.

McIlveen, Rose. "Custer's 'Last Stand' Takes Place in an IU Moot Courtroom." Indiana University Home Pages. 2 Oct. 1998. Indiana University. 6 Apr. 2000 <http://www.iuinfo.indiana.edu/HomePages/100298/text/custer.htm>.

Works Cited List
- Identifies sources credited in the report
- Presents entries in alphabetical order
- Gives complete publication information
- Contains correct punctuation in entries
- Is double-spaced throughout
- Follows a preferred style such as the MLA guidelines

CHAPTER 27

Do It Yourself

Find a topic that interests you and write a research report about it.

Purpose To educate others about your topic

Audience Teacher, classmates, anyone interested in the topic

❶ Developing a Research Plan

A proper research report uses several sources and is focused enough for you to supply in-depth information on your topic. If your topic is too broad, which is often the case, your first task will be to narrow its focus.

Narrowing Your Topic

When you begin to narrow your topic, keep these points in mind:
- The topic should interest you.
- You should be able to cover it in the pages you have available.
- You need to know enough about your broad topic to make a wise choice about how to narrow it.

Here are a few ways to find out more about your broad topic.
- Skim books on your topic. Check the table of contents, the introduction, picture captions, or other possible sources of quick information, such as quotations that begin chapters.
- Ask questions of other people.
- Browse the Internet.

Developing Research Questions

You can sharpen your research by developing a set of questions to guide your investigation. For example, the writer of the report on the Battle of the Little Bighorn was interested in the long-term effects of the battle. His research questions included the following:
- What happened during the actual battle?
- What happened to the people who survived?
- Why was the battle considered important?

As you begin to get answers, the information may lead you into unexpected areas. If so, feel free to change your direction.

❷ Finding Information

Locating Sources

The best way to locate sources is to start with the places that have the most information. You can find most of these sources at your library.

Information Resources

• Newspapers	• Atlases	• Encyclopedias
• Books	• Thesauri	• CD-ROM encyclopedias
• Magazines	• Dictionaries	• Statistical abstracts
• Almanacs	• Internet	• Online databases

For more information on how to find useful sources, see pp. 505–515.

Evaluating Sources

You will need several sources, but they will help you only if they are good sources. Ask these questions about your sources:

- Is the material on my topic up-to-date?
- Is the author qualified? What credentials does he or she have?
- Is the author fair?

For more information, see "Choosing and Evaluating Sources," pp. 514–515.

Making Source Cards

When you find a good source, write the publication information about it on an index card. This becomes your source card. You will need to make one for every source you find. Later, you will use your source cards to compile a Works Cited list. (You will learn more about the Works Cited list on page 497.)

Number each source card. Then, as you take notes from a source, you can use the number on the card to identify the source instead of writing the title and author again and again. The following chart and examples will guide you in making source cards.

- **Book** Write the author's name, the title, the city of the publisher, the publisher's name, the copyright date, and the library call number.
- **Magazine or newspaper article** Write the author's name (if one is given), the title of the article, the name and date of the publication, and the page numbers of the article.
- **Encyclopedia article** Write the author's name (if one is given), the article title, and the name and copyright date of the encyclopedia.
- **Internet site** Write the author's name (if one is given), the title of the document, publication information for any print version, the date you accessed the document, and the document's network address (in angle brackets).

Source Cards

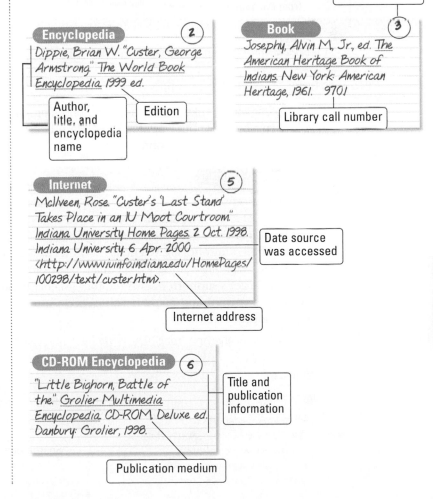

Source number

Encyclopedia ②

Dippie, Brian W. "Custer, George Armstrong." *The World Book Encyclopedia.* 1999 ed.

Author, title, and encyclopedia name

Edition

Book ③

Josephy, Alvin M., Jr., ed. *The American Heritage Book of Indians.* New York: American Heritage, 1961. 970.1

Library call number

Internet ⑤

McIlveen, Rose. "Custer's 'Last Stand' Takes Place in an IU Moot Courtroom." *Indiana University Home Pages.* 2 Oct. 1998. Indiana University. 6 Apr. 2000 <http://www.iuinfo.indiana.edu/HomePages/100298/text/custer.htm>.

Date source was accessed

Internet address

CD-ROM Encyclopedia ⑥

"Little Bighorn, Battle of the." *Grolier Multimedia Encyclopedia.* CD-ROM. Deluxe ed. Danbury: Grolier, 1998.

Title and publication information

Publication medium

REPORT

❸ Taking Notes

If you find some information that might be useful for your paper, take notes on it. Keep index cards handy, and write each piece of information on a separate card.

> **Here's How** **Making Note Cards**
>
> - **Use a separate index card** for each item of information.
> - **Give each card a heading** to show what the focus is.
> - **Write the source card number** on each note card.
> - **Write the page number** where you found the information in the source.
> - **Put quotation marks around anything** you copy word for word from the source.

For more information on taking notes, see pp. 524–526.

Paraphrasing

The simplest way to take notes is by paraphrasing, or rewriting in your own words what the source says. Here is a paragraph, followed by a note card paraphrasing it.

> **PROFESSIONAL MODEL**
>
> Americans found it almost impossible to believe that any group of Indians could have killed such a well-known officer and all his men. Custer's enemies accused him of disobeying [General] Terry by attacking the Indians without waiting for the main body of soldiers. Custer's supporters charged that [Major] Reno had been a coward, and could have rescued Custer if he had not retreated.
>
> —"Custer, George Armstrong" *The World Book Encyclopedia*

Note Card

> **Paraphrase**
> Why was Custer defeated?
> Two ideas: (1) Custer should have
> waited for more soldiers.
> (2) Major Reno was a coward
> and failed to rescue Custer.   2

Heading shows focus

Source number

Quoting

A good quotation from one of your sources can make your paper stronger. Use quotation marks when you copy an author's exact words. You might use a quotation in cases like these:

- You want to share with your readers the impact of an especially striking statement.
- The author's point needs to be stated exactly because it is so important.

Avoiding Plagiarism

Plagiarism is passing off the ideas of others as your own. It is easy to see that if you use an author's exact words without giving credit, you are stealing from the author. However, you also commit plagiarism if you use an author's ideas in a paraphrase without giving credit. Sometimes it is easy to let paraphrasing slip into plagiarism.

ORIGINAL

Every man in this surrounded group of cavalrymen was killed in a desperate, blazing fight that lasted less than half an hour.

The attacking force . . . had been led by Lieutenant Colonel Custer, who died in the battle along with more than 260 of his men.

—Alvin M. Josephy, Jr., ed.,
The American Heritage Book of Indians

PLAGIARIZED VERSION

In less than half an hour, every one of the surrounded cavalrymen was killed in a desperate, blazing battle. And their famous commander, Lieutenant Colonel Custer, died in the battle along with his men.

The writer shortened the original sentences and changed the word order in them. However, he did not credit his source. Here is a version that credits the source and avoids plagiarism.

STUDENT MODEL

Lieutenant Colonel George Custer and more than 260 of his men were killed in a fierce battle that lasted less than half an hour (Josephy 347).

Source is credited

❹ Organizing and Outlining

Planning Your Report

An **introduction,** a **body,** and a **conclusion** will be the three parts of your research report.

Introduction Come up with an interesting way to begin your report. Be sure to include your thesis statement, or main idea. A good thesis statement

- states clearly what you are writing about
- is one that can be supported with facts.

Body The body of your paper is where you support your thesis statement. The body should

- have unity, with the topic sentence in every paragraph supporting the thesis statement
- be organized and coherent, with paragraphs that are structured so that one idea flows smoothly and logically to the next idea

Conclusion At the end of your paper, you should restate your thesis, using different words, and sum up the ideas you used to support it.

Making an Outline

How can you be sure that you will have a well-organized paper that supports your thesis statement? Make and follow an outline. Here is the outline for the start of the research paper on the Battle of the Little Bighorn.

> ### The Battle of the Little Bighorn
> **Thesis statement:** I think it was not a victory at all. The Battle of the Little Bighorn was a battle that everyone lost.
>
> I. Introduction
> II. How the Indians lost
> III. How Custer lost
> IV. How Reno lost

For more about creating outlines, see p. 527.

CHAPTER 27

⑤ Drafting

Use your notes and your outline to begin your draft. You don't have to begin at the beginning and work straight through to the end. If you like, you can start with the section you have the strongest ideas about. As you work, follow these guidelines:

- **Follow your outline.** Write one or more paragraphs for every major part of your outline. (If you don't have enough material to make a paragraph, either do more research or revise your plan.)

- **Support your thesis.** Remember that everything in your paper should support your main idea.

- **Put paragraphs in order.** Make sure your paragraphs are in order before you begin your revision.

Integrating Your Notes into Your Paper

When you made your outline, you probably grouped your note cards according to their focus. Here is how the writer of the paper on the Battle of the Little Bighorn used information from his notes to write part of his report.

Reno's role ⑦

Reno and troops supposed to attack when Custer did. Reno did not attack. Some said he was a coward. Reno said he tried to attack but was turned back by Indians, who had more troops.

Reno's role ⑦

Reno was tried and cleared by military court in 1879. Next year dishonorably discharged for drunkenness and conduct unbecoming an officer. People disagreed about him for years. In 1967, army posthumously granted honorable discharge.

STUDENT MODEL

People who supported Custer believed that Reno's retreat was cowardly. Reno was cleared of such a charge by a military court in 1879, but the following year he was dishonorably discharged from the army on other charges. It wasn't until 1967 that the army posthumously granted him an honorable discharge ("Reno").

⑥ Documenting Information

There are some facts that you can expect most people to know. For example, most Americans know that wars were fought between Native Americans and settlers who moved into their territory. However, you need to document, or give a source for, any facts that aren't widely known.

The most common way to document information in a report is to put a reference in parentheses following the information. This method is called **parenthetical documentation.** The reference tells which work in the Works Cited list is your source for the information. You should use parenthetical documentation to give the source of each quotation or paraphrase in your report.

> **Here's How** **Guidelines for Parenthetical Documentation**
>
> • **One Author** Usually, you will cite the author's last name and the page number in parentheses. However, if you mention the author's name in the sentence, cite only the page number.
>
> > In Bernard DeVoto's view, "George Armstrong Custer's private blend of egotism and stupidity would get the Seventh Cavalry massacred" (125).
>
> If the writer had not mentioned the author's name in the sentence, the documentation would have looked like this:
>
> > "George Armstrong Custer's private blend of egotism and stupidity would get the Seventh Cavalry massacred" (DeVoto 125).
>
> • **No Author Given** Cite the title (or a short version of the title) and the page number if there is one.
>
> > The battle has been called "the last major Indian victory in the Indian Wars of the American West" ("Little Bighorn").
>
> • **Electronic Source** Cite the author's last name. If no author is given, list the title.
>
> > He was found not guilty of disobeying orders but guilty of negligent conduct and neglect of duty (McIlveen).

Preparing a Works Cited List

- First, gather up your source cards.
- Next, read through your report.
- If you used a source, put a check mark by the reference in the report and keep the card handy.
- If you didn't use a source, put its card aside. The only sources you will include in your Works Cited list are those you actually used for your paper.
- Place your source cards in alphabetical order according to the authors' last names. If a work has more than one author, use the first author's name. If there is no author, use the first word of the title. (Don't count *A, An,* or *The.*)

The list below shows how you should format your Works Cited list.

Brown 4

> Center the title, "Works Cited."

Works Cited

DeVoto, Bernard. Across the Wide Missouri. Boston: Houghton, 1947.

Dippie, Brian W. "Custer, George Armstrong." The World Book Encyclopedia. 1999 ed.

Josephy, Alvin M., Jr., ed. The American Heritage Book of Indians. New York: American Heritage, 1961.

"Little Bighorn, Battle of the." Grolier Multimedia Encyclopedia. CD-ROM. Deluxe ed. Danbury: Grolier, 1998.

McIlveen, Rose. "Custer's 'Last Stand' Takes Place in an IU Moot Courtroom." Indiana University Home Pages. 2 Oct. 1998. Indiana University. 6 Apr. 2000 <http://www.iuinfo.indiana.edu/HomePages/100298/text/custer.htm>.

> Indent the second line and additional lines of each entry 1/2 inch or five spaces.

> Double-space the whole list.

For more about documenting sources, see MLA Citation Guidelines, pp. 662–669.

REPORT

❼ Revising

TARGET SKILL ▶ Varying Sentences Your report will be more interesting to read if you vary the sentence structures. It can be boring to read sentences that all begin with subjects. For more help with revision, review the rubric on page 486.

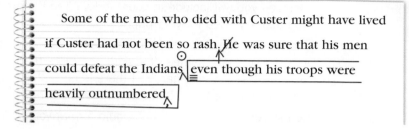

> Some of the men who died with Custer might have lived if Custer had not been so rash. He was sure that his men could defeat the Indians even though his troops were heavily outnumbered.

❽ Editing and Proofreading

TARGET SKILL ▶ *Who* and *Whom* Use *who* as the subject of a sentence or a clause. Use *whom* as an object of a verb or a preposition.

> One of the other people was Major Marcus A. Reno,
> ~~whom~~ *who* was in command of one of the three groups that
> Custer created.

For help with *who* and *whom*, see pp. 194–196.

❾ Sharing and Reflecting

Share your report with others who are interested in your topic. Listen carefully to their comments after they've read the report.

For Your Working Portfolio How did sharing your report help you evaluate your own research? Make notes on what you like about your report and what you would change if you were to continue your investigation. What are some new questions you could investigate to expand your research? Attach your notes to your finished report and save both in your ▱ **Working Portfolio.**

Speak for Yourself: *Multimedia Presentation*

"Even though Custer's troops were heavily outnumbered, he was sure that his men could defeat the Indians."

Power Presentation

George Custer   Sitting Bull

When you give a multimedia presentation of your **report** you will be able to use different visual tools to make your report come alive for your audience. Showing pictures, slides, and video clips will help you to introduce your topic more dynamically and effectively.

Here's How Creating a Multimedia Presentation

- Your presentation will be a summary of a much longer report, so you'll need to briefly tell your audience the *who, what, when, where, why,* and *how* of your information. Use note cards to keep you on track.

- Find pictures, maps, or graphs that will help illustrate your topic. Are there pictures or paintings of people involved in your topic? Are there maps of places where events took place?

- Find out if any movies or TV shows were made about your topic. You could show a brief scene from a video to illustrate part of your report.

- If applicable, make a graph or chart to clearly show an aspect of your topic. Is there a timeline you could show? Are there things being compared that you could show on a chart?

- Practice with your visuals before you give your presentation.

For more information on speaking skills, see pp. 563–565.

Student Help Desk

Research Report at a Glance

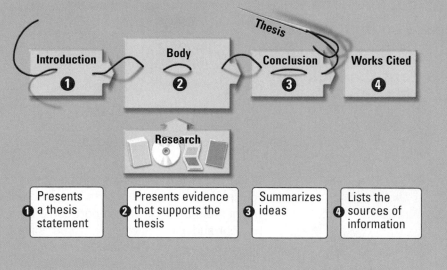

Introduction **1**	Body **2**	Conclusion **3**	Works Cited **4**
1 Presents a thesis statement	**2** Presents evidence that supports the thesis	**3** Summarizes ideas	**4** Lists the sources of information

Research

Idea Bank

Help for Your Topic Search

What do you want to know? Think about some of the things you would like to know more about. Make a list.

What do you already know? List some things or people that you know something about but that other people might not know so well.

Flip through an encyclopedia. List as a possibility everything that catches your eye.

Consider famous mysteries. What is the latest word on UFOs? Is there really a Loch Ness monster? What do we know about black holes? Does your area have any famous haunted houses or ghost stories?

Read literature. You probably have read some good authors this year, such as Mark Twain and Jack London. Consider topics they may have raised that you would like to know more about. What more you would like to know these authors?

Friendly Feedback

Questions for Your Peer Reader

- What was the main idea of my report?
- What did you like best about the report?
- What parts weren't clear?
- What should have been added?
- What should have been left out?

Publishing Options

Print	Create a class encyclopedia. Gather your research reports and arrange them alphabetically by subject.
Oral Communication	Make a tape recording that can be used by students working on the subject dealt with in your report. You might consider using presentation software to help present your information in an oral report.
Online	Check out **mcdougallittell.com** for more publishing options.

The Bottom Line

Checklist for Research Report

Have I . . .

____ written a strong introduction?

____ included a clear thesis statement?

____ used evidence from several sources to support my ideas?

____ credited my sources of information?

____ used a logical pattern of organization?

____ used transitions between ideas?

____ written a strong summary for the conclusion?

____ included a correctly formatted Works Cited list?

Communicating in the Information Age

Riding the Wave

With the information age in full swing, you need to get in the flow, ride the wave, and stay on your feet. Yet, it's easy to get overloaded and wiped out. You can keep your balance by using the right skills to find and use information.

Power Words
Vocabulary for Precise Writing

Be Informed

Whether you already know or need to find out, these words can help you describe the situation.

The Latest on the Newest

Who is **hot** on the entertainment scene? Who are the **cutting-edge** musicians? What clothes are **cool, fashionable,** and in **style?** Do you have the most **timely, up-to-date** news? If you want to stay **with it,** get a **contemporary** viewpoint from people who are **abreast of the news** and completely **in the know.** Getting **up-to-the-minute** news keeps you informed about what's **all the rage.**

Yesterday's News

It won't do you much good to look in an old newspaper or magazine. The information there will be **stale** and **out-of-date.** The clothes will all be **behind the times.** They will probably look **old-fashioned, tired, stodgy,** and **fusty.** News about music groups will be hopelessly **dated** and **passé.** If you rely on old news, you might feel **out of it** and totally **behind the times.**

▷ **Your Turn** How Do They Know?

With a partner, take a poll of 10 people to find out how they stay informed. Work with your partner to create a form that records the results of your poll. What words from this page would you use to describe the outcome?

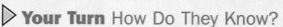

Finding Information

INFO BEAT

SEPTEMBER 2004

The Magazine for the Information Age

What Do Librarians Know That You Don't? Find Out Inside.

Don't Wipe Out on the Web—Use Our Surfing Tips!

Can You Do the Dewey? We'll Show You How!

Get Ready for Readers' Guide . . .

Also Inside: The Info Lady answers your questions about finding information.

Welcome to the Information Age

This is the Information Age—a time when there are more ways to find information than ever before. You can get information from books, magazines, newspapers, Web sites, and e-mail, to name just a few ways. You'll never need all of the information that's available, but you'll always need some of it. This chapter will help you get a handle on finding the information you need.

Write Away: Where Do You Go?
Think about the last time you had to look something up. What information were you looking for? How did you plan to use this information? Where did you find the information? Write a paragraph to answer these questions. Save your paragraph in your 📁 **Working Portfolio.**

FINDING INFO.

ClassZone at mcdougallittell.com

The Library and Media Center

The library and media center is full of facts, ideas, and answers. Don't worry if you're not exactly sure how to find the information you need—the library has tools that will help you and experts who can answer your questions.

❶ The Library Collection

A library's **collection** is made up of all the materials the library owns. These materials are kept in clearly marked sections of the library. The chart below describes these sections.

Sections of the Library	
Book stacks	Shelves of fiction, nonfiction, poetry, plays, and biographies
Catalog and indexes	The card catalog or computer catalog, and periodical indexes
Reference	Encyclopedias, dictionaries, atlases, almanacs, and other reference materials
Periodicals	Newspapers, magazines, and journals
Audiovisual	Videotapes, audiotapes, CDs, and CD-ROMs
Young adult and juvenile	Books written especially for teenagers and younger children
Computer resources	Access to the World Wide Web, word-processing programs, and databases
Microfiche and microfilm	Old issues of newspapers and magazines reproduced on film

❷ Special Services

Many libraries have special collections of manuscripts, rare books, photographs, family histories, and other interesting items. Ask the librarian whether your library has any special collections.

Librarians and media specialists are experts at finding information. They can recommend information sources and teach you how to use them.

Finding the Right Sources

Books and magazine articles are excellent sources of information. This lesson will teach you about tools to use to find books and articles on a specific topic.

❶ The Computer Catalog

A library catalog lists all of the items in the library. There are two kinds of catalogs: computer catalogs and card catalogs. Each library item in a computer catalog has its own record, or screen. A record for a nonfiction book is shown below.

Catalog

Location: **Public Library**

Searching: Ravenswood Public Library -- Holdings Display
❶ Find   Options   Backup   Startover   Quit   Help

❷ Call Number: 791.435 G524f
    Author: Glut, Donald F.
    Title: The Frankenstein legend: a tribute to Mary Shelley and Boris Karloff/Donald F. Glut.
  Published: Metuchen, NJ: Scarecrow Press, 1973.
    Paging: 372 p. : ill.; 22 cm.
❸ Subjects: Shelley, Mary Wollstonecraft, 1797–1851.
    Frankenstein. Karloff, Boris, 1887–1969.

❹ Library Holdings at
Floor 2 - Nonfiction
1. Call Number: 791.435 G524f Glut.D—Adult Book—Available ❺

❶ The Find command lets you begin a search.

❷ Call number, author's name, book title, publisher, and copyright date

❸ A description of the subjects covered in the book

❹ The book's location

❺ "Available" means the book is on the shelf.

To use the computer catalog, you type in an author's name, the title of a source, or the subject. The computer does the searching.

Keyword searching When you're not sure how to look up your topic, or if you're not getting many useful results from a subject search, you should search by keyword. **Keywords** are words, phrases, or synonyms that describe your topic. To create a list of keywords, first write down questions you have about your topic. Then circle words and phrases in your questions. These are your keywords.

If you don't know a lot about your topic, you should read an encyclopedia article about it to help you come up with questions and keywords. One student's questions are shown below.

What is a Gothic novel?

Is Frankenstein a Gothic novel?

When did Mary Shelley write Frankenstein?

❷ The Card Catalog

A card catalog holds alphabetically arranged cards that give basic information about library items. There are three kinds of cards in this catalog: author cards, title cards, and subject cards. Here's a sample subject card.

❶ FRANKENSTEIN

❷ 791.435 G524f

❸ Glut, Donald F.

❹ The Frankenstein legend: a tribute to Mary Shelley and Boris Karloff/Donald F. Glut.

❺ Metuchen, NJ: Scarecrow Press, 1973.

❻ 372 p. : ill.; 22 cm.

❼ 1. Karloff, Boris.   2. Shelley, Mary
I. Title II. Author

❶ Subject

❷ Call number

❸ Author

❹ Title

❺ Publisher and copyright date

❻ Number of pages illustrated

❼ Other entries in the card catalog for this book

The Dewey decimal system Most school and public libraries use the Dewey decimal classification system to organize their nonfiction books. In this system, nonfiction books are sorted into subject areas, such as literature, geography, and science. Each subject area is assigned a range of numbers. Using these numbers, each book is given a code, called a call number. A call number identifies a book's subject area and helps you locate the book in the stacks.

For more information on the Dewey decimal system, see p. 516.

791.435 G524f

A call number is listed in the library catalog and printed on a book's spine.

CHAPTER 28

❸ Using a Periodical Index

Current magazine articles are good sources of up-to-date information. Older articles can provide you with details and opinions from the past. To find individual articles on a specific topic, use a periodical index.

The *Readers' Guide to Periodical Literature*, one popular index, is a monthly list of articles that have appeared in well-known magazines. Articles are listed by author and by subject. Here's a sample subject listing from the *Readers' Guide*.

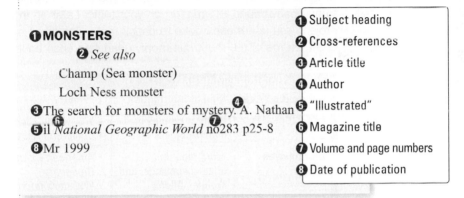

❶MONSTERS

   ❷ *See also*

   Champ (Sea monster)

   Loch Ness monster

❸The search for monsters of mystery. ❹A. Nathan

❺il *National Geographic World* ❼no283 p25-8

❽Mr 1999

❶ Subject heading

❷ Cross-references

❸ Article title

❹ Author

❺ "Illustrated"

❻ Magazine title

❼ Volume and page numbers

❽ Date of publication

At the end of each year, the monthly *Readers' Guide* indexes are collected into a single volume and labeled by that year.

Other Indexes

Libraries usually have a variety of indexes. Some list general articles in popular magazines, and others list magazine and journal articles in particular subject areas.

Many libraries also have access to computerized periodical indexes, such as Electric Library and InfoTrac. The *Readers' Guide* is also available on CD-ROM and through various online subscription services. Certain newspapers, such as the *New York Times* and the *Washington Post*, compile indexes to articles that have appeared in their pages.

Using Reference Materials

The reference section of a library has dictionaries, encyclopedias, and many other useful books. In general, these books are reliable sources because the information within them has been written and checked by experts.

❶ Print References

At the beginning of a research project, you use reference books to find background information on your topic. Later on in your project, you use these books to check facts. The chart below shows some of the most commonly used reference books.

Library Reference Materials		
Reference Work	**Kind of Information**	**Examples**
Encyclopedias	General articles on many subjects	• *World Book Encyclopedia* • *Compton's Encyclopedia*
Dictionaries	Word meanings, origins, spellings, and pronunciations	• *American Heritage Dictionary* • *Webster's Intermediate Dictionary*
Biographical dictionaries	Detailed information on the lives and careers of noteworthy people	• *Who's Who in America* • *Dictionary of American Biography*
Atlases	Maps and geographical information	• *National Geographic Atlas of the World* • *Cultural Atlas of Africa*
Almanacs	Facts and statistics	• *Information Please Almanac* • *World Almanac*
Chronologies	Time lines of historical, political, scientific, and cultural events	• *Asimov's Chronology of Science and Discovery*

Information in reference sources is organized in different ways, such as alphabetically by topic, keyword, personal name, geographic region, or category. Figure out the organization before you try to use a reference source. Many reference books include a section near the front that explains how to use the book.

❷ Electronic References

Many print references are also available in electronic form. The CD-ROM encyclopedia offers articles as well as special features such as sound, video clips, and links to other encyclopedia articles and to related Web sites.

In the illustration below, the large screen shows a CD-ROM encyclopedia article about the movie *Frankenstein.* The smaller screens show a second picture from the movie and a related article.

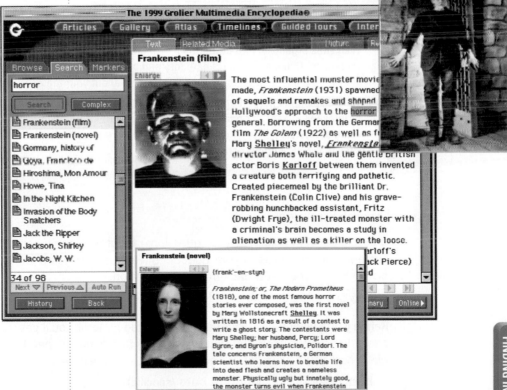

You can access the different features of an electronic encyclopedia by clicking on pictures, buttons, and highlighted words within an article.

Using the World Wide Web

The World Wide Web is made up of hundreds of millions of Web sites. To be a successful Web surfer, you need to know how to find useful sites and how to judge whether the information they contain is correct.

❶ Beginning Your Online Search

Directories and search engines are two tools you can use to search the Web. Without search tools, finding the information you need would be like looking for a needle in a haystack.

> **Here's How** **Choosing a Search Tool**
>
> - To find general information about your topic, use a **directory,** which is part of most search tools. A directory is a collection of Web sites organized into categories, such as art, politics, and recreation. Choose a general category and browse through the sites it contains to get background information about your topic.
>
> - To find specific information, use a **search engine,** such as AltaVista or Infoseek. A search engine allows you to look for information by using a keyword. Once you enter a keyword, the engine finds Web sites that contain that word.

Keyword Search Strategies

Create a list of keywords. Write questions about your topic and circle important words in your questions. Read an encyclopedia article first if you need background information.

Do (vampire bats) really exist?

Refine your keywords. If your keywords are too general, you'll get a long list of Web sites that don't have the information you need. Make sure you have a list of several keywords you can use.

bats (general)   **vampire bats** (specific)

Use the help button. Go to the help section of any search engine you use to find out about techniques that will help you get better search results. One common technique is to put quotation marks around a phrase you plan to search with.
   "vampire bats"

❷ Understanding Your Results

After you've entered a keyword, the search engine will come up with a list of Web pages. Not all of these pages will be useful, however. Here are some tips for interpreting your results.

L-Net

| Back | Forward | Reload | Home | Images | Print | Security | Stop |

Location:

Search Results

"Edgar Allan Poe"   **Search Again**

Select words to add to your search. . .
- ☐ Gothic literature
- ☐ The Raven
- ☐ American authors
- ☐ The E. A. Poe Society

842 pages found; best matches first   **About Your Results**

Display: ⦿ Full Descriptions ◯ No Descriptions ◯ Web Site Only   **Change Display**

100% House of Usher
Information on **Edgar Allan Poe**, including biographical information and his complete works.
http://www.comnet.ca/~forrest/
More Like This

❶

94% National Historic Site: Edgar Allan Poe
History of **Poe's** house, located in a suburban district of Philadelphia called Spring Garden.
http://www.nps.gov/ndal/ ❸
More Like This

❷

❶ Start at the Top
Search results are returned in a ranked order. The sites most closely related to your keyword are at the top of the list.

❷ Read Summaries
Search results usually include a short description of each Web site. Read these summaries to figure out whether a site will be helpful.

❸ Read Addresses Many Web site addresses contain three-letter clues that tell you what kind of group created the site.

Clue	Site was created by
.edu	an educational institution
.gov	government agency
.com	a commercial business
.org	a nonprofit organization

There are many different search engines, and each search engine scans a variety of sites. To get a range of results, try out several search engines.

FINDING INFO.

Choosing and Evaluating Sources

❶ How to Choose

After you've located some books, magazine articles, and Web sites, you need to choose the ones you will use for your research. First review your research questions to remind yourself what kinds of information you need. Then use the steps below to choose the best sources.

Choosing a Book or a Magazine Article

Step 1 Look at the copyright date of a book or the issue date of a magazine to see if the information about your topic is current.

Step 2 In a book, scan the table of contents and the index to see if your topic is listed in either place.

Step 3 Read the chapter or section titles and any highlighted words and phrases to see if they relate to your topic.

Step 4 Examine maps, charts, illustrations, and captions for any related information.

Step 5 Browse through a book or article to make sure it is not too difficult to read.

Choosing a Web Site

Step 1 Look for a summary section (sometimes called "About This Site") that gives an overview of the site's content.

Step 2 Read the opening page of the Web site to see whether the tone seems to match your needs.

Step 3 Check whether the site was updated recently.

Step 4 Make sure the site is easy to use. If you find it difficult to move around the site, you may not want to use it.

Step 5 If the Web site has links to other sites, try a few to see if they seem helpful.

❷ How to Evaluate

A book may look scholarly or a Web site may look professional, but you can't judge an information source by looks alone. Use the following questions to evaluate a source's accuracy.

Is the author an expert on the subject?
• Find out if the author of a book or article or the creator of a Web site is a specialist on the subject.
• Don't use a source if its author has a general interest in the subject but no expert knowledge about it.

Is the information correct?
• Try to find at least three different sources that agree on the information.

EVALUATING INFORMATION SOURCES

Does the source give a balanced point of view?
• An author or Web site creator may be trying to persuade you to believe something.
• Use several different sources to make sure you learn about all points of view on your topic.

Is the information on your topic up-to-date?
• Look at the copyright dates of books, the issue dates of articles, and the revision dates of Web sites.
• If you need current information, don't use a source that is more than five years old.

Being Web Wise

Many students believe the Web is the best place to look for information. After all, it's new, it's fast, and it's easy to use. However, you should always use caution when you use the Web. Anyone can put information on the Web. The author of a Web site may not care about accuracy. For your research, focus on sites run by established institutions, such as museums, libraries, universities, and government agencies.

You can't get all the information you need from just one book, one article, or one Web site. Use a variety of information sources when you conduct research.

Student Help Desk

Finding Information at a Glance

Use a variety of information sources.
- Books
- Articles
- Reference sources
- Web sites

Use a variety of search strategies.
- Subject
- Keyword
- Author's name
- Title

Use a variety of search tools.
- Library catalogs
- Periodical indexes
- Search engines
- Web directories

Dewey Decimal System — Decoding Dewey

Most libraries use the Dewey Decimal system to classify nonfiction books.

Numbers	Subject Areas	Examples
000–099	General Works	Encyclopedias, bibliographies
100–199	Philosophy	Psychology, ethics, logic
200–299	Religion	Mythology, theology
300–399	Social Sciences	Economics, law, education
400–499	Language	Dictionaries, language, grammar
500–599	Science	Biology, chemistry, mathematics
600–699	Technology	Engineering, agriculture, medicine
700–799	The Arts	Music, theater, painting, recreation
800–899	Literature	Poetry, plays, essays, novels
900–999	History	Biography, geography, travel

Web Search Strategy — Smart Surfing

Step 1: Before You Search
- Figure out what you want to know.
- Develop a list of keywords.

Step 2: Start Your Engine
- Use several search engines.
- Use specific keywords.
- Spell your keywords correctly.

Step 3: Use Clues to Choose
- Begin looking at sites at the top of the list of search results.
- Read site summaries.
- Use sites created by government agencies, libraries, museums, and educational institutions.

Step 4: Check It Out
- Ask and answer these questions:
  - Who created the site?
  - Is the information correct?
  - Is the information well balanced?
  - Is the source up to date?

The Bottom Line

Checklist for Finding Information

Have I . . .

____ looked up books on my topic in the library catalog?

____ looked up articles on my topic in a periodical index?

____ used a directory or a search engine to locate sources on the Web?

____ used different keywords to search for my topic?

____ used reference sources to find basic information on my topic and to check facts?

____ evaluated the reliability of my sources?

____ used three or more sources of information?

Obstacles

There are just as many words for obstacles as there are for overcoming them.

Plotting the Course

Many **difficulties, hurdles,** and **roadblocks** may lie in your way before you become what you really want to be. Many a **hitch** and **stumbling block** can put a **crimp** in your plans. There may be **struggles** and **hardships** when you start out. Not having proper training is an **impediment,** and in certain lines of work, lack of education is a **drawback. Distractions** may **sidetrack** and **detour** you into a line of work that's not the best for you. Bad luck can be a major **fly in the ointment** to your career. Whatever you do, **snags** and **hang-ups** are bound to turn up, so it's best to be ready for them.

Push toward the Finish Line

Many successful people learn to **overcome** obstacles and **rise to** the challenges they face. They learn how to **surmount** fear, **prevail over** doubt, and **whip** problems into shape, leaving them **triumphant** in the end. It may take time, but staying positive can help you **conquer** your goals, and eventually **rule the day.**

▷ **Your Turn** Name the Game

With a small group, name some hobbies, sports, and special interests that you find challenging. What obstacles make these activities difficult, and why?

Study and Test-Taking Skills

What is the symbol for iron?

What is the past participle form of the verb *drive*?

What is the formula for the area of a circle?

Clearing the Hurdles

If you can answer the questions on these hurdles, you probably gained the knowledge from reading and remembering what you read. Practicing good study habits, reading intelligently, and using proven test-taking strategies will help you feel less anxious about tests, improve your test scores, and retain more of the information you learn. This chapter will help strengthen your test-taking skills.

Write Away: Personal Best
Write a paragraph describing one of your accomplishments and the steps you took to achieve it. Save the paragraph in your
📁 **Working Portfolio.**

STUDY SKILLS

Reading for Information

Using Aids to Reading

When you read for information, you look for main ideas, important terms, examples, and details. These parts of the text are often signaled by titles, subheads, and boldface or italic type. Certain strategies will help you find more detailed information as well.

Preview

- Skim the pages.
- Read section titles, introductions, and conclusions for an overview.
- Note subheads, keywords, pronunciation guides, and marginal features.
- Read any questions at the end of the material to get an idea of the information you'll need to learn.
- Note maps, diagrams, and other graphics.

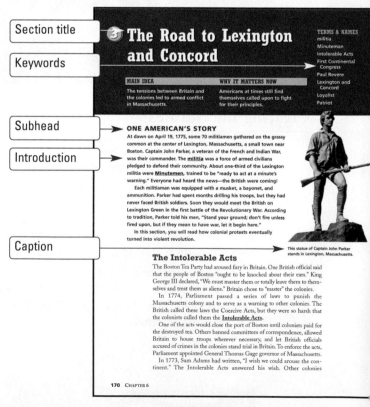

Section title

Keywords

Subhead

Introduction

Caption

③ The Road to Lexington and Concord

TERMS & NAMES
militia
Minuteman
Intolerable Acts
First Continental Congress
Paul Revere
Lexington and Concord
Loyalist
Patriot

MAIN IDEA	WHY IT MATTERS NOW
The tensions between Britain and the colonies led to armed conflict in Massachusetts.	Americans at times still find themselves called upon to fight for their principles.

ONE AMERICAN'S STORY

At dawn on April 19, 1775, some 70 militiamen gathered on the grassy common at the center of Lexington, Massachusetts, a small town near Boston. Captain John Parker, a veteran of the French and Indian War, was their commander. The **militia** was a force of armed civilians pledged to defend their community. About one-third of the Lexington militia were **Minutemen**, trained to be "ready to act at a minute's warning." Everyone had heard the news—the British were coming!

Each militiaman was equipped with a musket, a bayonet, and ammunition. Parker had spent months drilling his troops, but they had never faced British soldiers. Soon they would meet the British on Lexington Green in the first battle of the Revolutionary War. According to tradition, Parker told his men, "Stand your ground; don't fire unless fired upon, but if they mean to have war, let it begin here."

In this section, you will read how colonial protests eventually turned into violent revolution.

This statue of Captain John Parker stands in Lexington, Massachusetts.

The Intolerable Acts

The Boston Tea Party had aroused fury in Britain. One British official said that the people of Boston "ought to be knocked about their ears." King George III declared, "We must master them or totally leave them to themselves and treat them as aliens." Britain chose to "master" the colonies.

In 1774, Parliament passed a series of laws to punish the Massachusetts colony and to serve as a warning to other colonies. The British called these laws the Coercive Acts, but they were so harsh that the colonists called them the **Intolerable Acts.**

One of the acts would close the port of Boston until colonists paid for the destroyed tea. Others banned committees of correspondence, allowed Britain to house troops wherever necessary, and let British officials accused of crimes in the colonies stand trial in Britain. To enforce the acts, Parliament appointed General Thomas Gage governor of Massachusetts.

In 1773, Sam Adams had written, "I wish we could arouse the continent." The Intolerable Acts answered his wish. Other colonies

170 CHAPTER 6

Read actively
- Read the text thoroughly.
- Read the first sentence of every paragraph for main ideas.
- Examine and answer all questions posed by the text.

Interpret graphic aids
- Read the labels, captions, and explanations of graphic aids.
- Look through the text for reference to the graphic aids.
- Compare text information with graphic aids.

Review and take notes
- Reread difficult sections.
- Jot down important words, phrases, and facts.

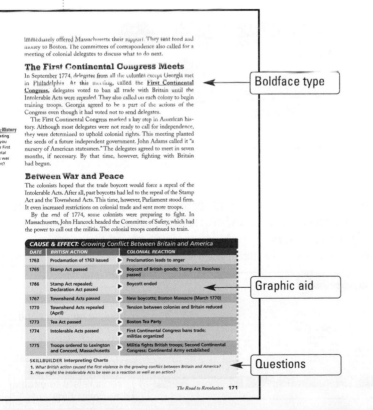

Immediately offered Massachusetts their support. They sent food and money to Boston. The committees of correspondence also called for a meeting of colonial delegates to discuss what to do next.

The First Continental Congress Meets

In September 1774, delegates from all the colonies except Georgia met in Philadelphia. At this meeting, called the **First Continental Congress**, delegates voted to ban all trade with Britain until the Intolerable Acts were repealed. They also called on each colony to begin training troops. Georgia agreed to be a part of the actions of the Congress even though it had voted not to send delegates.

The First Continental Congress marked a key step in American history. Although most delegates were not ready to call for independence, they were determined to uphold colonial rights. This meeting planted the seeds of a future independent government. John Adams called it "a nursery of American statesmen." The delegates agreed to meet in seven months, if necessary. By that time, however, fighting with Britain had begun.

Reading **History**
A. Evaluating
Why do you think the First Continental Congress was important?

Between War and Peace

The colonists hoped that the trade boycott would force a repeal of the Intolerable Acts. After all, past boycotts had led to the repeal of the Stamp Act and the Townshend Acts. This time, however, Parliament stood firm. It even increased restrictions on colonial trade and sent more troops.

By the end of 1774, some colonists were preparing to fight. In Massachusetts, John Hancock headed the Committee of Safety, which had the power to call out the militia. The colonial troops continued to train.

CAUSE & EFFECT: *Growing Conflict Between Britain and America*

DATE	BRITISH ACTION		COLONIAL REACTION
1763	Proclamation of 1763 issued	▶	Proclamation leads to anger
1765	Stamp Act passed	▶	Boycott of British goods; Stamp Act Resolves passed
1766	Stamp Act repealed; Declaration Act passed	▶	Boycott ended
1767	Townshend Acts passed	▶	New boycotts; Boston Massacre (March 1770)
1770	Townshend Acts repealed (April)	▶	Tension between colonies and Britain reduced
1773	Tea Act passed	▶	Boston Tea Party
1774	Intolerable Acts passed	▶	First Continental Congress bans trade; militias organized
1775	Troops ordered to Lexington and Concord, Massachusetts	▶	Militia fights British troops; Second Continental Congress; Continental Army established

SKILLBUILDER Interpreting Charts
1. *What British action caused the first violence in the growing conflict between Britain and America?*
2. *How might the Intolerable Acts be seen as a reaction as well as an action?*

The Road to Revolution **171**

Boldface type ◀

Graphic aid ◀

Questions ◀

STUDY SKILLS

Understanding Visuals

Many kinds of information are easier to understand when they are presented in a graphic, or visual, way. When visuals appear with text, study them. They can help to simplify even the most complicated ideas.

Types of Graphic Aids

Many kinds of visuals are used to simplify text or highlight important ideas. Three that you will use frequently are graphs, time lines, and maps.

Graphs and Charts

Graphs are useful visuals for comparing numerical values. Bar graphs, circle graphs, and line graphs make important numbers easier to understand. Notice how this circle graph depicts the diversity of the American colonies in the years preceding the Revolution.

Read titles.

Look at each piece of the circle.

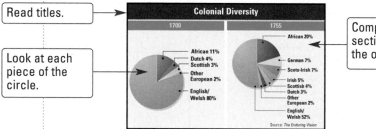

Compare each section with the others.

Time Lines

Time lines show events that occurred over time. Time lines are usually horizontal, with important dates and captions marked along the line. Time lines help you understand the order of events, especially in history.

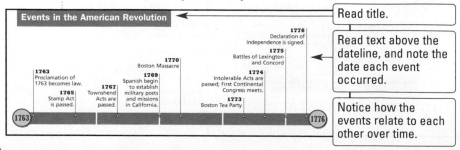

Read title.

Read text above the dateline, and note the date each event occurred.

Notice how the events relate to each other over time.

Maps

Maps are visual representations of an area. Use the legend or key for help in understanding the symbols and colors on the map.

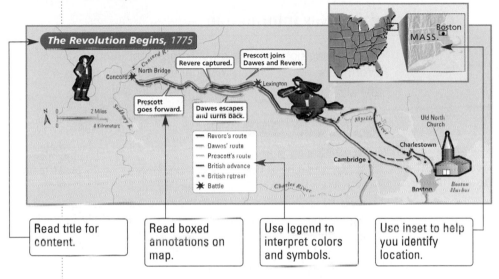

The Revolution Begins, 1775

Concord R.
North Bridge
Concord
Prescott goes forward.
Revere captured.
Prescott joins Dawes and Revere.
Lexington
Dawes escapes and turns back.
N
0   2 Miles
0   4 Kilometers

— Revere's route
— Dawes' route
— Prescott's route
— British advance
• • British retreat
✶ Battle

Mystic River
Old North Church
Charlestown
Cambridge
Charles River
Boston
Boston Harbor

Boston
MASS.

Read title for content.

Read boxed annotations on map.

Use legend to interpret colors and symbols.

Use inset to help you identify location.

Always search the text for a reference to the graphic aid you are using. The text will give you more information about the visual.

PRACTICE ▸ **Using Graphic Aids**

Use the circle graph, time line, and map to answer the following questions.

1. Look at the circle graph. Which ethnic group made up the largest percentage of colonial residents in 1755?
2. Look at the circle graph. Which ethnic group made up the second-largest percentage of colonial residents in 1755?
3. Look at the time line. Which action happened first, the Stamp Act or the Intolerable Acts?
4. Look at the map. Which river did the British cross on their way to Lexington?
5. Look at the map. Which town is situated farthest from Boston?

STUDY SKILLS

Taking Notes

Knowing how to take good notes from written material will help you in studying for tests and writing papers. You remember facts more easily when you write them down.

❶ Recognizing Key Information

When taking notes, focus on only the most important information. Most written material is presented in a way designed to help you easily find important points.

PROFESSIONAL MODEL

Revolutionary War in America
Tension had been building between Great Britain and the American Colonies for more than 10 years before the Revolutionary War began. Starting in the mid-1760s, the British government passed a series of laws to increase its control over the colonies. Americans had grown used to a large measure of self-government. They strongly resisted the new laws, especially tax laws. Fierce debate developed over the British Parliament's right to tax the colonies without their consent.

—*The World Book Encyclopedia*

> **Heading** gives the broad topic.

> **Topic sentence** gives the main idea.

> Look for **supporting details.**

Beginning of American Revolution
- *British government enacts laws.*
- *Colonies resist laws.*
- *Debate starts over British Parliament's right to tax.*

> The note card lists the main idea and the most important details from the passage.

❶ Paraphrasing

Paraphrasing means restating someone else's ideas in your own words. Information often is easier to remember when you write it in your own words. But be sure to change the wording as much as possible. Copying someone's written words without giving that person credit for authorship is called **plagiarism** and is unlawful.

Compare the two versions of the student model, each based on the following example.

Starting in the mid-1760s, the British government passed a series of laws to increase its control over the colonies.

STUDENT MODEL

PLAGIARIZED VERSION
Beginning in the 1760s, the British enacted a series of laws to better control the Colonies.

PARAPHRASED VERSION
To firmly establish its control, the British government began to impose new laws on the American Colonies in the 1760s.

❸ Summarizing

Summarizing means taking the main points of a written passage and rewriting them in a short account. You can do this by leaving out nonessential details and using your own words to make connections between the ideas and details. The summary should be about one-third as long as the original. The example below is a summary of the professional model on page 524.

STUDENT MODEL

The British government imposed new laws on the American Colonies in the 1760s. The colonists resisted the new laws, which were enacted without their consent.

❹ Using Note Cards

When you are doing research for a paper, you will be writing a number of note cards. These cards contain the ideas and information that will form the basis of your paper. Use a different card for each idea, quotation, or statistic. Give each card a heading that describes the note. Be sure to write the source information on the card. As you prepare to write your paper, you will need to organize the cards around specific points in your paper.

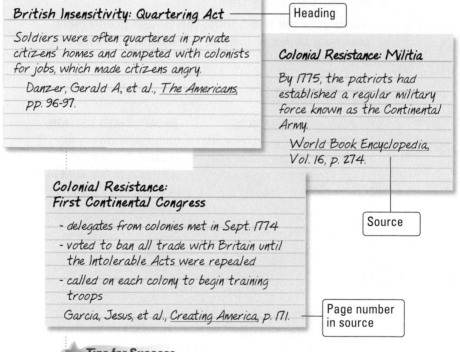

British Insensitivity: Quartering Act ——— Heading

Soldiers were often quartered in private citizens' homes and competed with colonists for jobs, which made citizens angry.

Danzer, Gerald A, et al., *The Americans,* pp. 96-97.

Colonial Resistance: Militia

By 1775, the patriots had established a regular military force known as the Continental Army.

World Book Encyclopedia, Vol. 16, p. 274.

Source

Colonial Resistance:
First Continental Congress

- delegates from colonies met in Sept. 1774
- voted to ban all trade with Britain until the Intolerable Acts were repealed
- called on each colony to begin training troops

Garcia, Jesus, et al., *Creating America,* p. 171.

Page number in source

⭐ Tips for Success

- Divide your cards into separate stacks by topics.
- In each stack, identify the main ideas.
- Look for patterns of information in each stack and between stacks.
- Arrange the cards so the ideas flow logically from one to the next. For example, arrange information from most general to most specific.

To avoid having to write source information on every note card, create source cards. For more on source cards, see page 490.

Creating an Outline

Creating a Formal Outline

An outline helps you organize information. An **informal outline** is a simple listing of key ideas and words. You can use it to take notes on class lectures. A **formal outline** is a logical arrangement of the main ideas, subtopics, and details that will go into a written paper. Here is an example of a formal outline for a paper on the causes of the Revolutionary War.

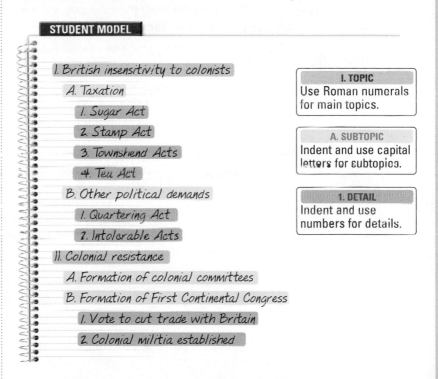

STUDENT MODEL

I. British insensitivity to colonists

   A. Taxation

      1. Sugar Act

      2. Stamp Act

      3. Townshend Acts

      4. Tea Act

   B. Other political demands

      1. Quartering Act

      2. Intolerable Acts

II. Colonial resistance

   A. Formation of colonial committees

   B. Formation of First Continental Congress

      1. Vote to cut trade with Britain

      2. Colonial militia established

I. TOPIC
Use Roman numerals for main topics.

A. SUBTOPIC
Indent and use capital letters for subtopics.

1. DETAIL
Indent and use numbers for details.

When outlining, remember to keep all items of the same rank in parallel form. If subtopic *A* is expressed as a noun, then *B* and *C* also should be expressed as nouns. Also, remember that when subtopics follow a topic or are followed by details, there must be two or more of each: for every *I*, there must be a *II*; for every *A*, a *B*; and for every *1*, a *2*.

HOT TIP

When the sequence of events is important to a subject, organize your outline from earliest event to latest event.

Taking Objective Tests

Objective tests measure your ability to recall facts, ideas, names, and dates. Sometimes your reasoning skills are tested also.

❶ Objective Questions

Objective questions include the following test formats: true-false, matching, and multiple choice. Read test directions carefully to determine whether there is only one correct answer to each question or there can be more than one.

True-False Questions

A **true-false question** asks you to decide whether a statement is accurate or not. If any word or phrase in the statement makes the statement untrue, then it must be declared false.

> **Directions:** Mark each statement T (true) or F (false):
>
> ____ Crispus Attucks, a colonist of African-American/Native American ancestry, was killed in the Boston Tea Party.

Answer: F (false). *Crispus Attucks was a colonist of African-American/Native American ancestry, but he was killed in the Boston Massacre.*

> ____ Committees of correspondence were colonial groups that exchanged letters about colonial affairs.

Answer: T (true). *All parts of this statement are true.*

⭐ Tips for Success

- For an answer to be true, the entire statement must be true.
- Beware of statements that contain words such as *all, none, always, never, every,* and *only.* If there is one exception, the entire statement is false.

Matching Questions

Matching questions ask you to connect an item from one column with another item in a second column. The two items matched should be related in a specific way.

Directions: Match each term in column A with a description in column B.

_____ **1.** boycott   **a.** search warrant

_____ **2.** revenue   **b.** income

_____ **3.** writ of assistance   **c.** refusal to buy goods from someone

Answers: **1-c; 2-b; 3-a**

Directions: Match each term in column A with a description in column B.

_____ **1.** Sugar Act   **a.** a law requiring legal and commercial documents to carry a stamp showing a tax had been paid

_____ **2.** Stamp Act   **b.** a law requiring colonists to house British soldiers and provide them with supplies

_____ **3.** Quartering Act   **c.** a law placing a tax on certain imported items, including molasses, and punishing smugglers

Answers: **1-c; 2-a; 3-b**

⭐ Tips for Success

- Match items you are sure of first.
- Cross out each answer as you use it.
- Check to see if an answer may be used more than once or not at all.
- Check to see if there are extra items in the answer column.

If you are not sure of an answer and want to guess, make sure the test doesn't subtract points for wrong answers. If your guess is wrong, you would lose a point.

Multiple-Choice Questions

Multiple-choice questions test your ability to select the correct answer from among several choices. Usually, the multiple-choice question has only one correct answer, but sometimes the directions ask you to mark *all* the correct answers.

> **Directions:** Choose the best answer for the following question.
>
> Why was Thomas Jefferson chosen to author the Declaration of Independence?
> **a.** He was the only delegate to the Continental Congress who was a slaveholder.
> **b.** He was an excellent writer who came from the key colony of Virginia.
> **c.** No other delegate had the language skills to craft such a document.
> **d.** Most delegates were afraid to put their names to a document called "Declaration of Independence."

Answer: **b**

❷ Short-Answer Questions

For **short-answer questions,** you must provide the answer yourself. It may be one word, a phrase, or a sentence or two.

> **Directions:** Fill in each blank with the name of a colonial town.
>
> **1.** The first battle of the Revolution took place at
>
> _____ .
>
> **2.** After the first battle, the British moved on to
> _____ , where supplies were stored.

Answers: **1.** Lexington; **2.** Concord (both in Massachusetts)

⭐ Tips for Success

- If the question asks for more than one answer, be sure you give all the information asked for.
- Be sure your answer fits grammatically into the sentence.

Standardized Tests

Standardized tests, sometimes called achievement tests, compare your understanding of several subject areas with that of students at other schools.

① Vocabulary

Synonyms and Antonyms

Synonym questions require you to find a word that is nearly the same in meaning as a given word. **Antonym questions** require you to find a word that is nearly the opposite in meaning.

> **Directions:** Choose a synonym for the underlined word.
>
> An <u>impartial</u> judge
>   **a.** unqualified
>   **b.** unprejudiced
>   **c.** Impertinent
>   **d.** punishment

Answer: **b**

> **Directions:** Choose an antonym for the underlined word.
>
> Their <u>cordial</u> reception
>   **a.** warm
>   **b.** unfriendly
>   **c.** early
>   **d.** important

Answer: **b**

★ Tips for Success

- Watch out for antonyms among the answers in a synonym question and vice versa.
- Be sure the word you choose is the same part of speech as the word in the question.
- Don't choose answers simply because they sound alike or are spelled similarly to the question word.

Analogies

An **analogy** compares two things. On a test, analogy questions ask you to find a second pair of words that are related in the same way as the first pair of words listed.

> **Directions:** Find a pair of words that are related in the same way as the pair of words in capital letters.
>
> WHOLE : PART : :
> **a.** piece : pie
> **b.** group : couple
> **c.** corner : box
> **d.** ensemble : individual

Answer: **d**

⭐ Tips for Success

- Put the original pair of words into a sentence that asks a question: "A *whole* is to a *part* as a *what* is to a *what*?"
- Think of the relationship between the words and make up a sentence that shows the relationship: "A *whole* has a *part* in it." Using the same sentence, insert the answer choices in the same order as the original pair: "A *piece* has a *pie* in it." Keep trying until you find one that fits.
- Don't be fooled by pairs in the wrong order. For instance, though a corner is part of a box, the words are in the wrong order.
- Don't fall for alternatives that are not exactly related. For instance, though a couple could be part of a group, it may not always be.
- Don't choose a pair simply because it contains the same parts of speech as the original pair.
- If two pairs fit the sentence, choose the pair that is most like the original pair.

In the chart on the next page are common relationships that appear on analogy tests. Study them to understand the relationships.

Common Relationships in Analogies	
Relationship	**Example**
Synonyms	CAMARADERIE : FRIENDSHIP : : enmity : hostility
Antonyms	ABSENCE : PRESENCE : : abundance : scarcity
Tool to user	HAMMER : CARPENTER : : needle : seamstress
Action to object	PULVERIZE : ROCK : : shatter : glass
Part to whole	CITIZEN : NATION : : individual : group
Cause to effect	BOMB : EXPLOSION : : germ : epidemic
Product to source	WORDS : LYRICIST : : music : composer
Connotative differences/degree	DIRTY : FILTHY : : annoying : obnoxious

PRACTICE Matching Pairs

Choose the pair of words that expresses a relationship most like the one expressed in the original pair.

1. AUNT : NIECE : :
   a. uncle : nephew
   b. father : brother
   c. mother : daughter
   d. sister : brother

2. PLAYER : TEAM : :
   a. television : sport
   b. player : coach
   c. team : sport
   d. team : league

3. TRIANGLE : CIRCLE : :
   a. square : cube
   b. inches : feet
   c. pentagon : rectangle
   d. pyramid : sphere

4. SIZE : ENORMOUS : :
   a. hue : mauve
   b. hundred : ten
   c. weight : height
   d. heavy : light

5. DESTROY : CREATE : :
   a. demolish : produce
   b. guess : know
   c. exaggerate : lie
   d. natural : man-made

6. VENOM : SNAKE : :
   a. design : artist
   b. quills : porcupine
   c. shell : turtle
   d. arsenic : poison

7. SUNDIAL : CLOCK : :
   a. car : motorcycle
   b. food : meal
   c. abacus : calculator
   d. misery : happiness

8. OPERATION : SURGEON : :
   a. money : banker
   b. brushes : painter
   c. plankton : fish
   d. litigation : lawyer

❷ Reading Comprehension

Reading comprehension tests measure your ability to understand material you are reading for the first time.

⭐ **Tips for Success**

- Skim the passage to see what it's about.
- Review the questions to find out what you're supposed to learn.
- Go back and read the passage with the questions in mind.
- Underline key words and phrases, dates, and other information you think you may need to answer the questions.

Directions: Read the following passage and choose the best answer for each question.

In the early years of the Revolution, Benedict Arnold, a popular Patriot soldier and leader, helped defend New England and then served as the American commandant of Philadelphia. In the later years of the war, however, he married a wealthy woman with British sympathies. Over time, Arnold accumulated debts to support his wife, and she convinced him to <u>pin his hopes on</u> the British.

Despite Arnold's suspicious connections, Washington gave him an assignment he requested—command of West Point, a strategic fort on the Hudson River, north of New York City. Arnold had secretly decided to turn traitor and hand West Point over to the British, but the Americans discovered the plot at the last minute. Arnold escaped to the British and ultimately died in Britain, scorned by both sides as a traitor.

—*The Americans*, p. 115

1. Benedict Arnold originally served in the
   a. American army   c. West Point Military Academy
   b. British army   d. Green Mountain Boys

2. The phrase "pin his hopes on" most likely means
   a. hope that the British would lose the war
   b. pin down the British about some financial help
   c. trust and rely on someone or something
   d. set down in writing his hopes and dreams

Answers: **1-a; 2-c**

Essay and Writing Prompts

Essay and writing questions ask you to write paragraphs that pull together all the information you've learned about topics. Your answers demonstrate your ability to organize and express your thoughts as well as your knowledge of facts.

❶ Understanding the Essay Question

On a social studies or science test, you may be asked to write an essay in response to a test question. Before you try to answer, make sure you clearly understand the question. Here is an example.

Directions: Write an essay to answer the following question.

1. Discuss two ways the American colonists resisted the 1765 Stamp Act.

- Asks for **essay**
- Asks you to **discuss**
- Asks for **two ways**

For more on essay questions, see p. 537.

❷ Understanding the Writing Prompt

For state and district tests, you'll be asked to respond to writing questions. Here is an example of one.

Write a letter telling your social studies teacher about one local historical site you would like to visit. Try to convince your teacher that the place you have suggested would be a good choice. Be sure to support your choice with convincing reasons and to explain your reasons in detail.

FORMAT

AUDIENCE

CONTENT

PURPOSE

Here's How   Analyzing the Prompt

- **Format** Look for words, such as *letter, memo,* and *essay,* that tell you the type of structure you will need to use in your response.
- **Audience** Look for the person or group you will address.
- **Content** Look for words that define the topic and details needed.
- **Purpose** Look for words that suggest the purpose of your response.

STUDY SKILLS

Student Help Desk

Study and Test-Taking Skills at a Glance

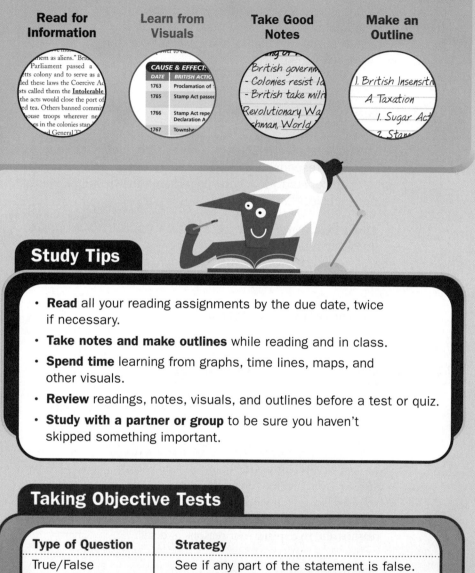

Read for Information	Learn from Visuals	Take Good Notes	Make an Outline

Study Tips

- **Read** all your reading assignments by the due date, twice if necessary.
- **Take notes and make outlines** while reading and in class.
- **Spend time** learning from graphs, time lines, maps, and other visuals.
- **Review** readings, notes, visuals, and outlines before a test or quiz.
- **Study with a partner or group** to be sure you haven't skipped something important.

Taking Objective Tests

Type of Question	Strategy
True/False	See if any part of the statement is false.
Multiple Choice	Cross out incorrect answers.
Matching	Match the ones you know first.
Short Answer	Key words, phrases, and main ideas you memorized are useful here.

Essays and Writing Prompts

- Jot down key ideas, topic sentences, and supporting details.
- Draft a quick outline.
- Choose words and phrases that are precise.
- Include examples and details.
- Avoid padding your answer with irrelevant information.
- Proofread your essay and correct any errors you find.

Types of Essay Questions

If the question asks you to . . .	You should . . .
Compare/contrast	show similarities and differences between two or more topics
Describe	explain the most important aspects of a topic
Define	explain the basic meaning of a term
Discuss	look at a topic from many viewpoints
Explain	describe how and why something happened or how something works
Analyze	examine the individual parts of a whole
Evaluate	examine and judge the topic carefully
Summarize/outline	give a brief overview of a topic

The Bottom Line

Checklist for Developing Study and Test-Taking Skills

Have I . . .

____ read to obtain information?

____ taken careful notes and reviewed the material?

____ become familiar with different types of test questions?

____ understood different types of vocabulary questions?

Power Words
Vocabulary for Precise Writing

In the Spotlight

Try using these words to describe things that pull you in and things that go unnoticed.

Look! Look!

Have you ever seen the **attention-getting** signs in Times Square, New York City? They are colorful and **showy,** with **vivid** neon lights and **bold, in-your-face** images. These **audacious** signs and billboards are meant to look **splashy** and **flamboyant.** You can't miss them—they are truly **ostentatious.**

A successful sign in Times Square **arrests** and **engages** you. It **piques your curiosity,** and **draws you in.** Its creators hope to **attract, entice,** and **lure** you. For their advertisement to work, it must be the **center of attention** and really **stand out from the crowd.**

Easy to Overlook

Now imagine a more **tasteful, low-key** sign in such a place. Would you even see such a **restrained** ad, with **unobtrusive** images and a **subtle** message? If you are going to sell here, your sign can't be **modest, quiet,** or **plain. Toned-down** and **laid-back** just don't cut it in Times Square!

▶ **Your Turn** First Loud, Then Soft

With a partner, create an attention-getting ad for a music video. Then create a low-key one for a nature program on public television. Use visuals for each ad.

bold

flamboyant

audacious

showy

splashy

572

vivid

Critical Thinking Skills

Eat More Chocolate, Grow Faster

The Flash

Killer Flies
Swarm City

No One Escapes
Deadly Storm

Surprise!
**Chess Best
Sport Ever**

Think Again

Sometimes headlines like the ones above purposely overstate ideas, present opinions as facts, or appeal to your emotions. However, you can use critical thinking skills to carefully consider the ideas presented to you and keep your own thinking clear. **Critical thinking skills** are ways of judging ideas and information. This chapter will help you sharpen your thinking skills, so that you won't be fooled by a flashy headline or other appeals.

Write Away: Reading Between the Lines
Study the headlines on the magazine cover above. What kind of articles would you expect to find for each headline? Write a brief magazine article based on one of the headlines shown. Save your paragraph in your 📁 **Working Portfolio.**

CRITICAL THINKING

Relationships Between Ideas

The first step in critical thinking is finding the main idea in a speech or in writing. The next step is understanding how the rest of the ideas are related to the main one and to each other. Ideas are often presented in comparisons, analogies, and cause-effect relationships.

❶ Main Ideas and Supporting Details

A **main idea** is the most important point in someone's speech or writing. A main idea is explained by **supporting details** that offer examples and credibility.

> **Here's How** **Finding Main Ideas and Details**
>
> **To find the topic in any piece of writing,** look at the first sentence or paragraph as well as at titles, heads, and subheads.
>
> **To find the main idea,** look for
>
> - ideas that follow statements, such as "The point is . . ." or "This is important because . . ."
> - the beginning and end of a selection, where the main idea is often introduced or summarized
> - ideas that are emphasized through repetition, boldface and italics, or forceful gestures
>
> **To find supporting details,** look for examples, explanations, and phrases such as, "For instance . . ." and "To illustrate the point . . ."

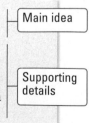

PROFESSIONAL MODEL

Greg Maddux of the Atlanta Braves is a [pitching] artist. He uses pinpoint control and half a dozen pitches to paint the corners of the strike zone. The ace right-hander won the National League Cy Young Award four times in a row (1992–95), a major league record.

— *Sports Illustrated for Kids*

Main idea

Supporting details

❷ Comparison and Contrast

Sometimes writers and speakers compare or contrast ideas. A **comparison** points out the similarities between things, while a **contrast** shows the differences.

STUDENT MODEL

Both Mars and Earth have roughly 24-hour days, warm summers, and clouds that drift in the sky. Yet, Mars is barely half the size of Earth and has some nights as cold as –200° F. Mars also has volcanoes that are much larger than Earth's, such as Olympus Mons, which is 75,000 feet tall. That's two and a half times the height of Everest!

Mars
Colder nights
75,000-ft Olympus Mons

Both
Approx. 24-hr days
Warm summers
Clouds

Earth
Nearly twice as large as Mars

PRACTICE Alike and Different

Study the images below. Create a Venn diagram to compare and contrast the football and rugby players.

Football

Rugby

➌ Cause-and-Effect Relationships

Cause-and-effect relationships show how one event (the **cause**) can result in another (the **effect**). You can find cause-and-effect relationships in anything—from news reports to history books—that discusses the reasons *why* something happens.

Because Henry Ford developed assembly lines to build the Model T, car manufacturing costs became cheaper.

CAUSE

EFFECT

➍ Analogies

An **analogy** is an extended comparison between two subjects. It's often used to help explain unfamiliar concepts by comparing them to more familiar ones.

STUDENT MODEL

You might say that Henry Ford was the Bill Gates of the early 1900s. With the Model T, Ford changed the lives of Americans as much as Gates did with the computer. Suddenly, people could do something faster than ever before. Ford's revolutionary thinking resulted in greater freedom for many Americans. Like Gates, Ford also became one of the richest men in America.

Writer compares Ford to a more current figure to show who Ford was in his own time.

Analyzing Facts and Opinions

LESSON 2

Simply gathering information isn't enough; you also need to evaluate it. To accurately evaluate information you must know how to tell the difference between facts and opinions.

❶ Identifying Facts

A **fact** is a statement that can be proved. Prove a statement by using one of the following methods.

> **Here's How** **Checking Statements for Facts**
>
> Your friend says a tennis ball weighs about two ounces.
>
> - **Make a personal observation.** (Weigh it for yourself.)
> - **Consult an authoritative source.** (Look in a tennis book.)
> - **Ask an expert.** (Write to the manufacturer.)

❷ Identifying Opinions

An **opinion** is a statement of personal belief that cannot be proved. When you're trying to identify opinions, look for the following types of signal words.

Words that Identify Opinions		
Word Type	**Examples**	**Example Sentence**
Judgment words	excellent, terrible, awful, clever, boring	She's a *terrific* singer!
Command words	should, ought to, must, mustn't	You *must* buy her new CD!
Thinking/ feeling words	think, feel, would argue, would agree, believe	I *think* she'll win a Grammy!

Sometimes, a speaker or writer may not use any signal words with an opinion. However, you can mentally insert such words to test whether a statement is an opinion. For example:

[I think] The music's much too loud.

❸ Evaluating Opinions

An opinion can be a valuable source of information, if it's well-supported. Learn how to evaluate an opinion for reliability.

Not All Opinions Are Created Equal

−	+	Why
"Mozart's music is a waste of time." **Raul Gomez** Eighth grader	"Mozart's operas can be challenging to play well." **Anna Romero** Pianist	The pianist has experience with and interest in Mozart's music. Raul just doesn't like it.

Here's How Evaluating Opinions

Ask yourself: is the opinion supported by facts?

Well-researched facts can support a thoughtful opinion.

Ask yourself: is the opinion reliable or made by an expert?

An expert brings special knowledge and interest to an area.

Ask yourself: is the opinion based on experience?

Experience can lead to an informed opinion.

PRACTICE Is That a Fact?

Decide whether each of the following statements is a fact or an opinion.

1. Eddie Carmel, well over eight feet tall, was called a giant.
2. Being a giant would lead to many challenges.
3. Carmel grew uncontrollably because of a glandular disease.
4. Carmel worked in the circus and in B-movies.
5. People should be aware of the special problems faced by giants and others with physical differences.

Going Beyond the Facts

You can learn to evaluate ideas by combining new information with what you already know. Two ways to do this are by making inferences and by drawing conclusions. You can also make generalizations when you have enough information.

❶ Making Inferences

An **inference** is a logical guess based on facts and common sense.

New Information	**+**	**Prior Knowledge**	**=**	**Inference**
My sister saw 12 hot air balloons this morning.		Our town hosts a hot air balloon festival every summer. Today is June 3.		The festival must be taking place today.

❷ Drawing Conclusions

Drawing conclusions goes beyond making an inference or guess. A **conclusion** is a judgment or decision reached after serious consideration of all related facts, prior knowledge, new knowledge, and inferences.

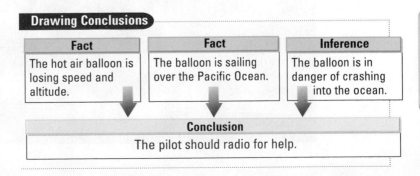

Drawing Conclusions

Fact	Fact	Inference
The hot air balloon is losing speed and altitude.	The balloon is sailing over the Pacific Ocean.	The balloon is in danger of crashing into the ocean.

Conclusion

The pilot should radio for help.

CRITICAL THINKING

❸ Making Generalizations

A **generalization** is a broad statement based on several specific cases or examples. Make generalizations to help you organize and understand large amounts of information.

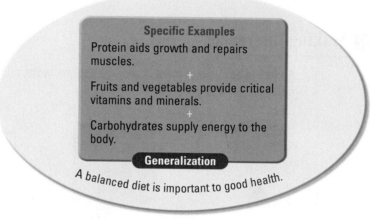

Specific Examples

Protein aids growth and repairs muscles.

+

Fruits and vegetables provide critical vitamins and minerals.

+

Carbohydrates supply energy to the body.

Generalization

A balanced diet is important to good health.

PRACTICE ⟩ **Isn't It Obvious?**

Make an **inference** about what is happening in the photo.

Draw a **conclusion** about what happened just before the photo was taken.

CHAPTER 30

Recognizing Errors in Reasoning

LESSON 4

In trying to persuade you to believe or do something, writers and speakers may use **faulty reasoning**. Detecting errors in thinking is an important skill in evaluating information. Carefully examine what you hear and read to see if the reasoning behind the words is sound.

❶ Overgeneralizations

An **overgeneralization** is a statement so broad that it cannot possibly be true. An overgeneralization often includes words such as *everyone, no one, always, all,* and *never.*

Everyone loves the Bellow Boys' new song.

Consider: There is probably at least one person who doesn't like the group's music.

Many people love the Bellow Boys' new song.

Stereotypes

Suppose that you go to a department store and are served by a woman who is very rude. If you decide that *all* female salespeople are rude, then you are guilty of stereotyping.

A **stereotype** is an overgeneralization about an entire group of people. Stereotypes are illogical and unreasonable.

Musicians are extroverted.

Consider: This lumps all types of people who are musicians together. Who knows how many of them are extroverted?

Some musicians are extroverted.

❷ Either/Or Argument

An **either/or statement** suggests that there are only two choices available in a situation. Most of the time this is not the case. When faced with an either/or statement, think about all the other possibilities that aren't mentioned.

Either you join the new recycling club, or you don't care about the environment.

⬇

Consider: Some students may care about recycling but may be unable to join the club for some reason.

⬇

If you care about the environment, you might join the new recycling club.

❸ False Cause-and-Effect Statement

A **false cause-and-effect statement** wrongly implies that one event caused another. Be careful not to assume that Event A caused Event B just because Event A happened first. Consider other possible causes and facts, as well.

Sid didn't buy those new running shoes, and as a result she lost the race.

⬇

Consider: Sid skipped training all week.

⬇

New running shoes may have helped Sid in the race, but not training enough may have been the real reason why she lost.

❹ Circular Reasoning

Circular reasoning attempts to prove a statement simply by repeating it in different words, instead of giving good reasons to support it.

Cross-country skiing may be difficult for a beginner because it is hard to do.

⬇

Consider: But difficult and hard mean the same thing! What are the real reasons that it's difficult?

⬇

Cross-country skiing can be difficult for a beginner because it requires a lot of strength and stamina.

PRACTICE A ▸ **Finding Faulty Reasoning**

Find and label the faulty reasoning in the posters below.

A dirty car just doesn't look clean. Come to the 8th graders' Car Wash, and your car will sparkle.

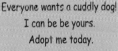

Everyone wants a cuddly dog! I can be be yours. Adopt me today.

Come to the Pep Rally on Friday at 3 PM in the gym! If you have spirit, you'll be there.

PRACTICE B ▸ **Fixing Faulty Reasoning**

Identify the kind of error in reasoning that is illustrated in each statement below. Then rewrite the statement so that it's logical.

1. Either you help me study, or I'll flunk the test.
2. The library book was overdue because it was late.
3. Everybody loves basketball.
4. John didn't get his homework done because he had to take the dog for a walk.

Recognizing Emotional Appeals

Some speakers and writers appeal to people's emotions to get a point across. Emotional appeals can often be found in ads and commercials, as well as in persuasive writing.

❶ Loaded Language

Some writers and speakers use strong words, or **loaded language**, to stir up positive or negative feelings in people. Such language is often used in place of facts to sway the opinions of readers and listeners.

Example:

Positive language:
Mia Hamm is a *dynamic* and *competitive* soccer player!

Negative language:
Mia Hamm is a *pushy* and *aggressive* soccer player!

When you notice loaded language, ask yourself "Where are the facts?" A speaker or writer may use loaded language to try to hide a lack of facts to support his or her opinions.

PRACTICE A Spotting Loaded Language

Bring in a copy of your favorite ad or commercial that uses loaded language. Exchange ads with a classmate, and discuss the types of loaded language that you find.

❷ Name-Calling

Name-calling is a way of getting people to reject someone's ideas by attacking the person instead. People who use this strategy fail to address what's really important—the *ideas*.

Example: Don't vote for Gene! He's an airhead.

What does Gene have to say? His ideas should be the issue.

❸ Bandwagon and Snob Appeal

Some of us want to fit in and be accepted. **Bandwagon** statements appeal to a person's desire to be just like everyone else.

Example: Why aren't you eating Super Snacks? Everyone else is!

Other people like to stand out in a crowd. **Snob appeal** targets those people who want to be different from everyone else.

Example: Don't be just another face in the crowd! Wear Cool Shades!

PRACTICE B Spotting Emotional Appeals

Label the different types of emotional appeals used in this advertisement.

Don't be a loser. Let Power Cleats get you goals! Everyone knows you have to give your best to win. And Power Cleats are the very best in soccer. That's why every great player wears these premium shoes. Their amazing traction gives you the grip you need.

Be a *winner* with *Power Cleats!*

Student Help Desk

Critical Thinking at a Glance

Do look for main ideas and supporting details.

Do gather enough information to make inferences and draw conclusions.

Don't confuse facts and opinions.

Don't be fooled by emotional appeals.

Don't fall for faulty reasoning.

Is It Fact or Opinion? Go Ahead and Prove It!

Statement	Check It Out
It's too cold to wear a T-shirt!	Go outside. **Personal observation** tells you this is true.
It's freezing outside!	Check the thermometer. This **authoritative source** tells you it is just below freezing.
This is the worst snowstorm this decade!	Consult the weather report. **Experts** say it's the second worst.

Signal Words

Type of Idea	Signal Words	Example
Cause-Effect	*because, therefore, so, since, as a result*	Because of the snowstorm, school is closed.
Comparison	*also, as well, both, in the same way, likewise, similarly*	Both this year and last year, we had snowstorms.
Contrast	*but, instead, however, on the other hand, unlike, yet*	However, last year we didn't miss any school.

Fact
My uncle is cooking dinner for us tonight.

Fact
The kitchen is filled with smoke and smells awful.

Inference
He burned the dinner again.

Conclusion
My uncle is not a good cook.

Using Thinking Skills   No Winter Coat?

I don't want to wear my winter coat today because . . .

I don't feel like wearing it. (CIRCULAR REASONING)

No one wears a winter coat in April! (OVERGENERALIZATION)

Either I got a new coat, or I'll just freeze! (EITHER/OR THINKING)

This hideous coat is ridiculous! (LOADED LANGUAGE)

Chris isn't wearing his, so why should I? (BANDWAGON)

I'm too cool to wear a winter coat. (SNOB APPEAL)

It's 70° F outside today. (REASONABLE!)

The Bottom Line

Checklist for Critical Thinking Skills

Have I . . .

____ located main ideas and supporting details?

____ identified relationships between ideas?

____ separated facts from opinions?

____ made inferences and drawn conclusions?

____ avoided errors in reasoning?

____ evaluated emotional appeals?

Power Words
Vocabulary for Precise Writing

harangue

tirade

Getting the Message Across

There is a word for each of the many ways in which we speak. Let's hope someone is listening!

Tell Me More

What a pleasure it is to hear a good **talk.** An inspiring **speech,** a fine graduation **address,** a great **sermon** by a religious leader, or a **lecture** given by a teacher or professor can all teach us something. It is the same when we hear a **eulogy,** which is a form of **praise** for someone held in high regard. All these forms of **oratory** can inspire us.

You'll Want to Cover Your Ears

What is not so inspiring is an angry **tirade** or a wild **rant.** Who enjoys getting a **tongue-lashing** for doing something wrong? But sometimes you just have to sit through a long **harangue** and hope the **diatribe** ends soon!

Why Is Nobody Listening?

If you **brag** or **boast** about yourself, people tend not to listen. You don't want to **run off at the mouth—drone on, filibuster,** or **climb on a soapbox** until your listeners shout *"Boring!"* If you **lie, falsify, prevaricate,** or **tell whoppers,** no one will believe you anymore. How much better to **convey** sincerity and to **disclose** honestly your desire to be heard!

lecture

RANT

oratory

address

▷ **Your Turn** Truth or Whopper?

In a group, hold a contest to see who can tell the most convincing tale. Before your turn, choose whether you will tell a true story or a made-up story. When everyone in the group has had a turn, guess whose story was true and whose was a giant whopper. (Limit turns to one minute.)

boast

PRAISE

Oral Communication

Can anybody hear me?

What Is Communication?

Try to answer this riddle: If someone is speaking, but no one is listening, is anybody communicating? The answer depends on what is meant by *communicating*. Many people mistakenly believe that communicating simply means speaking. In fact, oral communication is made up of three parts: the speaker, the audience or listener, and the message. If one of these elements is missing, communication stops. Read the riddle again. What do you think the answer is?

Write Away: What Did You Say?
Talking to someone who isn't listening is a frustrating situation. Think about a time when a friend or family member was not listening to you. In a paragraph, describe the situation and then describe how you felt as a result of the situation. Put your paragraph in your ☐ **Working Portfolio.**

ORAL COMM.

Listening Effectively

LESSON 1

Don't confuse listening with hearing. When you hear, you use your ears to take in sounds, but you don't necessarily pay attention to these sounds. When you listen, you use your ears and eyes to focus on the speaker, and your mind to understand and evaluate what is being said.

❶ Listening with a Purpose

People who are effective listeners know their purpose for listening. They use listening techniques that match their purpose.

Purposes for Listening		
Situation	**Purpose for Listening**	**Listening Techniques**
Your friend tells you about his vacation.	**For enjoyment,** to provide your friend with an audience	Look the speaker in the eye, nod to show you understand what he or she is saying, and make comments when appropriate.
A guest speaker in your classroom tells you about her career.	**For information,** to learn something new	Think about what you already know about the subject, and listen for ideas that interest you or add to your own knowledge.
You and your teacher discuss how to improve your grades.	**For problem-solving,** to generate ideas	Identify goals and possible problems; listen closely to each other's ideas and build on them.
Your father explains why you can't have a pet tarantula.	**For an explanation,** to understand a point of view, to find opportunities to share your own ideas	Listen carefully to what is being said, respond positively to the good points, and listen for opportunities to share your reasons.

CHAPTER 31

❷ Becoming an Active Listener

As a student, you listen every day for information. How well do you think you listen? Listening for information can be challenging when the information is difficult to understand. Resist the urge to give up. Instead, use the strategies below to become an active listener.

Strategies for Active Listening

Before You Listen

- Find out what the topic is.
- Think about what you know and what you want to know about the topic.
- Have the materials you need to take notes, if necessary.

As You Listen

- Keep your eyes on the speaker.
- Don't let your mind wander.
- Identify the speaker's purpose and main ideas.
- Listen for supporting details.
- Notice repeated ideas. They may signal main ideas.
- Be aware of statements that begin, "My point is . . ." Important information will follow.
- Listen for words and phrases that signal important points, such as *more important, next, as a result.*
- Look for and interpret nonverbal messages, such as posture, facial expression, and tone of voice.

After You Listen

- Review any notes you have taken.
- Ask follow-up questions to clarify points.
- Fill in any missing information in your notes.

ORAL COMM.

❸ Evaluating What You Hear

You should always listen with a critical ear. This means you should decide whether the information in a speaker's message makes sense and is supported with facts and examples. Use the statements below to evaluate the **content,** or the meaning, of a speaker's message.

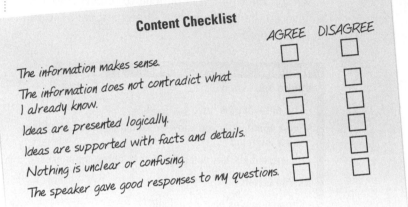

Content Checklist

AGREE DISAGREE

The information makes sense.

The information does not contradict what I already know.

Ideas are presented logically.

Ideas are supported with facts and details.

Nothing is unclear or confusing.

The speaker gave good responses to my questions.

If you disagree with several of these statements, you'll need to consider whether the speaker's information is reliable.

The way a speaker presents information—the **delivery**—is also important. Use the following statements to evaluate the delivery of information.

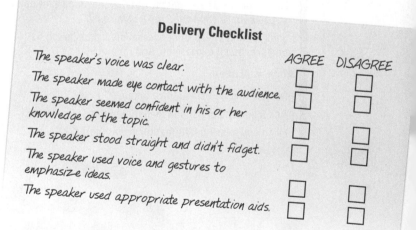

Delivery Checklist

The speaker's voice was clear.

AGREE DISAGREE

The speaker made eye contact with the audience.

The speaker seemed confident in his or her knowledge of the topic.

The speaker stood straight and didn't fidget.

The speaker used voice and gestures to emphasize ideas.

The speaker used appropriate presentation aids.

Interviewing

Interviewing someone who is knowledgeable about a particular subject is a good way to get in-depth information. As an interviewer, your job is to use listening skills and interviewing techniques to make sure you get all the information you need.

❶ Planning an Interview

Before you can interview someone, you need to do some basic planning. The first step is to find an expert—someone with extensive knowledge of your subject area.

> **Here's How** **Finding an Expert**
>
> - Ask teachers, parents, and neighbors for suggestions.
> - Consider people you know who work in fields connected to your subject area.
> - Conduct a keyword search on the Web.
> - Look in the phone book for businesses related to your subject.
> - Ask the librarian to show you how to find the names of organizations involved in your subject area.

List two or three experts you would like to interview. Then conduct background research to be sure these people have the kind of knowledge you're looking for.

Setting Up an Interview

Telephone, write, or e-mail the person you want to interview and cover these points:

- Identify who you are and why you want to interview the person.
- Arrange a time, date, and place that would be convenient for both of you to meet.
- Ask permission to audiotape or videotape the interview.
- State where you can be contacted in case the person needs to change plans.

❷ Preparing for an Interview

Do some more background research on the person you'll be interviewing to help you write questions. Then decide what you want to know from this person, and write questions that will get this information. You will get more information if you ask open-ended questions that don't allow for just a simple yes or no answer. Open-ended questions often begin with *what*, *why*, *how*, *explain*, or *describe*.

Yes-or-no question Would you recommend this job to someone else?

Open-ended question What advice would you give to someone interested in your field?

Call the person a day or two before the interview to remind her or him of your appointment.

❸ Conducting an Interview

Show the person that you appreciate his or her time by arriving on time and by bringing all the supplies you need.

> **Here's How** **Conducting an Interview**
>
> - Ask questions clearly, listen carefully, and don't interrupt.
> - Give the person time to answer.
> - Help the person stay on topic.
> - Ask follow-up questions if something is confusing or if you need more information.
> - Take notes, even if you're recording the interview.
> - Thank the person at the end of the interview and ask if you may call him or her to check facts or get additional information.

Following Up

After the interview, write a brief summary of your notes while the information is still fresh in your mind. Write out the interview if you recorded it. You should send a thank-you note to the person you interviewed no later than the day after the interview. When your material is final, send a copy to this person.

Participating in Groups

You've participated in groups both in and out of school, so you probably know how complicated group discussions can become. The key to successful group participation is cooperation.

❶ The Group's Purpose

In order for a group to be successful, it must have a purpose for forming. Some common reasons for working in groups, and an example of each, are listed below.

To make a decision: The editors of the school newspaper meet to choose the cover story for the next issue.

To solve a problem: Members of the school band get together to decide how to raise money for new band uniforms.

To brainstorm ideas: Several classmates get together to come up with a theme for the next school dance.

Group members need to work together to achieve their purpose. This means individual members must help the group come up with the best ideas instead of pushing their own ideas.

Group Roles

Before getting down to business, groups need to assign roles to their members. These roles distribute responsibility among the members and help the group achieve its purpose.

Group Roles	
Role	**Responsibilities**
Chairperson	Keeps group members focused on the purpose
Note-taker	Takes notes and reports on past meetings
Materials manager	Brings necessary supplies to each meeting
Participants	Contribute ideas, respond to each other's ideas, help the group reach agreement

ORAL COMM.

Remember that the success of the group relies on individuals performing their roles in the best way they can. Group members should work toward the *group's* goals, not their personal goals.

❷ Discussion Skills

Group members need to be both good listeners and good speakers. In addition, they need to be considerate of each other's feelings. Differences of opinion are bound to exist. To effectively handle these differences, use the suggestions below.

> **Here's How**) **Conducting a Group Discussion**
>
> - Be informed about the topic and purpose beforehand.
> - Take turns speaking and don't interrupt others.
> - Listen attentively to all ideas, and jot down notes and questions.
> - Focus on members' ideas and not on how you feel about each member.
> - Stay on the subject and avoid distractions.
> - Be respectful of others, even if you disagree.
> - Look for common ground to reach a solution together.

❸ Evaluating Discussions

Ask yourself the questions below to evaluate your individual performance as a group member. Use your answers to improve your group communication skills.

Contribution Checklist

- ✓ Did I listen attentively to other group members?
- ✓ Did I respond constructively to others' ideas?
- ✓ Did I contribute my own ideas to the discussion?
- ✓ Did I speak clearly, confidently, and respectfully?
- ✓ Did I cooperate well with other group members?
- ✓ Did I stay on track during the discussion?

Presenting an Oral Report

LESSON 4

Some students get so nervous about giving an oral report that they put off working on it until the last minute. Instead of making them feel calmer, waiting makes them even more nervous because they are unprepared. Don't let this happen to you! Instead, plan ahead, prepare your materials, and practice, practice, practice.

❶ From Writing to Speaking

One way to prepare an oral report is to use material you've already written. Keep in mind that an audience of listeners is different from an audience of readers. Readers can reread sections they don't understand, but listeners have only one chance to understand information. Use these techniques to change a written report into an oral report.

Adapting Written Reports	
Timing	Shorten the material so your report runs no longer than 15 minutes.
Introduction	Create an attention-getting opener that clearly introduces your topic.
Main section	Simplify your wording and shorten your sentences. Be specific in your descriptions and in the connections you make between ideas.
Body language	Use facial expressions and body movement to emphasize ideas. Look at your audience as you speak.
Presentation aids	Help your audience understand ideas by using visual aids (such as pictures, graphs, charts, and maps), and audio aids (such as music and sound effects).

The changes you make to a written report will depend in part on the kind of writing you're working with and your original purpose for writing the report. Was your purpose to inform? to persuade? to entertain? Make sure your oral report has the same purpose.

For more information on turning your writing into an oral presentation, see the Speak for Yourself feature at the end of every Writing Workshop.

ORAL COMM.

Choosing Presentation Aids

Presentation aids are useful for several reasons. They help your audience understand your ideas, give your audience something to look at, and help keep you focused. Think about your purpose, topic, and audience as you choose presentation aids. Which ones will be most helpful in emphasizing your main points?

Presentation Aids		
Aids	**Reasons for Using**	**Special Considerations**
Slides	To show real people, places, and things; to display charts and to show reproductions of fine art	Require special projection equipment
Maps	To show specific locations and relations of events	Must be large, simple, and well labeled
Diagrams	To illustrate real or imaginary ideas or things	Must be large, simple, and well labeled
Photos	To show real people, places, and things	Probably should be passed around the room
CDs	To provide sound effects and music that help create an atmosphere or illustrate a point	Require special sound equipment
Web sites	To provide additional sources of information on your topic	Require a computer and, for larger audiences, a special projector that projects images onto a large screen

WATCH OUT Don't overuse visual aids. They should be part of your presentation but not the focus of it.

❷ Presentation Skills

Create report notes to guide you as you speak. Mark your notes to remind you when to use your presentation aids. Practice your report a few times, using all of your presentation aids. As you practice, think about the way your voice sounds and about how you stand and move.

Using Voice and Body Language

The success of an oral presentation partly depends on how well it's delivered. Use the techniques listed below to keep your audience's attention and interest.

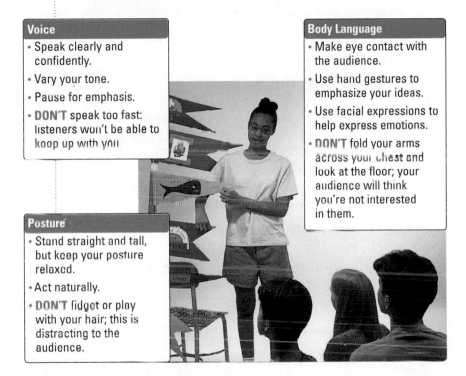

Voice
- Speak clearly and confidently.
- Vary your tone.
- Pause for emphasis.
- **DON'T** speak too fast: listeners won't be able to keep up with you.

Body Language
- Make eye contact with the audience.
- Use hand gestures to emphasize your ideas.
- Use facial expressions to help express emotions.
- **DON'T** fold your arms across your chest and look at the floor; your audience will think you're not interested in them.

Posture
- Stand straight and tall, but keep your posture relaxed.
- Act naturally.
- **DON'T** fidget or play with your hair; this is distracting to the audience.

Overcoming Stage Fright

Everybody gets stage fright. Here are some typical symptoms of stage fright and tips for getting rid of them.

Dry mouth Drink plenty of water, and keep a glass nearby while you speak.

Tripping over your words Slow down until you begin to speak more smoothly.

Inability to look at the audience Start by looking just over the tops of people's heads. Slowly begin to focus on a few friendly faces in the audience.

Presenting an Oral Interpretation

An oral interpretation is a way to show the meaning of a piece of writing through a performance. Using vocal and facial expressions, movement, sound effects, and other techniques, you can bring a piece of literature to life for an audience.

❶ Choosing a Selection

Choose a short selection for your oral interpretation, such as a short poem or a scene from a story, memoir, novel, or play. The selection may be something written by a friend, by a professional writer, or by you. Make sure the selection is truly interesting to you and includes one or more of these characteristics:

- dramatic action
- interesting rhythm
- interesting characters and settings

Use your imagination when you interpret the selection. Are there lines for speakers to say? Are there sounds you could recreate or images you could develop?

Here's How Interpreting a Selection

Figure out the mood of your interpretation. What emotion do you want to highlight in your interpretation? Anger? Sadness? Joy?

Find parts of the text to highlight. What actions, settings, ideas, or words do you want to emphasize?

Choose methods of interpretation. What will you use to interpret your selection? Sound? Movement? Speaking? Costumes? How will you show different characters? By changing your voice, posture, or facial expression? Choose methods that will emphasize the mood and meaning of the selection.

Make notes about your ideas for your interpretation and about the kinds of sounds and actions you want to include in it. You may need to try out several ideas before you find the ones that work. Later on, you will use these notes to create a script for your performance.

❷ Practicing and Presenting

Once you're satisfied with your interpretation, you'll need to prepare a **reading script.** A reading script is a neatly typed or handwritten copy of your selection, marked with notes and cues to remind you when to pause, move, or emphasize something. At the top of your script, include a list of props, such as costumes, you will use in your interpretation.

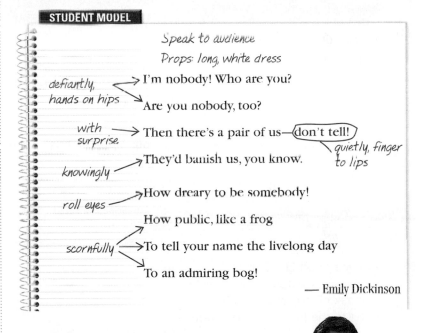

STUDENT MODEL

Speak to audience
Props: long, white dress

defiantly,
hands on hips → I'm nobody! Who are you?

Are you nobody, too?

with
surprise → Then there's a pair of us—(don't tell!)

quietly, finger
to lips

They'd banish us, you know.
knowingly

roll eyes → How dreary to be somebody!

How public, like a frog

scornfully → To tell your name the livelong day

To an admiring bog!

— Emily Dickinson

Use these suggestions to prepare yourself for your performance:

- Make sure you have all the props and equipment you need.

- Rehearse several times using all of your props.

- Present your interpretation for your friends and family, and use their suggestions to improve your performance.

Student Help Desk

Oral Communication at a Glance

Think about what you're going to say.

Speak clearly and confidently.

Consider your listeners.

Listen actively.

Evaluate what you hear.

Respect others' opinions.

Listening for Information   Listen Up!

- Find out in advance what the topic is.
- Think about what you know and what you want to know about the topic.
- Keep your eyes and your attention on the speaker.
- Listen for main ideas and supporting details.
- Take notes.
- After the speaker is finished, review your notes and ask follow-up questions.

Speaking Tips   Say It Like You Mean It!

In any speaking situation . . .
- Know your purpose for speaking.
- Speak clearly and confidently.
- Get to the point and don't ramble.

When you're speaking to an audience . . .
- Stand up straight but stay relaxed.
- Be enthusiastic to keep your audience interested.
- Avoid repeating empty words such as "like" and "you know."
- Use voice, facial expressions, and body movement to emphasize ideas.
- Make eye contact with people in your audience.

When you're speaking in a group . . .
- Take turns speaking.
- Don't use disrespectful language.
- Do ask questions, and comment on others' ideas.

Interviewing Checklist

Ask the Experts

Planning

Identify an expert who's willing to be interviewed.

Set up a time, date, and place for the interview.

Research the expert and your subject.

Write a set of open-ended questions.

Call the expert to remind him or her of your appointment.

Conducting

Ask questions clearly and listen carefully.

Allow plenty of time for answers and don't interrupt.

Ask follow-up questions when necessary.

Take notes on main ideas.

Thank the expert at the end of the interview.

Following Up

Review your notes and write a brief summary of them.

Write out the interview if you recorded it.

Send a thank-you note to the expert you interviewed.

When your final draft is finished, send a copy to the expert.

The Bottom Line

Checklist for Oral Communication Skills

Have I . . .

____ paid careful attention to the speaker?

____ listened for main ideas and supporting details?

____ identified relationships between ideas?

____ asked questions if necessary?

____ evaluated the content and the delivery?

____ waited for my turn to speak in a group?

____ spoken confidently and clearly?

____ varied my voice for emphasis and effect?

____ used appropriate gestures and facial expressions?

____ included presentation aids or props when possible?

nut

FAN

freak

buff

ENTHUSIASTS

devotees

Cheers!

When you have something you want to lend your support to, these words will help express your level of commitment.

Who's the Nut?

Do you know a sports **fan,** a movie **buff,** or a nature **enthusiast?** Does someone in your life fit the description of a **nut,** as in "baseball nut", or **freak,** as in "computer freak"?

Maybe you know people so **committed** to their interests that you would call them **adherents, devotees,** or even **zealots.**

Going Overboard

We think of being **devoted** and **faithful** as positive qualities. It feels good to know people we consider **true-blue, committed,** and **loyal.** Some forms of **enthusiasts—fanatics** and **radicals—**can hardly think of anything but the object of their interest. If their interest makes them **obsessed, wild-eyed,** or **crazy,** this kind of **exuberance** could become a little scary to others!

zealots

▷ **Your Turn** What's Yours?

Pick something you are enthusiastic about and, using the words above, describe your level of interest. Then, read your description to a partner and talk about why you chose the words you did.

LOYA

FAITHFUL obsessed

Learning About Media

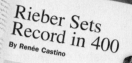

Rieber Sets Record in 400

By Renée Castino

LEICESTER, ENGLAND—"It was the last thing I expected," Beverly Rieber said of her record-shattering performance in the 400 meters at the Track and Field International Championships. "I'm pretty sure it was the last thing anybody else expected, either."

20-year-old Texan d-field world minutes 50 rld cham- so, she nd off the hich was Consti- stralia,

Nerves? How could I be nervous? Rieber said laughingly. "It's impossible to be nervous when none of the experts thinks you have a chance. I had the jitters during my first few events, but I was so calm before this race that I just knew I was going to do well. I didn't know how well, though."

Carried Away by Media

When you watch sports or a movie on TV, do you ever get so involved that you yell and cheer at the screen? Media such as TV, movies, video games, and recorded music can make you feel as if you're someplace else. When you get back down to earth, you may want to take a closer look at the media. What messages are you really getting? This chapter will help you examine the many media messages coming at you.

Write Away: If You Were in Charge
Imagine that you had your own TV or radio program or your own magazine, newspaper, or Web site. What kind of information would you send out to your audience? You might want to give information on a favorite sport or hobby, or you might focus on an issue you consider important. Write a paragraph describing your idea, and save it in your ◁ **Working Portfolio.**

MEDIA

Media Focus

Comparing Media

Medium means a system of communication. **Mass media** are forms of communication that are meant to reach a large audience. Newspapers, magazines, radio, TV, and movies are all types of mass media. Other types include books, recorded music, Web sites, advertisements, billboards, cartoons, comic books, and video games.

Just about all media products depend on **verbal communication**— written or spoken words. Most also use **nonverbal** ways to communicate, such as images, graphics, design, music, and sound effects.

All the examples in this lesson focus on skating. As you look at them, think about how each type of media uses verbal and nonverbal communication differently.

❶ Electronic and Film Media

A screen with moving pictures and sound—that's what carries you away in electronic and film media.

Television News Report

Television news reports present information in an easy-to-understand format. The reports often include brief video clips of dramatic events. An announcer "anchors" the broadcast, guiding viewers through the day's news.

Video replays of dramatic moments clarify what happened.

The producers want viewers to think of the **announcer,** or **anchor,** as friendly and trustworthy.

USA Medal Tally

Gold 5
Silver 2
Bronze 4

Graphics give information at a glance.

Web Site

Web sites can give in-depth information on specialized subjects. Unlike television news, Web sites allow you to choose which information you receive by clicking on underlined words, or **links**. This site offers news, images, and an interactive quiz.

This is truly a multimedia site. The **menu** of options includes text, still images, and video.

Clicking here lets users see skating sites created by other people and organizations.

Users can see when the site was **last updated**—especially important when looking for up-to-the-minute information.

L-Net

| Back | Forward | Reload | Home | Images | Print | Security | Stop |

Location:

The Association of American Figure Skaters presents

Figure **Skating Central**

Please visit regularly for the latest information on figure skating—professional and amateur, singles and pairs, men's and women's competitions.

This page was last updated April 23.

News	Competition Results
Upcoming Events	Photographs/Video
History of Figure Skating	Join the AAFS

You are visitor number

001054

Documentary

Documentaries are not as up-to-the-minute as TV newscasts or Web sites can be, but they often provide much more in-depth information. This documentary follows a skater who hopes to win an Olympic medal.

Narration, music, and **camera angles** all help to communicate the message.

Like TV newscasts, documentaries do not allow you to control the pace or flow of information.

Footage and **interviews** help viewers understand the skater's personality.

MEDIA

❷ Print Media

Newspapers, magazines, and other types of print media rely heavily on written words, of course. Dramatic photos, headlines, graphics, and design also help them deliver their message.

Newspaper Article

Once it's printed, a newspaper article can't be updated the way a TV news story or Web site can—you have to wait for the next day's paper. However, newspapers provide detailed information and dramatic photographs. Like a Web site, a newspaper article lets you take in information at your own pace and choose the stories that most interest you.

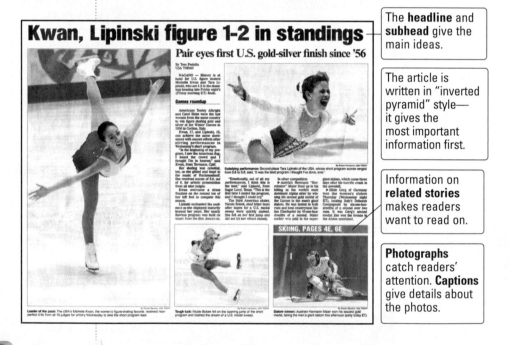

The **headline** and **subhead** give the main ideas.

The article is written in "inverted pyramid" style— it gives the most important information first.

Information on **related stories** makes readers want to read on.

Photographs catch readers' attention. **Captions** give details about the photos.

 PRACTICE Choose Your Media

In your 🗂 **Working Portfolio,** find your **Write Away** exercise from page 571. Write a paragraph about how you would present your information using at least two different media, one electronic (or film) and one print. Explain how the presentation is changed when you change media.

Understanding Media Influence

You've probably noticed that your friends and family try to influence you, or affect how you think and act. But did you ever think that TV, radio, and video games might influence you? Anything that has the power to attract you has influence over you. The trick is to understand that influence.

❶ Recognizing Purposes

Every media product, whether it's a comic book or a news story, is created for a specific reason, or **purpose.** Identifying why a media product was created is the first step in understanding how it can influence you.

Purpose and Influence in the Media	
Purpose	**Examples**
To inform: present facts or analyze something	News reports, some magazine articles, public service announcements, some Web sites
To persuade: try to sway the feelings or actions of an audience	Advertisements, movie previews, editorials, reviews, political cartoons, some novels
To entertain: amuse or delight	TV shows, movies, sports coverage, novels, recorded music, electronic games, comics

Keep in mind that most media have more than one purpose—and if you aren't aware of those purposes, you may be influenced without knowing it! This chart gives you some examples.

Main and Other Purposes in Media		
Media program or product	**Main purpose**	**Other purposes**
Sports coverage	To entertain you	To inform you about sports or athletes
Advertisement	To persuade you to buy something	To entertain you; to inform you about a product
News broadcast	To inform you about current events	To persuade you that an issue or idea is important

❷ Who Shapes the Message?

People who control the media are known as **gatekeepers.** Here's a diagram that gives some examples.

Who Controls the Media?

Media Owners
TV networks
Recording companies
Publishing companies

Media Products
Television
Radio
Magazines
Movies

Media Creators
Actors
Writers
Directors
Webmasters

Media Sponsors
Clothing manufacturers
Fast-food restaurants
Department stores

Media **sponsors** are companies that pay for their products to be advertised. It's important to be aware of sponsors and other gatekeepers because they control much of what you see and hear. For example, if a TV show is sponsored by a soft-drink company, you probably won't see or hear about competing brands of soft drinks on that show.

❸ Determining the Target Audience

Every TV show, magazine, and ad is designed for a certain **target audience**. That's a group of people who have things in common, such as age, interests, and buying habits. You are part of several target audiences. Many TV shows and commercials with young characters are created to appeal to your age group. Why? The shows' and ads' creators hope that you will watch, listen, and buy! Be aware of the media's sometimes subtle attempts to persuade you.

Beware of **bias,** the presentation of only one side of an issue. News reports usually try to give both sides, but ads are always biased. Many Web sites and specialty magazines are too.

Decoding Media Messages

What Messages Are You Getting?

To understand the influence of the media, you need to look beyond the surface of a message. To be a smarter consumer of media, keep these questions in mind the next time you see or hear a media message.

> **Here's How** **Deciphering a Media Message**
>
> - What is the message?
> - What is the purpose? Is there more than one purpose?
> - Who do you think is the target audience?
> - What methods are used to achieve the purpose?
> - Do you think the message is effective? Why or why not?
> - How could you prove or disprove the claims made in the message?

This lesson has messages from different media on the same subject—fast food. Notice the conflicting information.

Billboard

This advertisement promises an easy solution to a common problem.

Purpose: To persuade you to buy Heavenly Hamburgers.

Target audience: Parents who drive past the sign on their way home from work.

No **time** to **cook?**

Stop by Heavenly Hamburgers after work and pick up the perfect family meal!

Methods: The large, attractive photo entices the viewer. The text encourages people who have little time to cook to buy Heavenly Hamburgers instead.

Evaluate: How is a fast-food meal "perfect"? Does it have great taste, great nutrition, or just great convenience? Do facts support any of the claims in this ad?

MEDIA

TV News Report

This news segment compares the nutritional content of several fast-food products.

Purpose: To inform viewers about the high fat content of most fast foods.

Target audience: Viewers who frequently eat fast food and who are health conscious.

Hamburger: 36g fat

Methods: A serious, trustworthy announcer delivers the message. Facts are given in the report and in graphics on the screen to support the claim of high fat in fast food.

Evaluate: What is the source of the information—a scientific study, a government report, or some other source? How do you decide whether a message is reliable?

PRACTICE ▸ **Your Turn**

Analyze and evaluate this magazine ad. Be sure to answer the questions in the Here's How box on the previous page.

Tired of kids' stuff?

Grow Up!

When you were a kid, you liked fizzy sodas. Now that you know that sodas are loaded with empty calories, you've made orange juice your choice. An eight-ounce glass has a full day's supply of vitamin C and tastes better than soft drinks!

Drink the good stuff that's good for you.

Orange Juice from Florida: A better choice than soft drinks

Creating Media: Video

Now that you've studied the techniques used by the professionals, you can use these methods to shape your own media product, a video. With video you can create a short fictional movie, a documentary, a news or sports story, a funny skit, an interview, or a music video. Creating a video involves planning, production, and editing.

❶ Planning

Before you begin to videotape, you will need to plan your video. Here are the steps you should follow.

> **Here's How** **Planning a Video Production**
>
> 1. **Write an outline or overview.** Explain the message of your video and define its purpose and target audience.
> 2. **Write the script.** Whether you use actors or an off-camera narrator, you need to write down all the words that will be spoken.
> 3. **Prepare a storyboard.** Show the sequence and types of shots you'll videotape.
> 4. **Choose places and people.** Scout locations that have the right lighting and background for your video. Select participants and give each a defined role.
> 5. **Select and prepare equipment.** Choose and gather all the equipment you will need, including cameras, microphones, lights, and props.

A **storyboard** is a series of drawings that show the sequence of shots in your video. It also includes the dialogue or narration that goes with each shot.

Narrator: Bell Middle School hadn't won a basketball game in a long time . . .

Coach Williams was getting discouraged . . .

the fans were silent . . .

❷ Production

During the **production** stage, you actually videotape, or shoot, each scene. As the director, you'll use your script and storyboard to guide you through the taping. Here's what you'll need to do for each new scene.

- **Get Ready** Make sure props are in place and the participants know what they're supposed to do and say. Before taping, rehearse scenes that are acted out or have written dialogue.
- **Quiet on the Set** Record only those sounds that you've scripted—make sure there are no distracting background noises like barking dogs or sirens.
- **Lights!** Make sure lighting is appropriate for the scene. Dark, light, shadow, and contrast can all affect the mood of your video.
- **Camera!** Set up the camera to get the right angle at the proper distance from the subject.
- **Action!** Start the camera rolling.

Tape each scene several times so you have a backup if something goes wrong. Try experimenting with different camera angles for different effects.

❸ Editing

Once you finish shooting your video, you will need to edit it. Editing involves

- Placing scenes in a logical sequence
- Cutting out slow or lengthy scenes
- Adding sound effects, music, and special effects
- Making sure sound and image are matched up properly
- Adding graphics, titles, and credits

Here's what you can do when you add different design elements.

Photos and graphics provide additional information, statistics, data, and background.

Background music sets or intensifies the mood of a scene.

Sound effects emphasize a point or exaggerate humor.

Narration explains information that is not easily understood by viewing the images.

Special visual effects exaggerate a certain aspect of the scene or the subject or give a perspective of the subject.

You can edit your video with machinery, software, or in-camera editing. Find out what resources are available in your school.

❹ Evaluating and Revising

Hold a sneak preview, or screen your video before a group of friends or family members to find out its strengths and weaknesses. After the screening, hold a discussion or have your audience members fill out a questionnaire that includes these questions:

1. What message did you get from the video?
2. Did the scenes flow smoothly in a logical sequence?
3. What did you like best about the video?
4. What parts still need work?

PRACTICE ▸ **Imagine the Images**

List three topics that you think would make a good five-minute video. Then pick one and write an overview of how you would make the video. Include a description of your message, purpose, and target audience.

Student Help Desk

Learning About Media at a Glance

Identify the type of media, its purpose, and the message.

Recognize who is sending and receiving the message.

Analyze the design elements and techniques.

Evaluating Media Messages

Developing Media Literacy

- Who created the message and why?
- What techniques are used to attract your attention?
- What lifestyles, values, and viewpoints are represented in the message?
- How might others understand the message differently?
- What do you think is omitted from the message?

CHAPTER 32

Design Elements That Communicate   A Picture's Worth

Images	art, photos, and illustrations
Visual aids	maps, charts, graphs, and diagrams
Graphics	icons, logos, labels, decorations, and patterns
Type	the way the print looks and how it is used
Color	vivid or pale, contrasts, and black-and-white
Contrast	dark/light, loud/quiet, and simple/complex
Movement	film, video, animation, and words moving on a screen
Sound	narration, dialogue, music, and sound effects
Special effects	added or enhanced images and manipulation of scenes

Tips for Creating a Great Video

- Write an outline and plan.
- Write a script that includes dialogue, narration, stage directions, and sound effects.
- Draw a detailed storyboard.
- Gather the equipment you will need.
- Use lighting and sound that are appropriate to your video.
- Edit for pace and continuity, adding background music, sound effects, graphics, and special effects where needed.
- Screen your video with a group of friends.

The Bottom Line

Checklist for Learning About Media

Have I . . .

____ identified the message and its purpose?

____ understood different ways that media messages are communicated?

____ recognized how the media try to influence me?

____ analyzed ways the media appeal to a target audience?

____ understood how to create my own media message?

MEDIA

Power Words
Vocabulary for Precise Writing

cryptographer

It's All in the Name

Who does that and what is it called? Try out these fancy names for careers and professions.

What to Do for Fun

How about a hobby for your spare time? If there's an actor in you, try becoming a **thespian.** Or, you could be a **philatelist** and collect rare stamps, or a **numismatist** and collect rare coins. If you like postcards or flags, you could try being a **deltiologist** or a **vexillologist.** The more adventurous **spelunker** explores and studies caves.

Be What You Want to Be

Maybe you're giving thought to your future career. Do you like nature? An **ornithologist** studies birds, and a **botanist** specializes in plants. How about being a **linguist** or a **philologist?** Both study language. A **dermatologist** is a skin doctor, a **podiatrist** a foot doctor, and an **otolaryngologist** takes care of the ears, nose, and throat.

If you want more mystery, a **paleontologist** digs for dinosaur bones, an **oceanographer** examines sea life, and a **cryptographer** interprets messages written in code.

spelunker

deltiologist

▷ **Your Turn** Try Not to Get Cross

With a group, choose six or more of these complex names for professions and make a crossword puzzle with them. Give the blank puzzle to another group, with clues. Keep the answers for yourself. Time your group's effort to see how long it takes to complete the puzzle correctly!

Developing Your Vocabulary

Copyright © 1999 by Rick Stromoski

Dramatic Confusion?

If you had been the student above looking for the drama club, do you think you would have found it? Why or why not?

Encounters with unfamiliar words don't always result in dramatic confusion, but they can. You may want to arm yourself with some strategies for figuring out the meanings of words when you can't just look them up in a dictionary. This chapter will help you do that.

Write Away: What Do You Know?
Are you a thespian? a philatelist? a newbie? You're probably an expert in some hobby or area of study that has its own special terms. Take a moment to think of ten words that are specifically used to talk about a subject, sport, or hobby you know well. Then define each word and put your list in your ▭ **Working Portfolio.**

VOCABULARY

ClassZone at
mcdougallittell.com

Using Vocabulary Strategies

❶ Here's the Idea

You can usually figure out a word's meaning in one of these ways:
- by looking at the word's **context**—that is, the words and sentences surrounding it
- by analyzing the meanings of the word's parts
- by considering the meanings of related words you know
- by looking it up in a dictionary

Notice how one student used these strategies to figure out the meanings of the unfamiliar words in the following passage.

PROFESSIONAL MODEL

Octopuses are **invertebrates**—primitive animals without backbones—and according to Roland Anderson, a marine biologist at the aquarium, invertebrates have long been thought **incapable** of play. "But octopuses," he says, "are intelligent animals—the most intelligent invertebrates." And perhaps we're **underestimating** them.

Anderson and Jennifer Mather, an **animal psychologist** from Canada's University of Lethbridge, decided to see just how playful octopuses could be. They put eight giant Pacific octopuses in tanks and dropped an empty pill bottle into each tank. Two of the animals played with the bottle, said Anderson. "One blew the bottle back and forth against a water inlet, a little like bouncing a ball, and one blew the bottle around the tank."

In spite of their **apparent** dribbling and bottle-handling skills, neither octopus has been drafted by the NBA.

—John D. Allen, "Octoplay"

> The words between the dashes define *invertebrates.*

> Since *in-* means "not," *incapable* must mean "not capable."

> *Under-* means "below" and *estimating* has to do with forming an opinion. So, *underestimating* must mean "forming too low of an opinion."

> If *-ist* means "one who practices" and *psychology* is the study of the mind, an *animal psychologist* must be someone who practices the study of animals' minds.

> *Apparent* may have to do with looking or seeming since it's similar to *appearance.*

Using Context Clues

You can often determine a word's meaning from its context, or the words and sentences surrounding it. The context may present the meaning as an actual definition or restatement. On the other hand, it may just provide clues to the word's meaning, such as examples.

❶ Definitions and Restatements

Definitions and restatements of meaning are often signaled by the following words.

Words That Signal a Definition or Restatement

which	in other words	that is	or
this means	is, are	are called	are defined as

Punctuation marks such as commas, dashes, parentheses, or a colon may also signal the presence of a definition or a restatement.

Try to spot the clues to the definitions in these sentences about a girl named Bo-Bo, whose life was saved by brain surgery.

PROFESSIONAL MODEL

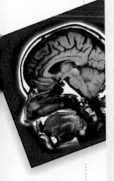

It was early Monday morning, and I was making rounds. When I came to Bo-Bo, the house officer explained her situation. "Just about the only thing she has left is **pupillary response**," he said. (That meant that her pupils still responded to light.) . . .

Bo-Bo was gently positioned on an **"egg crate,"** a soft, flexible pad covering the operating table. . . .

Then I opened the covering of her brain—the **dura**.

—Ben Carson, M.D., *Gifted Hands*

The words *that meant* and the parentheses are clues signaling the definition of *pupillary response*.

The meaning of *egg crate* is presented as a restatement signaled by a comma.

A dash helps to signal that *dura* is being defined. Here, the definition comes before the term being defined.

❷ Examples

Writers frequently give examples that suggest the meanings of words.

We may experience some turbulence, including minor bumps and sudden drops in altitude. So please remain in your seats, with your seat belts fastened.

The following words often introduce examples.

Words That Signal Examples		
such as	like	for example
especially	for instance	including

Sometimes examples merely follow a colon or a dash. They can come before a dash as well. Here, the items before the dash are examples of things that make up a decor.

Pearl-gray walls, light-gray couch, silver pillows, and glass-topped steel tables—the sleek decor gave the room a cool, modern look.

❸ Comparisons and Contrasts

A **comparison clue** suggests an unfamiliar word's meaning by pointing out a similarity. In the sentences below, the comparison is signaled by *as . . . as*.

People often say that my sister is as argumentative as a courtroom lawyer.

An argumentative person must be one who is challenging or confrontational, like a courtroom lawyer.

A **contrast clue** suggests the meaning of an unfamiliar word by pointing out a difference.

Ordinarily she is very argumentative, but this morning she was extremely conciliatory.

Since *conciliatory* is contrasted with *argumentative,* the words must be opposite in meaning. In other words, *conciliatory* must mean something like "pleasant" or "agreeable."

Comparisons and contrasts are typically signaled by words and phrases such as these.

Words That Signal Comparison and Contrast			
like	similarly	but	not
likewise	in contrast to	on the other hand	unlike
as	instead of		

④ General Context

The **general context** of an unfamiliar word is the information around it, or the larger setting in which it appears. For example, notice how the following passage helps you understand the meaning of *poignant*.

PROFESSIONAL MODEL

At the end of the story the boys were close to tears. Even Matsuzo found himself deeply touched. He wondered why the farmer had told his sons such a **poignant** bedtime story. Wouldn't they worry all evening instead of going to sleep?

—Lensey Namioka, "The Inn of Lost Time"

PRACTICE   **Using Context Clues**

In your 🗀 **Working Portfolio,** find your **Write Away** list from page 585. Then use what you learned in this lesson to create five sentences that contain five of the ten words you listed and clues to their meanings. Use a specific context clue in each sentence.
- a definition
- a restatement
- examples
- a comparison
- a contrast

Then underline your five terms, swap your sentences with those of a classmate, and see who can be the first one to figure out the meanings of the other person's underlined terms.

Analyzing Word Parts

Sometimes you can infer, or figure out, the meaning of a word from the meanings of its parts. Words can have four different kinds of parts: base words, word roots, prefixes, and suffixes.

❶ Base Words

A **base word** is a complete word that can stand alone. However, other words or word parts may be added to base words to form new words.

> search + light = searchlight
>
> re + search = research

When two or more base words are joined to make a new word, that new word is called a **compound word.** For example, *bookend* and *searchlight* are compound words.

❷ Prefixes and Suffixes

A **prefix** is a word part attached to the beginning of a base word or a word part. The meaning of the newly formed word is often a combination of the meaning of the prefix and the word or word part to which it is attached. For example, the prefix *re-* means "again, back, or backward." When it is added to the word *view*, the new word, *review*, means "to examine again, look back over, or study."

Some Common Prefixes		
Prefix	**Meanings**	**Examples**
a-	on, in, without	aboard, ablaze, amoral
dis-	absence of, not, undo, away	dislike, disapprove, disconnect
em-, en-	in	embed, encourage
inter-	among, between	interact, interlock
over-	too much	overextended, overload
pro-	before, in place of	provision, pronoun

A **suffix** is a word part attached to the end of a base word or a word part. A suffix usually determines the part of speech of a word. For example, by adding different suffixes to the adjective *short* you can create *short**en*** (verb), *short**ness*** (noun), and *short**ly*** (adverb).

For more on prefixes and suffixes, see p. 598.

You can create many new words from just one base word by adding different prefixes and suffixes to it. See how many words you can make by combining these word parts with *act*.

Did you notice that while *react* and *overact* have the same base word, the different prefixes give the words very different meanings?

Likewise, although *active* and *actor* are very similar words, the suffix *-ive* makes *active* an adjective while the suffix *-or* makes *actor* a noun.

You may have to change the spelling of some base words when adding suffixes. For example, *monster + ous = monstrous*.

For more about spelling changes, see Quick Fix Spelling Machine, p. 648.

PRACTICE A   **Using Prefixes and Suffixes**

See how many words you can build from the word parts below. Check your answers and spelling in a dictionary.

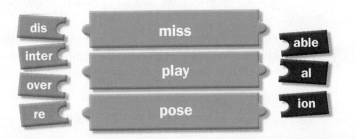

VOCABULARY

❸ Roots

A **word root** is a word part to which a prefix, a suffix, or another root must be added. Word roots cannot stand alone. Many English words contain ancient Greek and Latin roots.

Common Roots

Roots	Meanings	Examples
aster, astr	star	asterisk, astronomy
chron	time	chronicle, chronology
cycl	circle	bicycle, cyclone
dem	people	democracy, epidemic
ge	earth	geography, geology
gnos	know	diagnosis, prognosis
log	speech, word	apology, monologue
morph	form, shape	amorphous, metamorphosis
onym	name, word	antonym, synonym
phys	nature	physical, physician

(GREEK)

Roots	Meanings	Examples
duc, duct	lead, bring	aqueduct, conduct
fract, frag	break	fracture, fragile
ject	cast, hurl	eject, reject
mitt, miss	send, throw	emit, missile
pli	fold, bend	pliable, plier
popul	people	popular, population
scend	climb	ascend, descend
son	sound	sonata, unison
tract	pull, draw	distract, tractor
volv, volu, volut	roll, turn	revolution, involve

(LATIN)

Sometimes roots reveal a bit of history. For example, *volume*, which means "book," contains the root *volu*, which means "roll," because books were once written on rolls of parchment.

CHAPTER 33

❹ Word Families

A **word family** is a group of words that contain the same root. For example, this word family shares the Latin root *fac* or *fact,* from *facere,* meaning "to do or make."

fact
fact or
arti **fact**

fact ual
fac simile
bene **fact** or
fact ion

fact ory
manu **fact** ure
fact itious

Here's How) **Using Word Families**

• To figure out the meaning of the word *facsimile,* first look at the root.	*fac, fact*
• Think of other words with the same root.	*factory, manufacture*
• Figure out the meaning they share.	"to make"
• Look for prefixes, suffixes, base words, and other roots that may affect the meaning of your word.	*simile* is from *similis,* "similar"
• Use all these clues to guess the word's meaning.	*Facsimile* means "a copy or reproduction," "something made to be similar."

PRACTICE B > **Analyzing Word Parts**

Use what you have learned about word parts to figure out the definitions of the highlighted words in the paragraph below. Be prepared to explain how you arrived at your definitions.

    Unlike the image that science fiction movies tend to present of them, not all **asteroids** are speeding toward the earth like huge, dangerous **projectiles.** Many asteroids and even smaller **fragments** of matter actually **revolve** around the sun in regular orbits. However, meteoroids and other space rubble do occasionally strike the earth, so we can't entirely **dismiss** the possibility of something huge hitting us one day.

Using Vocabulary Reference Books

❶ Dictionaries

Dictionaries tell more than just the meanings of words. For example, look at the information you can learn from this entry.

---

brave / break — GUIDE WORDS: FIRST AND LAST ENTRY WORDS ON THE PAGE

brave (brāv) *adj.* **brav·er, brav·est.** Having or showing courage: *a brave defiance of danger.* —*n.* A Native American warrior. —*tr.v.* **braved, brav·ing, braves.** To undergo or face with courage: *Fire-fighters brave many dangers in the line of duty.* [First written down in 1485 in Middle English, from Old French, probably from Latin *barbarus,* like a barbarian.] ——**brave'ly** *adv.* —**brave'ness** *n.*

Synonyms: **courageous, fearless, bold.** Antonym: **cowardly.**

brav·er·y (brā'və rē *or* brāv'rē) *n., pl.* **brav·er·ies.** The quality or condition of being brave; courage.

bra·vo (brä'vō *or* brä vō') *interj.* An expression used to show approval, as for a musical performance. —*n., pl.* **bra·vos.** A shout or cry of "bravo."

ENTRY WORD DIVIDED INTO SYLLABLES

PRONUNCIATION GUIDE

PART OF SPEECH

DEFINITION

SAMPLE SENTENCE

ETYMOLOGY (WORD ORIGINS)

OTHER FORMS OF THE WORD

SYNONYMS

ANTONYM

—adapted from *The American Heritage Student Dictionary*

Here's How **Choosing the Right Definition**

1. Rule out any that don't make sense, given what you're reading about. If you're reading about firefighters rescuing someone, you could probably rule out the "Native American warrior" definition of *brave.*

2. Determine the word's part of speech in the sentence. In "The brave firefighter rescued the child," *brave* is an adjective, so you would choose the adjective definition. In "The brave began the ritual," *brave* is a noun, so you would choose the noun definition.

3. When there's more than one meaning for a word as a particular part of speech, use synonyms in place of the word to see which meaning makes the most sense in the sentence.

❷ Other Vocabulary References

You can also build your vocabulary by using thesauruses, synonym finders, and glossaries.

Thesauruses

A **thesaurus** is a dictionary of **synonyms**—words that have similar meanings. Many thesaurus entries also note **antonyms** —words that have the opposite meaning—of the entry word.

brave, *adj.*
Having or showing no fear when dealing with something difficult, dangerous, or scary. **syn:** bold, courageous, fearless, gallant, stout, stouthearted, unafraid, undaunted, valiant. **ant:** cowardly, craven, daunted, faint-hearted, fearful

ENTRY WORD
PART OF SPEECH
DEFINITION
SYNONYMS
ANTONYMS

Not all synonyms can be substituted for each other. Some words are used only in certain ways. For example, although *convey* and *transport* have similar meanings, you wouldn't ask, "Did I transport what I meant here?"

Synonym Finders

A **synonym finder** is a tool that's often in word-processing software. It enables you to display synonyms for a highlighted word—but does not tell you as much as a thesaurus does.

Glossaries

A **glossary** is a list of specialized terms and their definitions. Many books, especially textbooks and nonfiction books, contain glossaries—usually at the back of the book. Consider using a glossary when you can't find context clues for a key word or you are studying for a quiz or an exam.

Exploring Shades of Meaning

"Use the right word, not its second cousin," said the famous American writer Mark Twain. That's good advice. However, to be able to recognize the right word, you must be able to distinguish even slight differences between words—that is, you need to consider their shades of meaning.

Denotation and Connotation

A **denotation** is the literal meaning of a word—the definition you can find in the dictionary. A **connotation** is an attitude or feeling linked with the word. Connotations can have a big impact on the meaning a word conveys.

For example, *fragrant* and *reeking* share the meaning "producing a smell," but would you want to wear a cologne that was advertised as "reeking"? Think about it.

Enjoy the fragrant aroma of this fresh scent!

Enjoy the reeking smell of this pungent cologne!

That choice was probably fairly easy—but why? *Fragrant* has positive connotations, while *reeking* has negative ones. Many words have only positive or negative connotations.

Sometimes, though, making a decision about which product to wear—or which word to use—involves distinguishing between finer shades of meaning. When that's the case, connotations are extremely important.

For example, cover up the connotations of *brusque* and *crusty* below. From their denotations alone, can you say which you'd rather be labeled? Now look at their connotations. Those connotations make a difference, don't they?

brusque	crusty
Denotation Behaving or speaking in a way that's quick, to the point, or gruff	**Denotation** Behaving or speaking in a way that seems rough or gruff
Connotation An abrupt, blunt, discourteous, rude, or gruff manner	**Connotation** A manner that seems rough or gruff but that may actually be a way of covering up a soft heart or sentimental feelings

Always consider the connotations of words. Whether you're looking at a string of synonyms for a particular word or a list of antonyms to find the word's opposite, don't assume each word will work equally well. *Intentional, deliberate, careful,* and *willful* are all antonyms of *impulsive,* but each has different connotations.

> **Her actions weren't impulsive at all.**
> **They were _deliberate_.**

PRACTICE > **Distinguishing Shades of Meaning**

Use five of the ten pairs of synonyms below to write sentences that demonstrate how their connotations differ. You may want to refer to a dictionary for help.

1. sleep, stupor
2. speechless, silent
3. admiration, amazement
4. march, stride
5. fussy, conscientious
6. starving, hungry
7. commanding, bossy
8. reckless, adventurous
9. comfort, pamper
10. quarrel, feud

VOCABULARY

Student Help Desk

Developing Your Vocabulary at a Glance

1 **Look for context clues.**

Marissa was **unpretentious.** For example, she never bragged about being able to speak three languages.

2 **Analyze the familiar parts of a word.**

unpretentious

prefix: un- = not

suffix: -ious = full of

3 **Consider the meanings of related words.**

pretend	**pretender**
pretense	**pretentious**

4 **Use a dictionary.**

un·pre·ten·tious (ŭn'prĭ-těn'shəs) *adj.* Not demanding recognition; not exaggerating one's own worth or importance

Piece Together Word Meanings

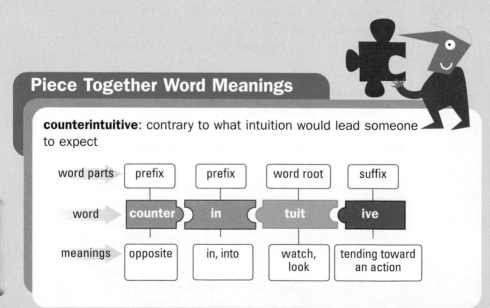

counterintuitive: contrary to what intuition would lead someone to expect

word parts	prefix	prefix	word root	suffix
word	**counter**	**in**	**tuit**	**ive**
meanings	opposite	in, into	watch, look	tending toward an action

Watch for Suffix Signals

	Suffix	Meaning	Examples
Noun suffixes	-er, -ist, -or	doer, performer	writer, typist, innovator
	-ation, -ment	action, process	consideration, wonderment
	-ism	process, theory	escapism
	-ity,-ness, -ship, -tude	condition, quality, state	tranquillity, foolishness, hardship, longitude
Verb suffixes	-ate	to become or produce	validate
	-en	to become, to cause to have	frighten
	-ize	to cause to be, to become	realize
Adjective suffixes	-able, -ible	able, inclined to, worthy of	washable, sensible
	-ate	having, resembling	collegiate
Adverb suffix	-ly	in the manner of, like	drearily, softly

The Bottom Line

Checklist for Developing Your Vocabulary

Have I . . .

_____ looked at the context of the word to find clues to its meaning?

_____ analyzed the parts of the word?

_____ tried to think of other words in the same family?

_____ looked up the word in a dictionary or glossary?

_____ used a thesaurus or synonym finder to find synonyms of the word?

_____ considered the word's denotations and connotations?

600

Student Resources

Exercise Bank

Boost your grammar fitness! Use the circled arrows ➡ to find the answers to the Self-Check items. In addition, you can complete exercises in this section to get extra practice in a skill you've just learned.

① The Sentence and Its Parts

1. Complete Subjects and Predicates (links to exercise on p. 7)

➡ **1.** complete subject (CS): *Species of plants and animals;* complete predicate (CP): *are disappearing near cities*
2. CS: *Urban sprawl;* CP: *harms their habitats*

On a sheet of paper, label one column "Complete Subjects" and another "Complete Predicates." For each sentence write the complete subject and complete predicate in the proper columns.

1. The goal of settlement houses is the improvement of neighborhoods.
2. Their services include recreational and educational activities.
3. Various types of counseling are also offered at settlement houses.
4. The first settlement house was founded in London in 1884.
5. Neighborhood Guild opened in New York two years later.
6. Hull House was one of the most famous settlement houses.
7. Jane Addams helped found this Chicago institution in 1889.
8. People of many different nationalities sought help at Hull House.
9. Addams worked tirelessly for social reform.
10. Her efforts won her the Nobel Peace Prize in 1931.

2. Simple Subjects (links to exercise A, p. 9)

➡ **1.** Industrial Revolution   **2.** industries

Write the simple subject of each sentence.

1. Early humans wandered from place to place.
2. Farming families began settling in villages about 11,000 years ago.
3. The first cities developed several thousand years later.
4. Technological advances allowed cities to grow.
5. Ancient Rome had nearly a million residents at its height.
6. Most cities were fairly small during the Middle Ages.
7. Modern industry created dramatic changes in urban life.
8. Large factories needed many workers.

9. The populations of older cities increased rapidly.
10. Other industrial cities sprang up in open areas.

3. Simple Predicates, or Verbs (links to exercise A, p. 11)

➡ **1.** is   **2.** hold

Write the simple predicate, or verb, of each sentence.

1. The Aztecs founded the city of Tenochtitlán in the 1300s.
2. This site became Mexico City after the Spanish conquest.
3. Mexico City is the capital of Mexico.
4. The city has a population of over 9 million.
5. Another 7 million people live in the metropolitan area.
6. Mexico City lies on an ancient lake bed.
7. Residents enjoy a mild climate.
8. The high altitude creates breathing problems for some people.
9. Splendid public buildings grace the center of Mexico City.
10. The city dominates Mexico's political, cultural, and economic activities.

4. Verb Phrases (links to exercise on p. 13)

➡ **1.** have allowed   **2.** can cause

Write the verb phrase found in each sentence below.

1. The United States has been called a "throwaway society."
2. The average American is throwing out over three pounds of waste per day.
3. City dwellers may be even more wasteful.
4. For example, New Yorkers are discarding nearly seven pounds per person.
5. Landfills have been filling up throughout the country.
6. New locations for landfills are becoming hard to find.
7. Some cities are burning their excess waste.
8. However, incinerators can cause air pollution.
9. Recycling might be the best solution.
10. Americans also should reduce their level of waste production.

5. Compound Sentence Parts (links to exercise A, p. 15)

➡ **1.** compound subject: *Juneau, cities*
   5. compound verb: *survived, profited*

Write and identify the compound subject (CS) or compound verb (CV) in each sentence.

1. Cities and towns may take years to recover from a natural disaster.
2. Powerful hurricanes have killed and destroyed on a vast scale.
3. High winds and heavy rains make these storms dangerous.
4. Weather balloons, radar, and satellites help meteorologists track hurricanes.
5. Seismologists study and measure earthquakes.
6. Sections of Earth's crust shift and break during these events.
7. The shaking of the ground can damage or topple buildings.
8. Architects and engineers can create earthquake-resistant structures.
9. Well-designed homes, schools, and office buildings may save many lives.
10. However, no precautions or safety measures can eliminate the danger of earthquakes.

6. Kinds of Sentences (links to exercise A, p. 17)

→ **1.** INT   **2.** D

Identify each of the following sentences as declarative (D), interrogative (INT), exclamatory (E), or imperative (IMP).

1. How much time do you spend in your local mall?
2. Shopping malls have become the social centers of many cities and towns.
3. Consider the different forms of entertainment in malls.
4. Does your local mall have movie theaters and game arcades?
5. Many malls also offer live entertainment, such as concerts.
6. Of course, shopping is the main activity in malls.
7. One mall in Canada has over 800 stores!
8. Imagine how long it would take to visit all of them.
9. There is even a mall just for kids, in Michigan.
10. A restaurant in the food court serves 50 types of peanut butter and jelly sandwiches!

7. Subjects in Unusual Order (links to exercise A, p. 20)

→ **1.** subject: *you;* verb phrase: *Have heard*
   2. subject: *amusement park;* verb: *lies*

Make two columns on a separate sheet of paper, and write the simple subject and verb (or verb phrase) of each sentence in the appropriately labeled column.

1. Would you like a trip to the past?
2. Visit the historic town of Williamsburg, Virginia.
3. Between the James and York rivers lies this popular tourist attraction.
4. Here is a brief description.
5. Within the town are over 80 homes and other buildings from the 1700s.
6. There are also more than 400 reconstructed buildings.
7. Along the streets stroll actors in colonial costumes.
8. Inside some buildings are demonstrations of crafts.
9. Are you planning a trip to Williamsburg?
10. Read a brochure or travel book for more information.

8. Complements: Subject Complements (links to exercise A, p. 22)

➜ **1.** Windy City—PN **4.** high—PA

Write the subject complement found in each sentence, and identify it as a predicate noun (PN) or predicate adjective (PA).

1. New Orleans is a city in Louisiana.
2. It was the birthplace of jazz.
3. Preservation Hall is famous for its jazz concerts.
4. The restaurants of New Orleans are another attraction.
5. The Cajun dishes taste spicy.
6. The city seems especially exciting during the annual Mardi Gras festival.
7. The architecture of New Orleans is a blend of old and new.
8. The historic French Quarter neighborhood is picturesque.
9. New Orleans is a major seaport.
10. The city is also a center for business and industry.

9. Complements: Objects of Verbs (links to exercise on p. 24)

➜ **1.** cities, IO; connection, DO   **2.** system, DO

Write the objects in these sentences, identifying each as a direct object (DO) or an indirect object (IO).

1. Most city dwellers cherish their urban parks.
2. These open spaces add variety to a city.
3. They give residents opportunities for recreation.
4. Chicago's Lincoln Park hugs the shore of Lake Michigan.
5. The park's free zoo teaches children lessons about nature.
6. Fairmount Park in Philadelphia provides tours of its seven colonial mansions.

7. Many filmmakers have shot scenes in Central Park.
8. The park offers visitors splendid views of New York City.
9. San Francisco's Golden Gate Park includes a Japanese teahouse.
10. The staff serves customers tea in the traditional Japanese way.

10. Fragments and Run-Ons (links to exercise A, p. 27)

➔ **1.** RO   **2.** F

Identify the following items as fragments (F), run-ons (RO), or complete sentences (CS).

1. Beijing is home to one of three great Chinese cooking styles, this style is called Beijing or Mandarin cuisine.
2. The food generally mild.
3. Wheat an important ingredient in many recipes.
4. Noodle dishes popular in Beijing cuisine.
5. Stuffed buns and filled dumplings are served as snacks or meals.
6. Beijing duck a famous dish.
7. This delicious meal takes a long time to prepare, it is served in three separate courses.
8. Chefs in Shanghai base their meals on rice rather than wheat.
9. Many Shanghai dishes feature seafood, the city is close to the sea.
10. Shanghai recipes often have interesting names, such as hairy crab and lion's head casserole.

2 Nouns

1. Kinds of Nouns (links to exercise A, p. 38)

➔ **1.** astronauts, food, tubes: common
2. Astronauts, tray, forks, spoons: common; Space Shuttle Program: proper

List the nouns found in each sentence, and identify them as common or proper. Then write three collective nouns from your list.

1. The Soviet Union launched the first satellite into orbit in 1957.
2. Yuri Gagarin of the Soviet Union became the first person to orbit Earth four years later.
3. President John F. Kennedy then challenged the United States to put an astronaut on the moon.
4. Teams of scientists worked to develop a suitable spacecraft.
5. The project to land astronauts on the moon was named *Apollo*.
6. American astronauts finally reached the moon in July 1969.

7. Neil Armstrong was the first person to stand on the moon.
8. As he stepped onto the surface, Armstrong said, "That's one small step for man, one giant leap for mankind."
9. Many Americans expressed pride in this historic achievement.
10. Soviet and American crews worked closely together on some later missions.

2. Singular and Plural Nouns (links to exercise A, p. 40)

➜ **1.** quantities   **2.** amounts

Rewrite the nouns in parentheses in their plural forms.

1. Sally Ride made (headline) in 1983 when she became the first American woman in space.
2. Yet a Russian woman had beaten her there by two (decade).
3. Valentina Vladimirovna Tereshkova's life was similar to the (life) of other ordinary Soviet citizens.
4. As a teenager, she worked in (factory) that produced tires and textiles.
5. However, at night she took (class) to continue her education.
6. She began making parachute (jump) in her spare time.
7. She showed (flash) of courage and strength while pursuing her goal of becoming a cosmonaut.
8. Soviet officals finally admitted her and four other (woman) into the training program.
9. She orbited Earth for nearly three (day) during her historic mission in 1963.
10. Russians regarded her as one of the country's (hero) when she returned home safely.

3. Possessive Nouns (links to exercise A, p. 43)

➜ **1.** *Astronomy's,* singular   **2.** *Babylonians',* plural

Write the possessive form of each noun in parentheses. Then label each possessive noun *singular* or *plural.*

1. Maria Mitchell was (America) first professional woman astronomer.
2. She inherited her (parents) passion for education.
3. As a teenager she began participating in her (father) astronomical studies.
4. One day she looked through his telescope and noticed a (star) unusual position.
5. (Mitchell) observations convinced her that the star was really a comet.

6. She received a gold medal from (Denmark) king in 1848 for her discovery.
7. She was the first female member of the American Academy of Arts and Sciences, one of the (country) oldest educational societies.
8. Vassar College eventually hired her as a professor and director of the (school) observatory.
9. Her research at the observatory included the study of (planets) surfaces.
10. Mitchell also became an important spokesperson for the advancement of (women) rights.

4. Compound Nouns (links to exercise A, p. 45)

➡ 1. *mountaintop;* singular
   2. *headaches,* plural; *sea level,* singular

Write each compound noun in these sentences, and label it *singular* or *plural.*

1. NASA launched a spacecraft to increase our understanding of Mars.
2. It landed with the aid of parachutes, rockets, and airbags.
3. Then it bounced like a basketball for two and a half minutes.
4. It finally came to a successful touchdown.
5. A small vehicle rolled out of a doorway onto the Martian surface.
6. The vehicle examined rocks and collected data according to a planned timetable for exploration.
7. Scientists at NASA headquarters gave silly names like Barnacle Bill and Flat Top to the rocks that were found.
8. Anchorpersons told television viewers about these discoveries on evening newscasts.
9. NASA received praise for the mission in many newspapers.
10. My great-grandmother finds space exploration fascinating.

5. Nouns as Subjects and Complements (links to exercise on p. 47)

➡ 1. subject; complement   2. subject

Identify each underlined noun as a subject or complement.

1. The <u>Hubble Space Telescope</u> (HST) is the first <u>telescope</u> based in space.
2. It avoids the <u>distortions</u> of Earth's atmosphere by orbiting the planet.
3. <u>NASA</u> launched <u>HST</u> into orbit in 1990.

4. <u>Astronomers</u> soon discovered a <u>flaw</u> in the telescope's mirror.

5. The <u>flaw</u> prevented the <u>telescope</u> from focusing properly.

6. <u>NASA</u> sent <u>HST</u> a <u>repair crew</u> in 1993.

7. The <u>crew</u> captured <u>HST</u> as it orbited the earth.

8. They installed corrective <u>mirrors</u> on the telescope.

9. <u>HST</u> then began to send <u>astronomers</u> astonishingly clear <u>images</u>.

10. <u>HST</u> is now a great <u>success</u> instead of a failure.

6. Nouns in Phrases (links to exercise on p. 49)

➡ **1.** appositive **2.** appositive

Identify each underlined noun as an object of a preposition or as an appositive.

1. Some of the most important space missions were accomplished without <u>astronauts</u>.

2. They were carried out by space probes, unmanned <u>spacecraft</u> that transmit information.

3. Space probes can be sent into <u>areas</u> too dangerous for humans.

4. They have provided much of our information about p<u>lanets</u>.

5. Venus and Mars, the <u>planets</u> nearest Earth, are frequent targets of space probes.

6. The probe *Mariner 2* reached Venus in 1962.

7. *Mariner 4*, the first <u>probe</u> to explore Mars, sent back important pictures of the planet.

8. *Magellan* spent four years taking photographs as it orbited the planet <u>Venus</u>.

9. It completed its mission by plunging into Venus's <u>atmosphere</u>.

10. *Magellan* and the other probes often performed beyond <u>expectations</u>.

③ Pronouns

1. What Is a Pronoun? (links to exercise A, p. 59)

➡ **1.** her **2.** She, they

List the personal pronoun(s) in each sentence.

1. Have you ever gone on a backpacking trip?

2. Backpackers need to consider safety aspects when planning their trips.

3. They need to know what to do in an emergency.

4. One experienced backpacker explained his most important rule: to avoid dangerous situations.

5. Whenever I go backpacking, I always take the latest weather report with me.
6. Careful backpackers never ignore any threatening weather heading toward them.
7. Electrical storms, snowstorms, or flash floods can cause you serious problems.
8. We need to know how to build sturdy temporary shelters in case our trip is interrupted by dangerous weather.
9. In my opinion, surviving in snow is the greatest weather challenge a backpacker can face.
10. Safe backpacking is one of the most exciting activities in my life, and it could also be a big part of yours.

2. Subject Pronouns (links to exercise on p. 62)

➡ **1.** I   **3.** They

Write the correct form of the pronoun to complete each sentence. Choose from the words given in parentheses.

1. My friends and (I, me) enjoy reading novels about young people who survive dangerous situations.
2. (We, Us) especially enjoyed *Hatchet* by Gary Paulsen.
3. In the novel, Brian Robeson's small plane crashes, and (he, him) is forced to survive by himself in the Canadian wilderness.
4. The pilot of Brian's plane dies, and the only survivor is (he, him).
5. For more than 50 days, (he, him) must use his skills to find food, build shelter, and keep safe.
6. Another terrific novel about survival is *Julie of the Wolves* by Jean Craighead George; (she, her) has written many popular books.
7. Miyax, also called Julie, is an Inuit, or Eskimo, girl; (she, her) struggles to survive a cross-country journey through the harsh Alaskan forests.
8. The only human for many miles around is (she, her).
9. Miyax befriends a pack of wolves, and (they, them) become like brothers to her.
10. It is (they, them) who help Miyax survive her ordeal in the Arctic wilderness.

3. Object Pronouns (links to exercise on p. 64)

➡ **1.** *me,* object   **3.** *him,* object

Write the correct pronoun to complete each sentence. Label each pronoun subject (S) or object (O).

1. About 50,000 noticeable earthquakes occur each year somewhere on earth, but only about 100 of (they, them) are strong enough to cause serious damage.
2. On January 17, 1995, residents of the Kobe-Osaka region of Japan awoke when the ground shook beneath (they, them).
3. The earthquake claimed about 6,000 lives and damaged thousands of buildings; at least 100,000 of (them, they) were destroyed.
4. The extent of the damage shocked (we, us) and other people around the world.
5. Kobe is the world's sixth-busiest port, serving many of Japan's ships. (They, Them) came almost to a halt following the quake.
6. To my friends and (I, me), the response of the Japanese people to the disaster was amazing.
7. In the six months following the Kobe earthquake, the Japanese people built 40,000 temporary houses; more than 300,000 homeless people used (they, them) for shelter.
8. Today, the people of Kobe have rebuilt much of their city, but the memory of that terrible morning will be with (they, them) forever.
9. When the next major earthquake strikes, will (we, us) be prepared?
10. What important lessons can the Kobe earthquake, and the tremendous relief efforts of the Japanese people, teach (we, us) about surviving disasters?

4. Possessive Pronouns (links to exercise A, p. 67)

➔ **2.** their   **3.** its

Write the correct pronoun or contraction for each sentence.

1. Caves are one fascinating element of this natural world of (ours, our's).
2. Caves can be formed by the sea, lava, glaciers, or the wearing away of underground rock; depending on (their, they're) origins, caves have different characteristics.
3. Is exploring a cave (you're, your) idea of fun?
4. The exploration of caves has (it's, its) own name—(it's, its) called spelunking.
5. If (you're, your) thinking of becoming a spelunker, it's important to learn the proper safety techniques.
6. (It's, Its) not dangerous to explore a cave if you follow the safety rules and use good judgment.
7. If people don't pay attention in a cave, (their, they're) more likely to fall down or get lost.

8. Rescuing an injured person from a cave can be quite difficult, especially if (its, it's) passageways are narrow and crooked.

9. You can sometimes find (you're, your) way out of a cave by following underground water downstream to the mouth of the cave.

10. Many caves have strong echoes; any shout you hear could be (your's, yours)!

5. Reflexive and Intensive Pronouns (links to exercise on p. 69)

➡ **1.** himself, (R)   **3.** herself, (I)

Write the reflexive or intensive pronoun in each sentence. Then identify it as reflexive (R) or intensive (I).

1. Have you ever asked yourself how you might deal with a disability?

2. Basketball player Mahmoud Abdul-Rauf has found the strength within himself to succeed, in spite of a disorder.

3. He suffers from Tourette's syndrome, a nerve disease that causes him to twitch and shout in spite of himself.

4. A star with the NBA's Denver Nuggets in the mid-1990s, Abdul-Rauf inspired many people who have struggled themselves with disabilities.

5. People with this condition sometimes isolate themselves from others because the disorder causes such embarrassment.

6. Abdul-Rauf believes that the disorder itself has made him into a better person and athlete.

7. It has caused him to push himself and practice harder.

8. He dedicated himself to overcoming the condition and becoming the best basketball player he could be.

9. The player's faith and dedication are qualities we ourselves can admire and try to imitate.

10. I myself have seen Abdul-Rauf play many times on television.

6. Interrogatives and Demonstratives (links to exercise A, p. 72)

➡ **3.** That   **4.** whom

For each sentence, choose the correct pronoun from the words in parentheses.

1. (This, That) is the story of how I survived the fishing trip during my week at summer camp.

2. (Whose, Who's) bright idea was it to collect earthworms for the fishing trip?

3. Of course, you need bait to go fishing, but (who, what) is the best bait?

4. Our counselor said red wigglers and night crawlers were good earthworms to use for (this, these).

5. Of course, there are always (those, these) who hate to handle worms.

6. (Who, Whom) was responsible for holding the flashlight while I tried to grab the red wigglers with my bare hands?

7. (This, That) was about the worst job I've ever had— digging in the dirt and trying to hold the squirming mess of worms.

8. (Who, Which) was the longest worm we caught? It must have been six inches long.

9. After all my trouble, guess (whom, who) didn't catch a single fish the next day?

10. (What, Which) do you mean, I didn't try hard enough?

7. Pronoun-Antecedent Agreement (links to exercise A, p. 75)

➜ **1.** their (cultures)　　**3.** She (Rose Robinson)

Write the pronouns in these sentences, along with their antecedents.

1. Over the years, the people of the Sea Islands of Georgia and South Carolina have kept alive their ancestral culture and language.

2. Enslaved Africans, brought to the islands during colonial times, mixed their West African languages with English.

3. Before the Civil War, the Sea Islands were known for their rice and cotton plantations.

4. After the war, many of them were given to freed slaves.

5. The culture that developed on the islands is known as Gullah. It has its roots in the cultures of West Africa.

6. The Gullah language is still a mixture, containing almost 6,000 African words; most of them are personal names.

7. You probably have several Gullah words in your own vocabulary.

8. The words *gumbo, voodoo, goober,* and *jukebox* come from Gullah. They are familiar, aren't they?

9. Students of languages are fascinated when they encounter a mixed language like Gullah.

10. When people visit the Sea Islands, they see evidence of a culture's survival and development over centuries.

8. Indefinite-Pronoun Agreement (links to exercise A, p. 78)

➡ **1.** he or she   **3.** them

Write the pronoun that agrees with the indefinite-pronoun antecedent.

1. Has anyone ever read about prehistoric cave paintings in (their, his or her) trips to the library?
2. No one who has ever seen prehistoric cave paintings will forget the powerful impression they make on (them, him or her).
3. Many have written about (his, their) impressions of prehistoric paintings of horses, deer, bears, bison, and aurochs, an ancient breed of cattle.
4. One of the horses in a cave in Chauvet, France, tosses (their, its) mane proudly while others watch.
5. Several are so skillfully painted that it looks as if (it, they) could stampede right off the cave walls!
6. Some of the animals are shown making (its, their) way across the cave walls in large herds.
7. Another raises (its, their) head to challenge a rival in battle.
8. All of the prehistoric artists who left (his, their) drawings on the cave walls are unknown.
9. None of the artists were able to sign (his or her, their) names to the paintings because written language had not yet been developed.
10. However, each has left (his or her, their) mark through the beauty and power of the paintings that have survived for more than 30,000 years.

9. Pronoun Problems (links to exercise A, p. 80)

➡ **1.** we

Choose the better noun or pronoun from the words in parentheses.

1. There is a special animal that (we, us) Americans have always admired as a symbol of the West and its wide-open spaces.
2. The American bison, or buffalo, gives (we, us) animal lovers a thrill because of its great size, majesty, and interesting habits.
3. Last year, a scientist talked to (we, us) students about the near extinction and comeback of the bison herds on the Great Plains.
4. During the last century, millions of American bison roamed the Great Plains. (They, The Great Plains) stretched from the Mississippi River to the Rocky Mountains.
5. Native Americans of the Great Plains and other areas of the West depended on the bison herds for food, clothing, and shelter. (They, the Native Americans) even used the bison's bones to make tools.

6. There may have been 60 million bison spread across the region before the European settlers came to the West. (They, The bison) lived together in gigantic herds.

7. But European hunters slaughtered (them, the bison), often for sport and target practice.

8. By 1900, animal conservationists were alarmed that fewer than a thousand bison were left in North America. With the help of President Theodore Roosevelt, they created successful programs to ensure (their, the bison's) survival.

9. If anyone enjoys learning about interesting animals and their struggle for survival, it's (we, us) members of the school environmental club.

10. The bison makes (we, us) lovers of the old West think about times past.

10. More Pronoun Problems (links to exercise A, p. 82)

→ **1.** me   **2.** him

For each sentence, write the correct pronoun from the choice given in parentheses.

1. When our teacher asked Jason and (I, me) to do a presentation on an explorer, we chose the Frenchwoman Alexandra David-Néel.

2. David-Néel, the daughter of French parents, made (her, their) way into the forbidden Tibetan city of Lhasa, becoming the first Western woman to do so.

3. Jason and (I, me) read about David-Néel's great interest in Buddhism, the religion of Tibet and other countries in Asia.

4. David-Néel, who spent much time away from home, still enjoyed a strong and lasting relationship with (she, her) husband.

5. In 1912, David-Néel met the Dalai Lama, leader of the world's Buddhists; she and (he, him) became friends.

6. While living and studying in a Buddhist monastery in the Himalayan kingdom of Sikkim, she met a boy named Aphur Yongden, who became (her, his) adopted son.

7. (He, Him) and David-Néel explored Tibet and its capital, Lhasa, which was forbidden to Westerners.

8. One winter, freezing temperatures forced Aphur and (she, her) to seek refuge in a mountain cave, where they had a dinner of shoe-leather soup!

9. Disguised as a Tibetan peasant, (she, her) and Aphur spent two months exploring the secret city.

10. The current Dalai Lama, the 14th leader to hold the title, and many of (his, their) followers live in India, far away from the city of Lhasa.

4 Verbs

1. What Is a Verb? (links to exercise A, p. 94)

➡ **1.** has ridden   **3.** is

Write the verb or verb phrase found in each of the following sentences. Then write *A* if it is an action verb or *L* if it is a linking verb.

1. People have slid down icy hillsides for thousands of years.
2. Since 1914, one form of sliding down hills has been a championship sport.
3. The sport's name is luge.
4. To some people, luge appears similar to bobsledding.
5. Both sports occur on a rounded, icy track built on the side of a hill.
6. However, many important differences separate the two sports.
7. In luge, the sled is a small platform with steel runners.
8. In some ways, luge seems similar to riding down an icy hill on a cafeteria tray!
9. The luge racer lies faceup on the luge, with feet forward.
10. In competitions such as the Winter Olympics, top speeds can approach 90 miles an hour!

2. Action Verbs and Objects (links to exercise A, p. 97)

➡ **1.** feat, DO   **3.** himself, IO; vehicle, DO

The following sentences contain 7 direct objects and 4 indirect objects. For each sentence, write and label each direct object (DO) and each indirect object (IO). Then, write *T* if the verb is transitive or *I* if it is intransitive.

1. One of the most famous automobile races in the world occurs around Memorial Day each year.
2. Since 1911, the Indianapolis 500 has given spectators thrills.
3. The 33 fastest cars and drivers compete in the race each year.
4. Hundreds of thousands of fans cheer the drivers during the race.
5. The race begins with the announcement for drivers to start their engines.
6. Television shows people around the world the spectacular auto race.
7. Could you send me a list of the drivers in this year's race?
8. Indy cars use special tires for better control.
9. A black-and-white checkered flag signals the end of the race.
10. Race officials traditionally give the winner of the race a bottle of milk.

3. Linking Verbs and Predicate Words (links to exercise on p. 99)

➡ **1.** was, mild (PA) **3.** felt, calm (PA)

Each sentence in the following paragraph contains a linking verb. Write the linking verb and the subject complement. Then write *PN* if the subject complement is a predicate noun. Write *PA* if the subject complement is a predicate adjective.

For many people, the Tournament of Roses Parade is the highlight of New Year's Day. This parade first became popular in the 1890s. Parade watchers in Pasadena, California, and TV viewers around the world grow excited as the parade approaches. The more than 60 gorgeous floats are probably the parade's biggest attraction. Their roses, camellias, carnations, and other flowers smell divine. The music of the numerous marching bands sounds cheerful. The beautifully decorated horses and riders look very elegant. Riding on a float at the end of the parade, the Rose Queen is often a college student from the Los Angeles area. The volunteers who work hard every year to create the parade must feel extremely proud. Memories of the beautiful floats remain strong for years.

4. Principal Parts of Verbs (links to exercise on p. 101)

➡ **1.** past   **2.** present

Identify each underlined principal part as the present, the present participle, the past, or the past participle.

1. During the 1950s and 1960s, African Americans <u>struggled</u> for equal rights.
2. In many Southern states, waiting rooms and restaurants in bus stations <u>segregated</u> African Americans.
3. In 1961, 70,000 "Freedom Riders" of all races <u>challenged</u> segregation in these bus stations and on buses.
4. By traveling throughout the South on buses and risking arrest, the Freedom Riders <u>focused</u> attention on segregation and injustice.
5. The bravery of the Freedom Riders has <u>inspired</u> many Americans.
6. In September 1961, a government commission <u>ruled</u> that all interstate buses and stations must be integrated.
7. Thanks to young people like the Freedom Riders, many Americans are <u>benefiting</u> from the civil rights campaigns of the 1960s.
8. Since the successful Freedom Rides of 1961, American minorities have <u>gained</u> many rights, as well as new responsibilities.
9. Today, all Americans <u>enjoy</u> equal rights under the law.
10. However, the campaign to make equal rights a reality for all Americans is <u>continuing</u>.

5. Irregular Verbs (links to exercise on p. 104)

➜ **1.** won　　**2.** gave

Write the correct form of the verb in parentheses.

1. Peter Cooper (builded, built) the first American railroad locomotive.
2. Cooper (began, beginned) his career as a builder and designer of horse-drawn carriages.
3. But Cooper soon (feeled, felt) that a railroad could compete with the newly opened Erie Canal and carry freight to the growing western states.
4. *Tom Thumb* was the name Cooper (gave, give) to the small but powerful locomotive he built.
5. In 1830, *Tom Thumb* (taked, took) 40 passengers on a historic ride through the hilly Maryland countryside at the breathtaking speed of 10 miles an hour.
6. Several other inventions of Cooper's have also (did, done) much to shape modern life.
7. For example, most Americans have (make, made) use of a washing machine to do laundry.
8. The New York City educational institution he founded, Cooper Union, has probably (become, became) the inventor's best-known gift to the nation.
9. Many people have (gone, went) to free classes in art and science at Cooper Union.
10. Late in his life, Peter Cooper (write, wrote), "The object of life is to do good."

6. Simple Tenses (links to exercise A, p. 107)

➜ **1.** past　　　　**2.** present

Identify the tense of each underlined verb as present, past, future, present progressive, past progressive, or future progressive.

1. Nellie Bly <u>became</u> one of the most famous reporters in American newspaper history.
2. In 1889, many people <u>were reading</u> Jules Verne's popular novel, *Around the World in Eighty Days.*
3. The novel's main character, Phileas Fogg, <u>journeys</u> around the world in exactly 80 days.
4. Nellie Bly's newspaper, the *New York World,* <u>sent</u> its star reporter on a round-the-world journey just like Phileas Fogg's.
5. Newspaper readers <u>were wondering</u> breathlessly if Bly would match Fogg's time.

6. "Nellie <u>will go</u> around the world in 80 days!" claimed her enthusiastic supporters.
7. "No," answered others. "She <u>is attempting</u> a feat that is impossible."
8. In early 1890, readers cried, "Nellie <u>will be arriving</u> in New York soon!"
9. The world-famous traveler <u>finished</u> her journey in 72 days, 6 hours, more than a week faster than Phileas Fogg.
10. Perhaps you <u>are wondering</u> how long such a journey would take today.

7. Perfect Tenses (links to exercise A, p. 110)

→ 1. *had compared,* past perfect
2. *will have experienced,* future perfect

Write each verb in the following paragraphs. Identify the two examples each of the present perfect, past perfect, and future perfect tenses.

The sport of rodeo has entertained people for more than a hundred years. Because riding and roping have always been necessary skills for cowboys on the Western ranges, cowboys had developed skills demanded in rodeo events today.

During the early 20th century, the adventurous cowboy Bill Pickett had wrestled a steer to the ground by biting its lip! From this feat developed the rodeo event called steer wrestling. The five standard events in a modern rodeo are calf roping, bull riding, steer wrestling, saddle bronc riding, and bareback bronc riding. A cowboy or cowgirl who begins to practice for any rodeo event will have accepted a major challenge.

Even today's audiences, notorious for their short attention spans, enjoy the entertainment a rodeo provides. The bronc riding events may be the most spectacular. A rider must remain on a bucking horse for eight to ten seconds, holding on with only one hand. Anyone staying on the bronco this long will have accomplished quite a feat!

8. Using Verb Tenses (links to exercise A, p. 114)

→ 1. patrol   2. have ridden

For each sentence, write the correct verb form in parentheses. Then identify the form as present, past, or future and as simple, perfect, or progressive.

1. Thousands of people (have dreamed, will be dreaming) of traveling into space and exploring our solar system.
2. Maybe you too (long, had longed) to take a ride aboard the space shuttle or another spacecraft when you are older.
3. By the time Sally Ride entered Stanford University, she (will give, had given) up her goal of playing professional tennis.
4. She (earned, earn) a Ph.D. in physics in 1978.
5. Before 1978, the National Aeronautics and Space Administration, known as NASA, (is not considering, was not considering) women as mission specialists.
6. "Sally Ride (Will Be, Has Been) America's First Female in Space" read the newspaper headlines in 1983 before she was sent into space.
7. Sally Ride flew two missions on the space shuttle after she (had qualified, will have qualified) as America's first woman astronaut.
8. Some scientists predict that people (took, will be taking) space flights often in the coming centuries.
9. Perhaps many women (fly, will have flown) into space by the middle of the 21st century.
10. (Are you thinking, Will you think) you'd like to follow in Sally Ride's footsteps?

9. Troublesome Verb Pairs (links to exercise A, p. 117)

➜ **1.** Let   **2.** sits

Choose the correct verb in parentheses for each of the following sentences.

1. Have you ever had the chance to (set, sit) on a camel's hump?
2. Camels used as transportation in the Arabian Desert can often be seen (lying, laying) in the shade.
3. Years ago, large camel caravans (left, let) trading cities loaded with goods to cross the desert.
4. A driver riding on a camel might (raise, rise) more than ten feet above the ground.
5. An Arabian camel, which has one hump, can (raise, rise) its speed to nearly ten miles an hour.
6. (Leave, Let) me tell you about the day we went to the zoo to see the new camel exhibit.
7. I had (lain, laid) my book about camels next to my bed so I'd be sure to remember to take it with me.
8. At the zoo, I (sat, set) the book on the railing while we watched the camels walk around.

9. One camel (rose, raised) its head to look at my book.
10. Then it leaned over the railing and took a bite out of my book, (letting, leaving) me with half a camel book!

5 Adjectives and Adverbs

1. What Is an Adjective? (links to exercise on p. 128)

→ 1. terrific, power
2. circular, winds; strong, tornadoes; more, damage; other, storms; similar, size

Write each adjective in these sentences, along with the noun or pronoun it modifies. Do not include articles.

1. In 1900, a severe hurricane in Galveston, Texas, caused many deaths.
2. When the ferocious storm hit, it was a complete surprise.
3. The average Galvestonian expected a regular hurricane with minor flooding and little damage.
4. But Galveston lay on a small island along the southern shore of Texas.
5. The high point in the city was only nine feet above the sea.
6. The constant winds of the unusual hurricane pushed the heavy water into mountainous waves.
7. This frightening phenomenon is known as a storm surge.
8. Waves of 20 feet and shrieking winds destroyed the unfortunate city.
9. About 6,000 people died.
10. Galvestonians rebuilt the city behind tall walls to protect it from the Gulf of Mexico.

2. Predicate Adjectives (links to exercise A, p. 130)

→ 1. brave, Anna Edson Taylor   2. certain, She

Write each predicate adjective in these sentences, along with the noun or pronoun it modifies.

1. Joshua Norton, a merchant who moved to San Francisco during the gold rush, was rich.
2. He became indispensable to companies and individuals.
3. Norton grew so successful that people referred to him as an empire builder.
4. The businessman was friendly, and people began calling him the Emperor.

5. Norton dismissed this, insisting that the country's democracy remained strong.
6. Then Norton lost his money and became poor.
7. He appeared insane, declaring himself emperor and dressing in an officer's uniform.
8. Instead of mocking him, the kind residents of San Francisco were happy to honor him.
9. They felt glad to see Norton with his two dogs, Bummer and Lazarus.
10. When Norton died, the *San Francisco Chronicle* announced, "The king is dead."

3. Other Words Used as Adjectives (links to exercise A, p. 133)

➡ **1.** your, fingerprints; their, marks   **2.** skin, ridges; their, surface

Write each noun or pronoun that is used as an adjective, followed by the noun or pronoun that it modifies.

1. DNA determines the hair color and other characteristics of you and your friends.
2. DNA is found in every blood cell and skin cell in our bodies.
3. Your DNA is unique to you, unless you have an identical twin.
4. If I commit a crime, my DNA may be found at the scene, not yours.
5. Detectives appreciate this fact, because it makes their jobs somewhat easier.
6. Crime labs can always analyze DNA from body tissue.
7. Sometimes the labs can analyze DNA from sweat stains and saliva on cigarette butts.
8. These samples are put through a complex process to form an identification for each person.
9. Millions of these DNA "fingerprints" are entered in a national database.
10. This kind of evidence has freed some innocent crime suspects and convicted many others.

4. What Is an Adverb? (links to exercise A, p. 136)

➡ **1.** professionally, climb (verb)   **2.** quite, extraordinary (adjective)

Write each adverb and the word or words it modifies. Then identify the modified word as a verb, an adjective, or an adverb. There may be more than one adverb in a sentence.

1. Makonnen David Blake Hannah, a high school student, often dreams about computers.
2. He wants to see computers everywhere in Jamaica.
3. Hannah has the very long title of youth technology consultant to Jamaica's minister of commerce and technology.
4. You may have already guessed that Hannah is a computer genius.
5. He lives on the Caribbean island, and he serves there as the youngest government advisor in Jamaica's history.
6. He talks passionately to schoolkids about computers.
7. He quite regularly reports to the technology minister about computer issues.
8. Hannah learned computers early.
9. Today he often designs computer software.
10. He is particularly happy to surf, both on the Web and off the Caribbean shore.

5. Making Comparisons (links to exercise A, p. 139)

➡ **1.** most fascinating   **2.** wetter

For each sentence, choose the correct comparative or superlative form from the choice in parentheses.

1. In 1994, people saw what may have been the (more spectacular, most spectacular) event of the century.
2. In 1992, Comet Shoemaker-Levy 9 passed Jupiter (more closely, more closer) than it had done before.
3. Jupiter's massive gravity shattered the huge comet into 21 pieces that were (smaller, smallest) than the original.
4. Using the (best, better) data available, astronomers determined that the comet's pieces would collide with Jupiter during their next flyby in 1994.
5. In mid-July, the (more powerful, most powerful) telescopes in the world were turned on Jupiter.
6. People without telescopes could see the event (more better, better) on their televisions than with the naked eye.
7. The (worse, worst) predictions of all said there would be nothing to see, while the (most positive, positivest) ones said the collision would be the greatest show not on Earth.
8. The first comet piece hit Jupiter (harder, more hardly) than anything viewed before.
9. The impacts were seen (more clearly, clearlier) than anyone had believed possible.
10. For a week, people watched the impact sites, which appeared (darker, more darker) than the rest of Jupiter's surface.

6. Adjective or Adverb? (links to exercise on p. 141)

➡ **1.** good, adjective   **2.** badly, adverb; really, adverb

For each sentence, choose the correct modifier from those given in parentheses. Identify each word you choose as an adjective or an adverb.

1. The "magnet lady" has a (real, really) thing for magnets.
2. Her name is (real, really) Louise Greenfarb.
3. She began her collection of over 26,000 magnets because she wanted to do (good, well) by her children.
4. When her young children got magnets as prizes in toy machines, Greenfarb thought this was a (bad, badly) thing.
5. What if they choked on these (real, really) small objects?
6. So Greenfarb chose (good, well) by sticking the magnets to her refrigerator.
7. Her collection (real, really) grew, and soon she started collecting magnets from all over the world.
8. She did so (good, well) that she was written up in the newspapers and eventually set a Guinness world record.
9. "The magnets are a (real, really) conversation piece," she says.
10. Greenfarb's magnet collection is the largest on record in the world—not (bad, badly) for a (good, well) mother.

7. Avoiding Double Negatives (links to exercise A, p. 143)

➡ **1.** can   **3.** is

Write the word in parentheses that is correct for each sentence.

1. You (can, can't) hardly have an anteater as a pet.
2. You (would, wouldn't) never be able to feed this animal, because it eats mostly ants and termites.
3. I (can, can't) scarcely believe that an anteater could eat 30,000 ants a day.
4. No animal (has, hasn't) a longer tongue than an anteater.
5. I (can't, can't hardly) believe that its tongue may be two feet long!
6. Anteaters don't have (any, no) teeth to chew their food.
7. You (will, won't) never mistake an anteater for another animal, because of its long, slender muzzle.
8. Anteaters don't live (anywhere, nowhere) but in southern Mexico and Central and South America.
9. Baby anteaters don't (ever, never) leave their mothers during their first year of life.

10. There isn't (nothing, anything) more threatening to anteaters than the humans who destroy the forests and grasslands where anteaters live.

6 Prepositions, Conjunctions, and Interjections ....

1. What Is a Preposition? (links to exercise on p. 154)

→ **1.** in, outer space **2.** with; instructions, rules

Write the preposition and the object or objects of the preposition in each sentence.

1. The word *robot* was coined by playwright Karel Čapek.
2. Čapek introduced *robot* in his 1921 play *R.U.R.*
3. In the early 1800s, Mary Shelley wrote *Frankenstein*.
4. Frankenstein's creation was an android composed of human parts.
5. Stories about robots and androids are still popular.
6. There is a difference between androids and robots.
7. An android is made with actual human parts or parts that resemble human parts.
8. A robot is a machine made from hardware.
9. According to the precise definition, the *Star Wars* character C-3PO is technically a robot.
10. Real computer-driven robots are all around us.

2. Using Prepositional Phrases (links to exercise A, p. 157)

→ **1.** around the world, manufacturers **2.** In factories, work

Write the prepositional phrase and the word it modifies for each of the following sentences.

1. Scientists create robots for new tasks and experiments.
2. A robot surgeon, or robodoc, can drill a perfect cavity in a bone.
3. This helps human doctors fit an implant precisely into the bone.
4. Robots that are powered by the sun can locate unexploded land mines.
5. Robots equipped with artificial intelligence explore the ocean floor.
6. These robots gather data beneath the icy surface.
7. A six-foot-long lunar rover is an expert explorer of the moon's rough terrain.
8. A robotic helicopter, Cypher, pilots itself through takeoff and landing.
9. A computer operator controls this new breed of autonomous flier.

10. Some futurists speculate that robots may replace humans as Earth's dominant creatures.

3. Conjunctions (links to exercise A, p. 160)

→ **1.** and; Cog, Kismet
2. but; The robot Cog has an upper body, it doesn't have any legs

For each sentence, write the coordinating or correlative conjunction and the words or groups of words that it joins.

1. First, study computer programming, for you must write a program that gives the robot its instructions.
2. Do you want an expensive or an inexpensive robot?
3. You can use a garbage can and wheels for its body.
4. Neither arms nor legs are needed for a hobby robot.
5. Three wheels set in a triangular pattern can propel the robot either forward, backward, or sideways.
6. The wheels are controlled by the brain and a stepper motor.
7. The robot's brain is the computer power source, and it is housed in the body.
8. The power source can be lead-acid batteries, but they are heavy.
9. Nickel-cadmium batteries are better than lead-acid, yet they are very expensive.
10. Many robots are equipped with sonar sensors, for these devices detect obstacles.

7 Verbals and Verbal Phrases

1. Gerunds and Gerund Phrases (links to exercise A, p. 171)

→ **1.** creating the Gothic novel *Frankenstein*
2. Completing *Frankenstein* at 19

Write the gerund or gerund phrase in each sentence, and identify it as a subject, a predicate noun, a direct object, or an object of a preposition. If a sentence does not contain a gerund, write *None*.

1. It was time for sleeping.
2. But tossing in bed was all that 14-year-old Jenny could do.
3. Why won't that dog stop barking, she thought?
4. Even the clock's ticking annoyed her.
5. Jenny tried reading for a while.
6. Soon she was poring over a story by Edgar Allan Poe.
7. Reading scary stories is not a good way to invite sleep.

8. The beating of Jenny's heart grew louder than the ticking clock!
9. She began noticing shadows that weren't there before!
10. Next time, she'll try counting sheep.

2. Participles and Participial Phrases (links to exercise A, p. 174)

➔ **1.** frightening, story
3. annoyed by Ichabod's flirtations, Brom Bones

Write the participles or participial phrases in the following sentences. Give the word or words that each phrase modifies.

1. The bubonic plague, also called the Black Death, was once a terrible killer.
2. Its grim rampage during the Middle Ages is a horrifying story.
3. Killing two-thirds of some populations, the bubonic plague swept through Europe in the 1300s.
4. An estimated 30,000 people died in London alone.
5. Victims, suffering terribly, ran high fevers.
6. A tongue turned yellow or brown was a telltale sign of the disease.
7. Known for its awful speed, the plague killed its victims within five days.
8. The dreaded disease was spread by fleas.
9. The fleas picked up the plague germs from infected rats.
10. Cities in the Middle Ages, lacking good sanitation, were easy targets for the spread of disease.

3. Infinitives and Infinitive Phrases (links to exercise A, p. 177)

➔ **1.** to scare an entire nation with an imaginary story
2. to broadcast a radio play about a Martian invasion

Identify the infinitive phrase found in each sentence, and tell whether it acts as a noun, adjective, or adverb. If a sentence doesn't have an infinitive phrase, write *none*.

1. *The Island of Lost Souls* was made to entertain moviegoers in the 1930s.
2. In the movie, a mad scientist tries to turn animals into humans.
3. To accomplish this feat, he performs painful operations on the animals.
4. The doctor teaches his animal people to be gentle.
5. They are totally unaware of their ability to be violent.
6. Only the doctor has the power to be cruel, they believe.
7. Then the scientist tells one of his ape men to commit a murder.
8. Realizing they are able to revolt, the animals attack the scientist.
9. They take him to his own operating room.

10. Is this film a warning to be kind to animals?

8 Sentence Structure

1. What Is a Clause? (links to exercise A, p. 187)

➜ **1.** independent   **2.** dependent

Identify each underlined group of words as an independent clause or a dependent clause.

1. <u>Enrico is the head chef at Ristorante Roma</u>.
2. He arrives at the restaurant <u>before his assistants show up</u>.
3. <u>While Enrico puts on his chef's apron</u>, he reviews the menu.
4. Before he approves the menu, <u>he checks the quality and freshness of the ingredients</u>.
5. <u>While Enrico works</u>, his assistant chefs arrive at the restaurant.
6. <u>Because the scallops are not satisfactory</u>, Enrico crosses them off the menu.
7. <u>Enrico replaces the scallops with shrimp</u> because they look very fresh.
8. Then he creates a dish of shrimp with pasta <u>that includes a light cream sauce</u>.
9. <u>When he's done</u>, he invites the other chefs to sample the dish.
10. <u>He does this</u> so that the staff knows what is being served.

2. Simple and Compound Sentences (links to exercise A, p. 190)

➜ **3.** simple   **4.** simple

Identify each sentence as simple or compound.

1. Frank Webber is in the eighth grade and is proud of his perfect attendance record.
2. He woke up with a sore throat on Tuesday, and he soon felt feverish.
3. Frank's mother told him to stay in bed; Frank protested without success.
4. His mother called the school nurse and reported his illness.
5. Frank buried his head in his pillow; his perfect attendance record was ruined.
6. Frank's dog tried to cheer him up.
7. His little brother Kevin wanted to play a game.
8. Frank's mother quickly banished Kevin from Frank's room, and she told him to stay away until Frank felt better.
9. The dog snuggled on the end of Frank's bed.

10. Frank sank into a deep sleep and dreamed of next year's perfect attendance record.

3. Complex Sentences (links to exercise on p. 193)

→ **4.** <u>Aunty Misery</u>, <u>who lives alone</u>, <u>is teased by children</u>.
5. <u>When these children yell insults at the old woman</u>, <u>Mr. Hernandez makes his voice squeaky and high-pitched</u>.

Write these sentences on a sheet of paper. Underline each independent clause once and each dependent clause twice.

1. When Dr. Poulas first started her dental practice, very few women were in the field.
2. Many people are afraid of going to the dentist because they fear the experience will be painful.
3. Dr. Poulas, who practices in a large city, lives near her office and walks to work.
4. Before seeing her first patient, she reviews his case.
5. Since Billy Walters's last check-up was a year ago, Dr. Poulas expects Billy to have one or two cavities.
6. Dr. Poulas calls Billy into the room where she will examine his teeth.
7. Billy has brushed and flossed every day so that his teeth would stay healthy.
8. Because of Billy's efforts, he has no cavities.
9. Billy smiles when Dr. Poulas finishes cleaning his teeth.
10. As Billy leaves, Dr. Poulas gives him a new toothbrush as a gift.

4. Kinds of Dependent Clauses (links to exercise A, p. 197)

→ **1.** Rex is a yellow Labrador retriever <u>who loves to chase squirrels</u>. adjective clause
2. <u>As soon as he sees a squirrel</u>, he yelps with delight. adverb clause

Write these sentences on a sheet of paper. Underline each dependent clause, and identify it as an adjective clause, an adverb clause, or a noun clause.

1. Katrina approached the parallel bars, which loomed above her, and took a deep breath.
2. Katrina's coach, Mr. Franklin, told her to begin whenever she was ready.
3. Mr. Franklin was the coach whom Katrina always depended on for encouragement and support.
4. Katrina brushed aside whatever fears had lodged in her mind.

5. Katrina grabbed the first bar as if she'd done it a million times.

6. She tried out moves that Mr. Franklin had taught her last week.

7. That Mr. Franklin was impressed was obvious.

8. Mr. Franklin's words of encouragement were what she remembered while twisting from one bar to the next.

9. When the set was nearly finished, Katrina somersaulted off the top bar.

10. Mr. Franklin shouted his praise before she even landed on the mat.

5. Mixed Review (links to exercise A, p. 199)

➜ **3.** complex   **4.** complex

Identify each sentence as compound, complex, or compound-complex.

1. When he opened the town post office Friday morning, Mr. Biggley had a line of customers waiting for him.

2. Mr. and Mrs. Cousins, Mrs. Garcia, and the Nickerson kids waited patiently while Mr. Biggley wrestled with the rusty lock.

3. Mr. and Mrs. Cousins needed their pension checks, and Mrs. Garcia wished to mail a parcel.

4. Allie and Ben Nickerson, who lived with their grandmother, often visited the post office to see the latest stamps; both of the children were avid stamp collectors.

5. After Mr. Biggley tended to the other customers, he pulled out the latest sheets of stamps, and they all looked at the new selections.

6. Allie and Ben bought a few new stamps so that they could add them to their collections.

7. Mr. Biggley rang up the sale, and he handed Ben and Allie their new stamps.

8. While Ben and Allie looked at their stamps once again, the bell above the door rang, and Ms. Prescott, who was the new English teacher, entered the shop.

9. Ms. Prescott wished everyone good morning, and the Nickerson kids swiftly ran out of the post office.

10. Since Ms. Prescott was a new customer, Mr. Biggley introduced himself, and hoping to make a good impression, he straightened his postmaster's hat.

9 Subject-Verb Agreement ....

1. Agreement in Number (links to exercise A, p. 210)

➡ **1.** is   **3.** spoil

For each sentence, write the form of the verb that agrees with the subject. Choose from the words in parentheses.

1. Personality types (has, have) been studied for centuries.
2. However, classification (is, are) difficult.
3. Scientists often (refers, refer) to two personality types, Type A and Type B.
4. A Type A person (seems, seem) competitive.
5. A Type A person also (behaves, behave) impatiently.
6. Typically, a Type A individual (doesn't, don't) relax.
7. On the other hand, Type B individuals (has, have) an easygoing, relaxed temperament.
8. Your friends probably (has, have) displayed either Type A or Type B traits.
9. Some people (possesses, possess) a combination of both types.
10. Research (suggests, suggest) that people with a Type A personality may be at higher risk for heart disease.

2. Compound Subjects (links to exercise A, p. 212)

➡ **1.** Correct   **2.** attracts

Proofread each of the following sentences to find the mistakes in subject-verb agreement. Then rewrite the sentences correctly. If a sentence contains no error, write *Correct*.

1. External pressure and internal pressure sometimes affect athletic performance.
2. Fear and anger is experienced by most athletes.
3. Competition and success requires emotional control.
4. Neither trainers nor a fitness instructor teach an athlete how to deal with mental mistakes.
5. Many athletes and their coaches consult sports psychologists.
6. Some problems and solutions seems easy.
7. Team players or solo athletes learns how to think rationally.
8. Emotional control and focus results in a competitive edge.
9. These skills and techniques help others besides athletes.
10. Even school or work demand a degree of self-control.

3. Agreement Problems in Sentences (links to exercise A, p. 215)

➡ **1.** Do   **4.** are

Write the form of the verb that agrees with the subject of each sentence. Choose from the verbs in parentheses.

1. (Has, Have) you seen the classic movie *The Three Faces of Eve?*
2. Multiple personality disorder (is, are) the subject of the film.
3. Severe traumas (is, are) often a cause of this disorder.
4. People with this rare condition (develops, develop) two or more distinct personalities.
5. There (is, are) periods of time when one personality takes full control.
6. (Does, Do) the different personalities know about one another?
7. The personalities of a person with this disorder (reflects, reflect) different traits and emotions.
8. There (is, are) usually a dominant, or central, personality.
9. An individual with multiple personalities (refers, refer) to himself or herself as "we."
10. To merge all of the personalities gradually (is, are) the goal of treatment.

4. Indefinite Pronouns as Subjects (links to exercise A, p. 218)

➡ **2.** Correct   **3.** has explained

Proofread each of the following sentences. Then rewrite the sentences in which the verb does not agree with its subject. If a sentence is correct, write *Correct*.

1. Everyone value the opinions and lifestyles of others.
2. Some of the movie stars, athletes, and models who are popular today serve as role models.
3. But none of these celebrities affects you directly.
4. Few actually meets you in person.
5. Maybe someone in your school or community inspire you.
6. Some of your friends and classmates exert a powerful influence on your personality.
7. No one learn how to behave properly without positive role models.
8. Most of your behavior has been learned through modeling.
9. Several of your family members is significant role models.
10. Something in their actions keep you on the right track.

5. Problem Subjects (links to exercise A, p. 221)

➡ **1.** is   **3.** is

Find the mistakes in subject-verb agreement in the following sentences. Then write the correct verb to agree with each subject.

1. My brother's college class study the human personality.
2. The faculty often disagrees on the topics to teach.
3. About 15 pounds are the weight of all the course books.
4. *The Ego and the Id* by Sigmund Freud describe parts of the personality.
5. Twenty-five pages are the length of each reading assignment for the class.
6. Economics prevent some students from taking a course field trip.
7. Two-thirds of the students plans to major in psychology.
8. Mathematics are useful in analyzing psychological data.
9. *Psychology Today* publish interesting articles.
10. Two weeks are how much time it takes to write the final paper.

10 Capitalization

1. People and Cultures (links to exercise on p. 232)

➜ 1. Giovanni, Caselll   2. Helios

For each sentence, find the words that should be capitalized but aren't. Write the words, giving them the proper capitalization.

1. When philo of Byzantium created his list of wonders, he included the Hanging Gardens of Babylon.
2. Unlike the wonders that were built to pay tribute to greek gods, the Hanging Gardens were built to show a king's love for his wife.
3. The Hanging Gardens were built around 600 B.C. on the orders of king nebuchadnezzar.
4. A powerful king, nebuchadnezzar conquered the Egyptians, the elamites, the Syrians, and the carians.
5. The only group of people the king did not try to defeat were the medes.
6. Instead, he united with the medes and married princess amytis.
7. Amytis had never lived anywhere but in the green, hilly persian land, which she missed when she moved to her new home.
8. The king built the beautiful terraced gardens to remind princess amytis of her homeland.
9. These babylonian gardens were a luxurious oasis in the Mesopotamian desert.
10. The Hanging Gardens still existed at the time of alexander the great, over 200 years later, and for generations after that.

2. First Words and Titles (links to exercise A, p. 235)

➡ **1.** What   **2.** It

Write the words that should be capitalized in each sentence. If there are no errors, write the word *correct.*

1. last summer my grandparents and I visited our family in Italy.
2. While we were visiting Pisa, my grandfather asked, "did you know that the Leaning Tower has been tipping inch by inch for 800 years?"
3. "why is it tipping?" I asked. "how far has it tipped?"
4. "the land beneath the tower," he explained, "is a mixture of sand, clay, and water."
5. "imagine placing 8,000 cars," he continued, "one on top of the other on soil that is as soft as sand."
6. "Today the Leaning Tower leans about 17 feet," he added, "but I read somewhere about an effort to stop it from tipping over."
7. "good!" I exclaimed. "i hope they can save it."
8. The PBS television show *Nova* aired a program called "fall of the Leaning Tower," about rescue efforts.
9. The program poses the question "can the Leaning Tower be saved through human intervention?"
10. A person interested in learning more about the Leaning Tower can use the following outline:
   I. Leaning Tower of Pisa
      A. construction of the Leaning Tower
         1. when built
         2. flaws in construction
      B. attempts to save the Leaning Tower
         1. restoring the building
         2. restoring the land

3. Places and Transportation (links to exercise A, p. 238)

➡ **2.** Eiffel, Tower

For each sentence, write the words that should be capitalized. Do not write words that are already capitalized.

1. Dr. Arnold Wollschlaeger's research for his new book *Modern Wonders of the World: Bridges* began in the united states and continued in europe.
2. From his home in the midwest, Dr. Wollschlaeger took the *zephyr* to the west coast.

3. When he arrived in San francisco, california, his first subject of research was the famed Golden Gate bridge.
4. The Golden Gate bridge, San francisco's deep-orange symbol since 1937, is one of the world's longest suspension bridges.
5. Dr. Wollschlaeger's next stop was london, england.
6. In london he boarded a bus called *the shropshire.*
7. The bus took him to the Iron bridge over the severn river.
8. Dr. Wollschlaeger continued his journey through the Channel tunnel and on to switzerland.
9. The subject of his research in switzerland was the kapellbrücke (Chapel bridge), which was europe's oldest wooden bridge.
10. Satisfied with his research, Dr. Wollschlaeger headed back to north america to begin his writing.

4. Organizations and Other Subjects (links to exercise A, p. 241)

➜ **1.** Springhill, Middle, School

Write the words that should be capitalized in each sentence. Do not write words that are already capitalized.

1. Before the christmas holiday, I had to turn in a research paper about a famous discovery.
2. Most of the people in my social studies II class had already selected their topics when I decided to write about Mount Everest.
3. Mount Everest was named after Sir George Everest, who had supervised the Great trigonometrical survey of India.
4. On may 29, 1953, at 11:30 a.m., Edmund Hillary and Tenzing Norgay became the first men to reach the summit of Mount Everest.
5. The expedition that they had been a part of was run by the Royal geographical society.
6. Their expedition had left Kathmandu, Nepal, on march 10, 1953, and had approached the mountain from the south side—the side previously thought unclimbable.
7. Hillary had previously made five expeditions on Himalayan peaks after world war II.
8. Since that friday, may 29, 1953, hundreds of climbers have attempted the dangerous feat of climbing Mount Everest.
9. For my research paper, I interviewed Phil Abernathy, co-owner of the right stuff.
10. Phil promised to tell me about his adventurous experience on Mount Everest if I purchased a woodland backpack.

11 Punctuation

1. Periods and Other End Marks (links to exercise A, p. 252)

➜ **1.** history?   **2.** armies.

Write the words in the paragraph that should be followed by periods, question marks, or exclamation points. Include these end marks in your answers.

The Inca people lived in the Andes Mts of South America. Runners carried messages from the capital to distant towns They relied on the roads to make their journey bearable. Do you believe that their road system covered thousands of miles A team of messengers could travel 150 miles in a day Amazing Can you imagine the fitness of these messengers In addition to having quick feet, they needed quick memories Messages were not written down but recited by messengers Such exhausting work Aren't you glad that you don't have to memorize messages

2. Commas in Sentences (links to exercise on p. 255)

➜ **1.** 1988   **3.** Fessenden

Write the words and numbers in the paragraph that should be followed by commas.

What happens folks, when a radio broadcast communicates the wrong message? On Halloween, 1938 Orson Welles's *Mercury Theater of the Air* had its regular broadcast. Welles a brilliant actor and director aired a play based on *The War of the Worlds* a science fiction novel by H. G. Wells. The play tells the story of a Martian invasion of New Jersey. Listeners heard explosions screams and strange noises coming over the airwaves. Unfortunately many listeners missed the announcements that the show was make-believe. Hundreds of people panicked understandably and fled their homes. Many were treated for shock and possible heart attacks at hospitals.

3. Commas: Dates, Addresses, and Letters (links to exercise A, p. 257)

➜ **1.** Providence   **2.** 22

Write the words and numbers in the letter that should be followed by commas.

177 S. Pinelog Trail
Casper WY 82601
Oct. 22 2004

Dear Maya

   Did you know that Paul Revere wasn't the only person to ride through the countryside warning colonists of British troops? It's true! On the night of April 26 1777 Sybil Ludington, a 16-year-old girl from Fredericksburg New York rode through Putnam County. Two thousand redcoats had landed in Westport Connecticut and marched inland. They raided Danbury, burned homes, and wrecked provisions. Sybil, the daughter of the area's commander, helped her father by carrying the news on horseback to the soldiers. In the end, the colonists defeated the British at Ridgefield Connecticut. It's amazing to discover what a major role a young person played in American history.

Your friend

Tori

4. Punctuating Quotations (links to exercise on p. 260)

➡ **1.** intelligence,"   **2.** Correct

Rewrite each sentence, adding quotation marks and other punctuation where needed. If a sentence is correct, write *Correct*.

1. "When did Alexander Graham Bell invent the telephone?" asked Nancy.
2. "I think it was about 1870," said Jack thoughtfully, "but I know it was over a century ago."
3. "Well, you'd be good on a quiz show! laughed Nancy. Now, who made the first phone call?
4. Jack told his sister that Bell tested his invention by calling his assistant, Mr. Watson.
5. Jack also added, Bell used the words *Hoy* and *Ahoy* as greetings, and Thomas Edison was the first person who used the greeting *Hello*

5. Semicolons and Colons (links to exercise on p. 263)

➜ **1.** mail: **2.** carriers;

Write the words from the paragraph that should be followed by semicolons or colons. Include these punctuation marks in your answers.

Several well-known people worked for the post office two of them even became president. Benjamin Franklin is called the Father of the United States Postal Service moreover, he seems to deserve the title. Franklin improved the service in three ways he found better routes, making mail delivery faster he allowed newspapers to be sent free, helping to spread the news and he increased the money collected by the postal system. Abraham Lincoln was postmaster of New Salem, Illinois, for three years he carried the mail in his hat. Harry Truman also served as postmaster he became president in 1945. Writer William Faulkner was once a postmaster, but people made several complaints against Faulkner he was rude, he refused to sort the mail, and he played cards when he should have been working. John Thompson was not known to the rest of the country however, the miners in the Sierra Nevada Mountains loved him. Thompson delivered the mail on skis through the high mountain drifts his nickname was Snowshoe Thompson.

6. Hyphens, Dashes, and Parentheses (links to exercise A, p. 265)

➜ **1.** (the early 1800s)   **2.** fifty-nine

Read the following passage for punctuation errors. Copy the underlined text, inserting hyphens, dashes, and parentheses where necessary. If the underlined text is correct, write *Correct.*

Colonial women in America were expected **(1)** <u>by all of society</u> to keep their homes clean and to stay out of politics. But as the colonies moved toward rebellion, some women began **(2)** <u>writing</u> about their anti-British feelings. Mercy Otis Warren wrote plays that made fun of Loyalists **(3)** <u>people who supported the British cause</u>. Warren was close to many politicians **(4)** <u>—her brother, James Otis, was a leader in the fight for independence</u>—and she never hesitated to speak her opinion. A defender of colonial freedom and women's rights, Warren died at the age of **(5)** <u>eighty six</u>. Phillis Wheatley also wrote in support of the colonial **(6)** <u>Patriot</u> viewpoint. When she was only **(7)** <u>twenty one</u> she wrote the poem "To the Right Honorable William, Earl of Dartmouth." This work compared the status of the colonies to that of a slave **(8)** <u>she herself was enslaved</u>. Mary Katherine Goddard, a publisher of a Baltimore newspaper, always sought to provide readers with the truth. Eventually, the Second Continental Congress

(9) <u>showing good judgment</u> chose her to produce **(10)** <u>copies</u> of the Declaration of Independence for distribution.

7. Apostrophes (links to exercise A, p. 267)

➡ **1.** he's   **2.** friends'

Find and correct the errors in the use of apostrophes.

Elizabeth Chapman is only 14, and already shes' an award-winning author. Her essay in an international contest won first place for it's description of living with cerebral palsy. Cerebral palsy affects a persons' muscles but not his or her mind. Elizabeth would like readers to change they're view of people who are physically challenged. She wrote, ". . . [people] act like just because I cant' walk, I cant hear either." She hopes her writing will help people understand what its like to have a physical disability. Elizabeths' learning to write by using computer software that is voice activated. A keyboards' demands tire her out. She hopes to have her first novel published soon. After all, whose going to stop her?

8. Punctuating Titles (links to exercise A, p. 269)

➡ **1.** <u>Odyssey</u>   **2.** <u>Gods of Mars</u>

Read the paragraph, and rewrite the titles and vehicle names, using either quotation marks or underlining as appropriate.

Our class played a quiz-show game. One person would make a riddle out of the title of a book, TV show, song, or other entertainment, and the first person to guess it correctly won a point. I guessed two movies—Jurassic Park and Star Wars—but I missed the movie Titanic. Sam is good with music, so he quickly guessed This Land Is Your Land and Heartbreak Hotel. I forgot the names of the spacecraft that photographed Venus and Mars. Shirl guessed Magellan and Viking correctly. I fooled Ken with a question about the Lusitania, the ship sunk by the Germans, and also with a riddle about the short story To Build a Fire. Manny finally won when he named the longest-running television news magazine. He guessed 60 Minutes.

Model Bank

Book Review

After reading *Across Five Aprils* by Irene Hunt, I felt a little bit like the main character, Jethro. At the beginning of the book, people are talking about the threat of civil war. Jethro, who is nine at the time, has very simple ideas about the war. In his eyes the North is good, the South is bad, and the North is sure to win because it is right.

He first begins to realize that things aren't this simple when his older brother Bill decides to go off and fight for the South. Bill says that slavery is wrong but that the North has its own kind of slavery with the workers in factories who aren't paid enough. He also doesn't blame the South for being upset at the idea of having their whole way of life changed by the government.

In school we are mostly taught that the North was the good side in the Civil War and that the South was bad, just like Jethro was taught. Hearing Bill's ideas about the situation was maybe the first time I had ever thought about the Civil War from the South's point of view. To Southerners it seemed that the Northerners were trying to tell them how to run their lives. I still think that the North needed to end slavery, but for everybody at the time, the situation wasn't that simple.

Ideas like these made this book so interesting to me. The events that take place in the book made me, like Jethro, realize that the issues surrounding the Civil War were much more complicated than I originally thought.

RUBRIC
IN ACTION

❶ Identifies the title and author and begins to tell about the story in the introduction

❷ Tells enough about the story for readers to understand the response

❸ Gives a clearly stated personal response to the book

❹ This writer ends by telling what the book meant to him.

Another option: End with a quotation from the story.

RESOURCES

Editorial

As anyone who has ever walked down by the bank and the sports shop knows, something needs to be done about the skateboarding situation in Greenville. There has been a big clash lately between the regular pedestrians and the teens with their boards, who like skating in that area because of all the ramps and planters and railings.

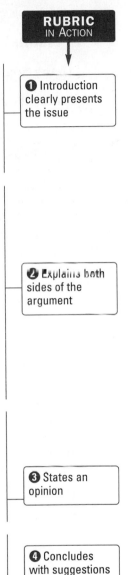

❶ Introduction clearly presents the issue

According to the skateboarders, they have no other place to go that would allow them to do the tricks and jumps that are the whole point of their sport. People should be glad to see them skating downtown, they say, because they're doing something athletic and healthy instead of getting into trouble. They see skateboarding as a craft and a sport.

❷ Explains both sides of the argument

Not everyone agrees. The store owners in the area chase the kids away when they can. They complain that the boards are damaging the cement and concrete around their stores. They are also convinced that having all these kids zipping by in front of their businesses is driving their customers away.

Both sides in this situation have valid arguments. It's important that some sort of compromise be reached so that the kids will still be able to pursue their hobby, but in a place where they won't be interfering with local businesses. If store owners and pedestrians don't want kids skateboarding downtown, they should realize that the answer isn't just to run them off.

❸ States an opinion

Parents are always concerned about how their kids are spending their time and what they are getting into. They should support these kids, who have found a healthy and athletic activity, and make sure they have a safe and challenging place to skate. That may mean building a new park or working out a time when kids would be allowed to skate downtown. Whatever the solution is, it's important that skateboarders don't just get chased away, because who knows where they'll end up?

❹ Concludes with suggestions and emphasizes the importance of solving the problem

Personal Writing

Thank-You Letter

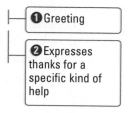
RUBRIC
IN ACTION

January 28, 2001

Dear Mrs. McGuiness,

    Thank you very much for helping me with my video presentation for my history class. Not only was it a huge hit with the class, but I also got an A! I couldn't have done it without you there to help me with the editing and working all that equipment.

    I was stopped by dozens of kids after class who told me it was one of the best presentations they had ever seen. They really got a lot out of it. Mr. Bouvier took me aside, too, and said it looked like a professional job!

    You spent a lot of after school time helping me and I wanted you to know that I truly appreciate it. Not only was my presentation a success, but working with the video equipment was more fun than I would have expected. It's given me tons of ideas, not only for other class projects, but also for short films that my friends and I could make. Don't worry, though. You won't have to help us with all of those. You taught me so well the first time, I'm sure I can do it on my own now.

Thanks again,

Davey Hatrick

❶ Greeting

❷ Expresses thanks for a specific kind of help

❸ Mentions a lasting effect the teacher's help will have on him

❹ Closing

Business Writing

Letter of Complaint

RUBRIC
IN ACTION

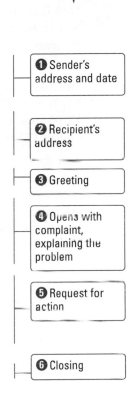

77 Dimaria Way
Columbia, MO 58475
September 21, 2001

❶ Sender's address and date

Peaks Publishing, Ltd.
1500 Taylor Avenue
Barkley, NY 10023

❷ Recipient's address

Dear Sir or Madam:

❸ Greeting

Two months ago I paid for a subscription to *Teen Dream* magazine, but since then I have been receiving copies of *Bug Collector* magazine. I've been saving the issues, assuming they'd stop coming, but they haven't, and the magazines I did pay for haven't shown up.

❹ Opens with complaint, explaining the problem

I am sending these bug magazines back to you. I trust you will reimburse me for the shipping cost and that you will arrange for me to get *Teen Dream* magazine. I look forward to reading it and hope there will be no more delays.

❺ Request for action

Sincerely,

Becky Polivka

Becky Polivka

❻ Closing

Letter of Request

1138 Beacon St.
Boston, MA. 02118
February 16, 2000

John E. Cook, Regional Director
Intermountain Area, National Park Service
P. O. Box 25287
12795 West Alameda Parkway
Denver, CO 80225-0287

Dear Mr. Cook:

    I am a middle school student doing a report on America's national parks. I was hoping to get some information from you about Yellowstone's geological history. I'm interested in exploring why it is so important that we preserve places like Yellowstone, in terms of both national heritage and scientific value.

    Any materials you could send me would be greatly appreciated.

Sincerely,

Carla Rudy

Carla Rudy

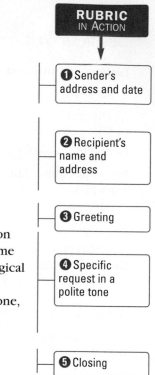

RUBRIC IN ACTION

❶ Sender's address and date

❷ Recipient's name and address

❸ Greeting

❹ Specific request in a polite tone

❺ Closing

Job Application Letter

101 Eberwine Terrace
Denver, CO 76758
September 18, 2000

Vera Siguel
The Center
45 Petosky Road
Denver, CO 76759

Dear Mrs. Siguel,

I am an eighth grader at Mather Junior High, and I would like very much to help with the organization and running of the new teen center. I am applying for the position of teen coordinator.

Last year I was on the Activities Committee for our school, planning dances and school events. We organized two very successful dances and a school fair, so I know what goes into making projects like this work. I know what kids my age are interested in, and I understand the types of things that will encourage them to come to the Center.

I would really love to be a part of this project. I look forward to hearing from you soon.

Sincerely,

Lise VanderVoort

Lise VanderVoort

RUBRIC
IN ACTION

❶ Sender's address and date

❷ Recipient's name and address

❸ Greeting

❹ Identifies the purpose of the letter

❺ Gives her specific qualifications for the job

❻ Closing

Cause-and-Effect Essay

RUBRIC IN ACTION

Among the major causes of the American War for Independence was a series of laws passed by the British Parliament between 1765 and 1775. These laws added to the already growing tension between the colonists and the British government and led to acts of rebellion.

❶ Begins with a clear statement of the cause-and-effect relationship

In 1765 the British Parliament passed the Stamp Act. This was extremely unpopular with the colonists because it was a tax on goods made within the colonies. As a result of the Stamp Act, the colonists united to protest the tax, with cries of "No taxation without representation!"

❷ Uses transitions to show the effects of specific causes

To aid in this protest, Samuel Adams formed a group called the Sons of Liberty. By destroying the homes of British officers and threatening merchants, they enforced a boycott of all British goods.

❸ Provides important background information

Because of this boycott and pressure from colonial delegates, Britain repealed the Stamp Act in 1766. At the same time, however, they passed the Declaratory Act, which said that Parliament could pass any laws without the colonists' consent.

❹ Gives more examples of cause-and-effect relationships

One of these new laws was the Tea Act, passed in 1773. This law gave the British East India Company the exclusive right to distribute tea in the colonies. That meant that the colonists would have to pay an import tax on tea. The colonists reacted with anger. The Sons of Liberty sneaked onto ships and dumped 342 chests of tea into the water. This protest became known as the Boston Tea Party.

As a result of the Boston Tea Party, Parliament passed the Coercive Acts, or Intolerable Acts. Included was the Port Act, which closed Boston Harbor until the ruined tea was paid for.

These events and many others led to the colonists' decision to break all ties with Britain. Less than a year later, the War for Independence would begin.

❺ Ends with the final effect, the war

Process Description

The building blocks of our planet, rocks, are formed in a process called the rock cycle. Rocks are usually thought of as being hard and unchanging. The truth is that rocks are constantly changing to and from each of their three forms: igneous, sedimentary, and metamorphic. These changes make up the rock cycle.

Igneous rock is formed from magma, molten rock beneath Earth's crust. Magma is lighter than the rock around it, so it rises to the surface. This is what happens when a volcano erupts. The liquid rock then cools and hardens. It becomes igneous rock.

Now the igneous rock is on the surface, where it is exposed to wind, rain, and ice. Water freezes in cracks in the rock, and pieces break off. These pieces are then worn down by wind and water and deposited in layers. The layers are pressed together over time until sedimentary rock is formed.

This sedimentary rock is then buried under more and more material. Heat and pressure beneath the surface change the sedimentary rock into metamorphic rock. Last, the metamorphic rock melts and becomes magma, and the cycle begins again.

The rock cycle can happen in many other ways, too. The changes that form rocks are steps in a never-ending process. They can happen in different sequences, depending on movements and conditions within Earth's crust.

Most of this process happens far too slowly to be seen by the naked eye. Understanding the cycle, though, helps scientists learn about how our planet was formed and how it is continually changing.

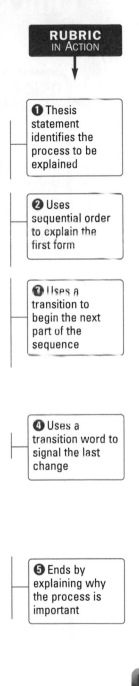

RUBRIC
IN ACTION

❶ Thesis statement identifies the process to be explained

❷ Uses sequential order to explain the first form

❸ Uses a transition to begin the next part of the sequence

❹ Uses a transition word to signal the last change

❺ Ends by explaining why the process is important

Quick-Fix Spelling Machine

QUICK–FIX SPELLING MACHINE: PLURALS OF NOUNS

SINGULAR	RULE	PLURAL
skateboard painting ticket	Add -s to most nouns.	skateboards paintings tickets

WATCH OUT The exceptions to this rule are nouns whose plurals are formed in special ways, such as *man* (*men*), *woman* (*women*), and *child* (*children*).

SINGULAR	RULE	PLURAL
hiss dish ditch box buzz	Add -es to nouns that end in s, sh, ch, x, or z.	hisses dishes ditches boxes buzzes
auto igloo radio	Add -s to most nouns that end in o.	autos igloos radios
potato tomato mosquito	Add -es to a few nouns that end in o.	potatoes tomatoes mosquitoes
flurry deputy battery dairy	For most nouns ending in y, change the y to i and add -es.	flurries deputies batteries dairies
alley play turkey	Just add -s when a vowel comes before the y.	alleys plays turkeys
calf thief wife leaf knife	For most nouns ending in f or fe, change the f to v and add -es or -s.	calves thieves wives leaves knives
belief muff safe	Just add -s to a few nouns that end in f or fe.	beliefs muffs safes
series sheep species aircraft	Keep the same spelling for some nouns.	series sheep species aircraft

RESOURCES

QUICK–FIX SPELLING MACHINE: POSSESSIVES

NOUN	RULE	POSSESSIVE
moon	Add an apostrophe and -s to singular nouns.	moon's light
student		student's locker
club		club's president
restaurant		restaurant's menus
school		school's teachers
bank		bank's assets
college		college's facilities
dog		dog's fur
garden		garden's scents
catalog		catalog's merchandise
museum		museum's exhibit
flower		flower's fragrance
book		book's cover
holiday		holiday's traditions
turkey		turkey's drumstick

WATCH OUT — The exception to this rule is that the *s* after the apostrophe is dropped after *Jesus', Moses',* and certain names in classical mythology. Dropping the *-s* makes these possessive forms easier to pronounce.

x-rays	Add an apostrophe to plural nouns that end in -s.	x-rays' envelopes
organizations		organizations' budgets
teams		teams' coaches
buildings		buildings' windows
cities		cities' mayors
airports		airports' schedules
babies		babies' toys
groceries		groceries' prices
violets		violets' buds
necklaces		necklaces' clasps
butterflies		butterflies' wings

deer	Add an apostrophe and -s to plural nouns not ending in -s.	deer's hooves
oxen		oxen's load
salmon		salmon's gills
stepchildren		stepchildren's names
herd		herd's cattle
sheep		sheep's wool
mice		mice's nests
people		people's languages

QUICK-FIX SPELLING MACHINE: WORDS ENDING IN SILENT *e*

WORD	RULE	CHANGE
home engage hope tune shame state	Keep the silent *e* when a suffix beginning with a consonant is added to a word that ends in a silent *e*.	homeless engagement hopeful tuneless shameful statement

WATCH OUT Some words that are exceptions include *truly, awful, argument, ninth,* and *wholly.*

WORD	RULE	CHANGE
peace courage manage salvage outrage charge	Keep the silent *e* when a suffix beginning with *a* or *o* is added to a silent *e* word if the *e* follows a soft *c* or *g*.	peaceable courageous manageably salvageable outrageous chargeable
agree woe	Keep the silent *e* when a suffix beginning with a vowel is added to a word ending in *ee* or *oe*.	agreeable woeful
flake elevate haze institute shake create	Drop the silent *e* from the base word when you add a suffix beginning with *y* or a vowel.	flaky elevation hazy institution shaky creative

QUICK–FIX SPELLING MACHINE: WORDS ENDING IN y

WORD	RULE	CHANGE
happy thirty merry greedy sneaky deputy	Change the *y* to *i* to add a suffix to a word ending in *y* if the *y* follows a consonant.	happiness thirtieth merriest greedily sneakier deputies
rally marry tally fry	Keep the *y* when adding *-ing* to a word ending in *y* if the *y* follows a consonant.	rallying marrying tallying frying
joy pay boy	Keep the *y* when adding a suffix to a word ending in a vowel and *y*.	joyous payable boyish

QUICK–FIX SPELLING MACHINE: WORDS ENDING IN A CONSONANT

WORD	RULE	CHANGE
mat slip hit dim	If a one-syllable word ends in a consonant preceded by a vowel, double the final consonant before adding a suffix beginning with a vowel.	matting slipped hitter dimmest
heap steal scoot meat	If a one-syllable word ends in a consonant preceded by two vowels, do not double the final consonant.	heaped stealing scooted meaty
transfer admit allot permit	Double the final consonant in a word of more than one syllable only if the word is accented on the last syllable.	transferring admitted allotting permitting

QUICK–FIX SPELLING MACHINE: ADVERBS

ADJECTIVE	RULE	ADVERB
sudden bad rapid	Add -ly.	suddenly badly rapidly
true	Drop e; add -ly.	truly
angry heavy steady	Change y to i; add -ly.	angrily heavily steadily

QUICK–FIX SPELLING MACHINE: COMPOUNDS

	SINGULAR	RULE	PLURAL
One word	dishcloth supermarket airport	Add -s to most words.	dishcloths supermarkets airports
Two or more words	feather bed atomic bomb attorney general	Make the main noun plural. The main noun is the noun that is modified.	feather beds atomic bombs attorneys general
Hyphenated words	son-in-law half-dollar vice-president	Make the main noun plural.	sons-in-law half-dollars vice-presidents

QUICK–FIX SPELLING MACHINE: OPEN AND CLOSED SYLLABLES

An *open syllable* ends in one vowel and has a long vowel sound.	baby labor fable cedar	ba by la bor fa ble ce dar
A *closed syllable* ends in a consonant and has a short vowel sound.	ladder mischief problem plunder	lad der mis chief prob lem plun der

QUICK–FIX SPELLING MACHINE: CONTRACTIONS

WORDS	RULE	CONTRACTION
I am	Combine a personal pronoun with a verb by adding an apostrophe in place of the missing letters.	I'm
you are		you're
he is		he's
she is		she's
it is		it's
we are		we're
they are		they're
I would		I'd
you would		you'd
he would		he'd
she would		she'd
we would		we'd
they would		they'd
I will		I'll
you will		you'll
he will		he'll
she will		she'll
it will		it'll
we will		we'll
they will		they'll
I have		I've
you have		you've
we have		we've
they have		they've
I had		I'd
you had		you'd
he had		he'd
she had		she'd
we had		we'd
they had		they'd
do not	Otherwise, combine two words into one by adding an apostrophe in place of the missing letters.	don't
where is		where's
there is		there's
could not		couldn't
would not		wouldn't
should not		shouldn't
is not		isn't
was not		wasn't
who is		who's

QUICK–FIX SPELLING MACHINE: SEED SORTER

Only one English word ends in *sede.*	super**sede**
Only three words end in *ceed.*	ex**ceed** pro**ceed** suc**ceed**
All other "seed" sound words end in *cede.*	ac**cede** con**cede** pre**cede** re**cede** se**cede**

QUICK–FIX SPELLING MACHINE: *ie* AND *ei* ENGINES

If you are unsure whether to use *ie* or *ei,* the better choice is usually *ie* unless the letters follow a *c* or sound like an *a.*

i BEFORE *e*	EXCEPT AFTER *c*	SOUND LIKE *a*	EXCEPTIONS
field	receipt	eight	their
chief	deceive	weight	height
piece	deceit	sleigh	counterfeit
grief	conceit	neigh	heir
belief	receive	feign	sheik
niece	perceive	vein	neither
priest	ceiling	skein	leisure
thief		rein	seize
relief		reign	either
brief		neighbor	weird
achieve			species
shield			financier
shriek			
believe			

QUICK-FIX SPELLING MACHINE: BORROWED WORDS

Over the centuries, as English speakers increased their contact with people from other lands, English speakers "borrowed" words from other languages. The English language began to grow in new directions and acquired new richness and flavor.

Spelling follows certain patterns in every language. For example, some letter patterns in French, Spanish, and Italian appear in words commonly used in English.

PATTERN	WORD

Some borrowed words keep their original spellings and pronunciations.

PATTERN	WORD
In many words taken from the French, the final *t* is silent.	ballet beret buffet
In both English and French, the soft *g* is usually followed by *e, i,* or *y.*	mirage region energy
The hard *g* is followed by *a, o,* or *u.*	vague
Many words taken from the Dutch language have *oo* in their spellings.	cookie snoop hook caboose
Many words borrowed from Spanish end in *o.*	taco tornado rodeo bronco
Many words that were plural in Italian end in *i.*	spaghetti macaroni ravioli

Some words from other languages were changed to fit English rules of pronunciation and spelling.

PATTERN	WORD
Many words in Native American languages contain sound combinations unlike those in English words. English speakers found these words useful but difficult to pronounce, so they used more familiar sounds and letter combinations.	topaghan = toboggan tamahaac = tomahawk pakani = pecan squa = squaw wampumpeag = wampum qajaq = kayak

Commonly Misspelled Words

A

abbreviate
accidentally
achievement
analyze
anonymous
answer
apologize
appearance
appreciate
appropriate
argument
awkward

B

beautiful
because
beginning
believe
bicycle
brief
bulletin
business

C

calendar
campaign
candidate
caught
certain
changeable
characteristic
clothes
column

committee
courageous
courteous
criticize
curiosity

D

decision
definitely
dependent
description
desirable
despair
desperate
development
dictionary
different
disappear
disappoint
discipline
dissatisfied

E

eighth
eligible
eliminate
embarrass
enthusiastic
especially
essay
exaggerate
exceed
existence
experience

F

familiar
fascinating
favorite
February
foreign
fourth
fragile

G

generally
government
grammar
guarantee
guard

H

height
humorous

I

immediately
independent
irritable

J, K, L

judgment
knowledge
laboratory
library
license
lightning

literature
loneliness

M

mathematics
minimum
mischievous

N

necessary
nickel
ninety
noticeable
nuclear
nuisance

O

obstacle
occasionally
once
opinion
opportunity
outrageous

P

parallel
particularly
people
permanent
persuade
pleasant
pneumonia

possess
possibility
prejudice
principal
privilege
probably
pursue
psychology

R

realize
receipt
receive
recognize
recommend
reference
rehearse
repetition
restaurant
rhythm
ridiculous

S

sandwich
schedule
scissors
separate
sergeant
similar
sincerely
souvenir
specifically
strategy
success
surprise
syllable
sympathy
symptom

T

temperature
thorough
throughout
tomorrow
traffic
tragedy
transferred
truly
Tuesday
twelfth

U

unnecessary
usable

V

vacuum
vicinity
village

W

weird

Commonly Confused Words

Good writers master words that are easy to misuse and misspell. Study the following words, noting how their meanings differ.

accept, except | *Accept* means "to agree to something" or "to receive something willingly." *Except* usually means "not including."
Did the teacher accept your report?
Everyone smiled for the photographer except Jody.

advice, advise | *Advice* is a noun that means "counsel given to someone." *Advise* is a verb that means "to give counsel."
Jim should take some of his own advice.
The mechanic advised me to get new brakes for my car.

affect, effect | *Affect* means "to move or influence" or "to wear or to pretend to have." *Effect* as a verb means "to bring about." As a noun, *effect* means "the result of an action."
The news from South Africa affected him deeply.
The band's singer affects a British accent.
The students tried to effect a change in school policy.
What effect did the acidic soil produce in the plants?

all ready, already | *All ready* means "all are ready" or "completely prepared." *Already* means "previously."
The students were all ready for the field trip.
We had already pitched our tent before it started raining.

all right | *All right* is the correct spelling. *Alright* is nonstandard and should not be used.

a lot | *A lot* may be used in informal writing. *Alot* is incorrect.

borrow, lend | *Borrow* means "to receive something on loan." *Lend* means "to give out temporarily."
Please lend me your book.
He borrowed five dollars from his sister.

bring, take | *Bring* refers to movement toward or with. *Take* refers to movement away from.
I'll bring you a glass of water.
Would you please take these apples to Pam and John?

can, may | *Can* means "to be able; to have the power to do something." *May* means "to have permission to do something." *May* can also mean "possibly will."

We *may* not use pesticides on our community garden.
Pesticides *may* not be necessary, anyway.
Vegetables *can* grow nicely without pesticides.

**capital, capitol,
the Capitol**   *Capital* means "excellent," "most serious," or "most important." It also means "seat of government." A *capitol* is a building in which a state legislature meets. *The Capitol* is the building in Washington, D.C., in which the U.S. Congress meets.
Proper nouns begin with *capital* letters.
Is Madison the *capital* of Wisconsin?
Protesters rallied at the state *capitol*.
A subway connects the Senate and House wings of *the Capitol*.

**desert,
dessert**   *Desert* (des´ ert) means "a dry, sandy, barren region." *Desert* (de sert´) means "to abandon." *Dessert* (des sert´) refers to a sweet, such as cake.
The Sahara in North Africa is the world's largest *desert*.
The night guard did not *desert* his post.
Alison's favorite *dessert* is chocolate cake.

fewer, less   *Fewer* refers to numbers of things that can be counted. *Less* refers to amount, degree, or value.
Fewer than ten students camped out.
We made *less* money this year on the walkathon than last year.

good, well   *Good* is always an adjective. *Well* is usually an adverb that modifies an action verb. *Well* can also be an adjective meaning "in good health."
Dana felt *good* when she finished painting her room.
Angela ran *well* in yesterday's race.
I felt *well* when I left my house.

its, it's   *Its* is a possessive pronoun. *It's* is a contraction of *it is* or *it has.*
Sanibel Island is known for *its* beautiful beaches.
It's great weather for a picnic.

lay, lie   *Lay* is a verb that means "to place." It takes a direct object. *Lie* is a verb that means "to be in a certain place." *Lie,* or its past form *lay,* never takes a direct object.
The carpenter will *lay* the planks on the bench.
My cat likes to *lie* under the bed.

lead, led	*Lead* can be a noun that refers to a heavy metal or a verb that means "to show the way." *Led* is the past tense form of the verb. **Lead is used in nuclear reactors.** **Raul always *leads* his team onto the field.** **She *led* the class as president of the student council.**
learn, teach	*Learn* means "to gain knowledge." *Teach* means "to instruct." **Enrique is *learning* about black holes in space.** **Marva *teaches* astronomy at a college in the city.**
leave, let	*Leave* means "to go away from" or "to allow to remain." *Leave* can be transitive or intransitive. *Let* is usually used with another verb. It means "to allow to." **Don't *leave* the refrigerator open.** **She *leaves* for Scotland tomorrow.** **The Cyclops wouldn't *let* Odysseus' men *leave* the cave.**
like	*Like* used as a conjunction before a clause is incorrect. Use *as* or *as if*. **Ramon talked *as if* he had a cold.**
lose, loose	*Lose* means "to mislay or suffer the loss of." *Loose* means "free" or "not fastened." **That tire will *lose* air unless you patch it.** **My little brother has three *loose* teeth.**
passed, past	*Passed* is the past tense of *pass* and means "went by." *Past* is an adjective that means "of a former time." *Past* is also a noun that means "time gone by." **We *passed* through the Florida Keys during our vacation.** **My *past* experiences have taught me to set my alarm.** **Ebenezer Scrooge is a character who relives his *past.***
peace, piece	*Peace* means "a state of calm or quiet." *Piece* means "a section or part of something." **Sitting still can bring a sense of *peace.*** **Here's another *piece* of the puzzle.**
principal, principle	*Principal* means "of chief or central importance" and refers to the head of a school. *Principle* means "a basic truth, standard, or rule of behavior." **Lack of customers is the *principal* reason for closing the store.** **The *principal* of our school awarded the trophy.** **One of my *principles* is to be honest with others.**

raise, rise	*Raise* means "to lift" or "to make something go up." It takes a direct object. *Rise* means "to go upward." It does not take a direct object. **The maintenance workers *raise* the flag each morning.** **The city's population is expected to *rise* steadily.**
set, sit	*Set* means "to place" and takes a direct object. *Sit* means "to occupy a seat or a place" and does not take a direct object. **He *set* the box down outside the shed.** **We *sit* in the last row of the upper balcony.**
stationary, stationery	*Stationary* means "fixed or unmoving." *Stationery* means "fine paper for writing letters." **The wheel pivots, but the seat is *stationary*.** **Rex wrote on special *stationery* imprinted with his name.**
than, then	*Than* is used to introduce the second part of a comparison. *Then* means "next in order." **Ramon is stronger *than* Mark.** **Cut the grass and *then* trim the hedges.**
their, there, they're	*Their* means "belonging to them." *There* means "in that place." *They're* is the contraction for *they are*. **All the campers returned to *their* cabins.** **I keep my card collection *there* in those folders.** **Lisa and Beth run daily; *they're* on the track team.**
to, too, two	*To* means "toward" or "in the direction of." *Too* means "also" or "very." *Two* is the number 2. **We went *to* the mall.** **It's *too* risky riding without a helmet.** **_Two_ amusement parks are offering reduced rates for admission.**
whose, who's	*Whose* is the possessive form of *who*. *Who's* is a contraction of *who is* or *who has*. **_Whose_ parents will drive us to the movies?** **_Who's_ going to the recycling center?**
your, you're	*Your* is the possessive form of *you*. *You're* is a contraction of *you are*. **What was *your* record in the fifty-yard dash?** **_You're_ one of the winners of the essay contest.**

MLA Citation Guidelines

Forms for Source Cards and Works Cited Entries

The following examples show some basic forms of bibliographic entries for research sources. Use these forms on source cards and in the list of works cited at the end of a report.

Whole Books

The following models can also be used for citing reports and pamphlets.

A. One author
Blackwood, Gary. The Shakespeare Stealer. New York: Dutton, 1998.

B. Two authors
Cummings, Pat, and Linda Cummings. Talking with Adventurers. Washington: Natl. Geographic Soc., 1998.

C. Three authors
Silverstein, Alvin, Virginia Silverstein, and Laura Silverstein Nunn. The California Condor. Brookfield: Millbrook, 1998.

D. Four or more authors
The abbreviation *et al.* means "and others." Use *et al.* instead of listing all the authors.

Brown, Richard G., et al. Algebra 1: Explorations and Applications. Evanston: McDougal, 1998.

E. No author given
Webster's Word Histories. Springfield: Merriam, 1989.

F. An editor but no single author
Silverberg, Robert, ed. The Science Fiction Hall of Fame. Garden City: Doubleday, 1970.

G. Two or three editors
Colbert, Jan, and Ann McMillan Harms, eds. Dear Dr. King: Letters from Today's Children to Dr. Martin Luther King, Jr. New York: Hyperion, 1998.

H. An author and a translator
Pressler, Mirjam. Halinka. Trans. Elizabeth D. Crawford. New York: Holt, 1998.

I. An author, a translator, and an editor
Hugo, Victor. <u>The Hunchback of Notre-Dame</u>. Trans. Walter J.
 Cobb. Ed. Robin Waterfield. London: Penguin, 1996.

J. An edition other than the first
Gibaldi, Joseph. <u>MLA Handbook for Writers of Research Papers</u>.
 5th ed. New York: MLA, 1999.

K. A book or a monograph that is part of a series
Latta, Sara L. <u>Allergies</u>. Diseases and People. Springfield: Enslow,
 1998.

L. A multivolume work
If you have used only one volume of a multivolume work, cite only
that volume.

Gonen, Amiram, ed. <u>Peoples of the World: Customs and Cultures</u>.
 Vol. 3. Danbury: Grolier, 1998. 10 vols.

If you have used more than one volume of a multivolume work,
cite the entire work.

Gonen, Amiram, ed. <u>Peoples of the World: Customs and Cultures</u>.
 10 vols. Danbury: Grolier, 1998.

**M. A volume with its own title that is part of a multivolume work
with a different title**
Dué, Andrea, ed. <u>The Modern World</u>. Danbury: Grolier, 1999. Vol.
 6 of <u>People and the Earth: An Environmental Atlas</u>. 6 vols.

**N. A republished book or a literary work available in several
editions**
Give the date of the original publication after the title. Then give
complete publication information, including the date, for the
edition that you have used.

Lewis, C. S. <u>The Voyage of the Dawn Treader</u>. 1952. New York:
 Harper, 1994.

O. A government publication
Give the name of the government (country or state). Then give the department if applicable, followed by the agency if applicable. Next give the title, followed by the author if known. Then give the publication information. The publisher of U.S. government documents is usually the Government Printing Office, or GPO.

United States. Dept. of Health and Human Services. Natl. Center for Health Statistics. <u>Health, United States, 1996–1997, and Injury Chartbook</u>. Washington: GPO, 1997.

Parts of Books

A. A poem, a short story, an essay, or a chapter in a collection of works by one author
Wilder, Laura Ingalls. "Whom Will You Marry?" <u>A Little House Reader: A Collection of Writings by Laura Ingalls Wilder</u>. Ed. William Anderson. New York: Harper, 1998. 130–43.

B. A poem, a short story, an essay, or a chapter in a collection of works by several authors
Angelou, Maya. "Still I Rise." <u>I, Too, Sing America: Three Centuries of African American Poetry</u>. Ed. Catherine Clinton. Boston: Houghton, 1998. 107–08.

C. A novel or a play in an anthology
Stone, Peter. <u>Titanic</u>. <u>The Best Plays of 1996–1997</u>. Ed. Otis L. Guernsey, Jr. New York: Limelight-Proscenium, 1997. 157–89.

D. An introduction, a preface, a foreword, or an afterword written by the author(s) of a work
Bradbury, Ray. Afterword. <u>Fahrenheit 451</u>. By Bradbury. New York: Ballantine, 1982. 167–73.

E. An introduction, a preface, a foreword, or an afterword written by someone other than the author(s) of a work
Allende, Isabel. Foreword. <u>Where Angels Glide at Dawn: New Stories from Latin America</u>. Ed. Lori M. Carlson and Cynthia L. Ventura. New York: Lippincott, 1990. ix–xii.

Magazines, Journals, Newspapers, and Encyclopedias

A. An article in a magazine, a journal, or a newspaper

Allen, Jodie. "Working Out Welfare." Time 29 July 1996: 53–54.

Abelson, Philip H. "Preparing Children for the Future." Science 13 Dec. 1996: 1819.

Voedisch, Lynn. "Have You Done Your Homework Yet?" Chicago Tribune 9 Oct. 1997, sec. 5: 5.

Fintor, Lou. "Cancer Control Efforts Reach Out to 'Culturally Isolated.'" Journal of the National Cancer Institute 90 (1998): 1424–27.

B. An article in an encyclopedia or other alphabetically organized reference work

Give the title of the article, the name of the reference work, and the year of the edition.

"Sioux Indians." The World Book Encyclopedia. 1999 ed.

C. A review

Crain, Caleb. "There but for Fortune." Rev. of Hearts in Atlantis by Stephen King. New York Times Book Review 12 Sept. 1999: 10.

Miscellaneous Print and Nonprint Sources

A. An interview you have conducted or a letter you have received

Sosa, Sammy. Letter to the author [or Personal interview]. 20 Oct. 1998.

B. A film

Ever After. Screenplay by Susannah Grant and Andy Tennant. Dir. Tennant. Perf. Drew Barrymore, Anjelica Huston, and Dougray Scott. 20th Century Fox, 1998.

C. A work of art (painting, photograph, sculpture)

Escher, M. C. Sky and Water I. National Gallery of Art, Washington.

D. A television or a radio program

Give the episode name (if applicable) and the series or program name. Include any information that you have about the program's writer and director. Then give the network, the local station, the city, and the date of the airing of the program.

"The Idol Maker." Narr. Vicki Mabrey. <u>60 Minutes II</u>. Prod. Aaron
    Wertheim. CBS. WBBM, Chicago. 29 Sept. 1999.

E. A musical composition

Mendelssohn, Felix. Symphony no. 4 in A major, op. 90.

F. A recording (compact disc, LP, or audiocassette)

If the recording is not a compact disc, include *LP* or *Audiocassette* before the manufacturer's name.

Johnson, James P. "Fascination." Perf. Marcus Roberts. <u>If I Could
    Be with You</u>. RCA, 1993.

Prado, Perez. "Mambo #8." <u>Que Rico Mambo</u>. Audiocassette.
    Rhino, 1989.

G. A lecture, a speech, or an address

Give the name of the speaker, followed by the name of the speech or the kind of speech (*Lecture, Introduction, Address*). Then give the event, the place, and the date.

Lowry, Lois. Speech. Newbery-Caldecott Awards Banquet.
    ALA Annual Conference. Convention Center, Miami Beach.
    26 June 1994.

Electronic Publications

The number of electronic information sources is great and increasing rapidly, so please refer to the most recent edition of the MLA Handbook for Writers of Research Papers *if you need more guidance. You can also refer to the page "MLA Style" at the Modern Language Association Web site <http://www.mla.org/>.*

Portable databases (CD-ROMs, DVDs, laserdiscs, diskettes, and videocassettes)

These products contain fixed information (information that cannot be changed unless a new version is produced and released). Citing them in a research paper is similar to citing printed sources. You should include the following information:

  • Name of the author (if applicable)

- Title of the part of the work used (underlined or in quotation marks)
- Title of the product or the database (underlined)
- Publication medium (CD-ROM, DVD, laser disc, diskette, or videocassette)
- Edition, release, or version if applicable
- City of publication
- Name of publisher
- Year of publication

If you cannot find some of this information, cite what is available.

Burke, James. "Yesterday, Tomorrow and You." Connections. Videocassette. Prod. BBC. Ambrose, 1978.

Antarctica. Dir. John Weiley. 1991. DVD. Slingshot, 1999.

"Boston Tea Party." Encarta 98 Encyclopedia. CD-ROM. 1998 ed. Redmond: Microsoft, 1998.

Nerds 2.0.1: A Brief History of the Internet. Prod. Oregon. 3 videocassettes. PBS, 1998.

Online Sources

Sources on the World Wide Web are numerous and include scholarly projects, reference databases, articles in periodicals, and professional and personal sites. Not all sites are equally reliable, and therefore material cited from the World Wide Web should be evaluated carefully. Entries for online sources in the Works Cited list should contain as much of the information listed below as is available.

- Name of the author, editor, compiler, or translator, followed by an abbreviation such as *ed., comp.,* or *trans.* if appropriate
- Title of the material accessed. Use quotation marks for titles of poems, short stories, articles, and similar short works. Underline the title of a book.
- Publication information for any print version of the source
- Title (underlined) of the scholarly project, database, periodical, or professional or personal site. For a professional or personal site with no title, add a description such as *Home page* (neither underlined nor in quotation marks).
- Name of the editor of the scholarly project or database

MLA Guidelines **667**

MLA GUIDELINES

- For a journal, the volume number, issue number, or other identifying number
- Date of electronic publication, of the latest update, or of posting
- For a work from a subscription service, list the name of the service and—if a library is the subscriber—the name of the library and the town or state where it is located.
- Range or total number of pages, paragraphs, or other sections if they are numbered
- Name of any institution or organization that sponsors or is associated with the Web site
- Date the source was accessed
- Electronic address, or URL, of the source. For a subscription service, use the URL of the service's main page (if known) or the keyword assigned by the service.

Scholarly project

Donlan, Leni, and Kathleen Ferenz. "Student Page." America Dreams Through the Decades. 21 Feb. 1999. Lib. of Congress American Memory Fellows Program. 6 Oct. 1999 <http://www.internet-catalyst.org/projects/amproject/student.html>.

Professional site

UNICEF. United Nations Children's Fund. 10 Oct. 1999 <http://www.unicef.org/>.

Personal site

Tomarkin, Craig. "World Series History." 6 Feb. 1998. BaseballGuru.com. 10 Oct. 1999 <http://members.aol.com/thebbguru/baseball/bbws1.html>.

Book

Twain, Mark. The Adventures of Tom Sawyer. New York: Harper, 1903. The Electronic Text Center. Ed. David Seaman. Aug. 1993. U of Virginia Lib. 10 Oct. 1999 <http://etext.lib.virginia.edu/etcbin/toccer-new?id=Twa2Tom&tag=public&images=images/modeng&data=/texts/english/modeng/parsed&part=0>.

Article in reference database

"Aztec." Encyclopedia.com. 1999. Infonautics Corp. 10 Oct. 1999 <http://www.encyclopedia.com/>.

Article in journal

Kientzler, Alesha Lynne. "Fifth- and Seventh-Grade Girls' Decisions about Participation in Physical Activity." <u>Elementary School Journal</u> 99.5 (1999): 391–414. 15 Oct. 1999 <http://www.journals.uchicago.edu/ESJ>.

Article in magazine

Warrick, Joby. "Death in the Gulf of Mexico." <u>National Wildlife</u> June/July 1999. 11 Oct. 1999 <http://www.nwf.org/nwf/natlwild/1999/mexico.html>.

Work from a subscription service

"Glasnost," <u>Merriam-Webster Collegiate Dictionary</u>. 1996. America Online. 7 Oct. 1999. Keyword: Collegiate.

Glossary for Writers

Alliteration : the repetition of beginning sounds of words in poetry or prose; for example, the "c" sound in "creeping cat"

Allusion : a reference to a historical or literary person, place, event, or aspect of culture

Analogy : a comparison used to explain an idea or support an argument. For example, an analogy for how a government works might be how a family works.

Analysis : a way of thinking that involves taking apart, examining, and explaining a subject or an idea

Anecdote : a brief story told to illustrate a point

Argument : speaking or writing that expresses a position or states an opinion with supporting evidence. An argument often takes into account other points of view.

Audience : one's readers or listeners

Autobiography : a biography (life story) told by the person whose life it is

Bias : a leaning toward one side in an argument. To be unbiased is to be neutral.

Bibliography : a list of sources (articles, books, encyclopedias) in a paper or report, used to document research or to recommend further study

Body : the main part of a composition, in which its ideas are developed

Brainstorming : a way of generating ideas that involves quickly listing ideas as they occur, without stopping to judge them

Cause and Effect : the relationship between an event (the cause) and an event it helps to bring about (the effect)

Characterization : the way people (characters) are portrayed by an author

Chronological : organized according to time sequence

Clarity : the quality of being clear and easy to understand

Classification	a way of organizing information by grouping or categorizing items according to some system or principle
Cliché	an overused expression, such as "quiet as a mouse"
Clustering	a brainstorming technique that involves creating an idea or topic map made up of circled groupings of related details
Coherence	connectedness; a sense that parts hold together. A paragraph has coherence when its sentences flow logically from one to the next. A composition has coherence when its paragraphs are connected logically and linked by transitional words and phrases.
Collaboration	the act of working with other people on projects or to problem solve
Comparison and Contrast	a pattern of organization in which two or more things are related on the basis of similarities and differences
Conclusion	a judgment or a decision that is reached based on evidence, experience, and logical reasoning; also, the final section of a composition that summarizes an argument or main idea, and points the reader toward action or further reflection
Connotation	an idea or feeling associated with a word, as opposed to the word's dictionary definition (denotation)
Context	the setting or situation in which something happens; the parts of a statement that occur just before and just after a specific word and help determine its meaning
Controversy	a disagreement, often one that has attracted public interest
Critical Thinking	what a writer *does* with information; thinking that goes beyond the facts to organize, analyze, evaluate, or draw conclusions from them
Criticism	an analysis (usually an essay) of something (usually a literary or artistic work) that evaluates how it does or does not succeed in communicating its meaning

Deductive Reasoning	the process of arriving at a specific conclusion by reasoning from a general premise or statement
Denotation	the dictionary definition of a word, as opposed to the ideas and feelings the word conveys (connotations)
Descriptive Writing	an account of what it is like to experience some object, scene, or person; writing that usually gives one basic impression and emphasizes sensory detail
Dialect	a form of a language (usually regional) that has a distinctive pronunciation, vocabulary, and word order
Dialogue	spoken conversation of fictional characters or actual persons; the conversation in novels, stories, plays, poems, or essays
Documentation	the identification of documents or other sources used to support the information reported in an essay or other types of analysis; usually cited in footnotes or in parentheses
Editorial	an article in a publication or a commentary on radio or television expressing an opinion about a public issue
Elaboration	the support or development of a main idea with facts, statistics, sensory details, incidents, examples, quotations, or visual representations
Evaluation	writing that purposefully judges the worth, quality, or success of something
Expository Writing	writing that explains an idea or teaches a process; also called informative writing
Expressive	characterized by expression; refers to descriptive communication of ideas that are full of meaning or feeling, often used by writers in personal writing to explore ideas
Fiction	made-up or imaginary happenings as opposed to statements of fact or nonfiction. Short stories and novels are fiction, even though they may be based on real events; essays, scientific articles, biographies, and news stories are nonfiction.

Figurative Language	language that displays the imaginative and poetic use of words; writing that contains figures of speech such as simile, metaphor, and personification
Formal Language	language in which rules of grammar and vocabulary standards are carefully observed; used in textbooks, reports, and other formal communications
Freewriting	a way of exploring ideas, thoughts, or feelings that involves writing freely—without stopping or otherwise limiting the flow of ideas—for a specific length of time
Gender Free	refers to language that includes both men and women when making reference to a role or a group that consists of people of both sexes. "A medic uses his or her skills to save lives" and "Medics use their skills to save lives" are two gender-free ways of expressing the same idea.
Generalization	a statement expressing a principle or drawing a conclusion based on examples or instances
Graphic Device	a visual way of organizing information. Graphic devices include charts, graphs, outlines, and cluster diagrams.
Idea Tree	a graphic device in which main ideas are written on "branches" and related details are noted on "twigs"
Imagery	figurative language and descriptions used to produce mental images
Inductive Reasoning	a method of thinking or organizing in which a general conclusion is reached by reasoning from specific pieces of information
Inference	a logical guess that is based on observed facts and one's own knowledge and experience
Informative Writing	writing that explains an idea or teaches a process; also called expository writing
Interpretation	an explanation of the meaning of any text, set of facts, object, gesture, or event. To interpret something is to try to make sense of it.
Introduction	the opening section of a composition, which presents the main idea, grabs the reader's attention, and sets the tone

Invisible Writing : writing done with a dimmed computer screen or with an empty ballpoint pen on two sheets of paper with carbon paper between them

Irony : a figure of speech in which the intended meaning is the opposite of the stated meaning—saying one thing and meaning another

Jargon : the special language and terminology used by people in the same profession or with specialized interests

Journal : a record of thoughts and impressions, mainly for personal use

Learning Log : a kind of journal used for recording and reflecting on what one has learned and for noting problems and questions

Literary Analysis : critical thinking and writing about literature, presenting a personal perspective

Looping : a repetitive process for discovering ideas on a topic through freewriting, stopping to find promising ideas, freewriting about those ideas, and repeating the loop several times

Media : various forms of mass communication, such as newspapers, magazines, radio, television, and the Internet; the editorial voice and influence of all of these

Memoir : an account of true events told by a narrator who witnessed or participated in the events; usually focuses on the personalities and actions of persons other than the writer

Metaphor : a figure of speech that makes a comparison without using the word *like* or *as.* "All the world's a stage" is a metaphor.

Monologue : a speech by one person without interruption by other voices. A dramatic monologue reveals the personality and experience of a person through a long speech.

Mood : the feeling about a scene or a subject created by a writer's selection of words and details. The mood of a piece of writing may be suspenseful, mysterious, peaceful, fearful, and so on.

Narrative Writing	writing that tells a story—either made up or true. Some common types of narrative writing are biographies, short stories, and novels.
Onomatopoeia	the use of words (usually in poetry) to suggest sounds; examples are "the clinking of knives and forks," and "the hissing of the fans of the losing team."
Order of Degree	a pattern of organization in which ideas, people, places, or things are presented in rank order on the basis of quantity or extent. An example is listing items in order from most important to least important.
Paraphrase	a restatement in one's own words that stays true to the ideas, tone, and general length of the original passage
Parenthetical Documentation	the placement of citations or other documentation in parentheses within a report
Peer Response	suggestions and comments on a piece of writing, provided by peers or classmates
Personal Writing	writing that focuses on expressing the writer's own thoughts, experiences, and feelings
Personification	a figure of speech in which an object, event, abstract idea, or animal is given human characteristics
Persuasive Writing	writing that is intended to convince the reader to believe a particular point of view or to follow a course of action
Plagiarism	the act of dishonestly presenting someone else's words or ideas as one's own
Point of View	the angle from which a story is told, such as first-, second-, or third-person point of view
Portfolio	a container (usually a folder) for notes on work in progress, drafts and revisions, finished pieces, and peer responses
Proofreading	the act of checking work to discover typographical and other errors; usually the last stage of the revising or editing process
Propaganda	any form of communication aimed at persuading an audience, often containing false or misleading information; usually refers to manipulative political material

Prose	the usual language of speech and writing, lacking the characteristics of poetry; any language that is not poetry
Sensory Details	words that appeal to any of the five senses—the way something looks, sounds, smells, tastes, or feels
Sequential Order	a pattern of organization in which events are presented in the order in which they occur, as in telling a story chronologically or describing the sequence of steps in a process
Simile	a figure of speech that uses the word *like* or *as* to make a comparison. "Trees like pencil strokes" is a simile.
Spatial Order	a pattern of organization in which details are arranged in the order that they appear in space, such as from left to right
Style	the distinctive features of a literary or artistic work that collectively characterize the work of a particular individual, group, period, or school
Summary	a brief restatement of the main idea of a passage
Symbol	something (word, object, or action) that stands for or suggests something else. For example, a flag can stand for or symbolize a nation; a withered plant may suggest or symbolize a failing relationship.
Theme	the central idea or message of a work of literature
Thesis Statement	a statement in one or two sentences of the main idea or purpose of a piece of writing
Tone	a writer's attitude or manner of expression—detached, ironic, serious, or angry, for example
Topic Sentence	a sentence that expresses the main idea of a paragraph
Transition	a connecting word or phrase that clarifies relationships between details, sentences, or paragraphs
Tree Diagram	a graphic way of showing the relationships among ideas; particularly useful in generating ideas; also known as an idea tree or spider map
Trite Phrase	an overused phrase whose use suggests a lack of imagination on the part of the user

Unity a quality of oneness. A paragraph has unity if all its sentences support the same main idea or purpose; a composition has unity if all its paragraphs support the thesis statement.

Venn Diagram a way of visually representing the relationship between two items that are distinct but that have common or overlapping elements

Voice an expression of a writer's personality through such stylistic elements as word choice and tone

Index

Amounts, subject-verb agreement with, 220

An, 127

Analogies, 542
  common relationships in, 533
  in standardized tests, 532–533

Analyzing a story, Writing Workshop for, 440–447

And
  both . . . *and,* 159, 333
  in compound sentences, 332
  as coordinating conjunction, 158
  subject-verb agreement with subjects joined by, 211, 226

Anecdotes
  in introduction of a composition, 371
  narrative paragraphs used in, 344

Antecedent of a pronoun, 58
  phrase between pronoun and, 81
  pronoun-antecedent agreement, 73–78, 89, 295

Antonyms
  in analogies, 533
  standardized tests on, 531
  in thesauruses, 595

Apostrophes, 266–267
  in contractions, 65, 266
  in plural possessives, 266
  in plurals of letters, numerals, or words referred to as words, 267
  in possessive nouns, 42, 266, 649
  possessive pronouns and, 65
  in singular possessives, 266

Appositive phrases
  commas before and after, 48, 255
  nouns in, 48

Appositives
  commas with, 255
  nouns as, 48

Argument. *See also* Logical reasoning
  in persuasive essay, 467, 468
  in problem-solution essay, 451

Articles (documents). *See also* Periodicals
  periodical indexes for, 509
  quotation marks for titles of, 268
  as sources of information, 507

Articles (grammatical), 127

Atlases
  as information source, 490
  in library collection, 506
  for reference, 510

Audience, 315
  for autobiographical incident, 428, 429

for comparison-contrast essay, 459, 461
  for eyewitness report, 435, 437
  language appropriate to, 470
  for persuasive essay, 467, 468, 471
  for poetry, 481
  for problem-solution essay, 451, 453
  for research report, 484, 499
  for short story, 477, 483
  for story analysis, 443, 445
  target, 576, 577–578

Audiovisual materials, in library collection, 506

Author cards, 508

Autobiographical incident, Writing Workshop for, 424–431

Auxiliary verbs. See Helping verbs

Awards, capitalization of, 240, 246

B
....

Bad
  as an adjective, 140, 148
  comparative and superlative of, 138

Badly, 140, 148

Bandwagon statements, 551, 553

Bar graphs, 391, 393, 522

B.C., capitalization of, 240

Be
  as helping verb, 12, 93
  as linking verb, 21, 81, 92
  predicate adjectives following, 129
  principal parts of, 103
  with progressive forms of verbs, 106

Before, dependent clauses introduced by, 186

Between, object pronouns after, 63

Bias in the media, 576

Billboards, 577

Biographical dictionaries, 510

Bodies of water, capitalization of, 236

Body (of a written work)
  autobiographical incident, 427
  compositions, 368, 372–375, 378
  oral reports, 563
  persuasive essay, 469
  problem-solution essay, 451
  research report, 494
  story analysis, 443

Body language, in oral reports, 563, 565

Boldface type, as reading aid, 520

Books
  capitalization of titles, 234
  citation forms for, 662–664
  as information source, 490, 507, 514
  italics for titles, 268

in library collection, 506
quotation marks for chapter names, 268
source cards for, 491
Both . . . and
combining sentences with, 333
as correlative conjunction, 159
Brainstorming, in topic selection, 314, 451, 481
Brand names, capitalization of, 240
Bridges, capitalization of, 237
Buildings, capitalization of, 237
Business abbreviations, capitalization of, 239
But
in compound sentences, 332
as coordinating conjunction, 158
signaling contrast, 588

C

Calendar items, capitalization of, 240, 246, 247
Call numbers, 508
Call to action, in conclusion of a composition, 376
Capitalization, 228–247
abbreviations in titles, 230
awards, 240, 246
bodies of the universe, 236
brand names, 240
bridge names, 237
building names, 237
business abbreviations, 239
calendar items, 240, 246, 247
directions, 237
ethnic groups, 232
family relationships, 231, 246, 247
first words, 233–234, 246, 259
geographical names, 236
historical documents, 239
historical events, 239
historical periods, 239
I, 231
initials, 230
institutions, 239
landmarks, 237
languages, 232
in letters, 234, 247
names, 230–241, 246
nationalities, 232
organizations, 239
outlines, 234
personal titles, 230
place names, 236–237, 246
poetry, 233, 234, 246
quotations, 233

races, 232
regions, 236, 237
religious terms, 231
special events, 240, 246
time abbreviations, 240
titles of works, 234, 246
vehicles, 237
Card catalog, 506, 508
Cars, capitalization of, 237
Case. *See also* Possessive nouns; Possessive pronouns
nominative, 58, 88
objective, 58, 88
of personal pronouns, 58–59, 88, 295
of predicate pronouns, 61
of pronouns in compounds, 81
of subject pronouns, 61
Catalog. *See* Library catalog
Cause-and-effect fallacy, 548
avoiding, 454, 469
Cause-and-effect order
in compositions, 374
in paragraphs, 358–359, 365, 366
Cause-and-effect relationships, 542
in analogies, 533
false, 454, 469, 548
as organizing principle, 358–359, 365, 366, 374
signal words for, 552
CD-ROM encyclopedias
as information source, 490
for reference, 511
source cards for, 491
CD-ROMs
citation form for, 666–667
in library collections, 506
CDs
citation form for, 666–667
in library collections, 506
in oral reports, 564
Character
in oral interpretation, 566
in short story, 477
Charts
for comparisons, 461
for elaboration, 391, 393
flow charts, 393
observation chart, 481
for organization, 459
pie charts, 391, 393
understanding, 522
Choppy sentences, 190, 404
Chronological order, 356
Chronologies, 510
Circle graphs, 522

Circular reasoning, 549, 553
avoiding, 454, 469
Cities, capitalization of, 236
Clarity
adverbs adding to, 135
complex sentences for, 192
specific nouns for, 96
Class names, capitalization of, 240
Clauses, 186–188. *See also* Dependent clauses; Independent clauses
diagramming, 284–286
kinds of, 186
Clichés, avoiding, 305, 417
Cluster diagram, 316
Coherence
in compositions, 374–375
in paragraphs, 351
Collaboration. *See* Group communication
Collective nouns, 37, 55
common collective nouns, 219
subject-verb agreement with, 219, 226
Colons
after greetings in business letters, 262, 263
between hours and minutes, 262, 263
in lists, 262
Commands. *See* Imperative sentences
Commas, 253–257
in addresses, 256–257
with adjective clauses beginning with *which,* 194, 204, 337
between adjectives modifying the same noun, 254, 274
with adverb clauses, 195, 204
with appositives, 48, 255
to avoid confusion, 255
in complex sentences, 195, 204
in compound sentences, 189, 204, 253
in dates, 256–257
definitions signaled by, 587
in direct quotations, 258
in divided quotations, 259
between independent clauses, 189, 204
and indirect quotations, 259
with interrupters, 254, 274
with introductory words and phrases, 254, 274
in letters, 256–257
missing or misplaced, 299

with nouns of direct address, 254, 274
with quotation marks, 258, 275
in sentences, 253–255
with series of items, 253, 274
Common adjectives, 127
Common nouns, 36
common adjectives formed from, 127
Communication. *See also* Language; Oral communication; Writing
design elements in, 583
verbal and nonverbal, 572
Companies, capitalization of, 239
Comparative degree, 137–139, 149
Compare-and-contrast order
in compositions, 374
in paragraphs, 360–361, 365, 366
Comparison. *See also* Analogies; Contrast
compare-and-contrast order, 360–361, 365, 366, 374
comparison-contrast essay, Writing Workshop for, 456–463
and contrast, 541
for elaboration, 384–385
meanings of words suggested by, 588–589
signal words for, 552, 588
Comparison-contrast essay, Writing Workshop for, 456–463
Comparisons (modifiers), 137–139
confusing, 297
double, 138, 149
irregular forms of, 138
regular forms of, 137–138
Complements, 21–24. *See also* Objects of verbs; Predicates; Subject complements
action verbs and, 95–97
kinds of, 33
nouns as, 46–47
Complete predicates, 6–7
identifying, 32
simple predicates as part of, 10
Complete sentences, 6
Complete subjects, 6–7
identifying, 32
simple subjects as part of, 8
Complex sentences, 192–193
conjunctions for, 333
diagramming, 285–286
forming, 333
punctuating, 195, 204
Compositions, 367–379
body, 368, 372–375, 378

coherence in, 374–375
conclusion, 368, 376–377, 378
introduction, 368, 370–371, 378
organizational patterns for, 374
paragraphs in, 368
parts of, 368, 378
thesis statement, 368, 370
unity in, 372–373
Compound-complex sentences,
198–199
Compound nouns, 44–45
hyphenated, 44, 264
plurals of, 44, 652
Compound numbers, hyphens with, 264
Compound objects
in prepositional phrases, 153
pronouns in, 81
Compound predicates, 14–15
in simple sentences, 189
Compound prepositions, 153
Compound sentences, 189–191
commas in, 189, 204, 253
conjunctions for, 332, 341
diagramming, 284
forming, 332
semicolons in, 189, 204, 262
Compound subjects, 14–15
diagramming, 276–277
pronouns as part of, 61, 81
subject-verb agreement with, 211–212,
226
Compound verbs
comma use with, 253
diagramming, 276–277
Compound words, hyphens in, 264
Computer catalog, 506, 507–508
Computers. See also Internet
resources in library collection, 506
Conclusion (of a written work)
autobiographical incident, 427
compositions, 368, 376–377, 378
persuasive essay, 469
problem-solution essay, 451
research report, 494
story analysis, 443
types of, 376–377, 379
Conclusions, drawing, 545, 553
Concrete nouns, 36, 55
Conjunctions, 158–160
in complex sentences, 333
in compound sentences, 332, 341
coordinating, 158, 189, 204
correlative, 159, 333
functions of, 166
subordinating, 192, 194
Connotation, 415, 420, 533, 596–597

Content
checking during revising, 319
evaluating a speaker's, 558
Context, in vocabulary development,
587–589
Continents, capitalization of, 236
Contractions
agreement of *doesn't* and *don't* with
subjects, 209
apostrophes in, 65, 266
possessive pronouns confused with,
65, 66, 266
spelling of, 66, 653
who's, 70
Contrast. See also Comparison
compare-and-contrast order,
360–361, 365, 366, 374
and comparison, 541
in comparison-contrast essay,
456–463
meanings of words suggested by,
588–589
signal words for, 552, 588
Conventions, checking during editing,
322
Coordinating conjunctions, 158
common, 158, 189
between independent clauses, 189,
204
Correlative conjunctions, 159, 333
Critical thinking, 539–553
analyzing facts and opinions,
543–544
going beyond the facts, 545–546
recognizing emotional appeals,
550–551
recognizing errors in, 547–549
relationships between ideas,
540–542

D

Dashes, 264
definitions signaled by, 587
Dates
capitalization in, 240
commas in, 256–257
Days, capitalization of, 240
Declarative sentences, 16
periods in, 16, 250
subject position in, 18
for variety, 407
Definite article, 127
Definitions
context clues signaling, 587
in dictionaries, 594
in glossaries, 595

Divisions of the world, capitalization of, 236
Do, as helping verb, 12, 93
Documentaries, 573
Documentation
    parenthetical, 496
    for research report, 496–497
Documents, capitalization of historical, 239
Doesn't, subject-verb agreement with, 209
Don't, subject-verb agreement with, 209
Double comparisons, 138, 149
Double negatives, 142–143, 149
Drafting, 317–318
    autobiographical incident, 427
    comparison-contrast essay, 459
    to discover, 317
    eyewitness report, 435
    peer response in, 318, 327
    persuasive essay, 469
    from a plan, 317
    poetry, 481
    problem-solution essay, 451
    research report, 494
    short story, 477
    story analysis, 443
Drama, 483

E

Earth, capitalization of, 236
East, capitalization of, 237
Editing and proofreading, 322–323
    autobiographical incident, 428
    clichés, 305
    commas, 299
    comparison-contrast essay, 460
    comparisons, 297
    for conventions, 322
    errors checklist for, 322
    eyewitness report, 436
    figurative language, 307
    fixing errors, 290–299
    improving style, 300–309
    incorrect pronoun case, 295
    paragraphing, 308–309
    persuasive essay, 470
    poetry, 482
    precise words, 306
    problem-solution essay, 452
    pronoun-antecedent agreement, 294
    quick-fix editing, 289–309
    research report, 498
    run-on sentences, 291
    sentence fragments, 290
    short story, 478

slang, 305
story analysis, 444
subject-verb agreement, 292–293
supporting details, 304
symbols for, 323
varying sentence length, 303
varying sentence structure, 302
verb forms and tenses, 298
video, 580–581
weak sentences, 300
who and *whom,* 296
wordiness, 300
Either . . . or
    combining sentences with, 333
    as correlative conjunctions, 159
Either/or fallacy, 548, 553
    avoiding, 454, 469
Elaboration, 381–393
    description as, 383, 384–385
    evidence as, 383, 386–387
    examples as, 386
    facts as, 387, 392
    methods of, 383, 392
    supporting opinions as, 383, 388–389
    visuals as, 383, 390–391, 393
Electronic media, 571–573. *See also* Internet; Television
    publishing your writing in, 323
    reference works, 511
Emotional appeals, recognizing, 550–551
Empty sentences, 396–397
Encyclopedias
    on CD-ROM, 490, 491, 511
    citation form for, 665
    as information source, 490
    as keyword source, 508, 512
    in library collection, 506
    for reference, 510
    source cards for, 491
End marks, 250–252. *See also* Periods (punctuation)
    exclamation points, 16, 251, 258, 275
    question marks, 16, 251, 258, 275
Epic poems, italics for titles of, 268
Essays. *See also* Compositions
    quotation marks for titles of, 268
Essay test questions, 535, 537
Ethnic groups, capitalization of, 232
Evaluation
    of discussions, 562
    of opinions, 544
    predicate adjectives for, 99
    of sources, 490, 515

types of, 522–523
understanding, 522–523
in video, 581
Graphs
bar, 391, 393, 522
circle, 522
as elaboration, 391, 393
line, 391, 393, 522
understanding, 522
Group communication, 561–562

H

Hand gestures, in oral reports, 429, 445, 453, 565
Have, as helping verb, 12, 93, 109
He, in compound subjects, 81
    for nouns or pronouns of unclear gender, 74
Helping verbs, 93
    agreement with subjects, 211, 226
    common, 12, 93
    in verb phrases, 12–13, 93, 122
Her, in compound objects, 81
Here
    demonstrative pronouns with, 72
    sentences beginning with, 19, 213, 227
Him, in compound objects, 81
Historical documents, capitalization of, 239
Historical events, capitalization of, 239
Historical periods, capitalization of, 239
Holidays, capitalization of, 240
How
    adverb phrases answering, 155
    adverbs answering, 134
    for choosing precise modifiers, 330
    noun clauses introduced by, 196
How many
    adjective phrases answering, 155
    adjectives answering, 126
Hyperbole, 416
Hyphens
    in compound nouns, 44, 264
    in compound numbers, 264
    in spelled-out fractions, 264
    in word at end of line, 264

I, J, K

I, capitalization of, 231
    in compound subjects, 81
    and *me,* 64, 82
Ideas. *See also* Main idea; Topics
    checking during revising, 319
    organizing in prewriting, 316

relationships between, 540–542
Idiom, 412–413
Imagery, in poetry, 481, 482
Imperative sentences, 16
    exclamation points in, 16
    periods in, 16, 250
    subject position in, 18
    for variety, 407
Implied main idea, 349
Implied topic sentence, 349
Indefinite articles, 127
Indefinite pronouns
    as adjectives, 131
    personal-pronoun agreement with, 76–78
    singular and plural, 76–78, 216
    subject-verb agreement with, 216–218, 226
Independent clauses, 186–188
    in complex sentences, 192
    in compound-complex sentences, 198
    in compound sentences, 189
    joining, 189, 204
    in simple sentences, 189
Indexes of periodicals, 506, 509
Indirect objects, 23
    action verbs and, 95
    as complements, 46
    diagramming, 279
    function of, 33
    noun clauses as, 195, 196
    nouns as, 55
    object pronouns as, 63, 88
    verbs that often take, 95
    whom for, 70
Indirect questions, periods with, 250
Indirect quotations, punctuation of, 259
Inferences, 545, 553
Infinitive phrases, 175–177
    diagramming, 282–283
    prepositional phrases distinguished from, 176, 182
    using, 175, 183
Infinitives, 175–177
    diagramming, 282
Informal language, 412
    for everyday conversation, 420
    idioms in, 412–413
    for monologue, 429
    slang in, 305, 413
    as style element, 411
Information
    complements for adding, 47
    finding, 505–517
    listening for, 568

quotation marks for titles, 268
Musicals, capitalization of titles, 234

N

Name-calling, 551
Names, 36
  capitalization of, 230–241, 246
  geographical, 236–237, 246
  personal, 230
Narrative/literary writing, 474–485
  paragraphs in, 344–345
  transition words for, 353
Nationalities, capitalization of, 232
Nations, capitalization of, 236
Negative language, 550
Negative tone, 411, 418
Negative words, 142–143
Neither . . . nor
  combining sentences with, 333
  as correlative conjunctions, 159
Newspapers, 574
  capitalization of titles, 234
  citation forms for, 665
  indexes to, 509
  as information source, 490
  in library collection, 506
  source cards for, 491
News reports
  bias in, 576
  creating, 437
  deciphering the message of, 578
  purpose of, 575
  on television, 572, 578
None, as singular or plural, 217
No one, in overgeneralization, 469,
    547, 553
Nor
  in compound sentences, 332
  as coordinating conjunction, 158
  neither . . . nor, 159, 333
  subject-verb agreement with
      subjects joined by, 211, 226
North, capitalization of, 237
Note cards, 526
  for research report, 492, 495
Note taking, 524–526
  in groups, 561
  in reading for information, 521
  for research report, 492–493
Not only . . . but also, as correlative
    conjunctions, 159
Noun clauses, 195–196
  diagramming, 286
  function of, 205
  words that introduce, 196

Nouns, 34–55. *See also* Predicate nouns
  abstract, 36–37, 55
  adjective phrases modifying, 155
  as adjectives, 132
  as appositives, 48, 55
  collective, 37, 55, 219, 226
  commas with nouns of direct
      address, 254, 274
  common, 36, 127
  as complements, 46–47
  compound, 44–45, 264, 652
  concrete, 36, 55
  as direct objects, 55
  as indirect objects, 55
  infinitive phrases used as, 175,
      183, 282
  kinds of, 54–55
  noun clauses, 195–196, 205, 286
  as objects of prepositions, 48, 55
  in phrases, 48–49
  plural, 39–41, 44, 51, 266, 648
  possessive, 42–43, 55, 266, 649
  pronouns used in place of, 58
  proper, 36, 127
  singular, 39–41, 219, 226, 266
  as subjects, 46–47, 55
  suffixes, 598
Number
  indefinite pronoun agreement, 76–78
  personal pronouns, 58–59
  pronoun-antecedent agreement in,
      73, 76–78, 89
  subject-verb agreement in, 208–227
Numbers
  apostrophes in plurals of, 267
  fractions, 220, 264
  hyphens with compound, 264
  in outlines, 251, 527
  subject-verb agreement with, 220

O

Object case, of personal pronouns,
    58–59, 88
Objective tests, 528–530, 536
Object of a preposition
  following *to* or *for,* 95
  gerunds as, 170
  noun clauses as, 195, 196
  nouns as, 48
  object pronoun as, 63, 70, 88
  whom as, 70
Object pronouns, 63–64
  after *between,* 63
  in compounds, 81
Objects of verbs, 23–24. *See also*
    Direct objects; Indirect objects
  compound, 81, 153

Observation chart, 481
Online databases, as information
source, 490
Online publishing
of autobiographical incident, 431
of comparison-contrast essay, 463
of eyewitness report, 439
of persuasive essay, 473
of poem, 485
of problem-solution essay, 455
of research report, 501
of short story, 485
of story analysis, 447
Opinions
analyzing, 543–544
evaluation of, 544
facts distinguished from, 552
identifying, 543
supporting, 383, 388–389, 452
Opposing views, in persuasive essay,
468
Or
in compound sentences, 332
as coordinating conjunction, 158
either . . . or, 159, 333
subject-verb agreement with
subjects joined by, 211, 226
whether . . . or, 159, 333
Oral communication, 555–569
of autobiographical incident, 429,
431
of comparison-contrast essay, 463
content checklist, 558
delivery checklist, 558
discussion skills, 562
of eyewitness report, 437, 439
in groups, 561–562
interviewing, 556–558
listening effectively, 556–558
oral interpretation, 566–567
oral reports, 563–565
of persuasive essay, 471, 473
of poem, 485
of problem-solution essay, 453, 455
of research report, 499, 501
of short story, 483, 485
speaking tips, 568
of story analysis, 445, 447
Oral interpretation, 566–567
choosing a selection, 566
creating, 445
interpreting a selection, 566
practicing and presenting, 567
Oral reports, 563–565
adapting written reports for, 563
body language, 563, 565
of comparison-contrast essay, 461

creating, 461
presentation aids, 563, 564
presentation skills, 564–565
stage fright, 565
voice, 565
Order of degree
in compositions, 374
in paragraphs, 362–363, 365, 366
Organization
checking during revising, 320
of comparison-contrast essay, 459
of compositions, 374
of eyewitness report, 435
feature-by-feature, 360, 459
of ideas in prewriting, 316
of paragraphs, 355–365
of persuasive essay, 469
of research report, 494
subject-by-subject, 360, 459
Organizations, capitalization of, 239
Outlines
capitalization of first words of, 234
creating, 527
for creating unity in a composition,
372
formal and informal, 527
periods after numbers and letters
in, 251
for research report, 494
for video production, 579
Overgeneralization, 547, 553
avoiding, 454, 469
critical thinking contrasted with, 553
Overloaded sentences, 400–401

P

Padded sentences, 397–398
Paintings, italics for titles of, 268
Paragraphs, 353–365
breaking up lengthy, 373
building, 343–353
cause-and-effect order for, 358–359,
365, 366
coherence in, 351
compare-and-contrast order for,
360–361, 365, 366
in compositions, 368
descriptive, 344, 353
fixing, 308–309
informative, 346, 353
main ideas of, 348–349, 521
narrative, 344–345, 353
order of degree for, 362–363, 365,
366
organizing, 355–365
paring down details in, 350

persuasive, 347, 353
sequential order for, 356, 365, 366
spatial order for, 357, 365, 366
topic sentences of, 348–349, 368, 372
transitional words and phrases in, 351, 353, 356, 359, 360, 373
types of, 344–347, 352
unity in, 348–350, 353
Parallelism, in outlines, 527
Paraphrasing, in note taking, 492, 525
Parentheses, 264
definitions signaled by, 587
Parenthetical documentation, 496
Participial phrases, 172–174
diagramming, 281
Participles, 172–174
diagramming, 281
gerunds and verbs distinguished from, 172, 182
kinds of, 172
past, 100, 102–103, 172, 281
present, 100, 172, 281
Passive voice, 338–339
Past participles, 172
diagramming, 281
of irregular verbs, 102–103
as principal part of verbs, 100
of regular verbs, 100
Past perfect tense, 108, 109
using, 112, 123
Past progressive form, 105, 106
using, 112
Past tense, 105
of irregular verbs, 102–103
as principal part of verbs, 100
of regular verbs, 100
using, 112, 123
Peer response
to autobiographical incident, 431
to comparison-contrast essay, 463
in drafting, 318, 327
to eyewitness report, 439
to persuasive essay, 473
to poem, 485
to problem-solution essay, 455
to research report, 501
to short story, 485
to story analysis, 447
Perfect tense, 108–110
forming, 109
future, 108, 109, 113, 123
past, 108, 109, 112, 123
present, 108, 109, 112, 123
Performance, publishing writing through, 323
Periodical indexes, 506, 509

Periodicals. *See also* Journals; Magazines; Newspapers
indexes of, 506, 509
Periods (historical), capitalization of, 239
Periods (punctuation), 250, 251
with abbreviations, 251
in declarative sentences, 16, 250
in imperative sentences, 16, 250
in indirect questions, 250
with initials, 251
in lists, 251
in outlines, 251
with quotation marks, 258, 275
Person
of personal pronouns, 58–59, 88
pronoun-antecedent agreement in, 73–74, 89
Personal names, capitalization of, 230
Personal pronouns, 58–60
case, number, and person of, 58–59, 88
gender of, 74, 88
as object pronouns, 63–64
possessive pronouns, 58, 59, 65–67, 88
unclear reference with, 79–80
Personal titles, capitalization of, 230
Personal writing, 424–431
Personification, 417
Persuasive essay, Writing Workshop for, 464–473
Persuasive speech, 453
Persuasive writing, 464–473
paragraphs in, 346
transition words for, 353
Photographs
as elaboration, 393
in newspapers, 574
in oral reports, 564
in video, 581
Phrases. *See also* Prepositional phrases; Transitional words and phrases; Verbal phrases
adding to sentences, 331
appositive, 48, 255
commas after introductory, 254, 274
diagramming, 280–283
inserting, to combine sentences, 335
misplaced, 428
nouns in, 48–49
participial phrases, 172–174, 281
between pronouns and antecedents, 81
rearranging, for sentence variety, 402
repeated, 375
Pie charts, for elaboration, 391, 393

Q

Question marks, 250
    with interrogative sentences, 16, 250
    with quotation marks, 258, 275
Questions
    for exploring and limiting a topic, 316
    indirect, 250
    interrogative pronouns for
      introducing, 70
    interrogative sentences, 16, 250
    for peers about your writing, 318
    for reflecting on your writing, 324
    for research report, 484
    subject position in, 18
    subject-verb agreement in, 213, 227
    in tests, 528–530
    for variety, 407
Quotation marks
    commas inside of, 258, 275
    in dialogue, 260, 478
    in direct quotations, 258
    in divided quotations, 259
    exclamation points with, 258, 275
    periods inside of, 258, 275
    punctuation with, 258, 275, 478
    question marks with, 258, 275
    for titles of works, 268, 274
Quotations
    capitalization of first words of, 233
    direct, 233, 258
    divided, 233, 259
    for elaboration, 389
    in eyewitness report, 438
    indirect, 259
    in note taking, 493
    punctuating, 258–261
    in story analysis, 443, 444, 446

R

Races, capitalization of, 232
Raise, rise, 116, 661
Readers' Guide to Periodical Literature,
    509
Reading
    for information, 520–521
    reading comprehension tests, 534
Reading script, 567
Real, as an adjective, 140, 148
Really, as an adverb, 140, 148
Reasoning. *See* Logical reasoning
Reasons, for elaboration, 388
Reference works, 510–511. *See also*
    Encyclopedias
    almanacs, 490, 506, 510
    atlases, 490, 506, 510

dictionaries, 490, 506, 510, 594
    electronic, 511
    in library collection, 506
    in print, 510
    thesauruses, 490, 595
    for vocabulary, 594–595
Reflecting on your writing, 324
    autobiographical incident, 428
    comparison-contrast essay, 460
    eyewitness report, 436
    persuasive essay, 470
    poetry, 482
    portfolios for, 324
    problem-solution essay, 452
    questions for reflection, 324
    research report, 498
    short story, 478
    story analysis, 444
Reflexive pronouns, 68–69
Regions, capitalization of, 236, 237
Regular verbs, 100, 122
Relative pronouns
    adjective clauses introduced by, 194
    common relative pronouns, 194
Religious terms, capitalization of, 231
Repeated words and phrases, 375
Research report, Writing Workshop for,
    486–501
    citing sources, 490–491, 497
    documenting information, 496
    drafting, 495
    editing and proofreading, 498
    evaluating sources, 490
    finding information for, 490
    note taking, 492–493
    organizing and outlining, 494
    plagiarism avoidance, 493
    questions for, 484
    research plan for, 489
    revising, 498
    sharing and reflecting on, 498
Restatements of meaning, 587
Revising, 319–321
    autobiographical incident, 428
    comparison-contrast essay, 460
    eyewitness report, 436
    for ideas and content, 319
    for organization, 320
    persuasive essay, 470
    poetry, 482
    problem-solution essay, 452
    research report, 498
    for sentence fluency, 321
    sentences, 395–407
    short story, 477
    story analysis, 444
    video, 581

INDEX

Title cards, 508
Titles (of works)
    capitalization in, 234, 246
    italics for, 268, 274
    quotation marks for, 268, 274
    as reading aids, 520
    subject-verb agreement with, 220,
        226
Titles (personal), capitalization of, 230
To
    in infinitive phrases, 176
    in infinitives, 175
    object of a preposition following, 95
Tone, 418
    in oral reports, 565
    in persuasive essay, 468
    as style element, 411
Tool-to-user relationship, 533
Topics
    for autobiographical incident, 428,
        430
    for comparison-contrast essay, 459,
        462
    exploring and limiting, 316, 467
    for eyewitness report, 438
    finding, 314, 326
    for persuasive essay, 467, 472
    for poem, 481, 484
    for problem-solution essay, 451, 454
    for research report, 484, 500
    for short story, 477, 484
    for story analysis, 443, 446
Topic sentence, 348–349
    composing, 348
    implied, 349
    in outline of a composition, 372
    thesis statement compared with,
        368
To what extent
    adverb phrases answering, 155
    adverbs answering, 134
Towns, capitalization of, 236
Trains
    capitalization of names, 237
    italics for names, 268
Transitional words and phrases
    for coherent compositions, 374
    for coherent paragraphs, 351, 353
    for paragraph organization, 356,
        359, 360, 364
    between paragraphs, 373
Transitive verbs, 96
True-false test questions, 528
TV. *See* Television

U, V

Underlining, italics and, 268
Unity
    in compositions, 372–373
    in paragraphs, 348–350, 353
Universe, capitalization of bodies of
        the, 236
Us
    in compound objects, 81
    and *we* with nouns, 79, 89
Vagueness, avoiding, 411, 451
Variety in sentences
    inverting word order for, 19
    in research report, 498
    sentence length and, 303, 404–405
    sentence structure and, 302,
        402–403
    sentence types and, 402–403, 407
Vehicles, capitalization of, 237
Venn diagrams, 360
Verbal phrases, 168–183
    gerund, 170–171, 282
    infinitive, 175–177, 182, 183,
        282–283
    participial, 172–174, 281
Verbals, 168–183
    gerunds, 170–171, 172, 182, 282
    infinitives, 175–177, 282
    kinds of, 170
    participles, 100, 102–103,
        172–174, 182, 281
Verb phrases
    helping verbs in, 12–13, 93, 122
    subject-verb agreement with, 208,
        226
Verbs, 90–123. *See also* Action verbs;
        Helping verbs; Linking verbs;
        Objects of verbs; Subject-verb
        agreement; Tenses of verbs;
        Verbals
    adverb phrases modifying, 155
    compound, 253, 276–277
    fixing incorrect forms, 298
    followed by indirect objects, 23
    gerunds and participles
        distinguished from, 172, 182
    in inverted sentences, 18–19
    irregular, 102–104
    principal parts of, 100–104, 122
    progressive forms of, 105, 106
    regular, 100, 122
    simple, 276
    as simple predicates, 10
    suffixes for forming, 598
    troublesome pairs of, 115–117
    voice, 338–339

Word families, 593
Wordiness, avoiding, 301, 406
Words. *See also* Meaning; Transitional
    words and phrases; Vocabulary;
    Word choice
  antonyms, 531, 533, 595
  apostrophes in plurals of words
      referred to as words, 267
  commas after introductory, 254, 274
  compound, 264
  definitions, 587, 594, 595
  families of, 593
  hyphenating at end of line, 264
  inserting, to combine sentences,
      334
  negative, 142–143
  parts of, 590–592, 599
  repeated, 375
  roots of, 592, 599
  signal, 552, 588
  synonyms, 531, 533, 595
Works Cited list, 490, 497
  forms for entries in, 662–669
Works of art
  capitalization of titles, 234
  italics for titles, 268
World Wide Web, 573. *See also*
    Internet.
  addresses, 513
  bias in, 576
  evaluating sites on, 515
  as information source, 514
  keyword searches on, 512–513,
      517
  for oral report, 564
  for reference, 512–513
Writing. *See also* Writing process
  fixing dull, 307
  six traits of good, 319
Writing process, 313–327. *See also*
    Drafting; Editing and proofreading;
    Prewriting; Publishing; Reflecting
    on your writing; Revising; Sharing
    your writing
Writing test questions, 535, 537

Writing Workshops
  analyzing a story, 440–447
  autobiographical incident, 424–431
  comparison-contrast essay, 456–463
  eyewitness report, 432–439
  persuasive essay, 464–473
  poem, 479–485
  problem-solution essay, 448–455
  research report, 486–501
  short story, 474–478, 484–485

X, Y, Z

Yet, as coordinating conjunction, 158
ZIP codes, punctuating, 256

Acknowledgments

For Literature and Text

American Heritage Student Dictionary: Entry for the word *brave* from *The American Heritage Student Dictionary.* Copyright © 1998 by Houghton Mifflin Company. Reproduced by permission from *The American Heritage Student Dictionary.*

Blackbirch Press: Excerpt from *Slime, Molds, and Fungi* by Elaine Pascoe. Copyright © 1999 by Blackbirch Press, Inc. Text © 1999 by Elaine Pascoe. Reprinted by permission of Blackbirch Press, Inc.

Brandt & Brandt Literary Agents: Excerpt from "The Third Wish," from *Not What You Expected: A Collection of Short Stories* by Joan Aiken. Copyright © 1974 by Joan Aiken. Reprinted by permission of Brandt & Brandt Literary Agents, Inc.

Cobblestone Publishing: Excerpt from "Elephants of War" by Malcolm C. Jensen, from *Calliope,* January 1999, p. 22. Reprinted with the permission of Cobblestone Publishing, Inc.

Cricket Magazine: Excerpt from "Octoplay" by John D. Allen, from *Muse* magazine, July/August 1999. Reprinted with the permission of Cricket Magazine Group.

Henry Holt & Company: Stanza from "Stopping by Woods on a Snowy Evening" by Robert Frost, from *The Poetry of Robert Frost,* edited by Edward Connery Lathem. Copyright © 1951 by Robert Frost. Copyright 1923, © 1969 by Henry Holt and Company, LLC. Reprinted by permission of Henry Holt and Company, LLC.

Excerpts from "The Clown," from *Real Ponies Don't Go Oink!* by Patrick F. McManus. Copyright © 1974, 1981, 1985, 1989, 1990, 1991 by Patrick F. McManus. Reprinted with the permission of Henry Holt and Company, Inc.

Gerda Weissmann Klein: Excerpt from "A Diary from Another World" by Gerda Weissmann Klein, *The Buffalo News,* November 12, 1978. Reprinted by permission of Gerda Weissmann Klein.

Danny Krantz: "9 Volt Batteries" by Danny Krantz, from *Signatures from Big Sky,* 1998, volume 8, p. 23. Reprinted with the permission of Danny Krantz.

National Geographic Society: Excerpt from "Exploring Galaxies," from *National Geographic World,* January 1992, p. 15. Reprinted with the permission of the National Geographic Society.

People Weekly: Excerpt from "Fallen Rider" by Gregory Cerio, from *People Weekly,* June 12, 1995. Copyright © 1995 by Time, Inc. Reprinted by permission of Time, Inc.

Katelyn Peters: "Sawdust" by Katelyn Peters, from *Signatures from Big Sky,* 1998, volume 8, p. 26. Reprinted with the permission of Katelyn Peters.

Random House: Excerpt from "Nature Seems So Unnatural" from *Not That You Asked* by Andy Rooney. Copyright © 1989 by Essay Productions, Inc. Reprinted by permission of Random House, Inc.

Marian Reiner: Stanza from "Simile: Willow and Ginkgo" from *A Sky Full of Poems* by Eve Merriam. Copyright © 1964, 1970, 1973 by Eve Merriam. Reprinted by permission of Marian Reiner.

Jewell Parker Rhodes: Excerpt from "Block Party" by Jewell Parker Rhodes. Copyright © 1993 by Jewell Parker Rhodes. Reprinted by permission of the author.

Scribner: Excerpts from "A Mother in Mannville," from *When the Whippoorwill* by Marjorie Kinnan Rawlings. Copyright © 1936, 1940 by Marjorie Kinnan Rawlings; copyright renewed © 1964, 1968 by Norton Baskin. Reprinted with the permission of Scribner, a division of Simon & Schuster.

Angela M. Tressler: "The Trap" by Angela M. Tressler, from *Illinois English Bulletin,* 1996. Reprinted with the permission of Angela M. Tressler.

Table of Contents

Illustrations by Todd Graveline

8, 32, 33, 39, 47, 55, 68, 72, 89, 105, 123, 149, 152, 166, 167, 182, 183, 189, 204, 205, 210, 227, 246, 247, 263, 275, 276, 288, 290, 318, 324 *top foreground,* **326, 327, 331** *top,* **332, 340, 341, 346, 350, 352, 353, 355** *right foreground,* **364, 365, 371, 378, 381, 403** *center,* **406** *top, center, bottom,* **407** *center,* **411, 415, 417, 421, 430, 431, 439, 517, 536, 545, 549, 552, 553, 557, 568, 569, 582** *top, bottom,* **585, 598, 599.**

Art Credits

COVER *center left* Copyright © David Young Wolff/Tony Stone Images; *center* Photo by Sharon Hoogstraten; *center right* Copyright © Christopher Thomas/Tony Stone Images.

CHAPTER 1 **2-3** Copyright © Tony Stone Images; **4** *top* Copyright © Ron Chapple/FPG International/PNI; *bottom left* Corbis; *bottom center* Copyright © T. J. Florian/PhotoNetwork/PNI; *bottom right* Mark Gibson/Corbis; **9** Photo by Dennis Kitchen Studio, Inc.; **17** Tony Brown, Eye Ubiquitous/Corbis; **19** Charles E. Rotkin/Corbis; **25** Michael T. Sedam/Corbis; **28** *Chinese Girl,* Emil Orlik, oil on canvas, Christie's Images/SuperStock.

CHAPTER 2 **34** Copyright © Jerry Schad/Photo Researchers, Inc.; **36, 38** NASA; **41** *left* Copyright © Chris Butler/Science Photo Library/Photo Researchers, Inc.; *right* NASA; **43** NASA; **46** Copyright © 1999 PhotoDisc, Inc.; **50** NASA; **52** Photo courtesy of U.S. Space Camp® .

CHAPTER 3 **56** Photofest; **60** Copyright © Myrleen Ferguson/PhotoEdit; **61, 66** Copyright © 1999 PhotoDisc, Inc.; **84** AP/Wide World Photos.

CHAPTER 4 **90** Copyright © Carol Bernson/Black Star/PNI; **92** Copyright © Bernard Boutrit/Woodfin Camp/PNI; **97** AP/Wide World Photos; **99** Corbis/Bettmann; **101, 104, 107** AP/Wide World Photos/NASA; **108** Copyright © Tom Bean/Corbis; **111** Copyright © Kevin Schafer, Martha Hill/All Stock/PNI; **112** Copyright © Peter Bianchi/NGS Image Collection; **120** AP/Wide World Photos.

CHAPTER 5 **124** *background* Charles Michael Murray/Corbis; *foreground* Copyright © 1999 PhotoDisc, Inc.; **126** AP/Wide World Photos; **130** *left, right* Copyright © 1999 PhotoDisc, Inc.; **132** Detail of *Dinner at Haddo House* (1884), Alfred Edward Emslie, National Portrait Gallery, London; **139** *left, center, right* Copyright © 1999 PhotoDisc, Inc.; **143** Copyright © Dave Watts/Natural Selection; **144** Max Seabaugh/MAX; **145** Copyright © 1999 PhotoDisc, Inc.; **148** Earl Kowall/Corbis.

CHAPTER 6 **150** Photofest; **154** Lowell Georgia/Corbis; **156** Copyright © Ed Kashi/Phototake/PNI; **157** Copyright © Richard Pasley/Stock Boston/PNI; **158** Copyright © Sam Ogden Photography; **161** *The 5th Wave* reprinted with permission of Rich Tennant; **162** *left, right* NASA; **163** *inset* Copyright © 1999 PhotoDisc, Inc.

CHAPTER 7 **168** Corbis/Bettmann; **173** Photo by Meighan Depke; **175** Copyright © 1999 PhotoDisc, Inc.; **179** Wallpaper design for *Swan, Rush and Iris,* Walter Crane (1845–1915), Victoria & Albert Museum, London, UK/Bridgeman Art Library, London/New York.